D1084127

STUDIES IN DANTE

THIRD SERIES

MOORE

STUDIES IN DANTE

THIRD SERIES

MISCELLANEOUS ESSAYS

BY

EDWARD MOORE, D.D.

HON. D.LITT. DUBLIN

GREENWOOD PRESS, PUBLISHERS
NEW YORK

Originally published in 1903
by Oxford at the Clarendon Press

First Greenwood Reprinting, 1968

Library of Congress Catalogue Card Number 68-57629

PRINTED IN UNITED STATES OF AMERICA

PREFACE

THE Preface to the Second Series of these *Studies* would almost serve *mutatis mutandis* for the present volume. The expressions both of thanks to others, and of apologies for myself, may be renewed, with few variations. As to the former, I must again gratefully acknowledge the kindness of the Delegates of the Clarendon Press in undertaking the publication of another series of *Studies*. Also my cordial thanks are again due to my friend Dr. Paget Toynbee for revising the proof-sheets of my work, and for many valuable corrections and suggestions which I owe to him.

I am very much indebted to Dr. Rambaut, the Radcliffe Observer at Oxford, for very kindly revising the Article on Astromomy.

Essays I and III are the only ones in this Series that have been published before, and these only partially. I have to thank the Editor and Proprietors of the *Quarterly Review* for permission to embody in these two Essays Articles which appeared originally in that Review. Both have been considerably added to. In the case of the former, I have endeavoured to work in explanations of all the passages in the writings of Dante, whether in prose or verse, which appear to me to present any serious astronomical difficulty. These have been introduced under the several divisions of the general description of Dante's astronomical system with which they seemed to be naturally connected. A list is added of the principal passages so discussed or explained, and the Essay is also provided (as are two others) with a Synopsis of its contents. By these means I hope it may be found useful to students who meet with such passages in the ordinary course of their reading, though they may not wish to embark on the study of the subject of Astronomy generally.

My obligations to such works as those of Sir G. Cornewall Lewis and Mr. Narrien on Astronomy, and those of Mr. Tozer and Mr. Beazley on Geography, are much greater than would be represented by the references and acknowledgements in the text, numerous as they will be found to be. My thanks are further due to Mr. Tozer for the kind permission to reproduce the map of the world according to Strabo from his volume of *Selections from Strabo*.

I am afraid that some statements or explanations may be found repeated in different parts of the book. This is partly inevitable, owing to the occasional points of contact between the subjects of the first three Essays. Also they were written at different times and for different audiences or readers. So far as such repetitions are due to the latter cause, I have endeavoured to eliminate them. But if they have sometimes escaped my notice, I must apologize to my readers for the oversight. I have been compelled, however, sometimes to repeat arguments or explanations that have appeared already in previous Essays (e. g. especially on the subject of Beatrice in Essay IV). This seemed inevitable, lest the subjects now in hand might appear to be incompletely treated, or indeed sometimes be almost unintelligible to those who might not have access to the earlier volumes of these *Studies*.

I cannot close without expressing my sincere regret at the death of Professor Earle, which has occurred while these sheets have been passing through the Press; and my sense of the great loss thereby sustained by all lovers of Dante, and by myself in particular. I have always differed strongly from the development of his views in recent years in reference to Beatrice, and the interpretation of the later Cantos of the *Purgatorio.* Consequently, in Essay IV I have had to appear as an adverse critic of those views. Had I known that my words would never meet his eye I might sometimes perhaps have expressed myself differently. But of this I am sure, that he would not now, any more than in the past, have resented any such antagonism, even had it proceeded from a much more formidable opponent than myself. Would that I had the advantage of his brilliant style and singular command of language.

E. MOORE.

THE PRECINCTS, CANTERBURY.
September, 1903.

NOTE.

I have adopted in this volume a simpler method of reference to the *Summa* of St. Thomas Aquinas, which I hope will be found convenient, but it needs explanation. That Treatise is divided into five main divisions, known as Pars Prima, Prima Secundae, Secunda Secundae, Tertia, and Tertiae Supplementum. These are indicated as I, II^1, II^2, III, and III Suppl. Each *Pars* is subdivided into *Quaestiones*, and these into *Articuli*. The general plan of each Article is (1) a statement of the subject ; (2) the view of opponents with their arguments under distinct heads ; (3) a general *Responsio* ; and then a separate *Responsio* to each of the opponents' arguments. The 'Questions' are here given in small Roman numerals, and the 'Articles' in Arabic numerals. The letters r, r_1, r_2, r_3, &c., refer to the general or the separate *responsiones* above described. Thus a full reference such as II^2 xcvi. 3, r_2 would mean that a quotation will be found in the Second Division of the Second Part, Question xcvi, Article 3, and in the answer to the second argument of the opponents.

I must also again warn my readers that my references to Scriptural quotations apply to the Vulgate, as the Version used by Dante himself. Not only does the numbering of most of the Psalms differ from that of our English Version, but sometimes also the division of verses in other Books is different, and especially in the Apocrypha. A variation in the Latin and English Translations may sometimes cause a reference to the English Version to appear irrelevant or mistaken. I repeat this warning, as I still occasionally receive kindly meant but mistaken suggestions for corrections in the Scriptural references of my previous volumes.

ERRATUM

P. 114, l. 6. *for* end of article *read* end of book.

CONTENTS

EDITIONS OF BOOKS AND AUTHORS QUOTED

[This does not profess to be a complete list of the authors quoted. It has been made chiefly with the view of enabling me to give references in an abbreviated form in the case of works cited more than once, and also to inform my readers of the edition employed when there might be any doubt on this point.]

Albertus Magnus, *Opera*, 21 vols. ; Lugduni, 1651.

Alfraganus, *Elementa Astronomica* (translated by Golius) ; Amsterdam, 1669.

Angelitti, *Sulla Data del Viaggio Dantesco* ; Naples, 1897.

———— *Sull' Anno della Visione Dantesca* ; Naples, 1898 (?).

Aquinas, S. Thomas, *Summa Theologica* ; in Migne's *Patrologia*, Paris, 1876.

Arci, Filippo, *Cronografia Dantesca*, ed. Paravia ; 1900.

Aroux, *Dante, Hérétique, Révolutionnaire, et Socialiste* ; Paris, 1854.

Augustine, S., *Opera Omnia*, 11 vols., ed. Bened. ; Paris, 1836–1839.

Bacon, Roger, *Opus Maius*, ed. J. H. Bridges ; 1897.

Bartoli, A., *Delle Opere di Dante Alighieri*, vol. vi of *Storia della Letteratura Italiana*.

Beazley, C. R., *Prince Henry the Navigator* ; London, 1895 (in Heroes of the Nations Series).

———————— *The Dawn of Modern Geography* ; London, 1897.

Bede, *Opera Historica*, ed. C. Plummer ; Oxford, 1896.

Benvenuto da Imola, *Comentum super Dantis Aldigherii Comoediam*, 5 vols., ed. Hon. W. Warren Vernon ; Florence, 1887.

Bernard, S., *Opera Omnia*, ed. Mabillon, 2 vols. ; Paris, 1719.

Boccaccio, *Comento sopra la Commedia*, ed. Milanesi, 2 vols. ; Florence, 1863.

———————— *Vita di Dante*, ed. Macrì-Leone ; Florence, 1888.

Butcher, S. (Bp. of Meath), *Theory and Construction of the Ecclesiastical Calendar* ; London, 1877.

Carpenter, G. R., *The Episode of the Donna Pietosa* (in the Eighth Annual Report of the American Dante Society) ; Cambridge, U.S.A., 1889.

Chaucer, *The Student's Chaucer*, ed. Skeat ; Oxford, 1895.

D'Alfonso, Roberto, *Note critiche sull' Autenticità della Epistola a Can Grande della Scala* ; Nicastro, 1899.

D'Ancona, A., *La Vita Nuova* (including *Discorso su Beatrice*) ; Pisa, 1884.

Della Valle, *Il senso geografico-astronomico della Divina Commedia* ; Faenza, 1869.

Dionisi, *Serie di Anettodi*; Verona, 1785.

Dizionario della Lingua Italiana (Tommaseo e Bellini), 4 vols., fol. (referred to as *Gran. Diz.*).

Döllinger, Dr., ' *Dante as a Prophet*,' in *Studies in European History* ; London, 1890.

D'Ovidio, F., *Studj sulla Divina Commedia* ; 1901.

Earle, Professor, *Introduction* to Part II of Dr. C. L. Shadwell's Translation of the *Purgatorio* ; 1899.

Farrar, F. W. (Dean), *Early Days of Christianity.*
———————— *Life and Work of St. Paul.*
Fraticelli, *Dissertazione sulla Vita Nuova* (in Dante, *Opere Minori*, vol. ii), third edition ; Florence, 1873.

Gardner, E. G., *Dante's Ten Heavens* ; Westminster, 1898.
Gaspary, A., *The History of Italian Literature to the Death of Dante*. Translated by Dr. Oelsner ; 1901.
Gelli, Giov. Battista, *Letture sopra la Commedia di Dante* ; Florence, 1887.
Giambullari, *Del sito, forma e misure dell' Inferno* ; Florence, 1544.
Ginsburg, *The Kabbalah* ; 1865.
Graesse, *Legenda Aurea Iacobi a Voragine* ; Leipzig, 1850.
Grant, R., *History of Physical Astronomy* ; 1852.
Gregorovius, *History of the City of Rome in the Middle Ages*. Translated by Annie Hamilton, 6 vols.; London, 1894–1898.
Grion, Giusto, *Che l'Anno della Visione di Dante è il MCCCI* ; Udine, 1865.
Guerrini e Ricci, *Studi e Polemiche Dantesche* ; Bologna, 1880.

Hegel, Carl, *Über den historischen Werth der älteren Dante-Commentare* ; Leipzig, 1878.
Hugh of St. Victor, *Opera*, 2 vols. ; Rothomagi, 1648.

Isidore, *Opera* ; in Migne, *Patrologia*, vols. 81–84.

Kraus, Dr. F. X., *Dante, sein Leben und sein Werk, etc.* ; Berlin, 1897.

Latini, Brunetto, *Il Tesoretto*, ed. Zannoni ; Florence, 1824.
———————— *Li Livres dou Trésor*, ed. Chabaille ; Paris, 1863.
Lewis, Sir G. Cornewall, *Historical Survey of the Astronomy of the Ancients* ; London, 1862.
Liddon, H. P., *Essays and Addresses* ; London, 1892.
Lowell, J. R., *Among my Books*, containing *Essay on Dante*, 2 vols. ; London, 1876.
Lubin, *Studi Preparativi Illustrativi* (ed. *Div. Comm.*) ; Padua, 1881.

Martène et Durand, *Veterum Scriptorum et Monumentorum Collectio*, 9 vols. ; Paris, 1724–1733.
Moore, E., *Time-References in the Divina Commedia* ; London, 1887.
———————— *Dante and his Early Biographers* ; London, 1890.
———————— *Contributions to the Textual Criticism of the Divina Commedia* ; University Press, Cambridge, 1889.
———————— *Studies in Dante*, Series I ; Clarendon Press, Oxford, 1896.
———————— ,, ,, Series II ; Clarendon Press, Oxford, 1899.
———————— *Gli Accenni al Tempo nella Divina Commedia* ; Florence, 1900.

Nannucci, *Manuale della Letteratura del primo secolo della Lingua Italiana*, 2 vols. ; Florence, 1874.
Narrien, *Origin and Progress of Astronomy* ; London, 1833.
Newcombe, S., *The Stars* ; London, 1902.

Ozanam, *Dante et la Philosophie Catholique au* 13me *siècle* ; Paris, 1845.

Pasquini, *La principale Allegoria della Divina Commedia* ; Milan, 1875.

Phillott, *Mediaeval Geography*, An Essay in illustration of the Hereford Mappa Mundi ; London, 1873.

Pliny, *Naturalis Historia*, ed. Sillig, 8 vols.; Hamburg, 1851.

Reusens, *Éléments de Paléographie* ; Louvain, 1899.

Richard of St. Victor, *Opera* ; Rothomagi, 1648.

Ristoro d' Arezzo, *La Composizione del Mondo*, ed. Narducci ; Rome, 1858. (The pagination of edd. 1858 and 1859 is the same.)

Rizzacasa d' Orsogna, *La Foce che quattro Cerchi giugne con tre Croci* ; Sciacca, 1901.

———————————— *Polemiche Dantesche* ; Sciacca, 1902.

Rossetti, D. G., *Dante and his Circle* ; London, 1874.

Rossetti, Gabriel, *Sullo Spirito Antipapale* ; London, 1832.

Rossetti, Miss M. F., *A Shadow of Dante* ; first edition, 1871.

Sacrobosco, Joannes de, *De Sphaera* ; Paris, 1545.

Scartazzini, G. A., *La Divina Commedia*, 3 vols. ; Leipzig, 1874-82.

———————————— *Prolegomeni della Divina Commedia* ; Leipzig, 1890.

———————————— *Dante-Handbuch*, in A. J. Butler's Translation ; 1895.

Scherillo, M., *Alcuni Capitoli della Biografia di Dante* ; Turin, 1896.

Scrocca, *Il Peccato di Dante* ; Rome, 1900.

Solerti, Angelo, *Per la Data della Visione Dantesca* ; in the *Giornale Dantesco*, 1898.

Strabo, *see* s. v. ' Tozer.'

Tocco, F., *Dante e l' Eresia* ; in the *Biblioteca Storica Critica*, no. vi, 1899.

Torraca, Francesco, *L' Epistola a Cangrande* ; Rome, 1899.

Torri, Alessandro, *Epistolae Dantis* ; Livorno, 1842.

Toynbee, Paget, *Dictionary of Proper Names and Notable Matters in the Works of Dante* ; Clarendon Press, 1898.

———————————— *Dante Studies and Researches* ; Methuen, 1902.

———————————— *Brunetto Latini's Obligations to Solinus* ; in *Romania*, vol. xxiii.

Tozer, *Selections from Strabo* ; Oxford, 1893.

—— *History of Ancient Geography* ; Cambridge, 1897.

—— *English Commentary on Dante's ' Divina Commedia '* ; Oxford, 1901.

Vandelli, Giuseppe, *Sull' Epistola a Cangrande* ; from *Bullettino della Società Dantesca*, N. S., vol. viii. pp. 137-164.

Vedovati, Filippo, *Esercitazioni cronologiche, storiche, etc.* ; Venice, 1864.

Vernon, Hon. William Warren, *Readings on the Inferno, Purgatorio, and Paradiso*, 6 vols. ; 1894-1900.

White, Andrew D., *Warfare of Science with Theology*, 2 vols. ; London and New York, 1898.

Wicksteed and Gardner, *Dante and Giovanni del Virgilio* ; 1902.

Witte, C., *Epistolae Dantis* ; Padua, 1827.

———————————— *Dante-Forschungen.* Series I, Heilbronn, *n. d.* (prob. 1868). Series II, Heilbronn, 1879.

Wright, Thomas, *St. Patrick's Purgatory* ; 1844.

SYNOPSIS OF ESSAYS I, II, AND III

I. The Astronomy of Dante

REFERENCES to Astronomy very numerous in Dante's works (pp. 1, 2). His chief authority Alfraganus (p. 3). Remarkable correctness of many results obtained by Ptolemaic Astronomy (p. 5). Three principal divisions of the subject proposed (p. 6).

I. *General Cosmogony* (pp. 6-32).

Eight Heavens revolving concentrically about the fixed Earth, each with a proper motion of its own besides the diurnal rotation common to all (pp. 7, 8). Discovery of the Precession of the Equinoxes by Hipparchus (pp. 8-11). This led to the supposition of a ninth Heaven, the *Primum Mobile* (pp. 11-13). Finally, a motionless tenth Heaven, the abode of God, made known by Revelation (pp. 13, 14). The system expounded by Cicero in *Somnium Scipionis* (p. 14). Passages in Dante illustrative of the above Cosmogony (pp. 14-19). Special discussions of *Conv.* II. xv (pp. 16-18); and *Par.* ii. 112 *seqq.* (pp. 18, 19). The nature of Dante's belief in 'Astrology' (pp. 19-21). Discussion of *Conv.* II. xv. 114 *seqq.* and the date of Creation (pp. 21, 22). Relative speed of revolution of the different heavens, and its Final Cause (pp. 23-5); the Efficient Cause of such motion due to 'Angeli Movitori' (p. 26). Order of succession of planetary heavens (pp. 27-9). Their several dimensions (pp. 29, 30). Extension of theory of concentric spheres to the Four Elements (pp. 30-2).

II. *Planetary Motions and Signs of the Zodiac* (pp. 32-91).

All Planetary Motions supposed circular (p. 32). Three principal theories of combined circular motions : (1) revolving spheres (pp. 33, 34) ; (2) eccentric orbits (p. 34); (3) epicycles (pp. 35-7). Application of this by Dante to the orbit of Venus (pp. 37-43). 'Synodical' and 'periodic' (or 'sidereal') revolutions distinguished (p. 39); a peculiarity in the motions of the two inferior planets explained in connexion with *Conv.* II. ii *init.*; and xiii. 49 *seqq.* (pp. 39-43). Passages in Dante relating to the Sun (pp. 43-74). The Sun the one source of light for all the other heavenly bodies (pp. 44, 45). Size and distance of the Sun (p. 45). Motions of the Sun (pp. 46 *seqq.*). Explanation of several passages in Dante relating to the Sun ; viz. : *Conv.* III. v (pp. 46-50) ; *Purg.* iv. 58 *seqq.* (pp. 50-2) ; *Purg.* xv. 1-5 (p. 51 *n.*) ; *Inf.* xxiv. 1-3 (p. 53) ; *Par.* xxviii. 116 (p. 54) ; *Par.* xxv. 101 (*ib.*) ; *Purg.* xxxii. 52-6 (p. 55) ; *Canz.* xv. 1-10 (p. 56) ; *Purg.* ii. 57 and xix. 1-6 (pp. 57, 58) ; *Par.* xxx. 1-9 (pp. 58,

59); *Par.* xvi. 37 *seqq.* (pp. 59, 60) ; *Par.* i. 37 *seqq.* (pp. 60-2) ; *Par.* xxii. 151-4 and xxvii. 79-87 (pp. 62-71) ; *Purg.* xviii. 79-81 (pp. 71-3); *Par.* xii. 49 (pp. 73, 74). Passages in Dante relating to the Moon (pp. 74-91). Explanation of *Purg.* ix. 1-9 (pp. 75-85); 'Real' and 'Calendar' Moon (pp. 85-7) ; Spots on surface of the Moon (pp. 87-91).

III. *The Measurement of Time* (pp. 91-106).

Regulation of the calendar originally a priestly function (pp. 91, 92). Earliest calendars lunar rather than solar (p. 92) ; compromises between these (p. 93) ; lunar and calendar months (p. 94) ; various lengths of the *year* (*ib.*): Julian calendar and its accumulating error (pp. 95, 96). Gregorian reformation of calendar (p. 97). ' Solar ' and ' sidereal ' *day* (pp. 98-100) ; length of day used to determine latitude (pp. 100-2). 'Temporal' and ' equal ' *hours* (pp. 102-6). Conclusion (p. 106).

II. THE GEOGRAPHY OF DANTE

No evidence that Dante had made a special study of Geography (p. 109). Chief authorities on the subject accessible to him were— B. Latini, Orosius (p. 110), Alfraganus, Solinus, Isidore, Albertus Magnus, and Roger Bacon, though the last-named is strangely never mentioned by him (pp. 111, 112). Geographical study hampered by theology (p. 113). Eight principal divisions of the subject (p. 114): I. The all-surrounding ocean (pp. 114-6). II. Distribution of land and water on the globe (pp. 116-20) ; southern hemisphere generally believed to be covered with water, or at any rate uninhabited, belief in antipodes being thought unscriptural (p. 117) ; legend of Ulysses in Dante (pp. 118) ; formation of the mountain of Purgatory (p. 119). III. Limits and extent of the habitable earth in longitude and latitude (pp. 120-2) ; illustrations of this from Dante (pp. 123, 124). IV. Relative size of the three continents (pp. 124, 125) ; Asia (including Egypt) equal to Europe and Africa together (*ib.*). V. Size of the Mediterranean supposed to be 90° in longitude (p. 126). VI. Central position of Jerusalem (pp. 127, 128). VII. Methods of computing longitude and latitude (pp. 129-34) ; longitude by differences of time, when obtainable (pp. 129, 130) ; latitude by the maximum length of the day; system of *Climata* pp. 130-4). VIII. Opinions as to the site of the Terrestrial Paradise (pp. 134-9) ; this, as well as the topography of the underworld, regarded as a geographical question (pp. 134-136) ; peculiar theory of Dante as to its situation in southern hemisphere on summit of mountain of Purgatory (p. 136) ; belief (Pagan as well as Christian) in a common source for Euphrates and Tigris (pp. 137-9). Three further points in conclusion (pp. 139-43) ; (i) Geographical or ethnical terms used anachronistically by Dante (pp. 139, 140); (ii) Dante's habit of describing towns allusively by the names of their rivers (p. 140) ; (iii) his apparent confusion of Babylon in Assyria and Babylon in Egypt (pp. 140-2). Discoveries in geography extremely slow in gaining admission either into geographical treatises or into maps (pp. 142, 143); even if Dante knew of such, they would have been out of place in the *Divina Commedia*, and the *Convito* offered no occasion for introducing them (p. 143).

III. THE DATE ASSUMED BY DANTE FOR THE VISION OF THE *DIVINA COMMEDIA*

This is generally held to be 1300, but the support of 1301 has recently been revived (p. 144). The assumed date, whatever it be, is never forgotten by Dante in his allusion to events as present or future from this standpoint. Hence we have (1) an *historical* argument, and also (2) an *astronomical* argument from references to the position of the Sun, Moon, and Planets, at the assumed time of the Vision (p. 145).

I. The *historical* arguments. Dante says that he entered the Inferno (1) on a Good Friday; (2) about the spring equinox; (3) in a 'centesim'-anno'; but all these three *data* have been variously understood (pp. 146, 147); further confusion from the various 'uses' as to the date of the beginning of the year, 'Roman,' 'Pisan,' 'Florentine' (pp. 147–9); reasons for supposing Dante to have followed the 'Roman' use (p. 150); another difficulty arises from different methods of describing the number of a series of years of which the last is incomplete (p. 151). Discussion of the principal passages brought into the controversy (a) *Inf.* xxi. 112–4 (pp. 151–4); (β) *Purg.* ii. 91–9 (pp. 155–7); (γ) *Inf.* x. 111 (p. 157); (δ) *Par.* xvii. 80, 81 (pp. 157–8); (ε) *Purg.* viii. 133–9 (p. 158); (ζ) *Par.* ix. 40 (*ib.*); (η) *Purg.* viii. 73–81 (p. 159); (θ) *Inf.* xviii. 28 (*ib.*). Later events may still be referred to sometimes in the way of similes or illustrations (pp. 160, 161). Next, passages where the inclusion, or otherwise, in counting an unfinished year is involved:—(a) *Purg.* xxxii. 2 (p. 161); (β) *Inf.* i. 1 (*ib.*); (γ) *Inf.* xix. 54 (p. 162); (δ) *Purg.* xxiii. 78 (*ib.*); (ε) *Purg.* xviii. 121 (*ib.*). Finally, passages containing prophecies of future events. Much uncertainty arises in identifying such events (pp. 162, 163); partly also in consequence of the limits of prescience on the part of the lost enounced in *Inf.* x. 100–8 (pp. 163, 164). Summary of the *historical* arguments, which seem very strongly to preponderate for 1300 (pp. 164, 165).

II. The *astronomical* arguments. Preliminary question whether Dante's astronomical references are scientifically precise, or to be understood more or less popularly. The latter view maintained here (pp. 165–7); Discussion of passages relating to the position of (a) the Moon (pp. 167–9); (β) the Sun (pp. 169, 170); (γ) Mars (pp. 170, 171); (δ) Saturn (pp. 171, 172); (ε) Venus (pp. 172–4); Summary of the astronomical arguments (pp. 174, 175). Special reasons leading Dante to the choice of 1300 (p. 175). Conclusion (pp. 175, 176).

STUDIES IN DANTE

I. THE ASTRONOMY OF DANTE [1]

IT is a matter of regret that even students of ability and culture often refuse so much as to attempt to understand Dante's astronomical references. They assume either that they are not to be understood at all, or at least not without special astronomical or mathematical training. The truth is, that, as I hope to be able to show, most of them are perfectly simple and clear to any one with a knowledge of the most rudimentary facts of astronomy, modified by the manner of their presentation on the Ptolemaic system. This, however, does not in any way increase the difficulty. Indeed it may be said to have this special advantage in the way of intelligibility and simplicity, that it treats of the motions of the heavenly bodies just as they appear to an ordinary observer, without applying any of the corrections of such *prima facie* appearances required by modern astronomy. Those who thus give up such passages in despair,

> ' Contented if they might enjoy (?)
> The things which others understand,'

may well remember the warning addressed by Beatrice to Dante :

> ' Se li tuoi diti non sono a tal nodo
> Sufficienti, non è maraviglia ;
> *Tanto per non tentar è fatto sodo.*

' If thy fingers are not equal to untying such a knot, it is no wonder. It has become so hard from not trying.' (*Par.* xxviii. 58–60.)

On the other hand many specialists have brought to bear upon these astronomical references and allusions in Dante such a wealth of technical knowledge, and have interpreted them by the aid of calculations so elaborate and minute, that

[1] This essay is founded upon an article in the *Quarterly Review*, April, 1898.

* * *

they seem to forget that Dante's object was not to compose a didactic poem for teaching astronomy, but to use astronomy, as well as other branches of his very varied and extensive knowledge, in the service of poetry. He was a poet first and an astronomer afterwards [1]. Some of the laborious investigations just referred to would seem to suggest the reversal of that order, and to leave us with the impression that one of the most indispensable adjuncts to the study of the *Divina Commedia* would be the *Nautical Almanac*.

It is quite true that astronomy occupies an exceptionally prominent position in the works of Dante. It is evident from the frequency, and often the somewhat elaborate character, of his references to it in the *Divina Commedia*, as well as from many lengthy discussions of astronomical phenomena in the *Convito*, that he was himself both profoundly learned and also specially interested in this branch of science. But besides this, the subject of the *Divina Commedia*, especially in the *Paradiso*, naturally invited a large number of such references. The grades of happiness of the redeemed are associated locally with the different spheres or 'heavens' of the current astronomical science. Besides this, the belief in stellar influences on human affairs and character, shared by Dante with most, if not all, thinkers of his age [2], imparted a special and very practical interest to the study of astronomical phenomena. We may add further the prevalent idea of the mystical inter-relation of the physical world generally with the spheres of moral and mental activity, which is illustrated by the minute and, to modern ideas, tedious discussion of the relation between the various sciences of the *Trivium* and *Quadrivium* and the planets and other heavenly bodies, in *Conv.* II. xiv. Some preliminary acquaintance therefore with at least the outlines of the Ptolemaic system and phraseology is necessary for the intelligent understanding of numerous

---

[1] This applies to the *Divina Commedia* with which most of the writers referred to are mainly, if not exclusively, concerned. The case is, of course, different with the *Convito*, a designedly philosophical treatise, the astronomy of which has as yet been most inadequately discussed. This subject is dealt with more fully in Essay III.

[2] See this subject discussed, *infra*, pp. 19-21.

passages in Dante. That acquaintance need not, however, be extensive or minute, and in some cases, not 'a little knowledge,' but the advanced study of a specialist has proved 'dangerous,' in tempting its possessor beyond the limits of the legitimate interpretation of poetical allusions.

When we seek for the *direct* source of Dante's astronomical knowledge we have no hesitation in assigning the chief place to the *Elementa Astronomica* of Alfraganus. This is an epitome of the great work of Ptolemy by an Arabian astronomer of the ninth century. It was translated from Arabic into Latin first in the twelfth century by Gerardus of Cremona (d. 1187), who was also the first translator into Latin of the Almagest itself[1]; and again, a little later[2], by Johannes Hispalensis (of Seville), so that it would thus have become accessible to Dante. It has been five times printed[3], the latest, and perhaps least inaccurate, edition being that from which my citations are made (Ed. Amsterdam, 1669). Alfraganus is quoted by Dante in *Conv.* II. xiv. 95 as his authority for the dimensions of the planet Mercury (the passage being found in *Alf.* c. xxii.). Again he quotes his work in *Conv.* II. vi. 134, under the title by which it is sometimes known, as *Libro dell' aggregazione delle stelle*. Besides this, most of the astronomical data, and sometimes even the comparisons and illustrations given by Dante, are found *totidem verbis* in Alfraganus[4]. This, therefore, or some similar epitome

---

[1] Both translations c. 1175, *auct.* Jourdain, pp. 121 *n*, 123.

[2] His date, though somewhat uncertain, probably fell in the reign of Alfonso X of Leon, 'the Astronomer' (d. 1284). See Jourdain, p. 115.

[3] Viz. (1) Ferrara, 1493; (2) Nürnberg, 1537; (3) Paris, 1546; (4) Frankfort, 1590; (5) Amsterdam, 1669. Dr. Toynbee informs me that (2) is a mere reprint of (1), and that both are full of errors; that (3), though still very inaccurate, is better than (1) and (2); and that the Latin version is revised in (4) and (5), which are much the best editions. Also that (4), or rather some MS. to which this edition is related, exhibits most nearly the type of text used by Dante. In this edition the colophon runs : 'Explicit Alfraganus *de aggregatione scientiae stellarum*' (see *Conv.* II. vi. 134), the usual title being *Elementa Astronomica*, as in seventeen out of twenty MSS. at Oxford.

[4] e. g. the graphic comparison of the horizontal revolution of the sun as seen from the poles at the equinox, in *Conv.* III. v. 147, to that of a millstone (*come una mola*). So Alfraganus, c. vii. (p. 29) 'caelum, *molae trusatilis instar*, in gyrum vertitur horizonti respondentem.'

of the Almagest, he evidently used freely, and that it was in fact this particular work is made most probable by these definite citations of it [1].

I wish at the outset to acknowledge my very large obligations to the elaborate and learned works of Professor Narrien [2] and Sir G. C. Lewis [3]. I have relied upon them for most of the facts relating to the early history of astronomy adduced in the following pages. After this I shall not consider it necessary to repeat this acknowledgement in respect of details from time to time. The latter of these works deals mainly with the historical aspect of the subject. The former in addition develops the mathematical problems involved in the theories of the early astronomers. Both writers, it will be understood, treat of the subject in its general aspect and without any reference to the works of Dante, who is never once mentioned by them in this connexion.

As my object is to help readers of Dante, whom Plato would describe as 'ἀγεωμέτρητοι,' to understand his astronomical references and allusions, I may be pardoned if I sometimes seem to err on the side of over-explanation of points which appear simple enough to those who are even moderately versed in the rudiments of astronomy.

The correctness of many of the results obtained under the Ptolemaic system is quite astonishing [4] when we consider the imperfection of the instruments of observation and time-keepers available, the paucity of recorded observations for comparison, and the falsity of the fundamental assumptions of the system. The last-mentioned defect, however, is not so serious a drawback as it might at first sight appear. The *apparent results* would not be affected by the falsity of the hypothesis

---

[1] Alfraganus is very frequently quoted by Roger Bacon in his *Opus Majus*, with definite references to the chapters of the work. It is also often cited by other writers of that period, as by Albertus Magnus, Sacrobosco, Ristoro d' Arezzo, &c.

[2] *An historical account of the Origin and Progress of Astronomy*; by John Narrien, F.R.A.S., London, 1833.

[3] *An historical survey of the Astronomy of the Ancients*; by the Right Hon. Sir George Cornewall Lewis, London, 1862.

[4] I have met somewhere with the statement that 'the ancients knew more about the *visible facts* of astronomy than many of their modern critics.'

by which they were explained. A familiar illustration of this
may be given from common experience. When one of two
trains is stationary and the other is moving slowly and
smoothly it is often impossible to detect by the sight whether
we are ourselves in the moving or the stationary train. So,
whether the sun revolves about the earth or the earth about
the sun, there is absolutely no difference in the resulting
visible phenomena, which are the subject of astronomical research and record. This is noticed by Cicero [1] in respect of
the rival suppositions of the daily revolution of the earth
about its axis, and that of the daily revolution of the heaven
about the stationary earth. The old theories of eccentrics
and epicycles did, in point of fact, embody and explain the
observed *facts* as far as they were known in early times. Hence
it was quite possible on these assumptions to construct Tables
by which the motions and positions of the heavenly bodies could
be predicted with as much accuracy as would correspond with
the imperfect means of observation then available. So, says
Bacon, 'The same phenomena in astronomy are satisfied by
the received astronomy (i. e. Ptolemaic) of the diurnal motion,
and of the proper motion of the planets with their eccentrics
and epicycles, and likewise by the theory of Copernicus, who
supposed the earth to move ; and the calculations are indifferently agreeable to both' (*Adv. of Learning* II. c. 8, § 5).
Bacon himself strongly opposed the Copernican system ; e. g.
'Therefore the opinion of Copernicus in astronomy, *which
astronomy itself cannot correct*, because it is not repugnant to
any of the appearances, *yet natural philosophy doth correct.*'
Interp. Nature, Works, iii. 229.

I propose to use the term 'Ptolemaic' as a convenient
designation of the geocentric or pre-Copernican system of
astronomy generally. Though Ptolemy was himself a skilful
geometer and astronomer, he was not the inventor, but only
the most distinguished expositor and historian of the system
that bears his name. Its leading features had already been

---

[1] *Acad.* II. xxxix. § 123 'Hicetas . . . caelum, solem, lunam, stellas, supera
denique omnia stare censet, neque praeter terram rem ullam in mundo moveri ;
quae cum circum axem se summa celeritate convertat et torqueat, eadem effici
omnia, quae si stante terra caelum moveretur.'

traced by the labours of Eudoxus, Plato, Aristotle, Aristar-
chus, Eratosthenes, and above all Apollonius of Perga and
Hipparchus, besides many others. On the other hand the
so-called Ptolemaic system includes some improvements or
discoveries subsequent to his date. For it was the habit of
Arabian translators and editors to introduce occasional up-to-
date improvements in the works of the authors thus handled
by them. There are some remarkable instances of this in
the case of Aristotle, who in one so-called 'translation' of his
works is actually made to quote the Almagest by name [1],
a work written more than 400 years after his death !

It will probably be found most convenient to divide our
subject under the following heads :—

(1) Cosmogony, or the general conception of the construction of the universe.

(2) The Planetary motions, and the signs of the Zodiac.

(3) The measurement of time, years, days and hours.

These subjects will be considered only so far as they are
connected with the Ptolemaic system, and as they are implied
or expounded in the writings of Dante himself.

I. COSMOGONY, OR THE GENERAL CONCEPTION OF THE CONSTRUCTION OF THE UNIVERSE.

Now the first and most obvious of astronomical facts is the
apparent *diurnal* rotation of the sun, moon, planets, and fixed
stars round the earth as a fixed centre from east to west ; and
another, which is almost equally obvious, is that the sun,
moon, and five visible planets (which I shall, in accordance
with Ptolemaic and Dantesque usage, describe as the seven
planets), are each severally affected by a peculiar [2] and much
slower motion of their own about the earth, over and above
that of diurnal rotation, and also, in the opposite direction,
from west to east [3]. These two primary facts of observation

---

[1] *Auct.* Jourdain, p. 213. See also *Studies in Dante*, I. p. 317 *n.*

[2] This is termed a 'peculiar' motion, because the sun, moon, and each of
the planets make this revolution in a period peculiar to itself; e. g. the sun in
one year ; the moon in one month ; Mercury in about eighty-eight days ; Saturn
in about twenty-nine years, and so on.

[3] It is necessary to have a perfectly clear conception of the difference intended

were in the earliest times accounted for by supposing each of these bodies to be carried round the earth as the central point of the universe in a series of concentric hollow spheres or shells. These were technically called 'heavens.' Thus there were at any rate seven of such heavens, one outside, or as the common phrase was, 'above,' the other ; corresponding to the Moon, Mercury, Venus, the Sun, Mars, Jupiter, and Saturn. Outside these again was an eighth heaven, that of the fixed stars. To these were afterwards added a ninth and a tenth, for reasons to be explained presently. Thus the whole universe resembled a set of those curiously carved Indian balls consisting of several hollow spheres or spherical shells, one within the other,

'Laborious orient ivory sphere in sphere.'

At first, as Dante explains in *Conv.* II. iii. (which should be carefully read in connexion with this part of the subject), there were thought to be only eight of these heavens, an error which he states was shared by Aristotle, 'seguitando solamente l'antica grossezza degli astrologi' (*Conv.* II. iii. 20), though in the next chapter (l. 33) he makes rather a vague and lame attempt to show that Aristotle himself was conscious of a truer view, 'a chi bene lo intende.' It was held that the eighth of these heavens was that of the fixed stars, and that beyond

---

between revolution from east to west, and revolution from west to east. These terms are technically used in reference to the direction of the passage of the south, or meridian, line. If it is passed from left to right, the spectator facing south, that is termed a revolution from east to west ; but if it is passed from right to left, that is termed a revolution from west to east. Or again thus : in east to west revolution the west is reached from the east through the south ; but in west to east revolution the west is reached from the east through the north. Hence in *Purg.* xviii. 79, Dante describes the west to east orbital motion of the moon by the words 'correa contra il ciel,' i. e. contrary to the diurnal motion of the whole body of the heavens as controlled by the *Primum Mobile.* So in *Par.* vi. 1, 2, when Constantine removed the seat of empire from Rome to Constantinople,

'l'aquila volse
Contra il corso del ciel.'

Finally, in *Par.* ix. 85, the length of the Mediterranean in longitude, as Dante is there explaining it, from west to east is again described as 'contra il sole.' Compare Pliny, *N. H.* II. viii. 32 'omnium errantium siderum meatus, inter quae solis et lunae, *contrarium mundo* (i. e. Primo Mobili) agere cursum, id est laevum, illo semper in dextro praecipiti.' Also Cicero, *infra*, p. 14 *med.*

this there was no other ('che di fuori da esso non fosse altro alcuno '). The diurnal rotation of this eighth heaven from east to west was communicated in some way[1] to the seven 'lower' heavens in addition to their own several proper rotations, which, as I have already noted, were all in the converse direction, viz. from west to east.

Then came the important and very remarkable discovery by Hipparchus (fl. c. 150 B.C.) of the 'Precession of the Equinoxes,' as it is called. This is frequently alluded to by Dante, and holds a conspicuous position among his astronomical references. It may be briefly explained thus. In *Conv.* III. v., a most important and difficult chapter, where Dante explains at length 'come il sol gira,' he clearly distinguishes his diurnal motion from east to west in a plane parallel to the equator from his annual motion from west to east in a plane obliquely inclined to the equator, viz., that of the ecliptic ('tortamente contra quello,' viz. 'il moto diurno,' l. 129)[2]. These two circles necessarily intersect in two points, where the sun passes from below to above the equator (as in March), or from above to below (as in September). These points are known as the equinoctial points, or, more briefly, as the equinoxes, because the sun being then on the equator his diurnal revolution will be practically along the line of the equator itself, and not merely parallel to it. This is clearly and graphically described by Dante in *Conv.* III. v. 142 *seqq.* Consequently there will then be equality of day and night *all over the earth.* At the terrestrial equator or ' equinoctial line' there is obviously at all times equality of day and night. The Zodiac is a band or zone extending about 8° north and south of the ecliptic, that being the limit within which the apparent

---

[1] Dante thinks it presumptuous to dogmatize. See *Conv.* II. vi. 145-51.

[2] It is hardly necessary, though it may perhaps be safer, to explain that the Ecliptic is the path traversed by the sun in his *annual* (apparent) revolution about the earth from west to east. This must by no means be confused with his (apparent) *diurnal* revolution from east to west, which being due to the earth's daily rotation *on its axis* from west to east is of course in a plane parallel to the *Equator.* The (apparent) annual revolution of the sun is due to the earth's annual revolution in its *orbit* in the plane of the Ecliptic, along which, consequently, the sun appears to move. The plane of the Ecliptic is inclined to that of the Equator at an angle of c. $23\frac{1}{2}°$, *v. infra*, p. 48.

paths of the moon and five planets are included. When it was first divided into twelve equal parts, each designated by one of the twelve constellations or signs occupying that region of the heavens through which it passed, it was so arranged that the first of these signs, viz. 'Aries,' should commence at the spring equinoctial point, extending thence eastwards over one-twelfth of the zodiac, i. e. 30°; and this point or 'equinox' was known as the 'first point of Aries.' But after two or three centuries it was noticed by Hipparchus that the sun no longer crossed the equator at the 'first point of Aries,' but some little way back westwards in the constellation Pisces. Considering the meagre nature of his appliances and resources, and the very minute amount of this annual displacement, this discovery of Hipparchus must be considered to be a very remarkable achievement. For this backward movement of the equinoctial points is no more than about 50″ of space in a year[1]. Hipparchus determined it approximately as being not less than 36″, or more than 50″. Ptolemy afterwards assumed it to be 36″. Hence it would amount to only $1° = 3600″$ in 100 years, and this is (as we shall see) the amount assigned to it in several places by Dante, as well as by Alfraganus in his *Elementa*. Consequently it would take, according to this estimate, just 36,000 years to traverse the whole circle of the ecliptic, after which the equinox would again be found to be at 'the first point of Aries[2].' As a matter of fact, the amount of 'precession' assumed by Ptolemy and accepted by Dante is too small, and the whole revolution will really be accomplished in about 26,000 years. The true cause of this important phenomenon was first explained by Sir Isaac Newton[3]. Its visible result will be practically the same as if

[1] Some idea of the minuteness may be gathered thus. Most people are familiar with the two stars in the Great Bear called 'The Pointers.' These are about 5° apart. The amount of annual movement due to Precession being only c. 50″ of space, this is considerably less than $\frac{1}{300}$ part of the distance between 'The Pointers.'

[2] See Grant's *Physical Astronomy*, p. 38.

[3] Whewell, *Inductive Sciences*, i. p. 175, mentions a curious and very retrograde alternative theory of 'Trepidation' of the Stars, proposed by the Arabian astronomer Arzachel in the eleventh century, involving alternate progression and regression of the apparent equinoxes, and also a change of latitude in the stars.

we suppose the whole firmament to be revolving slowly round the pole of the ecliptic from west to east, and the equinoctial points therefore to be gradually receding along the ecliptic from east to west, at this very slow, and as Dante calls it almost imperceptible, rate (' movimento quasi insensibile,' *Conv.* II. xv. 102). Now the longitude of all celestial bodies is measured along the ecliptic, the zero line (corresponding to the meridian of Greenwich in terrestrial longitude) being the meridian of the spring equinoctial point. This is always measured *eastwards* round the whole circle, so that a star 1° west of that meridian would be described as having a longitude of 359°. Consequently, as the true equinoctial point gradually recedes westward along the ecliptic, it is evident that the east longitude of all the stars, as measured from the meridian of that point, is correspondingly increased. And as this increase has now been going on for more than 2,000 years, since the first point of Aries corresponded with the true equinoctial point, it will be seen by a simple calculation, that, at the rate of about 50″ a year, the longitudes have now increased by nearly 30°, and consequently that the true ' equinox' has now worked back nearly through the whole constellation of Pisces.

Unastronomical readers should perhaps be cautioned against confusing seconds of space with seconds of time. I have said that the point where the sun crosses the equator is 50″ of space further westwards every year. Now if the sun takes one year to traverse 360° of space, it will appear by a simple rule-of-three sum that he will fake a little more than twenty minutes to traverse this 50″ [1]. Now as the sun is going from west to east along the zodiac, and the equinoctial point is coming, so to speak, to meet him in the opposite direction from east to west at the rate of 50″ a year, the sun will,

---

[1] Similarly, turning to *diurnal* rotation, if a complete revolution of 360° takes place in twenty-four hours, it is clear that 15°, i. e. $\frac{360}{24}$, will occupy one hour, and hence 15° of longitude will make the difference of one hour in time, and 90° of six hours. This is the simple principle underlying the numerous references which Dante makes to the difference of time on different parts of the earth's surface; e. g. *Purg.* ii. 1-9, iii. 25, iv. 137-9, xxvii. 1-6, &c. Cf. *Purg.* xxxiii. 104, 105.

as we may say, be saved from going over that amount of
space each year before he reaches the equator ; or in other
words, he will reach it rather more than twenty minutes
sooner each year. Hence the 'tropical' year, as it is called—
i. e. the year which is regulated by the *seasons*, and the
beginning and end of which is marked by the moment of the
sun's reaching the equator at the spring equinox—is about
twenty minutes shorter than the 'sidereal' year, which represents one exact revolution of the earth in its orbit. Thus the
equinox may be said to occur twenty minutes sooner every
year, and hence arose the expression '*precession* of the equinoxes.' Having regard to the *position* of the equinoctial point
among the 'signs of the zodiac,' we should rather regard the
process as a *retrocession*.

We next ask, how this discovery of (as was then supposed)
a slow eastward movement of $1°$ in a century of the whole
starry heavens round the pole of the ecliptic, contrary to their
diurnal westward motion round the pole of the equator, was
adapted to the theory of the eight revolving heavens which
we have already explained. It was done in two ways. In
the first instance astronomers supposed the eighth heaven
(that of the fixed stars) to be affected by this motion *in
combination with* that of diurnal rotation ; this second, or precessional, motion also being (according to some astronomers,
but not according to others) communicated to the seven lower
or planetary heavens [1], in the same manner in which we have
seen that the movement of diurnal rotation was communicated
to them. But, as Dante points out in *Conv.* II. iii. 36, it was
felt to be inconsistent with the symmetry and simplicity of
nature that the eighth heaven should be subject to complicated
movements of this kind, and in fact to two simultaneous
revolutions in contrary directions, and moreover in different
planes (l. 38), or round different poles [2]. (In the case of the
seven planetary heavens, in which the same objection might
seem to hold, one of the movements (the diurnal) was not
'proper' to them, but only 'communicated' from the eighth

---

[1] As it obviously ought to be, and as it is in Alfraganus, c. xiii., *sub init.*

[2] Dante is not always consistent on this point, see *infra*, p. 15.

heaven to them all alike, and in addition to their own 'proper' motion.) Hence Dante says that Ptolemy, compelled by philosophical principles—'costretto da' principii di filosofia '— which demand a *Primum Mobile* of absolute simplicity, assumed another and a ninth heaven, above and beyond the eighth, to which the simple diurnal revolution of all the other heavens from east to west was due [1]. Hence this ninth heaven was known as the *Primum Mobile*, since its motion was communicated to all the other heavens. It was also sometimes called the Crystalline heaven, i.e. transparent, or diaphanous, as Dante explains in *Conv.* II. iv. 11. This left only the slow motion of precession from west to east at the rate of $1°$ a century, to the eighth heaven, that of the fixed stars. Hence this is often referred to by Dante as the slowest, and the ninth as the swiftest of the heavens. Also in the beginning of *Conv.* II. iv., where Dante enumerates the nine heavens in order, he further observes of the ninth heaven that it is not visible to the senses except by the diurnal motion spoken of in the previous chapter. We see by the context that he means that the other eight heavens are manifest to the senses, by the planets or stars which are, so to speak, attached to them ; but there is no visible or sensible object thus associated with the ninth heaven, or *Primum Mobile*. Its existence is inferred by the mind to account for observed phenomena of sense [2].

[1] Hence the Pole Star is described as the point of the axis of the *Primum Mobile* in *Par.* xiii. 11, 12 :

'punta dello stelo
A cui la prima rota va dintorno.'

A few words of explanation of this rather fanciful passage may not be out of place. Dante has described the two garlands, each consisting of twelve Spirits, which are associated respectively with S. Thomas Aquinas and S. Bonaventura. He now likens them to two imaginary constellations of exceptional brilliancy composed of twenty-four stars made up from the fifteen most brilliant stars from all parts of the firmament (ll. 4-6) together with the seven stars of the Great Bear (ll. 7-9) and the two of the Little Bear (now known as β and γ) furthest from the Pole Star, which is indicated as above. These are described as forming the mouth of the horn to which the seven principal stars of the Little Bear are here likened (ll. 10-12). These twenty-four stars are supposed to form two new constellations resembling the Corona Borealis (ll. 13-15), revolving concentrically, one within the other, and in opposite directions (ll. 16-18).

[2] The long description of it in *Par.* xxvii. 99-120 should be read here.

Hence it is described by Milton as

> ' That swift
> Nocturnal and diurnal rhomb, *supposed*,
> *Invisible else*, above all stars, the wheel
> Of day and night.' (*Par. Lost*, viii. 133-136.)

The enumeration of the heavens was now complete as far as human observation or reflection could reveal them. But Dante adds that 'by the Catholic religion' we are bound to believe in a tenth heaven, the Empyrean, the calm and motionless abode of God and of His angels and the glorified saints. This is the teaching of the Catholic Church, which cannot say that which is false, ' che non può dire menzogna.' This is the supreme edifice of the universe, ' sovrano edificio del mondo,' beyond and above which there is nothing, and this itself has no local limitation[1], but was formed and abides in the Divine mind. And he adds that the Psalmist refers to this when he declares that God has set his glory *above* the heavens. This tenth heaven differs from all the others in that it does not revolve but is *absolutely motionless*. For all motion implies change and a desire for something better (see this explained in *Epist.* x, § 26, also *infr.* p. 24, and in Essay V). Therefore, ' quieto e pacifico è lo luogo di quella somma Deità che Sè sola compiutamente vede ' (*Conv.* II. iv. 28-30). It is the ' ciel della divina pace ' (*Par.* ii. 112). God himself

> ' Del suo lume fa il ciel sempre quieto,
> Nel qual si volge quel ch' ha maggior fretta '

(i. e. the *Primum Mobile, Par.* i. 122, 123).

Finally, see Par. xxii. 64-67 :—

> ' Ivi è perfetta, matura ed intera
>   Ciascuna disianza ; in quella sola
>   È ogni parte là dove sempr' era ;
>   Perchè non è in loco, e non s' impola.'

The words ' s'impola ' express that it has no pole or axis of revolution like all the other heavens. Its existence in the case of the other nine is clearly explained in *Conv.* II. iv. 48, *seqq.*

---

[1] ' Esso non è in luogo, ma formato fu solo nella prima Mente,' *Conv.* II. iv. 37. See further the fuller description of it in Epist. X. §§ 24, 25.

Thus the construction of the universe is finally completed with the recognition of these ten several heavens; the first eight by the evidence of the senses, the ninth, or *Primum Mobile*, by necessary inference, and the tenth by the aid of revelation. And so, as Dante says in *Conv.* II. iii. 18, in spite of the diverse opinions that have prevailed on this subject, 'the truth has at last been discovered.'

It is interesting to compare with this the system expounded by Cicero in the *Somnium Scipionis*, a work possibly, and even probably, known to Dante. Africanus discourses thus (§ 17): 'You find all things included within nine orbs or rather globes. Of these one is that of heaven itself, that which is the outermost, which embraces all the others, God Himself on high, enclosing and containing the rest. Within this are fixed those eternal courses of the stars which revolve. Underneath it lie seven [such] orbits, which *turn backwards with a motion contrary to that of the heaven* ('qui versantur retro contrario motu atque caelum '),' i. e. from west to east, or 'contro il ciel,' as we have had before. It will be seen that the spheres are here enumerated in the converse order to that usually adopted, the *first* being the *outermost*. Thus the first sphere or globe, which is called 'heaven,' is that which contains the fixed stars, and at the same time is the *Primum Mobile*. It also seems to be identified with God Himself. Nothing is said about the motion of Precession. It is also to be noticed that in the sense in which the term 'heavens' has been hitherto used (and as it is used by Dante) there are only eight heavens, since in the following section the earth itself is said to be the ninth ('terra *nona*, immobilis manens, ima sede semper haeret, complexa medium mundi locum ').

I will next draw attention to some of the chief passages in Dante, which are illustrated by the general system of cosmogony now expounded. First, as the old astronomers were not always agreed as to whether these spheres were material or not, we may remark that Dante clearly held them to be so. In *Par.* xxviii. 64, the heavens are described as 'cerchi corporai.' In *Par.* ii. 112, we read, 'Dentro dal ciel della divina pace, Si gira un *corpo*,' &c., and this is seen by the context to describe the ninth heaven or *Primum Mobile*. Again in *Par*. xxx. 38, 39 :—

> ' Noi semo usciti fuore
> Del maggior corpo al ciel ch' è pura luce ; '

the 'maggior corpo ' is the *Primum Mobile*. In *Conv*. II. iv. 87 he describes the very bright star of Venus as 'fixed' (*fissa*) upon its epicycle. And (not to quote other passages) in *Purg*. iii. 29 he compares the non-casting of any shadow by Virgil's 'spiritual body' to the permeability of the several heavens by the light of others—'Che l' uno all' altro raggio non ingombra[1].' Unless they were in some degree material, this would not afford a suitable illustration[2]. We may add *Par*. ii. 32 and 37 *seqq*. ; also our word 'firmament' ; and *Job* xxxvii. 18, 'caelos, qui solidissimi quasi aere fusi sunt.'

Next, it is to be observed that Dante is not always quite consistent in attributing the diurnal motion to the ninth and the precessional motion to the eighth sphere, as we have seen (p. 11) that he did in *Conv*. II. iii., justifying it there by philosophical necessity. This view moreover is implied in *Conv*. II. iv. 10, 19, and in vi. 140-3. Also in *V. N*. ii, 9 *seqq*., where the age of Beatrice at their first meeting is described in a very characteristically Dantesque manner. 'She had been so long in this life that during her time the starry heaven had moved in an eastward direction (i. e. from west to east) $\frac{1}{12}$ of a degree, so that she appeared to me almost at the beginning of her ninth year.' Now, as Dante conceived this precessional motion to be at the rate of 1° in a century, the age of Beatrice would be $\frac{100}{12} = 8\frac{1}{3}$ years. But notwithstanding, there is one place, viz. *Conv*. II. xv.12-14 and 95 *seqq*., in which he distinctly attributes *both* motions to the eighth or stellar

---

[1] Cf. *Summa*, I. lxvi. 3 *ad fin*. ' Sed quia corpus firmamenti etsi sit solidum, est tamen diaphanum quod lumen non impedit, ut patet per hoc quod lumen stellarum videmus non obstantibus mediis caelis,' &c.

[2] So Roger Bacon, *Mult. Spec*. II. iv. (ii. p. 472), argues that the light of the fixed stars is not refracted in passing through the celestial spheres of the planets, because they are all of uniform 'diaphaneity,' 'quamvis sint orbes (planetarum) contigui et diversarum superficierum ' (in explanation of 'contigui' v. *infra*, p. 29).

heaven, and he bases upon this a fanciful analogy between this heaven and the *two* sciences of physics and metaphysics, which is also elaborated by other arguments equally convincing[1]. Yet almost immediately afterwards, in the same chapter (ll. 133 *seqq.*), when tracing a similar analogy between the *Primum Mobile*, or crystalline heaven, and moral philosophy, he returns to his usual theory, and attributes to *that* heaven the diurnal motion, which governs that of all the other heavens without exception[2], and argues that in like manner all the actions of life are controlled by moral philosophy. And a very curious and difficult passage then follows, to *prove* this pervading and controlling influence of the *Primum Mobile* by a consideration of the impossible or disastrous conditions which would result from its absence, or from the suspension of its motion. Supposing, says Dante, that this ninth heaven had no motion, then the one-third part of the heavens would never yet have been visible from any place upon the earth. This seems at first a very hard saying; but its meaning comes out clearly on a little reflection. It being assumed that the earth is itself motionless, then on this further supposition that there was no *diurnal* revolution of the heavens, they too would remain fixed, and would always present the same hemispherical surface at any given spot; i.e. the same 180° would always be above the horizon,

---

[1] The occasion just cited is the only one, I believe, in which Dante abandons the theory which assigned the diurnal and precessional motions to separate spheres. It seems as if the temptation of securing so suitable an argument for the purpose in hand was irresistible, both theories having admittedly been sometimes held.

[2] In this sense it is described in *Par.* xxviii. 70 as

> 'costui, che tutto quanto rape
> L'altro universo seco:'

and again in *Par.* xxiii. 112, 113 as

> 'Lo real manto di tutti i volumi
> Del mondo.'

But, as all the lower heavens derive their motion from it, so it depends for all its vitality on the tenth heaven, the abode of God Himself. In *Par.* xxx. 106–108, Dante speaking of the tenth heaven says—

> 'Fassi di raggio tutta sua parvenza
> Riflesso al sommo del Mobile primo,
> Che prende quindi vivere e potenza.'

With this last passage we may compare *Summa*, I. lxvi. 3. r $_2$ 'Caelum empyreum habet influentiam super corpora quae moventur, licet ipsum non moveatur.'

and the other 180° would never be seen there at all. The only modification of this rigid condition would be due to the slow *precessional* motion of the heaven of the fixed stars, amounting to 1° in a century ; but in the approximately 6000 years since the beginning of creation this motion would have only traversed about 60°. Thus, besides the 180° at present visible, there would have been at one time or another since Creation a further 60° exposed to the eye of man at that spot. Hence, the total amount of the heavens ever seen up to the present moment anywhere would be 180° + 60° = 240°, though of course only the same 180° would ever be seen at any given period of time. Consequently, the remaining 120° would never yet have been visible at all. Since 120° is 360° × $\frac{1}{3}$, therefore, as Dante states, one-third of the whole heavens would never yet have been seen from any given place on the earth. So much for that. But another obvious result of this supposition would be that the sun, moon, and planets would perform one-half of their *orbital* revolution round the earth (the *diurnal* revolution being *ex hypothesi* abolished) behind our backs, so to speak ; i. e. in that 180° of the heavens which, on this hypothesis, would be always invisible to us. Hence, says Dante (ll. 142 *seqq.*), the sun would be invisible for half of each year, the moon for half of each month, Saturn for fourteen and a half years, Jupiter for six years, and so on of all the other planets. These figures in each case correspond to one-half of the time of each planet's year, or annual revolution, according to the elements given by the Ptolemaic system (which are in fact remarkably correct), and as Dante would have found them set forth in chap. xvii. of the *Elementa* of Alfraganus. All this would result in the death of animals and plants, the reduction of the world to chaos, and the complete frustration of all other celestial influences [1].

---

[1] Reading here (l. 157) *altri*, not the conjectural *astri*. We may compare a very similar passage in Ristoro d'Arezzo, *Dist.* vii. pt. ii. c. 4 (p. 101) :—'Se la virtude del cielo si cessasse e lo cielo non si movesse, le piante, e li animali e le minerie, le quali son fatti delli omori delli quattro elimenti, disceverereb-berosi e disfarebbensi tutte, e ciascheduno omore tornerebbe al suo elimento. ... E se la virtude del cielo tornasse nel cielo, e se 'l cielo non si movesse, non farebbe tutta la sua operazione, e mescolerebbe li elimenti insieme.'

* * *

The purpose or 'moral' of all this curious disquisition is to show that in like manner the suspension or removal of moral philosophy would reduce all human life and all human science to chaos and oblivion.

I will next invite attention to a passage which, though at first sight a little obscure and difficult, illustrates two points that have been incidentally noticed : (1) the communication of the diurnal motion of the *Primum Mobile* to the seven 'inferior' or 'lower' heavens, and (2) the influence of the stars or 'heavens' on human life, character, and events. I refer to *Par.* ii. 112 *seqq.*, which I will translate literally, interposing brief comments.

'Within the heaven of the Divine peace [i. e. the Empyrean or tenth heaven] there revolves a body [i. e. the *Primum Mobile* or ninth heaven] on whose virtue or influence depends the Being of all that is contained within it' [i. e., as in the passage last explained from the *Convito*, if the *Primum Mobile* ceased to operate, all things would return to chaos and nonentity. See *Conv.* II. xv. 152, 'Life would become extinct in plants and animals ; nights and days, and months and years would be no more, and all the universe would fall back into confusion'].

l. 115. 'The heaven which follows, which has so many objects of sight [1] [i. e. the eighth heaven with all the fixed stars], distributes that Being through diverse essences or existences, which are distinct from it and contained by it' [i. e. the numerous stars which this eighth heaven displays].

l. 118. 'The other revolving spheres through various differences dispose towards their several ends and their several productions the distinctive objects which they have within themselves' [i. e. the several planetary spheres or heavens, each according to its proper end and distinct purpose, bring about the diverse operations and productions suitable to each].

l. 121. 'These organs of the Universe [2] [i. e. sun, moon, and

---

[1] *Vedute*, exactly like 'viste' in *Par.* xxiii. 30; xxx. 9. Compare 'vedute' as used in *Par.* xiv. 80.

[2] They are called 'organi' as being the instruments by which God performs His operations in the world, comp. *Par.* viii. 97-9. See also *Mon.* II. ii. 15, and the other passages quoted p. 20.

planets, or, as Dante would say, the seven planets] proceed as thou now seest from step to step, for they receive from above and operate below' [1] ; i. e. they themselves receive influence from the higher spheres, the eighth and ninth heavens, from which the precessional and diurnal motions common to them all are derived, and they exercise influence on that which is below them, i. e. on the events and life of this earth ; the 'sublunary' sphere, as we still call it, because it was thought to lie below the lowest of the heavenly spheres, viz. that of the moon. The rest of the passage, though highly poetical in form and interesting in its teaching, scarcely falls within the scope of astronomy [2].

The same teaching is expressed in the plain prose of the *Conv.* II. xv. 132–8 : 'The said heaven [i. e. the ninth or *Primum Mobile*] regulates by its motion the daily revolution of all the others, *through which they below receive the virtue* [or vivifying influence] *of all their parts*. Because if the revolution of this heaven did not so order this, little of the influence of those heavens would come here below, or even the sight of them' ; in other words, their influence on human affairs would be almost entirely lost. The saving phrases, 'little' and 'almost entirely,' refer to the very slight 'precessional' motion which would still remain even if the diurnal were abolished. How the 'sight' of them would be lost has been already explained, *sup.* p. 17.

This explicit reference to the influence of the stars in human affairs, as well as the expression 'organi del mondo' in *Par.* ii. 121, suggests that we should here define precisely the nature of Dante's belief in 'astrology' in the modern sense of the word, though in his day the term was used convertibly with 'astronomy.' There is a striking passage in *Par.* viii. 97 *seqq.* in which Dante declares the difference in

---

[1] Compare *Par.* xxviii. 127–9,

   'Questi ordini di su tutti rimirano,
      E di giù vincon sì che verso Dio
      Tutti tirati sono e tutti tirano.'

[2] The passage here explained has several remarkable points of resemblance with the *Quaestio* xxi. 7–29.

human characters to be due to God's special providence [1]. The career of each individual is foreseen and fore-ordained of God (though it is often perversely departed from, ll. 139 *seqq.*), and his character and capacities are ordered suitably to it. See ll. 100–3 :—

> ' E non pur le nature provvedute
> Son nella mente ch' è da sè perfetta,
> Ma esse insieme con la lor salute.'

But the immediate efficient cause of these differences of character is found in the influence of the stars. See ll. 97–9 :—

> ' Lo ben che tutto il regno che tu scandi
> Volge e contenta, fa esser virtute
> Sua provvidenza in questi corpi grandi ; '

and again in ll. 127, 128, ' La circular natura ' [i. e. the re-volution of the heavens] is described as ' suggello alla cera mortal.'

Thus Dante firmly held that God's ' never-failing providence ordereth all things both in heaven and earth,' yet that He wills to use the stars as His instruments, just as the angels who effect the motions of those stars are His agents [2]. Hence, in the passage above quoted, the stars are called ' organi del mondo.' In *Mon.* II. ii. 15 we read, ' Est enim natura in mente primi motoris, qui Deus est, deinde in coelo *tanquam in organo* ' ; and *ibid.* 25 he speaks of ' instrumentum eius [*sc.* Dei] quod coelum est.' Similar language will be found in the *Quaestio* xx. 59 : ' quum organum suae virtutis sive influentiae sit ipsa luna.' So again, *ibid.* xxi. 16. See further, *Ep.* V. viii. 134, where God is said sometimes to carry out His purposes ' per homines, *tanquam per caelos novos.*' When in the important passage, *Purg.* xvi. 67–83, Dante insists that the stellar influence is never so overpowering as to destroy

---

[1] Otherwise children would always resemble their parents in character ; see ll. 133–5 :

> ' Natura generata il suo cammino
> Simil farebbe sempre ai generanti,
> Se non vincesse il provveder divino.'

[2] That the influence of the stars is not due to themselves but to the ' Angeli Movitori ' is distinetly asserted in *Conv.* II. v. 6 ; III. vi. 65 and elsewhere. See especially *Par.* iv. 61–3 where it is pointed out how ' Questo principio male inteso ' led to idolatry. On the ' Angeli Movitori,' see further *infra*, p. 26.

human responsibility [1], this is equivalent to the assertion of the freedom of the will side by side with the belief in God's foreknowledge, and in a special providence. The reality of the influence of the stars on human affairs (in this perfectly harmless form) Dante regarded as entirely indisputable (see *Conv.* II. xiv. 27) ; so much so that any one who doubted it was 'extra limitem philosophiae' (*Quaestio* xxi. 18).

The following are some of the other passages in Dante beyond those already referred to which bear upon this subject: *Purg.* xx. 13, xxx. 109-11 ; *Par.* xxiii. 21, xxvi. 129 ; *Conv.* II. xxiii. 50 [2].

I will next cite a few passages in which Dante refers to the extremely slow motion of the eighth, and the extremely swift motion of the ninth heaven.

The slowness of the eighth heaven is alluded to in *Purg.* xi. 103 *seqq.*, where the vanity of human fame is exhibited by the reflection that before 1000 years are passed [3] it will utterly have perished, and yet that period bears a less proportion to eternity than the twinkling of an eye to the revolution of the slowest sphere in the heaven, i. e. to the 36000 years occupied in the revolution of the eighth heaven. In connexion with this there is a passage in *Conv.* II. xv. 114, which calls for a word of explanation. Dante is here arguing for the appropriate connexion of each of the sciences of the *Trivium* and *Quadrivium* with one of the seven planetary spheres or heavens, and he says that the slow motion of the eighth heaven [4], being in fact endless, is a symbol of those incor-

---

[1] So S. Aug. *C. D.* v. i. says that, even if the stars influence human events, they themselves depend on the will of God, and our wicked acts are no more *caused* by them than by Him.

[2] Aquinas is fully in agreement with Dante on this point. The following among many other passages may be noticed :—I. cxv. 4 and 6; II¹. ix. 5; I². xcv. 5 *fin.* ; III. Suppl. lxxvii. 1.

[3] '1000 years' is a general expression for a long period (compare 'sexcenti' in Latin). The phrase is probably suggested to Dante by Scripture as in *Ps.* lxxxix. 4, and 2 *Pet.* iii. 8. See also *Purg.* xiv. 65, and *Conv.* IV. xi. 81. It has been imitated by Petrarch, *Trionfo d'Amore*, i. 81:
'fiati cosa piana
Anzi mill' anni.'
For a similar *litotes* in Dante cf. *Par.* xxvii. 142 (explained *infra*, p. 97).

[4] The slow motion of the eighth heaven is referred to by Roger Bacon (ii.

ruptible things which form the subject of metaphysics. That it is ' endless' he proves thus. Since the creation only a little more than one-sixth part of this revolution has been accomplished, and we are already in the last age of the world, awaiting the consummation of all things. Consequently this revolution will never be completed while the world lasts. It is at first sight rather puzzling to find Dante declaring that a little *more* than one-sixth of the revolution is already accomplished, for on his own *datum* of 1° in a century this would imply that in or about 1300 A.D. the world had existed for more than 6000 years. This, however, corresponds with the chronology which would be found by Dante in two authorities with which he was familiar. In Orosius I. 1. § 5 the time from Adam to Ninus is given as 3184 years, and that from Ninus (contemporary with Abraham) to Christ, 2015. This would make the Incarnation of Christ to be in the year 5199. If to this we add 1300, we have 6499 as the *Annus Mundi* in the time of Dante. Hence the statement, 'a little more than one-sixth,' in the passage just quoted, is explained. So, again, Brunetto Latini (Dante's so-called ' Master') gives the alternative dates of 5500 or 5290 as the year of the Incarnation. The same, or a somewhat similar computation, appears from other mediaeval writers to have been popularly accepted [1].

pp. 268, 269). He is misquoting Seneca, and very curiously misquoting him. ' At illa regio coelestis per triginta [sex millia] annorum velocissimo sideri viam praestat.' The words ' sex millia' are inserted by Bacon himself, and he applies the passage to 'precession.' Seneca says merely 'triginta,' and is referring to the revolution of Saturn! (Bridges's note *l. c.*). On the epithet ' velocissimo ' see next page.

[1] e. g. *Legenda Aurea*, Cap. vi. The author himself adopts the date 5228 for the Incarnation, but he gives the alternative dates 5090 (*auct.* Eusebius of Caesarea) and 6000, though he says of this last, 'inventa fuit a Methodio potius mystice quam chronice.' There are two other passages in Dante which imply the same chronology as the passage of the *Convito* just explained. In *Purg.* xxxiii. 62 Adam is said to have ' desired to see Christ's day' for 5000 years and more, i. e. since the Fall. And more precisely in *Par.* xxvi. 119, 120, Adam is made to say of the time that he was in Limbo, i. e. from his death to Christ's Resurrection,

> ' Quattromila trecento e due volumi
> Di sol desiderai questo concilio.'

Now 4302 added to 930 (the years of Adam's life on earth) will give 5232 ;

It seems, perhaps, at first sight inconsistent that Dante should describe the heaven of the moon in *Par.* iii. 51 as 'la spera più tarda,' especially as the proper motion of this heaven is evidently swifter than that of any other of the planetary spheres, its revolution being accomplished in one month as that of the sun is in one year, and that of the other planets in periods from about 88 days in the case of Mercury to about $29\frac{1}{2}$ years in the case of Saturn (see *Conv.* II. xiv. 228, and xv. 143). But the explanation is obviously this, that Dante is referring to the relative effect upon the heaven of the moon, as compared with the other heavens, of the common diurnal motion which they all receive from the *Primum Mobile.* It is clear that any point on the surface of concentric spheres or circles moving with a common rotation will revolve more or less quickly in proportion to their size, i. e. the length of their radii. This is expounded by Dante in *Par.* xxviii. 49–51 and 64–72. Hence the heaven of the moon, being the smallest ('quel ciel che ha minor li cerchi sui,' *Inf.* ii. 78), will experience the slowest diurnal rotation. On the same principle the equator of any revolving spherical body moves more quickly than any other part of it [1]. Dante not only points this out in *Conv.* II. iv. 59 *seqq.*, but here, and in other places, he insists on the greater degree of life, dignity, and nobleness, which is associated with swifter motion in all cases. Hence it is that greater influence on things below is exercised by the 'equatorial stars,' *Conv.* II. iv. 75 ; *Quaestio* xxi. 25.

The same considerations will explain the epithet 'velocissimo' applied to Saturn by Seneca in the passage quoted, p. 22 *n.* This is the exact converse to the case of the moon. The proper motion of the heaven of Saturn is the slowest. Hence in *Conv.* II. xiv. 226 Dante speaks of 'la tardezza del suo movimento per li dodici segni.' But his diurnal

and as the period referred to is that of Christ's descent into Limbo (see *Inf.* iv. 55–63) we must deduct thirty-three to find the date assigned to the Incarnation, viz. 5199, as above.

[1] Thus in the case of the earth, its surface moves 1040 miles an hour at the equator, 900 miles at lat. 30°, only 520 at lat. 60°, and so less and less till its velocity from rotation sinks to nothing at the Poles (Denison's *Astronomy, &c.,* p. 39).

rotation round the earth is the swiftest, owing to the greater length of the radius of his 'heaven.' Hence Dante (*ibid.* l. 230) describes Saturn as ' alto sopra tutti gli altri pianeti,' or in the words of Pliny, *N. H.* II. ix. 44, 'sidus altissimum' (see also *infra*, p. 29, *n.* 1).

The reason for this superiority of the swifter motion, and also for the extreme swiftness attributed to the revolution of the ninth heaven, may be thus explained. All motion whatsoever is regarded by Dante as an effect and striving after some higher condition ; and as this at last 'al sommo pinge noi di collo in collo,' it represents ultimately and in effect a struggle to attain the perfect rest and quiet of the Divine Essence, whose home is the Empyrean, or the motionless tenth heaven [1]. This is expounded clearly in *Epist.* x. § 26:—

'Omne quod movetur, movetur propter aliquid quod non habet, quod est terminus sui motus . . . Omne ergo quod movetur est in aliquo defectu et non habet totum suum esse simul. Illud igitur caelum quod a nullo movetur, in se et in qualibet sui parte habet quidquid potest modo perfecto, eo quod motu non indiget ad suam perfectionem.'

And in contrast with this, this tenth heaven is motionless, 'per avere in sè secondo ciascuna parte ciò che la sua materia vuole' (*Conv.* II. iv. 17–19). Hence, though it seems at first somewhat paradoxical, in any *created* object the swiftest motion is the most divine, because its swiftness is the evidence and the measure of the intensity of its desire to reach the Rest of God,

> 'Che tutto il ciel move,
> Non moto, con amore e con disio.' (*Par.* xxiv. 131.)

This exposition of the 'laws of motion' is a very favourite thought with Dante. Thus, in *Par.* i. 76, the general revolution of the heavens is described as

> 'La rota che tu (Dio) sempiterni
> Desiderato.'

And, again, in *Conv.* II. iv. 19 :—'This is the reason why the *Primum Mobile* moves with exceeding swiftness, because

---

[1] On this *vide supra*, p. 13.

through the most fervent longing of every part of the ninth heaven, which is next to this [i. e. to the Empyrean], to be united with every part of this tenth divine and peaceful heaven, it revolves within it with so much desire that its velocity is almost inconceivable [1].' On the same principle, swiftness of motion is the measure of the love and happiness of glorified spirits : see *Par.* viii. 19–21, xxiv. 16–18, xxviii. 25–27. The passage last referred to calls for a few words of explanation. Dante here describes how he saw a point of exceeding brightness, and the nine Orders of Angels revolving round it. The first of these circles of fire (afterwards explained to be the Order of Seraphim) 'revolved with a swiftness that would have surpassed that motion which most quickly engirdles the world' (l. 27) (i. e., as often elsewhere, that of the *Primum Mobile*). Then follow the other eight Orders, and 'each moved more slowly as its number was further removed from one' (l. 34). Dante is at once struck by this anomaly, for (as he declares to Beatrice) in the world of sense one can see that revolutions are so much more Godlike (i. e. swifter) in proportion as they are more remote from the centre (ll. 49–51), as e. g. that of the equator compared with any other part of the earth's surface (*Conv.* II. iv. 69). He cannot understand why the 'copy' and the 'exemplar' (i. e. the world of sense and the world of spirit) are thus out of conformity (ll. 55–7). For our present purpose it is not necessary to quote the solution which follows, but ll. 64–9 should be specially noted.

So much as to the *Final* Cause of all celestial motions. But the speculation of Dante and others as to the secondary or immediate *Efficient* Causes of these motions supplies another point of contact between the theological and physical theories of that time.

---

[1] It will be sufficient to enumerate, without comment, a few other passages in which the rapid motion of the *Primum Mobile* is referred to. See *Purg.* xxxiii. 90; *Par.* i. 123, xiii. 24, xxvii. 99, xxviii. 27, xxx. 106-8 ; *Conv.* II. iv. 27. In *Purg.* xxviii. 104 Dante explains that the leaves of the trees in the Earthly Paradise are gently inclined to the west (see l. 12 'U' la prim' ombra gitta il santo monte') by the equable motion of the whole atmosphere as it is carried round by the revolution of the *Primum Mobile* ('la prima volta '), and not by any local atmospheric disturbances (see ll. 7 and 106-8) from which the whole mountain of Purgatory is entirely exempt (see xxi. 43-57).

(1) Each heaven or sphere or star was thought to be under the control of 'Angeli Movitori[1];' see *Conv.* II. ii. 62 *seqq.*, where Dante is speaking specially of the 'terzo ciel,' that of Venus, 'certe Intelligenze, ovvero per più usato modo volemo dire Angeli, li quali sono alla rivoluzione del cielo di Venere, siccome movitori di quello:' and again II. v. 5, 'È da sapere primamente che li movitori di quello sono Sustanze separate da materia, cioè Intelligenze, le quali la volgare gente chiama Angeli.' (2) Further, Dante declares that the *modus operandi* of these Angels is not physical or mechanical, but mental or spiritual, through the action of pure volition. It was effected 'solo intendendo[2],' as this expression of the Canzone is explained in the commentary, II. vi. *fin.*: 'gira toccata da virtù motrice che questo *intende*; e dico toccata, non corporalmente, per tatto di virtù la quale si dirizza in quello.' (3) The belief thus enunciated was held to supply an argument for the creation of angels simultaneously with that of the material universe. Otherwise, reasons Dante, in opposition to the theory of Jerome that they were created many ages before, the 'motori' would have been all that time 'senza sua perfezion,' having no sphere for their operations[3]. *Par.* xxix. 37–45 (see further *Studies*, I. 79).

Perhaps it may seem that we have already been tempted too far from 'astronomy,' properly so called, in illustration of this point. But we must remember that Dante lived before the days when such *a priori* and semi-theological considerations came to be thought out of place in physical science. Consequently this explanation of the 'laws of celestial motion'

---

[1] An idea as old as Theodore of Mopsuestia (d. 429) and ridiculed by John Philoponus (seventh century) as treating the angels like porters to hold up and push about the heavenly bodies (Beazley, *Dawn of Geography*, p. 44). Cosmas Indicopleustes (c. 530) ridicules those who imagine the heavenly bodies to revolve by some natural uniform motion, and depicts their amazement when at the last day they discover the truth, for the angels will then cease their ministry, and as a consequence the stars will fall from heaven (Beazley, *op. cit.* p. 293).

[2] The meaning of 'intendere,' 'intenzione,' &c., as used by Dante, may be further illustrated by *Conv.* II. v. 94; viii. 9; III. xii. 82; and IV. i. 65.

[3] The same idea is found in Ristoro d' Arezzo, B. viii. c. 3, 'Adunque questi spiriti e questi intelligenze non deono istare oziose, e per ragione deono lavorare e fare operazione.'

would be held to be as real and legitimate a part of the
'science' of astronomy as the enunciation of the 'law of
gravitation' would be to a modern physicist.

In reference to the eighth heaven, that of the fixed stars,
there is just one other point to be noticed. Dante, following
Ptolemy and Alfraganus (c. xix.), held the total number of
the stars to be 1022, and he is at no loss for mystical reasons
to justify this precise number (see *Conv.* II. xv. 21). In regard
to the milky way or galaxy, or 'Via di San Jacopo,' as Dante
says it was vulgarly called (probably from a confusion, or
supposed connexion, between Galassia and Galizia)[1], he mentions three or four theories, including that which treated it
as a multitude of minute stars, which would of course upset
the above calculation of their definite number. He does not
formally adopt any definite conclusion on the subject, being
deprived here of the guidance of his master, Aristotle, for the
curious reason that 'his actual view cannot be ascertained,
owing to the discrepancy between the "old" translation and
the "new[2]" (*Conv.* II. xv. 45 *seqq.*).'

Before we leave this division of our subject, there are three
further points falling under the head of general Cosmogony to
be noted :

(i) The relative order assigned to the planetary heavens.

(ii) Their several magnitudes, or their distances from the
earth.

(iii) The relation of the ten heavenly spheres to the four
elemental spheres which were thought to be concentric with
them and to lie below them.

i. The relative order of the planetary spheres was much
disputed among the early astronomers, but the Greeks generally accepted that order which is found in Ptolemy[3], and is

---

[1] Dr. Toynbee informs me that Dante probably obtained this from Uguccione,
who says, 'Galaxias, id est lacteus circulus, qui vulgo dicitur, Via Sancti Jacobi.'
Uguccione is quoted by name only in *Conv.* IV. vi. 39, but Dr. Toynbee has shown
that Dante is much more often indebted to him. See *Dictionary*, s.v. ' Uguccione.'

[2] See a discussion of this passage, in which I have attempted to identify these
two types of translations, in *Studies*, I. p. 182.

[3] Dante, however, acknowledges that Aristotle erroneously supposed the
heaven of the sun to follow immediately after that of the moon, misled by

expounded by Dante in *Conv.* II. iv. *init.*, with a view to show
that 'terzo cielo' in the Canzone refers to Venus. That order
is—1, The Moon ; 2, Mercury; 3, Venus [1]; 4, The Sun ; 5,

earlier writers (see *Conv.* II iii. 25 *seqq.*). These earlier writers were probably
the Pythagoreans, Eudoxus, and Plato, who assumed the spheres of all the five
planets to be beyond or 'above' those of the sun and moon (Lewis, *Astronomy*,
&c., p. 246). But from Archimedes onwards, when geometry was more studied
and applied to astronomy, the order above given was almost universally accepted.
It is interesting to note, in connexion with the argument quoted in the text as
to the relative position of Mars and the moon, that some astronomers applied
a sort of converse argument—viz. that Mercury and Venus were *never* seen to
pass across the sun—to prove that the orbit of the sun must be *below* those of
these planets. Ptolemy replies to this that the reason may be that they may
never be in a plane between us and the sun (Lewis, *op. cit.* p. 247). In fact, such
an occurrence, especially in the case of Venus, is extremely rare.

[1] The transposition of Mercury and Venus in (I believe) all ancient systems
of Astronomy is probably to be explained thus. The ancients had no means of
measuring the *distances* of the heavenly bodies. The wildly inaccurate guesses
on this point may be seen in Alfraganus (c. xxi.), where it is assumed that the
maximum distance of any planet corresponded exactly with the minimum
distance of the next 'above' it. As a specimen we may mention the minimum
and maximum distances of the sun which are taken at 3,640,000 and 3,965,000
miles respectively. But their *orbital motions* were ascertained, as we have
seen, with remarkable accuracy. It was then not unnaturally assumed that
their relative proximity was proportionate to their periods of apparent revolution round the earth. Thus (1) the moon, one month ; (2) Mercury c. 88 days
(sidereal) or c. 116 (synodical) ; (3) Venus c. 225 (sidereal), c. 584 (synodical),
and so on. Pliny distinctly recognizes this principle in *N. H.* II. viii. 33, when
he says : 'multumque (esse) ex eo (*sc.* Saturno) *inferiorem* Iovis circulum et
ideo motu celeriore duodenis circumagi annis.' Again, § 44, he says of the
moon, 'Proxima ergo cardini *ideoque* minimo ambitu xxvii diebus,' &c. Another
curious indication of the prevalence of this order is found in the succession of
the seven 'planets' in the names of the seven days of the week, as explained
by Arago. Not only each day but also each hour of the day was under the
special influence of one of the planets. Thus, beginning with Saturn, the
oldest of the deities, and also as Tacitus says in *Hist.* v. 4 'de septem sideribus
quis mortales reguntur altissimo orbe et praecipua potentia,' the first series of
seven hours on his day would be assigned to Saturn, Jupiter, Mars, the Sun,
Venus, Mercury, the Moon ; so again would be the second and third series
of seven hours. Thus, the twenty-second, twenty-third, and twenty-fourth
hours would belong, as before, to Saturn, Jupiter, and Mars. Consequently
the first hour of the next day would be assigned to the sun, and for that reason
the day itself would be *dies Solis*. Following out this method it will be found
that the succeeding days would fall to the Moon, Mars, Mercury, Jupiter, Venus
(as is clear from the names of the week-days in French or Italian), in the order
with which we are all familiar. See Chambers, *Descriptive Astronomy*, p. 436.
A similar explanation will be found in B. Latini, *Trésor*, I. p. iii. c. 120, and
also in Roger Bacon, *Astrologia*, vol. i, p. 382.

Mars; 6, Jupiter; 7, Saturn. That the moon is 'below' at any rate both the sun and Mars is argued by Dante in *Conv.* II. 3 *fin.*, by appealing, in respect of the former fact, to eclipses of the sun by the moon ; and, in respect of the latter, to an occultation of Mars by the moon observed and recorded by Aristotle. We may further observe here that the name 'inferior' planets still applied to Mercury and Venus is an interesting survival of the old Ptolemaic idea that their spheres or heavens were *below* that of the sun, while those of the other planets (still called 'superior' planets) were above it [1]. The chief point, however, to notice in this generally accepted order is that the true position of Mercury and Venus relatively to the earth and to the sun is transposed. The same order is again implied in the orrery-like view of the solar system, which Dante describes as presented to his gaze from the sign Gemini in the eighth heaven, in *Par.* xxii. 139 *seqq.*

ii. The dimensions of the several heavens, or in other words their distance from the centre of the earth, are given by Alfraganus in c. xxi. It is evident that the combination of eccentrics and epicycles in the planetary orbits would cause the distance of those bodies from the earth to vary, even on a geocentric theory of the universe, which would not be the case if they revolved round her as a centre in circular orbits. Hence each planet has a maximum and a minimum distance, and Ptolemy assigns to them a very curious *a priori* law which seems to be quite independent of actual observations. He assumes the principle that 'inter orbes nihil est vacui,' and this can only be the case on the supposition that the maximum distance of each planet corresponds with the minimum distance of the one next beyond (or 'above') it [2]. This would seem to imply that the equatorial diameter of the *speretta* (*Conv.* II. iv. 8c) forming the epicycle of one heaven would just touch the similar diameter of the epicycle of the next heaven above it. Hence the greatest distance of the moon is stated to corre-

---

[1] Comp. *Quaestio*, xv. 13 'quum omne remotius e centro mundi sit altius.' Saturn is described by Dante as 'alto sopra tutti gli altri pianeti,' *Conv.* II. xiv. 230.

[2] This principle was applied also to the four elemental spheres. See next paragraph.

spond with the least distance of Mercury, and the greatest
distance of Mercury with the least distance of Venus, and so
on of all the rest. Alfraganus then gives the amounts of these
distances in multiples of the semi-diameter of the earth, which
is taken (as by Dante in *Conv.* II. xiv. and IV. viii.) at 3250
miles. We need not give these details, but they have a special
interest for us so far, that they throw light upon *Par.* ix. 118,
where Dante says that the heaven of Venus is that which is
reached by the conical shadow cast by the earth into space :

> ' Da questo cielo in cui l'ombra s'appunta
> Che il vostro mondo face[1].'

Now the length of this shadow is estimated by Ptolemy at
871,000 miles (see Alfraganus, c. xxviii.), and this will in fact
be found to pass beyond the sphere of Mercury, and to reach
into that of Venus, according to the Ptolemaic figures given by
Alfraganus in c. xxi.[2]

iii. The complete cosmical theory of Dante's time included an extension of the hypothesis of concentric spheres
to the four elements, fire, air, earth, and water. This is

---

[1] It has been suggested that Dante attaches an allegorical significance to
this astronomical fact, and that, as Miss Rossetti expresses it, some imperfection
of earthliness is symbolized by it as affecting even the saints who appear to
Dante in those spheres that are within its limits. In the heaven of the waxing
and waning moon, we find wills imperfect through instability ; in that of
Mercury wills imperfect as being stimulated by ambition and desire of worldly
fame ; in that of Venus wills imperfect through excess of earthly love (*Shadow
of Dante*, p. 203). As regards the denizens of the moon, the same imperfection
would be fitly symbolized by the dark portions, or flaws on the moon's surface,
as they are explained in *Par.* ii. *ad fin.* The same thought is worked out in
fuller detail in Mr. Gardner's admirable work, *Dante's Ten Heavens*, pp. 14, 90.
The word *appunta* in the quotation given above may be illustrated by the
expressions 'coni effigie' and 'coni umbrosi axis,' in reference to the earth's
shadow, in Alfraganus, c. xxviii. We may also compare Shelley's description
of death as 'the dreary cone of our life's shade' (*Epipsychidion*). See also
Milton, *Par. Lost*, iv. 776, quoted p. 76 *infra.*

[2] He states the maximum distance of Mercury and minimum of Venus at
542,750 miles, and the maximum of Venus and minimum of the sun as 3,640,000
miles. Evidently, therefore, the length of shadow, as given in the text, falls
within the sphere of Venus. This minimum distance of Venus is mentioned by
Dante in *Conv.* II. vii. *ad fin.* He insists on the very powerful influence
exercised on human affairs by that planet, although at her nearest point she
is distant from us 167 times the semi-diameter of the earth. Now $167 \times 3250 =$
542,750 miles, as given above.

found in numerous writers, e. g. in the pseudo-Aristotelian treatise *De Mundo*, c. 3. The passage is quoted in *Studies*, I. p. 124.

In contrast with these four elements, whose natural motion is either up or down in a straight line [1], there was assumed to be a fifth element whose motion was circular (and therefore perfect), which was described as 'aether' (in contrast with 'aer') or 'caelum' [2]. But, though the natural motion of the four elements was rectilinear, they were thought to exist in spheres which formed as it were a continuation of the system of the ten heavens. Next below the sphere of the moon was that of fire [3], then that of air, then that of water, and finally, and lowest of all, at the centre of the Universe, that of earth [4]. Further, the principle explained above ('inter orbes nihil vacui') was applied to the elemental spheres also, so that, as Ristoro frequently expresses it, the 'gibbosity' of one filled the concavity of the next. This (as I have observed

---

[1] Cf. *Quaestio*, § xii. ll. 39 *seqq.* 'grave et leve' 'sunt passiones corporum simplicium [i. e. elements] quae moventur *motu recto*; et levia moventur sursum, et gravia deorsum.'

[2] See further *Studies*, I. pp. 124, 300; II. pp. 322 *n* and 339. Also Milton, *Par. Lost*, B. iii. ll. 714 *seqq.* :

> Swift to their *several quarters* hasted then
> The cumbrous elements, earth, flood, air, fire ;
> And this ethereal quintessence of Heaven
> Flew upward, spirited with various forms,
> That *rolled orbicular* and turned to stars, &c.

The expression 'several quarters' corresponds with the statement of Dante as to the 'naturato amore' of the several elements in *Conv.* III. iii. 8 (*v.* next note).

[3] See *Par.* i. 115, and *Conv.* III. iii. 8–13 : 'le corpora semplici hanno amore naturato in sè al loro loco proprio, e però la terra sempre discende al centro ; il fuoco alla circonferenza di sopra lungo 'l cielo della luna, e però sempre sale a quello.' Hence when Dante was ascending from the summit of Purgatory before he reached the lowest of the heavenly spheres, that of the moon (*Par.* ii.), he passed through the sphere of fire. See *Par.* i. 58–63 ; 79–81.

[4] Hell being at the centre, and so the very lowest point, of the sphere of earth, and therefore as far as possible removed from God, whose glory is 'set above the heavens.' See *Inf.* xi. 64 ; xxxii. 8 ; *Par.* xxxiii. 22.

The way in which one element is enveloped by another is graphically compared by Bede to the constituent parts of an egg. Earth is like the yolk in the centre, water surrounds it like the white of the egg ; air corresponds with the membrane round the white ; and fire with the shell that includes the whole. (From Beazley, *Dawn of Geography*, p. 371.)

in *Studies*, II. p. 367) was also clearly asserted by Alfraganus, Albertus Magnus, Joannes de Sacrobosco, Brunetto Latini, and Roger Bacon. Hence it was that the emergence of dry land ('terra detecta') *above* the water presented a very difficult and hotly disputed problem. This it was that Dante (as I believe) claims to have finally determined in the *Quaestio de Aqua et Terra*[1].

So much for Cosmogony, or the general system of the Universe. We pass on next to consider

II. PLANETARY MOTIONS AND THE SIGNS OF THE ZODIAC.

It is obvious that these motions are very complicated and baffling, on the supposition of a circular revolution about the stationary earth. For, as a matter of fact, we now know (1) that the earth is not stationary; and (2) that the planets do not revolve about it at all, but round the sun. Consequently, when viewed from the earth, they seem sometimes to advance, sometimes to retrograde, and sometimes to be stationary for a time[2]. To complicate the difficulty still further, it was a fundamental assumption of all ancient astronomers that, the circle being the most perfect of all geometrical figures[3], only circular motion could possibly be attributed to the heavenly bodies. Yet we now know that they do not revolve in circles at all, but ellipses. Hence the most elaborate mechanical combinations of circular motions in different planes and various directions were invented or imagined in order to account for the motions of sun, moon, and planets, on the supposition that the earth was the centre of the universe, and that they all revolved about it through

---

[1] See *Studies*, II, Essay VII, and especially pp. 367-70, where the opinions of several writers on this apparent anomaly are given.

[2] See Lewis, *op. cit.* pp. 152, 3 ; Narrien, p. 182.

[3] As Dante states, on the authority of Euclid, in *Conv.* II. xiv. 211. It was probably nothing but a similar *a priori* notion as to the perfection of the sphere among solids that led the Pythagoreans to assert the sphericity of the earth. This was afterwards generally denied, and its first recorded assertion on scientific grounds occurs in Arist. *de Caelo*, ii. 14 (see *Studies*, II. p. 323). Compare also Ristoro d'Arezzo, *Dist.* vii. c. 21, p. 163 (ed. 1859) 'E questo movimento non potrebbe essere altro che circolare ; imperciò che 'l movimento del cielo dee essere perfetto ' (and similarly *ib.* p. 161).

a series or combination of movements, each one of which was circular.

Now there are three principal types under which such theories or devices fall; the problem being to explain all the phenomena by a combination of *circular* motions only [1]. They may be described as those of (1) revolving spheres; (2) eccentric orbits; (3) epicycles, either in combination with or in substitution for that of eccentric orbits. The first of these, and the earliest in date, seems to have been suggested rather than formulated by Plato, but to have been erected into a systematic theory by Eudoxus (406–350 B. C.). On this theory the complicated movements of the sun, moon, and planets, were explained on the supposition that they were controlled in each separate case by either three or four hollow spheres or spherical shells. One of these always corresponded in its revolution round the pole of the equator with that of the heaven of the fixed stars, or (as it was then held) of the *Primum Mobile*, with which, at that time at any rate, and before the discovery of precession, the heaven of the fixed stars was identified. A second revolved in a contrary direction round the pole of the ecliptic; and a third, and in some cases a fourth, or even a fifth, round a pole or poles different from either of these. Thus each separate planet had, in effect, a system of 'heavens' of its own, repeating in miniature that of the whole cosmical system already described. Dante recognizes this as a possible aspect of the case on the 'epicycle' system in *Conv.* II. iv. 88 *seqq.* The result was that the universe was thought to be composed of twenty-seven such revolving spheres or shells, including that of the *Primum Mobile*. Before long, however, as the planetary motions were more accurately observed, additional spheres were required to be added in order to explain them, raising the number to thirty-three. Aristotle increased the number further to fifty-five (*Metaph.* xi. 8). A short-lived revival of this theory in the sixteenth century by Fracastorius postulated as many as

---

[1] Thus Alfraganus concludes an elaborate discussion of the complicated Lunar motions :—' Ita ostensum est Lunae incessum ... *componi ex quinque motibus circularibus* ' (c. xiii. p. 53).

* * *

seventy-nine such spheres [1]. Of such a system it may indeed be said that 'mole ruit sua'; but even in early times it was felt that the growing complexity of this hypothetical machinery deprived it of all claim to afford a rational explanation of the phenomena.

The next attempt was the theory of eccentric circular revolutions, i. e. a revolution in some sense round the earth, but about some centre different from that of the earth. Each planet was supposed to be subject to two influences of revolution, besides, of course, the diurnal rotation common to all the heavenly bodies : (1) a circular movement of the planet itself round the earth as a centre in the direction of the signs of the zodiac, i e. from west to east ; and (2) a circular movement of its orbit [2], so to speak, round some different central point, and in the opposite direction. This latter was techni-

---

[1] See Narrien, *op. cit.*, p. 361.

[2] This 'orbit' seems to have been conceived as a sort of disk or plate revolving eccentrically about the earth from east to west. Meanwhile upon the surface of this disk or plate the planet was supposed to be itself revolving about the earth as a centre from west to east. The apparent motion of the planet, as seen from the earth, was the resultant of these combined motions. (See Narrien, pp. 213 *seqq.*).

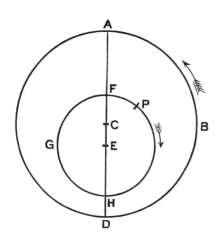

This will be explained by the following diagram :

E = Centre of earth.

C = Centre of planet's 'orbit.'

EC = Eccentricity.

⊙ DAB is the eccentric or the 'orbit' of the planet, but while this 'orbit' was revolving round the centre C, eccentrically to the earth, the planet itself (P) was revolving in an opposite direction on its own account round the earth as a centre. It will be observed that a combination of these motions will account for the planet, as seen from the earth, sometimes seeming to advance, sometimes to retrograde, and sometimes to be stationary, or, as Milton has expressed it,

'Progressive, retrograde, or standing still.' *Par. Lost*, viii. 127.

cally called its 'eccentric.' Now, by assigning different velocities
to these two revolutions and different degrees of eccentricity
in different cases, the irregular movements of the planets were
roughly accounted for, without abandoning the fundamental
axiom that all celestial motions must be circular. The author
of this theory was Apollonius of Perga (c. 230 B.C.). He,
however, soon abandoned it in favour of another and far more
celebrated theory, of which he was also the author, and one
which was destined to dominate the field of astronomical
research for more than 1,700 years, viz. that of epicycles. It is
this theory which it specially concerns us to explain, as it was
the system universally accepted in the time of Dante, and by
him frequently recognized and described. The epicycle was
a small revolving circle, to the circumference of which the
body of the planet was supposed to be attached. The centre
of this revolving circle was situated on a much larger circle,
which was the equator of the sphere, or heaven (as it was
called), of the planet itself, which sphere was revolving in an
opposite direction round the earth, either about its centre, or
as an 'eccentric' about some other centre, in the manner
previously explained. This circle was technically termed the
'deferent,' in relation to the epicycle which it carried. Alfraganus commonly refers to the 'deferent' as the 'eccentric[1].'
It is clear that the *principle* of the last two theories which we
have explained is the same, as is recognized by Ptolemy himself. It would therefore be more correct to say that the epicyclic
theory modified or supplemented rather than that it supplanted
the theory of eccentrics, since in some cases, and indeed

---

[1] e.g. c. xii. (p. 48) : 'Circulus ille in quo circumfertur epicycli centrum vocatus
fuit "excentricus deferens"': and again, 'epicyclorum vero sideribus quinque
reliquis competentium centra deferuntur in excentricis' (p. 47).

All this will be found very clearly set forth by Ristoro, i. c. 12 : 'Noi
troviamo ciascuno pianeta essere portato inverso oriente da uno suo grande
cerchio, lo quale è chiamato *deferente*, e ciascuno di questi cerchi, senonsè
quello del sole [for this exception *v.* p. 41, n. 3], porta un altro cerchielletto,
lo quale è chiamato *epiciclo*. E il centro di questo epiciclo siede in su questo
gran cerchio, il quale è chiamato deferente. E 'l centro del corpo del pianeta
istà in su questo cerchietto, lo quale è chiamato epiciclo.' Compare with this
Conv. II. iv. 78 *seqq.* quoted *infra,* p. 37.

generally, the eccentric was retained as the *locus* of the centre of the revolving epicycle[1]. A combination of these opposite movements of epicycle and deferent, due regard being had to their relative velocity and the magnitude of their diameters, was so contrived as to account fairly well for the more obvious, though still very complicated, phenomena of planetary motions. But, as in the case of the more primitive hypothesis of revolving spheres, the progress of observation required the assumption of a further epicycle, with its centre fixed on the revolving circumference of the original epicycle, and sometimes of another even on this, until this system, like the other, becomes impractically cumbrous and intricate. This is referred to in the well-known lines of Milton :—

> 'When they come to model heaven
> And calculate the stars, how they will wield
> The mighty frame, how build, unbuild, contrive,
> To save appearances[2], how gird the sphere
> With centric and eccentric scribbled o'er,
> Cycle and epicycle, orb in orb.' *Par. Lost*, viii. 79-85.

No wonder that King Alfonso of Leon, surnamed the Astronomer, who died when Dante was in his twentieth year, cynically declared that, if he had been consulted at the making of the universe, he could have suggested a much simpler arrangement[3]. It should, however, be remembered that, after all, the theory of epicycles did explain the known facts, and consequently admitted of remarkably accurate calculations (considering the appliances available) of the move-

---

[1] As Alfraganus maintains in c. xii. (p. 47) 'vehuntur earum [sc. planetarum] córpora non in excentrico, sed in orbibus exiguis, qui appellantur epicycli ; utpote qui *devehuntur ipsi in excentricis.*'

[2] There is an expression curiously like this in the *Summa*, I. xxxii. 1.r$_2$, where S. Thomas says that the assumption by astronomers of eccentrics and epicycles is made 'quod hac positione facta possunt *salvari apparentia sensibilia* circa motus caelestes,' but he acutely adds, ' non tamen ratio haec est sufficienter probans, quia etiam forte alia positione facta salvari possent.'

[3] Fuller, *Holy War*, iv. c. 20, takes this very seriously, and makes a characteristically quaint remark in reference to this saying, the tone of which moreover he considerably alters in his manner of quoting it :—' Alphonse, king of Castile, an admirable mathematician : but the ointment of his name is marred with the dead fly of his Atheisticall speech, " that if he had been in God's stead he could have framed the world better than now it is ".'

ments of the heavenly bodies. But it was too cumbrous and complex to be accepted as a *vera causa*. Even Copernicus held to the theory of epicycles, as applied heliocentrically. Moreover, some of the celestial phenomena—chiefly, I believe, the lunar motions—were more satisfactorily accounted for by the earlier geocentric system than by the Copernican theory. This remained as an objection to the latter till it was removed by the discovery of the law of gravitation[1]. Again, the absence of any trace of parallax in the stars, which no instruments were at that time, and for long after, capable of discovering, was felt to be a strong objection to the heliocentric system, which postulated so large an annual displacement of the earth's position in space. This led the eminent astronomer Tycho Brahe to suggest a combination of the Ptolemaic and Copernican systems, making the earth the centre round which the sun revolved, carrying with him the planets *en masse* which were revolving round *him* as their centre[2].

This theory of epicycles will be found very clearly described by Dante in the *Convito*, in reference to the planet Venus (see II. iv. 78 *seqq.*). After pointing out that in any revolving sphere or heaven the equator is the noblest part because its revolution is obviously the most rapid, he declares that ' on the back of this equatorial circle in the heaven of Venus (of which he is at present speaking, the same being applicable to all the planets alike) there is a little sphere (*speretta*) which has a revolution of its own within that heaven; the circle (i.e. equator) of which sphere astronomers call the epicycle: . . . and on the arch or back of this equatorial circle or epicycle is fixed (*è fissa*) the very brilliant star of Venus[3].' He then proceeds to say that in a certain sense this *speretta* might itself be called another heaven, and in that case the number will be much more than ten, but it is more convenient to consider it as one with the main heaven of the planet itself to which it is attached. Another clear and instructive passage occurs in c. vi. of the

[1] Hutton, *Aspects of Religious and Scientific Thought*, p. 41.

[2] Newcomb, *The Stars*, p. 140.

[3] Compare the language of Aquinas, *Summa*, I. lxx. 1. r₃, when, quoting Aristotle, he says, ' stellae fixae sunt in orbibus et non moventur nisi motu orbium.'

same book, where Dante quotes the 'Libro dell' aggregazione delle stelle,' i. e. Alfraganus, to show that the planet Venus is subject to three motions of rotation—(1) That by which the star moves upon its own epicycle. (2) That by which the epicycle moves together with the whole 'heaven' (i. e. of the planet) equally with that of the sun. These last words apply only to the motion of the 'eccentric' or 'deferent' of the two inferior planets, as may be seen on reference to Alfraganus, c. xvii. *sub fin*. This will be explained presently. (3) That motion by which the whole of the heaven (of the planet) moves, following the movement of the starry heaven (i. e. the eighth heaven) from west to east, $1°$ in one hundred years : in other words, the precessional motion already explained. Then Dante adds that, besides these three motions, there is also that of diurnal revolution, which is common to all the nine heavens alike [1]. It may be added, that the periods of revolution in the epicycle for the several planets, as given by Alfraganus, very fairly correspond with the true 'synodical' period of each planet, and those of the revolution of the eccentric or deferent, except in the case of the 'inferior' planets (for reasons which will be explained), with the true 'sidereal' period of each, or, as these elements are sometimes called, its 'synodical' and 'periodic' revolution. Even as early as Eudoxus, these periodic times (i. e. the length of their respective 'years') were given with considerable accuracy in the case of the three exterior planets, while those of Mercury and Venus are stated to be just one year in each case. All these periods are mentioned by Dante, as we have seen in *Conv.* II. xv. 142 *seqq.*

It may be well to explain here this important distinction of

---

[1] Though Dante is speaking here only of Venus, these three planetary motions—viz. (1) that of revolution on the epicycle; (2) that of the revolution of the centre of the epicycle on the orbit of the 'eccentric' or 'deferent'; (3) that of precession—are given by Alfraganus, c. xiv. (p. 60), as common to the four planets Venus, Mars, Jupiter, and Saturn. The motions of Mercury are more complex ('magis implicati sunt,' p. 57), and are in fact four in number, since a further revolution of the centre of the eccentric deferent in another 'circellus' of its own must be assumed (p. 59), and in the case of the moon five such circular motions (as we have already seen) must be postulated (p. 50). All this, as Milton says in the passage above quoted, 'to save appearances,' and not to abandon the assumption that only *circular* motions could be admitted.

'synodical' and 'periodic' (or, as it is in some cases called, 'sidereal') revolution. A 'periodic' or 'sidereal' revolution is when a heavenly body has just gone once round its orbit. A 'synodical' revolution is when it has come round again to the same position in reference to the earth and the sun, whatever the starting-point may be, but generally it is understood to be the point of 'conjunction' or that of 'opposition.' As the length of this revolution is affected by the motion of the sun or earth meanwhile, it will be greater or less, according to circumstances, than the planet's revolution in its own orbit[1]. The familiar illustration which has been given from the hands of a watch will make this distinction clear at once. Suppose the hands together, say, at twelve o'clock. A 'periodic' revolution of the minute hand occupies, of course, just one hour, and will be completed at one o'clock; but a 'synodical' revolution will have been completed when the two hands are exactly together again, and that will evidently be a little after five minutes past one. So, in fact, 1 hour and $5\frac{5}{11}$ minutes is the 'synodical' period of the minute hand in this particular case. I shall have occasion again to refer to this distinction later on.

The peculiarity in the motions of the inferior planets which is indicated in the above passage[2] respecting Venus—i. e. that its 'heaven' (as also that of Mercury) has the same period of revolution as that of the sun—will be best explained in connexion with another passage of some obscurity, and also of some special interest, in which Dante once again refers to the motions of the planet Venus. It occurs at the beginning of ch. ii. of the 2nd Trattato of the *Convito* :—

' The star of Venus had twice revolved in that circle of hers, which makes her appear as an evening and a morning star, according to her two different periods, since the passing away of that blessed Beatrice, who lives in heaven with the angels, and on the earth with my spirit, when, etc.'

Now as the inferior planets perform the whole of their revolutions *within* the orbit of the earth, and between it and the sun, any point on their orbits, as well as on that of the sun,

---

[1] See the diagram in reference to the moon, *infra*, p. 93.
[2] Viz., *Conv.* II. vi. 139, with which should be compared II. xv. 148.

must *appear* to revolve round the earth in a year. In other words, the earth (as we now know) revolves round the sun, and consequently also round the orbits of Venus and Mercury, which lie between it and the sun, in a year, as in the annexed diagram. So, if these planets were stationary, as the sun

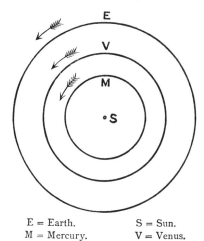

E = Earth.
M = Mercury.
S = Sun.
V = Venus.

(practically) is, they would necessarily appear to have just the same period of revolution round the earth as the sun has; for the annual revolution of the earth would make them as well as the sun, and for the same reason, *appear* to revolve round the earth exactly in one year. Such is in effect the motion attributed to the larger or 'deferent' circle, or in other words the 'heaven,' of those planets in the Ptolemaic astronomy, the principle of which system was to resolve a complicated motion into the two or more simple motions from which it might be taken to have resulted, and then to suppose these to be acting simultaneously and independently of one another. We have next then to take account of the fact that these planets are not stationary, but have their own proper orbital motion round the sun. In effect therefore they might be regarded as satellites of the sun from the point of view of the earth. Indeed, this actual suggestion was made by one or two writers quite early in the Christian era[1], but this curious foregleam of the truth

---

[1] e.g. by Vitruvius and one or two other authors quoted by Sir G. C. Lewis, *op. cit.* p. 248. This idea seems almost to be involved in *Par.* xxii. 143, 144 :—

  'e vidi come si move
  Circa e vicino a lui Maia [Mercury] e Dione [Venus].'

There is also an expression in the *Somnium Scipionis*, § 17, which at least falls in strikingly with this conception of the relations of the motions of Mercury and Venus to that of the sun. 'Hunc (sc. = solem) *ut comites consequuntur,*

seems to have passed unnoticed. The effect of this independent orbital motion, which is in each case much more rapid than that of the earth, is that these planets appear to us now on one side of the sun and now on the other, i. e. sometimes as morning and sometimes as evening stars [1]. The old astronomers did not know the true reason of this, but these observed facts had to be accounted for, and this they did by the motion attributed to the epicycle of the planet. Thus we find that the period of one complete revolution of the epicycle itself (i. e. the 'sidereal' as distinguished from the 'synodical' period), viz. c. 225 days for Venus and c. 88 days for Mercury, corresponds pretty nearly with the modern computation of the 'orbit' or 'year' of each of these planets. Hence when Dante speaks in the above passage of 'the revolution of Venus in that circle of hers which makes her appear as an evening and a morning star at different periods [2],' he describes in effect her revolution in her epicycle [3]. Taken thus, two of these revo-

alter Veneris, alter Mercurii cursus.' The idea of 'comites consequentes' comes very near to that of 'satellites.' See also so-called Aristotle, *De Mundo*, c. 6 (399 a 8) ἥλιος δὲ ἐν ἐνιαυτῷ [διαπεραίνεται κύκλον] καὶ οἱ τούτῳ ἰσοδρόμοι, ὅ τε Φωσφόρος καὶ ὁ Ἑρμῆς λεγόμενος. Narrien (pp. 284, 285) observes that a passage in Pliny might lead to an inference similar to that which Vitruvius first states thus explicitly: 'Mercurii autem et Veneris stellae circum solis radios, *solem ipsum*, *uti centrum, itineribus coronantes*, regressus retrorsum et retardationes faciunt. Etiam stationibus, *propter eam circinationem*, morantur in spatiis signorum.'

[1] Hence Venus is described in *Par.* viii. 11, 12, as: —
'la stella
Che 'l sol vagheggia, or da coppa, or da ciglio.'

[2] *Conv.* II. ii. 1–5.

[3] That the planets appear to retrograde or to be stationary is distinctly stated to be due to the epicycle by Ristoro d' Arezzo, i. c. 12. After describing these phenomena he adds : 'E per questi movimenti vedemo manifestamente essere li epicicli : e questo pare che sia incontro a coloro che contradicono li epicicli.' A little later he says : 'E troviamo che il sole non ha epiciclo, e questo è segno di ciò, che nol troviamo retrogradare, e nol troviamo stare fermo in nulla stagione . . . secondo che noi troviamo li altri pianeti.' So again in B. ii. c. 6. It seems strange that the true cause of this exceptional character of the sun's motions should never have been suspected. Once more we may compare Milton, who similarly describes the motion of the six planets (i. e. moon and the five planets) as :—

'Progressive, retrograde, or standing still';

while the heliocentric theory is tentatively suggested in the words :—

'what if seventh to these
The planet earth, so steadfast though she seem,
Insensibly three several motions move?' (*Par. Lost*, viii. 127–30.)

lutions of which he is speaking will therefore amount to 450 days, or, taken roughly, fifteen months. His statement is that this period had elapsed between the death of Beatrice, viz. June, 1290, and the first appearance to him of the Donna Gentile, who symbolized for him philosophy[1]. This vision therefore is thus fixed to have been in September, 1291.

A further, though not an astronomical, time-reference dependent on this in *Conv.* II. xiii. 49–69 opens the way to a touching incident connected with one of Dante's personal friendships, the interest of which may perhaps excuse this slight digression. At l. 45 of this chapter of the *Convito* Dante tells us that the influence of this Donna Gentile, or Philosophy, attracted him more and more, till in a short time, which he puts at about thirty months, he became wholly devoted to her, and that he then opened his mouth and composed the Canzone which forms the subject of this 2nd Trattato, viz. :—

> 'Voi che intendendo il terzo ciel movete.'

Counting thirty months then from September, 1291, the date of its composition would be found to be in March, 1294[2]. Now if we refer to *Par.* viii. 37 we find that Dante meets his friend Carlo Martello, titular king of Hungary, in the 'terzo ciel[3],' or heaven of Venus. Carlo greets him by quoting the first line of this very Canzone which Dante tells us was composed in March, 1294. Now we know from Villani that Carlo Martello was in Florence for a short time precisely in March, 1294[4]; we know also that he died not long after-

---

[1] This is clearly stated in *Conv.* II. xvi. *ad fin.*

[2] On this subject see Mr. G. R. Carpenter's interesting Essay on *The Episode of the Donna Pietosa* in the American Dante Society's Report for 1888.

[3] Hence the expression used of Venus, in the third line of this Canto, as 'volta nel terzo epiciclo.' We may compare Petrarch, Sonnet xxxiv. parte 2 :—
> 'Ivi fra lor che 'l terzo cerchio serra,'
and Shelley, *Epipsychidion* :—
> 'A splendour
> Leaving the third sphere pilotless.'

[4] This is proved by a document cited by Del Lungo from the Florentine archives dated March 31, 1294, including a bill for providing cloth of gold, &c., for the reception of 'Charles, king of Jerusalem, and Charles, king of Hungary.' Another document proves him to have been in Siena in the following May (see Mr. Vernon's *Paradiso*, i. p. 254 *n.*).

wards. It is natural to suppose that he saw, and probably expressed his admiration of, this newly-composed poem, of which Dante's mind was then full. He now therefore welcomes his friend to 'the everlasting habitations' with this touching reminiscence of their last meeting upon earth. Further, as I have noticed in my former volumes, Carlo Martello is the one personal friend whom Dante has honoured with a place in Paradise.

Venus is the only planet whose motions Dante refers to in such detail, and the reason of this is her mention by implication in the expression 'terzo ciel' in the Canzone here commented on. It will be remembered that the 'Convito,' 'Convivio,' or 'Banquet,' consists of a prose commentary on three of Dante's own Canzoni, the same plan having been further designed in reference to fourteen of these poems. A single word is often a sufficient peg on which to hang a long disquisition astronomical, physical, metaphysical, &c. Hence the *Convito* forms a sort of encyclopædia of Dante's knowledge or thoughts on almost all subjects, and by consequence an encyclopædia of the highest knowledge then current or attainable on all such subjects. Thus, all the passages already quoted from the *Convito* are merely introduced by way of commentary on the expression 'terzo ciel' in this Canzone, the first line of which is :—

'Voi che intendendo il terzo ciel movete.'

A still more elaborate disquisition on the motions of the sun originates from a passage in another Canzone, where the sun is mentioned in a manner involving no necessary astronomical knowledge whatever, as we shall see presently.

I now proceed to explain the opinions held by Dante as to the Sun.

In the first place it will not be forgotten that the sun was then regarded as one of the seven planets, revolving like the rest round the earth [1]. At the beginning of the *Inferno* it is spoken of as 'pianeta.' The mountain had its shoulders

'Vestite già de' raggi del pianeta
Che mena dritto altrui per ogni calle.' (*Inf.* i. 17, 18.)

[1] Cf. *supra*, p. 6, note a.

But in spite of the comparatively subordinate position thus assigned to the sun it was held to be the one source of light for the *whole Universe*, and that even the fixed stars as well as the moon and planets shone by its reflected light. This appears from *Par.* xxiii. 28–30 :—

> 'Vid' io sopra migliaia di lucerne [the glorified Saints]
>   Un sol [Christ] che tutte quante l'accendea,
>   Come fa il nostro le viste superne [1].'

Again in *Par.* xx. 4–6, after describing the setting of the sun, Dante adds :—

> 'Lo ciel, che sol di lui prima s' accende,
>   Subitamente si rifà parvente
>   Per molte luci, in che una [i. e. the Sun] risplende.'

This is quite explicitly stated in *Conv.* II. xiv. 125 : 'del suo lume tutte le altre stelle s'informano' : and this is the chief ground on which the Sun corresponds with arithmetic among the sciences, since upon it they all in like manner depend. Again in *Conv.* III. ii. 44 we read 'la natura del sole è partecipata nell' altre stelle.' Hence the Sun becomes a fit image of God, as we see in numerous instances in the *Paradiso* ; and this again Dante expressly states in *Conv.* III. xii. 55, 'Nullo sensibile in tutto 'l mondo è più degno di farsi esemplo di Dio, che 'l sole, lo quale di sensibile luce sè prima, e poi tutti i corpi celestiali ed elementali allumina.' Again *Canz.* ix. 16, 17, 'Feremi il core sempre la tua luce, Come 'l raggio la stella.' The same idea appears in the *Somnium Scipionis*, § 17, where the Sun is described as 'dux et princeps et moderator luminum reliquorum . . . tanta magnitudine ut cuncta sua luce illustret et compleat [2]' : and in the following beautiful

---

[1] I am aware that 'viste' *h. l.* is sometimes explained otherwise. But there can, I think, be no reasonable doubt that it means 'the stars,' being used exactly like 'vedute' in *Par.* ii. 115, and 'viste' itself in xxx. 9.

[2] The same (then common) view will be found in Roger Bacon, *Op. Majus*, Persp. Pars ii. Dist. iii. c. 2 (vol. ii. p. 104) 'certum tamen est quod lumen lunae causatur a sole, sicut omnium stellarum' ; and in Ristoro d' Arezzo, B. ii. c. vi. the sun is described as 'fonte della luce, e tutte le altre stelle e l' altre cose ricevono lume da lui.' Also in Albertus Magnus, *De Prop. Elem.* L. ii. c. i. ; *De Caelo et Mundo*, ii. Tr. iii. c. 6 ; and B. Latini, *Trésor* I. pt. iii. c. 113. But it should be carefully noted that, though the sun was thus believed to be the one source of all light, yet it was firmly maintained that the other stars and

passage of *Paradise Lost* (vii. 364 *seqq.*), where Milton, speaking of the sun, says:—

> ' Hither, as to their fountain, other stars
> Repairing, in their golden urns draw light.
>
> . . . .
>
> By tincture or reflection they augment
> Their small peculiar, though from human sight
> So far remote, by diminution seen.'

As to the size then assigned to the sun and its distance from the earth, Dante follows Alfraganus (c. xxii.), and consequently asserts (*Conv.* IV. viii. 56–64) that the sun's diameter is $5\frac{1}{2}$ times that of the earth and therefore amounts to 35,750 miles, though to ordinary people it seems to be about one foot [1]. I do not remember that he speaks of its comparative bulk ('corporis solaris quantitas'), but this is given by Alfraganus in the same passage as 166 times that of the earth [2].

planets, and notably the moon, had some inherent light of their own. It was thought important to insist upon this in the case of the moon, because it is expressly called 'a great light' in Gen. i. 16. This itself, however, was *originally* derived from the sun, but it was 'drunk in,' appropriated, and stored up, over and above the light which they merely reflect. And so, as Milton says (*v. supra*) :—

> 'By tincture or reflection they augment
> Their small peculiar.'

Thus Albertus Magnus (*C. et M.* II. iii. 8) objects to a certain theory as to the lunar spots, that it assumes the moon to be merely 'velut speculum,' and that 'lumen quod est in luna esset per reflexionem ipsam sicut ad speculum, et non per *imbitionem* luminis solis in profundum eius.' This is also very clearly put by Roger Bacon : 'Non est lumen solis reflexum a superficie stellarum, quod ad nos descendit ab eis, sed *proprium lumen et innatum*, eductum tamen de potentia materiae in corpore stellae *per virtutem solis venientis ad stellam*, quae . . . facit lumen in ea,' *Op. Majus*, Pars iv. Dist. iv. c. 1 (i. p. 129) ; comp. Perspect. Pars iii. Dist. i. Cap. 2 (ii. p. 133). Finally, Dante himself (*Mon.* III. iv. 140) argues that the moon must have some light of its own because it remains visible in a total eclipse ! He thus considers the common argument to be refuted which seeks to prove that, as the 'Lesser Light' is dependent on the 'Greater Light' (i.e. the moon upon the sun), therefore the authority of the Emperor is derived from the Pope. On the contrary, as the moon has 'influentiam ... a propriis suis radiis,' so the Emperor has authority independent of the Pope ! It is curious to set beside this Pliny's explanation of the moon being invisible to us when in conjunction (*coitu*) with the sun. This is 'quoniam haustum [cf. 'imbitionem' *supra*] omnem lucis adversa *illo regerat unde acceperit.*' *N. H.* II. ix. 46.

[1] Comp. Arist. *De An.* iii. 3 (428 b. 3).

[2] Ristoro, viii. 3, states it more precisely as $166 + \frac{1}{4} + \frac{1}{8}$ times (i.e. $166\frac{3}{8}$) that of the earth.

The most elaborate account of the Sun's motions is introduced by Dante, like that already explained in the case of the
planet Venus, by way of exposition of a passing reference to
him in one of the Canzoni, a reference which neither involves
nor requires any astronomical knowledge whatsoever.

To this remarkable chapter (*Conv.* III. v.) we now pass.
It is at first sight probably the most abstruse and difficult to
be found in the works of Dante. This difficulty is increased
by the corruption of the MSS. and by the officious would-be
corrections of some modern editors, especially Giuliani. It
would be impossible here to expound this chapter as a whole,
but I propose to reproduce some of the most salient passages,
which show the extraordinarily clear conception and accurate
knowledge which Dante possessed respecting the solar orbit.
The expression commented upon is merely this (see l. 19 of
the Canzone): ' The Sun, who encircles the whole world, sees
nothing so gracious as in that hour when he shines upon my
lady, &c.,' a sentiment which other poets have often felt, and
perhaps still more often expressed. Now when we come to
the commentary in III. v., Dante says that to understand this
we must have a perfectly clear conception (l. 20) of how the
sun revolves about the earth ; and then follows a long and
abstruse astronomical disquisition. To us this seems much
as if a modern divine were to preface a sermon on the text,
' Praise Him, sun and moon,' with a scientific explanation of
the lunar theory and the phenomena of nutation and evection.

After a preliminary explanation of the different views held
by Pythagoras, Plato, and Aristotle, as to the position of the
earth in the Universe, Dante emphatically declares that the
opinion of the last-named 'glorious philosopher to whom
Nature revealed her secrets beyond all others' has finally
settled the question. He therefore lays it down as a fundamental truth that the earth remains eternally fixed and
motionless in the centre of the Universe[1]. It would be
superfluous, he adds, to enter into Aristotle's reasons for this
assertion, since with those for whom he is writing such
authority is sufficient in itself.

---

[1] Cf. Milton :—'the sedentary earth ' (*Par. Lost*, viii. 32).

This being premised, Dante proceeds to explain the ceaseless diurnal revolution of the heavens round the earth as a fixed centre (l. 66). This revolution implies two poles and an equator equidistant between them. The north pole is marked by the pole-star; and, supposing a stone could be dropped from the north pole of the heavens, it would fall upon this earth on the surface of the sea (i. e. the circumambient 'Oceanus') at a spot where, if a man were standing, the pole-star would be directly above his head [1]. Dante adds that he believes that spot would be 2700 miles, more or less, to the north of Rome. To fix our thoughts (' per meglio vedere') he supposes a city on that spot called ' Maria,' and many of the subsequent phenomena are described as they would appear to the 'inhabitants of Maria.' A similar description is given of the south pole, and another imaginary city is supposed to exist there, to which Dante gives the name of ' Lucia [2].' This he believes to be about 7500 miles south of Rome, so that the cities of Maria and Lucia are exact antipodes, and the distance between them 10200 miles, which was then believed to be that of the semi-circumference of the globe. The place of the equator is then laid down, with sundry geographical details which do not concern us at present.

Next he proceeds to describe 'come il sol la [terra] gira,' or, in other words, the proper motion of the 'heaven' of the sun itself. It revolves from west to east, not directly, but obliquely, contrary to its diurnal motion from east to west. That is, its own orbital revolution is from west to east, and further it is not along the equator, but along a circle inclined to the equator [3], viz. the ecliptic, 'upon which is the body of

[1] 'La stella gli sarebbe sempre sul mezzo del capo.' It is almost incredible that ' la stella ' here has been explained as the sun by some commentators ! Compare the expression ' l' ago alla stella,' in *Par.* xii. 29.

[2] We are of course reminded of the prominent part played by Maria and Lucia in the recovery of Dante in *Inf.* ii., and also of the special assistance given to him by Lucia in *Purg.* ix.

[3] 'Non direttamente contra lo movimento diurno, cioè del dì e della notte, ma tortamente contra quello' (ll. 128-30). We may compare with this the description of the equinoctial point in *Par.* x. 8, 9, as :—

'quella parte
Dove l' un moto e l'altro si percote.'

the sun.' This intersects the equator, or 'il cerchio delli due primi poli,' in two points, viz. the first point of Aries, and the first point of Libra, i. e. the two equinoctial points already spoken of; and so it forms two arcs or loops (l. 136), one to the north and the other to the south of the equator; the highest points of which arcs are $23\frac{1}{2}°$ distant from the equator [1], one being at the first point of Cancer, and the other at the first point of Capricorn. Hence (and this graphic piece of description should be noted), the people of 'Maria,' when the sun is upon the equator at the first point of Aries, see it go round the world down upon the ground, or rather upon the sea [2], *like a millstone* [3] (i. e. with a horizontal revolution), *of which only the upper half of its body is visible*; and then they see the sun rising higher and higher day by day *like the screw of a press* [4], until it has completed a little more than ninety-one revolutions, i. e. for three months or $\frac{365}{4}$ days, which = $91\frac{1}{4}$ days: and a person in 'Maria,' looking directly at the sun, would see it always moving from left to right [5]. The sun will then have reached the first point of Cancer, or, as it is called, the 'tropic' of Cancer, because it then turns downwards again, having now reached the highest point of the ecliptic. The same spiral or screw-like revolution downwards occurs for $91\frac{1}{4}$ days, and then the sun passes below the equator, and the people of 'Maria' see it no more for six months, during which precisely the same phenomena are repeated before the eyes of the people of 'Lucia' at the south pole, where any one looking at the sun would see it always revolving from right to left. This is obviously the case, as

---

[1] Alfraganus says that according to Ptolemy the exact distance was 23° 51', but that it is more correctly given by Almámon, 'of pious memory,' at 23° 35' (c. v. p. 18). Hence, probably, the measure here given by Dante, viz. 'ventitrè gradi e uno punto più,' i. e. $23\frac{1}{2}°$.

[2] See this explained in the next Essay.

[3] This metaphor is used by Alfraganus, 'molae trusatilis instar,' c. vii.

[4] This upward motion of the sun in spring is again described in a similar way in *Par.* x. 32:

'Si girava per le *spire*
In che più tosto ognora s' appresenta.'

[5] Dante is of course referring here to the sun's *diurnal* revolution. His own proper motion in his orbit could not of course be 'seen' at any given time.

the sun is always north of them. Hence these cities will have only one day and one night, each of six months, in the course of the year.

The passage (ll. 151-154) in which Dante describes the altitude of the sun at the north pole at the time of the summer solstice is very obscure, doubtless owing to the corruption of the text, since Dante's own ideas were perfectly clear and definite on all such points. As a preliminary textual problem of some difficulty has to be dealt with, the explanation of this passage will be found in a supplementary note at the end of the present Essay (pp. 107, 108).

It is interesting to note how very graphically Dante proceeds to describe the solar phenomena at the equator, the actual experience of which was as impossible in his days as that of the phenomena at the poles. He considers the Garamantes, mentioned by Lucan, to be the nearest actual inhabitants to that spot (ll. 173 *seqq.*), and so describes what would be seen by them, using them, as he does the supposed inhabitants of Maria and Lucia, *per meglio vedere.* They would see the sun when at the first point of Aries revolve right over their heads, not *like a millstone, but like a wheel*[1], i. e. with *vertical,* and not *horizontal* revolution. Then it is seen to go away from them for $91\frac{1}{4}$ days towards Maria, and then to turn back to them for a like number of days, and after its passing into Libra the same phenomena are repeated in the direction of Lucia. This situation (*luogo*), which goes all round the earth (i. e. its equator), has perpetual equality of day and night. Now notice particularly this point, which could only be stated as the result of accurately conceived

---

[1] It is scarcely credible that this admirably clear and graphic illustration has been altered by Giuliani thus: 'non a modo di vite ma di mola,' thus obliterating the very point which Dante took such pains to make clear. Alfraganus describes the same phenomenon in this way : 'necesse est . . . caeli conversionem ad eosdem horizontes [i. e. of the equator, on whose horizon he has just said that the earth's poles will lie] *recte ferri sine ulla obliquitate*' (c. vi. p. 21). It may be observed that the vertical, or approximately vertical, plane of the sun's revolution in equatorial regions accounts for the familiar phenomenon of the comparative absence of twilight there. For the sun will obviously descend much more rapidly *below the horizon,* in proportion as he revolves more nearly vertically to it.

* * *

theory—*twice* in the year it has a summer of most intense heat, and it has two slight winters. Thus Dante perceived clearly that the two hottest times of the year on the equator must be at the equinoxes, when the sun is directly overhead, and the two coolest times (the 'two slight winters') at the times of the tropics, when the sun is furthest away either to the north or to the south of the equator. Finally, the varying aspects of the sun as presented to those dwelling between these extreme points are briefly touched upon, and the chapter ends with an outburst of admiration for the ineffable wisdom of God, by which all this is so ordered for the well-being of the 'habitable parts of the earth.' The same thought occurs in *Par.* x. 13–21, where the obliquity of the ecliptic ('L'obbliquo cerchio che i pianeti porta') is declared to be just such, neither more nor less, as to order the condition of the world in the best possible manner [1]. Again we may compare the language of Milton :

> 'Some say he bid his angels turn askance
> The poles of Earth twice ten degrees and more
> From the sun's axle; they with labour pushed
> Oblique the centric globe,' &c.   *Par. Lost,* x. 668 *seqq.*

And in the next twenty or thirty lines Milton describes the beneficial effects of this upon the seasons, very much as in the passage above referred to in Dante.

There is another passage relating to the sun's motions in *Purg.* iv. ll. 58 *seqq.*, which may be briefly noticed next. Dante, now supposed to be in the southern hemisphere, and outside the tropic, expresses his astonishment at seeing the sun in the north, it being then a few days after the spring equinox, and the sun consequently only a little above the equator. Virgil says that if it were later in the year, i.e. summer instead of spring, and the sun in Gemini [2], Dante

---

[1] This is also expounded at considerable length by Ristoro d'Arezzo. See passages quoted in *Studies*, II. p. 360.

[2] It may not perhaps be superfluous in the case of some readers to explain the meaning of the sun being 'in' Aries, Gemini, &c. The stars of the sign in which the sun is situated at any time are of course invisible : but supposing the sun could become a black patch, and the stars about him thus to become visible (as is the case on the occasion of a total eclipse), then he would be seen to be

would see him much further north (ll. 61 *seqq.*). His words
are :—' If Castor and Pollux [i. e. the sign of Gemini] were
in company with that mirror [the sun] which distributes of its
light both above and below [i. e. to the upper and lower
hemispheres in turn, as explained in the passage last commented upon from *Convito* III. v.], thou wouldst see the
zodiac ruddy with his light revolve still nearer to the Bears
[i. e. still further to the north], unless it were to stray from
its ancient course.' (This it was supposed to have done
once under the misguidance of Phaeton, and in doing so to
have left traces of its burning in the Milky Way, according,
at any rate, to one explanation, which is recognized by

surrounded by the stars of the sign 'in' which he is said to be. His position
in the signs can easily be inferred practically by observing what sign is on the
meridian at midnight, since the sun will be in that which is exactly opposite to
it, or 180° distant. This is in effect implied by Dante in *Purg.* ii. 4, 5 when
' the night [i. e. midnight, its central point], which revolves opposite to the sun,
was coming forth from the Ganges with the Scales.' In other words it was
midnight on the Ganges, and Libra (or the Scales) was on the meridian : consequently at Jerusalem, which was, according to Dante's system of geography,
90° further west, it would be six hours short of midnight, or in other words
6 p.m. or sunset, as is set forth in ll. 1–3 ; and the sign Aries, in which the sun was,
would be on the meridian where it was noon, i. e. in Spain, 180° west of India,
according to Dante's calculations. See further in the Essay on *Geography*,
infra, p. 123. Also compare *Purg.* xxvii. 1–4, where these conditions are
reversed and it is midnight in Spain (Libra being on the meridian of the Ebro, or
Spain, l. 3) and noon on the Ganges (l. 4). Another passage of the same kind
occurs in *Purg.* xxv. 2, 3, where the early afternoon (c. April 10) is described as
the hour when Taurus is on the meridian of the day (Aries with the sun being
then ' di mezzo il ciel cacciato,' to borrow the phrase used in *Purg.* ii. 57), and
Scorpio on the meridian of night, as would naturally follow, these signs being
opposite, or 180° apart.

It may be well to add a brief explanation of a similar curiously periphrastic
passage in which 3 p.m. is indicated, though no sign of the Zodiac is there
mentioned. I refer to *Purg.* xv. 1–5. It may be translated thus :—

' There remained so much of the sun's course towards evening (ll. 4, 5) as
between the end of the third hour [i. e. 9 a.m.] and the beginning of the day
there appears of that sphere whose restless motion is like that of a child at play
[i. e. of the swiftly moving *Primum Mobile* which causes the diurnal revolution].'
In plain words, about three hours of day remained, or the equivalent of the
interval between sunrise and 9 o'clock. We may either suppose Dante to be
referring to the period of the Equinox (as is probable), or that he is speaking of
the ' ore temporali,' ' which the Church employs,' as he says when explaining
the meaning of this term in *Conv.* III. vi. 20. Consequently (l. 6) in either case
it was evening there (i. e. in Purgatory), and midnight here (i. e. in Italy , with
a difference of c. 135° in longitude (comp. *Purg.* iii. 25).

Dante in *Inf.* xvii. 106–8, *Purg.* xxi. 118, and *Conv.* II xv. 47 *seqq.*)

Virgil further explains that Jerusalem and the Mountain of Purgatory are exact antipodes, so that they have 'different hemispheres and a common horizon' (ll. 70, 71), viz. that plane through the earth's centre which divides the whole heaven into two distinct hemispheres [1]. From this it results that the altitude of the equator is the same northwards in the one case as it is southwards in the other, since this is merely a question of latitude, and the latitude of antipodes is the same, though north in one case and south in the other. The equator is described as 'the mid-circle of the celestial motion, which always lies between the sun and the winter.' This is clearly the case, since in each hemisphere the six winter months are simply those in which the sun is on the *other* side of the equator.

Once more, in *Par.* xxix. 1–3 when the moon is full at the Equinox, and the sun is rising and the moon is setting (or *vice versa*), Dante describes them, under the title of 'ambo e due i figli di Latona,' as being the one in Aries (Montone) and the other in Libra. In this position they are compared to the scales of a balance, the apex or tongue of which is in the zenith. This exact balance, however, lasts but for a moment, since one body begins at once to set and the other to rise, thus 'cambiando l'emisperio.'

It will be observed that in two of the above passages (*Purg.* ii. 45, and xxv. 23) 'notte' is evidently used for the central point of night, or midnight, which is treated as if it were a point, or, as we might almost say, as a body (like the Pythagorean Antichthon), revolving invisibly directly opposite to the sun :—

'La notte che opposita a lui cerchia,' (ii. 4.)

---

[1] The amount of the heaven visible at any one time or place is (theoretically) 180°, i. e. 90° from the zenith in all directions. In other words just one half or one hemisphere of the heavens is visible. Obviously at the spot exactly opposite in the other hemisphere of the earth will be seen precisely the other hemisphere of the heavens, and the dividing line will be the same horizon as before, so that two places which are antipodes will, as Dante expresses it, have different hemispheres and a common horizon. We may compare the definition of horizon given by Alfraganus :—'circulus qui distinguit inter partem caeli supra nos conspicuam, et partem caeli sub terra conditam.'

and consequently in the sign 180° distant from that in which the sun was.

I lay some stress upon this use of 'notte' because it affords the key to the interpretation of a passage very often misunderstood, viz. *Inf.* xxiv. 1–3 :—

> 'In quella parte del giovinetto anno
> Che il sole i crin sotto l'Aquario tempra,
> *E già le notti al mezzodì sen vanno.*'

In l. 3, 'mezzodì' merely means south, and has nothing to do with either 'mid-day' or 'half the day' as it is sometimes explained. So the statement simply is that the nights are already going southwards. Now the sun being in Aquarius, the night (in the sense just explained) will be in Leo.

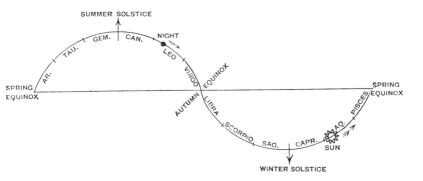

After the winter solstice, at the first point of Capricorn, the sun turned northwards, and the nights similarly turned southwards since the first point of Cancer. Then by late January or February the sun, being in Aquarius[1] (l. 2), will have already (*già* in l. 3) made considerable progress northwards, and the nights consequently southwards.

In connexion with the solar theory in Dante, I will next call attention to some of his numerous references to the signs

---

[1] Speaking popularly, as usual, and neglecting the effects of Precession. See next page, note 2.

of the zodiac, of which I have noted nearly thirty in the *Divina Commedia* alone, and these include allusions to every one of the signs, except, apparently, Virgo and Sagittarius. He often employs their position in relation to the sun to indicate the season of the year, or the hour of the day or night at a given season, that being generally the spring equinox, with which the whole Vision is associated. A few salient instances, or such as call for some comment, may be selected, for some of the allusions are rather far-fetched and obscure, not to say sometimes even fantastic. In *Par.* xxviii. 116, 117, we read of an eternal spring in Paradise, 'which no Ram rising by night despoils.' Now when the sun enters Libra, the Ram rises when the sun sets, so that it may thus be regarded as a night constellation after the autumnal equinox, and thus ' notturno Ariete' may be treated as a characteristic of the winter months, and in this way the passage implies that there is no winter in Paradise [1].

Not unlike this is the rather obscure manner in which Dante conveys to us that the apparition of St. John in Paradise was ' as the sun shineth in his strength' (see *Par.* xxv. 101). His words are : ' So that if the Crab (Cancer) possessed such a gem the winter would have one month of a single day.' Now in mid-winter the sun is in Capricorn (December—January) [2].

---

[1] The word *svernare*, in l. 118, is sometimes taken here in the sense in which it occurs in *Purg.* xxvii. 142, 'sets free from winter' (for a discussion of the passage see *infra*, p. 92). It seems more probable, however, that it means here ' to sing a song of spring,' as it is thus used by other writers, e. g. Guido Guinicelli—'Con dolce modo svernano nel mese di Maggio ' (*Gran Diz.* s. v.).

[2] Hence the description of winter in *Par.* xxvii. 68, 69—

'quando il corno
Della Capra del ciel col sol si tocca.'

In reference to this and the following passages discussed, it should be noted that, strictly speaking, owing to the Precession of the Equinoxes, the sun no longer enters Capricorn at the winter solstice. But popularly the spring was still associated with the sun entering Aries on Mar. 21, and the other months were associated with corresponding signs on this supposition. The sun, however, no longer enters the constellation Aries in March but about April 12. But in a poetic passage it would have been pedantic, and probably also misleading, to go beyond the popular conception. So in Gower's *Confessio Amantis*, B. vii., the signs of the zodiac are definitely assigned one to each month, Aries to March, Taurus to April, and so on. The same is found in Ristoro d'Arezzo. It would seem as if even in the *Convito* Dante adapts himself to such popular

Therefore Cancer is in 'opposition' with him, and is, consequently, the sign which is on the meridian at midnight. Hence,
if the day is 'ruled' by the sun in Capricorn, Cancer might
be said to 'govern the night,' and, if he had a gem similar to
the appearance presented by St. John wherewith to illuminate
the night, the winter would have one month of uninterrupted
day (the Sun shining by day, and Cancer by night).

Again, in *Purg.* xxxii. 52–6, the successive months and
stages of spring are thus indicated :—' The buds of plants
begin to swell when the great light [the sun] falls upon us
mingled with the rays of that [light] which beams behind the
celestial fish [i.e. when the sun is in Aries [1], the sign following
Pisces], and then the flowers burst forth anew each in its own
hue, before the sun yokes his coursers under another star ;'
i.e. before he enters Taurus. This amounts to saying that
the buds begin to swell at the end of March, and the flowers
to come out early in April. We may compare with l. 54,
Par. xxii. 110, where Gemini is described as

'il segno
'Che segue il Tauro.'

The particular constellation to which Dante is transported
when visiting the stellar heaven is that of the Twins or Gemini (see *Par.* xxii. 111 *seqq.*). He tells us that this was so
because he was born under the influence of this sign ; for
he who is the father of every mortal life (the sun being so
described by Aristotle [2]) with them was rising and with them
setting ' when first I felt the Tuscan air.' That is, the sun
was in Gemini, and therefore Dante's birthday was late in
May or early in June. Probably it was on one of the very

---

phraseology ; when, for instance, he describes the spring and autumn equinoxes
respectively as the times when the sun 'va sotto l'Ariete,' or 'va sotto la Libra '
(*Conv.* III. v. 178 and 182), unless it be maintained that he refers to the 'signs '
and not the 'constellations.' But (in company with some professed astronomers)
I very much doubt whether this distinction is to be found in Dante's language.
[See on this *infra*, p. 64 *n.*]

[1] Exactly as in *Canz.* xv. 40, 41 :

'Passato hanno lor termine le fronde
Che trasse fuor la virtù d'Ariete.'

[2] See *Studies*, I. p. 140.

last days of May[1]. And, in accordance with the current belief already alluded to, he traces to the influence of these stars whatever genius or ability he might have[2]. A somewhat obscure reference to Gemini occurs in the beginning of *Canz.* xv. (*Oxford Dante*, p. 166):—'I have come to that period of the revolving year, when the horizon, as the sun is setting, brings to birth for us the twin-bearing sky, *geminato cielo*' (ll. 1–3). In plain language, it was the time when the sign Gemini is rising as the sun is setting, or when that constellation is in opposition to the sun, and so the time indicated is when the sun is in Sagittarius, i. e. November or December. The passage as it proceeds being somewhat obscure in its astronomical allusions, a few words of explanation may not be amiss. Dante is here describing how all the influences that would excite love are absent. (1) It was the winter season, as ll. 1–3 have been explained ; (2) Venus, the planet of love (see *Purg.* i. 19), is in opposition with the earth, at her apogee, the sun therefore being between her and the earth, so that his rays fall right athwart her ('la 'nforca sì di traverso,' literally, bestride her), thereby veiling her light, and thus her influence is extinguished or minimized ; (3) the planet that intensifies cold (i. e. Saturn) is in the ascendent on the meridian (described as 'the great circle on which each of the planets casts little shadow,' i. e. shines upon us most vertically), and so his chilling influence is at a maximum.

---

[1] Dr. Witte, *Dante-Forschungen*, ii. No. 3, gives some ingenious reasons for supposing it to have been May 30. That it was within a day or two of this seems clear from the direct statement made to Boccaccio himself by Pier Giardino di Ravenna, that Dante upon his death-bed informed him that 'he had passed his fifty-sixth year by as much time as had gone by since the end of the preceding May up to that day.' Now this Pier Giardino is shown by existing documents to have been well known at Ravenna, and also to have been actually resident there in the year of Dante's death (1321).

[2] *Par.* xxii. ll. 112-4 :—

> 'O gloriose stelle, o lume pregno
> Di gran virtù, dal quale io riconosco
> Tutto, qual che si sia, lo mio ingegno.'

This is an allusion to the common belief of astrologers that poets and men of learning were specially developed by the influence of this constellation. See Jacopo della Lana on this passage :—'Colui che ha Gemini per ascendente si è ingeniero e adatto a scienzia litterale, e maggiormente quando lo Sole si trova in quel segno.'

Still under all these unfavourable conditions (l. 10) not a single thought of love that oppresses his soul is lightened thereby[1].

A somewhat similar calculation to that which is involved in the first three lines of the *Canzone* just commented upon is involved in the interpretation of the hour which is indicated in *Purg.* ii. 57 by the statement that the beams of the rising sun had 'chased Capricorn from the meridian.' Though that sign would not be visible under these circumstances, it is obvious that when the sun is in Aries (as he then was, shortly after the spring equinox), and also on the horizon, the first quadrant of the sky would be occupied by Aries, Pisces, and Aquarius (counting the signs backwards, as the sun travels through the zodiac from west to east), and therefore Capricorn would have entirely passed the meridian as soon as the whole of Aries had risen above the horizon. Again, a few hours earlier, and before sunrise that same morning, the beautiful morning star Venus, preceding the sunrise[2], quenches by her brilliancy the feeble stars of the constellation Pisces (see note 1, *infra*). And the dawn, or rather the termination of night, at a similar hour on the preceding morning in hell, is indicated by the statement that 'the Fishes are quivering on the horizon' (*Inf.* xi. 113). This aspect of the constellation is yet a third time referred to, though under some disguise, in the description of the dawn on the morning of the third day on the Mountain of Purgatory. See *Purg.* xix. 1–6. The hour before dawn is indicated as (1) the coldest of the twenty-four hours ; (2) that at which the geomancers (at the season of the spring

---

[1] The following references illustrate some of the thoughts and expressions in the above passage. 'Inforcare' is similarly used in *Purg.* viii. 135. The zodiac is described as the

'letto che il Montone

Con tutti e quattro i piè copre ed inforca.'

The light of Venus is veiled by the sun here just as Venus herself by her superior brilliancy veils the light of the stars in Pisces, as we read in *Purg.* i. 21 :—

'Velando i Pesci ch' erano in sua scorta.'

Finally, the chilling influence attributed to Saturn is again mentioned in *Purg.* xix. 1–3. Compare Pliny, *N. H.* II. viii. 33 : 'Saturni sidus gelidae et rigentis esse naturae.'

[2] In regard to an objection sometimes made that Venus was not in fact a morning star in the spring of 1300, see Essay III, *inf.* pp. 172–4.

equinox) can see in the eastern sky their 'greater fortune'
(*maggior fortuna*). This was the name given to a certain
arrangement of seven dots or points in geomancy. A similar
grouping was thought to be traceable in certain stars on the
confines of Aquarius and Pisces. These stars therefore would
be seen in the east just before sunrise.

It is perhaps interesting to observe here that Milton, wishing
to describe the creation of the sun at the spring equinox in
accordance with mediaeval belief (see *supra*, p. 7), has fallen,
as it appears to me, into a curious astronomical error. In
Paradise Lost, vii. 374 we read

> 'The gray
> Dawn and the Pleiades *before* him danced,
> Shedding sweet influence.'

'Before him,' in fact, and as Dante truly represents it, would be
the more unpoetical sign of the Fishes. It is possible this may
not be an error, but a poetic licence on the part of Milton, since
'the sweet influences of the Pleiades' afforded him a more
familiar and suitable picture. But in any case we have an
interesting contrast between the methods of Milton and Dante.
Milton thinks of the pictorial or poetic effect, Dante of the
actual fact. Dante never hesitates to set down the plainest
facts, and it would never occur to him to alter or distort them
for the sake of poetic effect, least of all in any description intended, as we might almost say, to give a datum of time[1].

There is a passage of some difficulty in *Par.* xxx. 1-9 which
has often been quite misunderstood as giving a note of time.
This is certainly not the case. It is clear from ll. 10-13 that
the previous nine lines merely introduce a simile, and the gist
of the first thirteen lines of the Canto is simply this : 'As in
the hour before dawn the stars gradually disappear till even
the brightest is quenched at the approach of the sun, so the
bright Angels [whose joyous movements have formed the subject of the last two Cantos] one by one disappeared from my
sight.' Now let us explain some of the details of this description of dawn. 'Say that some 6000 miles away we have the

---

[1] On this contrast between Dante and Milton see passages from Ruskin and
Macaulay, quoted in *Studies*, II. pp. 244, 245.

sixth hour glowing'—i.e. noon. (*Forse* thus introduces a purely hypothetical case.) We have already seen that Dante took the circumference of the earth at 20400 miles. This being traversed by the sun in twenty-four hours, a space of 5100 miles will have been traversed in six hours, so that, if it be noon c. 6000 miles to the eastward, it will be sunrise c. 900 miles distant from the spectator in that direction [1]. Consequently in the actual position of the spectator it will still be rather more than an hour before sunrise, assuming as usual the average equinoctial period.

The next feature mentioned is that the earth's shadow is projected nearly upon an horizontal plane ('letto piano'). If the sun were actually on the horizon it would be exactly so, but, as he is still an hour or more below it, this is only the case approximately. *Quasi* is thus used exactly as in *Par.* i. 44, as is explained *infra*, p. 62. In ll. 4–9 another descriptive feature is added : 'The vault of heaven high above us [*profondo* is here used in the sense of *caelumque profundum* in *Georg.* iv. 222] begins so to appear [i.e. to grow so bright] that some stars are lost to sight down here below (*a questo fondo*). And as the most brilliant handmaid [2] of the sun comes further on, so the heaven shuts out one star after another, even at last to the very brightest.' In this way the Angels disappeared from sight one by one till all were gone (ll. 10–13).

There are two allusions to the sun being in the constellation Leo, one implying that in the spring of 1300 Saturn ('settimo splendore') was in that sign [3] (*Par.* xxi. 14); the other giving a chronological datum, the explanation of which is very much disputed, the difficulty being complicated by a difference of reading. In *Par.* xvi. 37 *seqq.* the birth of

[1] Or the computation may be put thus :—A distance of 6000 miles in longitude implies a retardation of a little over seven hours of time, as will appear from a simple proportion sum (see also Essay on *Geography*, *infra*, p. 129). Hence when it is mid-day at any given point it will be seven and a quarter hours earlier at a place 6000 miles westward. And so again it will be a little before 5 a.m. at the time of equinox.

[2] *Ancella* is used for the hours of the day, as in *Purg.* xii. 81, and xxii. 118.

[3] On this see further, Essay III, *inf.* p. 171.

Cacciaguida[1] is said to have occurred when Mars (where Dante then was) had returned to rekindle himself beneath the feet of his Lion 500 and 50 and 30 times (*var. lect.* 553 times), the *terminus a quo* no doubt being the Christian era. Now the sidereal period of Mars, according to Ptolemy, and as Dante might have seen it in Alfraganus, c. xvii., was 1 year, 10 months, and 22 days, nearly (*ferme*), i. e. c. 687 days: and 687 × 580 = 398,460 days, which would give the date 1091 for Cacciaguida's birth, making him 56 at the time of his death in the 2nd Crusade in 1147. This seems quite a suitable chronology. Some commentators, however, objecting to this date, and appealing to *Conv.* II. xv. 145,—where Dante is speaking professedly in round numbers (*quasi*) as was suitable to the object for which the reference is *then* made, whereas *here* it is for the purpose of giving a very precise date,—suppose him to have taken the period of Mars at two years, or 730 days, and use this as an argument for reading ' tre ' instead of ' trenta[2],' though it is a reading almost entirely devoid of manuscript support. It is true that thus an improbable supposition, combined with an unsupported reading, supplies quite a suitable date, viz. 1106. But there is no reason for preferring it to the date 1091 obtained by a more reasonable process. In fact, the only objection made to it is the absurd one that at 56 Cacciaguida was too old to go crusading!

There is another, at first sight extremely obscure passage, relating to the sun's position on the ecliptic, which should be explained before we leave this part of our subject, viz. *Par.* i. 37 *seqq.*:—

' The lamp of the world rises upon mortals through several points, or passages, but from that which combines four circles with three crosses,' it is most propitious, &c.

Now if we were asked, first of all, to say what particular

---

[1] Observe how appropriately the brave crusader is represented as being born under the sign of Leo.

[2] For the period of two years, or 730 days, combined with the reading ' trenta ' would give the impossible date 1160. The ' synodical ' period of 780 days (also given by Alfraganus) is still more out of the question with either reading, besides being totally out of place in this context.

point was likely to be thought thus most favourable, we should say without any hesitation the Vernal Equinox. For then the sun returns from the 'mondo senza gente' to the more favoured hemisphere of the north ; then is the beginning of the season when all nature 'feels the gladness of the spring' in renewed life and hope ; that was, according to mediaeval belief, the time of Creation [1], of the Annunciation, of our Redemption, i.e. the Crucifixion ; it was also the beginning of the year according to Florentine usage [2] ; finally, the sun, being then on the equator, partook of its most 'noble' and perfect motion according to the idea expounded in *Conv.* II. iv. 68 *seqq.* We feel sure that Dante could not possibly mean to indicate any other time. Moreover, the date for the Vision is indicated (*inter alia*) by the statement (three times repeated) that the constellation Pisces was upon the horizon just before sunrise, the sun being in the next following sign of Aries. See *Inf.* xi. 113 ; *Purg.* i. 21 and xix. 4 [3].

Now if we turn to any good globe we shall see, at the point where the equator and the ecliptic intersect, another great circle passing through the same point. This is one of the circles known by astronomers as the colures [4]. These were two great circles cutting the equator at right angles, one of which passed through the two poles of the earth (or of the equator) and the two equinoctial points, and the other through the poles of the equator and of the ecliptic and the two solstitial points, or tropics. The former was called the equinoctial, and the latter the solstitial colure. Here Dante is speaking of the point of sunrise upon the horizon (see *foci* and *surge* in l. 37). Now the actual point of sunrise evidently differs each day as the days lengthen or shorten. And these points are the *foci* (= *fauces*), through which the sun passes at rising. The most perfect then of these spots is the due east point, at which the

---

[1] See *Inf.* i. 38-40. Also *Time References in the Divina Commedia*, pp. 14-16, and Supplementary Note III, pp. 118 *seqq.* ; or *Accenni*, &c., pp. 116 *seqq.* We may note in this connexion the curious 'storia ideale' of a Venetian chronicler who puts the foundation of Venice on *March* 25, *about mid-day*, in the year 421.

[2] On the different usages in Italy and elsewhere see *ibid.*, p. 48, and more fully in *Accenni*, &c., p. 53, and authors cited there. Also *infra*, in Essay III.

[3] See the allusion in this passage explained *supra*, p. 58.

[4] See, *inter al.*, Alfraganus, c. v., p. 17.

sun rises at the vernal equinox, and at that point the three circles above mentioned—i. e. the equator, the ecliptic, and the equinoctial colure—all intersect the fourth circle of the horizon, and so make three crosses with it [1]. It will be observed that Dante uses the qualifying word *quasi* here, because the actual day of the equinox was already past, whatever explanation we adopt of the initial day of the vision ; and, according to what I hold to be the most probable theory, the day on which Dante is now speaking, when he entered Paradise at noon [2] (the ' colmo del dì '), was April 13, 1300.

We have now to consider together two passages in the *Paradiso* relating to the sun's position, the explanation of which, taken in combination, presents, as I think, the most difficult problem arising out of any passages of this class in the *Divina Commedia*.

I refer to *Par.* xxii. 151-4 and *Par.* xxvii. 79-87 :—

> ' L' aiuola che ci fa tanto feroci,
>   Volgendom' io con gli eterni Gemelli,
>   Tutta m' apparve dai colli alle foci :
> Poscia rivolsi gli occhi agli occhi belli.'

> ' Dall' ora ch' io avea guardato prima,
>   Io vidi mosso me per tutto l' arco
>   Che fa dal mezzo al fine il primo clima ;
> Sì ch' io vedea di là da Gade il varco
>   Folle d' Ulisse, e di qua presso il lito
>   Nel qual si fece Europa dolce carco.
> E più mi fora discoperto il sito
>   Di questa aiuola ; ma il sol procedea
>   Sotto i miei piedi un segno e più partito.'

---

[1] All this has no doubt its allegorical meaning also. The four circles represent the four cardinal virtues, and the three crosses the three theological virtues. Benvenuto comments thus :—' Sol iustitiae, Deus, qui est lux mundi, oritur hominibus per diversas vias, sed potissime per quattuor virtutes cardinales et tres divinas.' Compare the symbolism of the seven maidens, four on the left and three on the right of the triumphal car of Beatrice in *Purg.* xxix. 121-32, xxxi. 103-11, 130-2, and probably also that of the four stars of *Purg.* i. 23, in contrast with the three in viii. 89-93. Note also the ' Settentrion del primo cielo' (i. e. the Empyrean) in *Purg.* xxx. 1.

[2] Noon is involved in the statement that the *whole* of the south hemisphere was light, the mountain of Purgatory being its central point, just as Jerusalem was of the north hemisphere, the *whole* of which was consequently dark (ll. 44, 45).

In the former passage Dante is supposed to be looking down from the constellation Gemini (l. 152 and *supra*, l. 111) on the solar system. After describing the position and appearance of the several planets (ll. 139–50), he adds respecting the earth : ' As to this little floor [1] which makes us so proud, as I revolved with the eternal Twins, the whole of it appeared to me from its hill-tops to its river mouths.' (This seems to mean that the whole habitable earth was seen by him in one glance. Compare *supra*, l. 135: ' So that I smiled at its paltry appearance.')

In the latter passage Dante says that he looked down again upon the earth, and ' from the time when I had first looked, I saw that I had moved through the whole arc that the first " clime " makes from its middle to its end [i. e., in plain language, just half of the arc described by the first ' clime '], so that I saw beyond Gades the mad track of Ulysses [i. e. the Atlantic Ocean, see *Inf.* xxvi.], and on the other side, nearly to that shore [or, perhaps, hard by me that shore] on which Europa became a sweet burden [i. e. the coast of Phoenicia, whence Europa was carried away to Crete by Jupiter in the form of a bull]. And still more of the site of this little floor would have been disclosed to me, but that the sun

---

[1] *Aiuola*, cf. *De Mon.* III. xvi. 90 : ' in areola ista mortalium.' The insignificant size of the earth is a favourite thought with writers of various classes. Alfraganus declares, ' terrae moli . . . nullam esse quantitatem perceptibilem respectu caeli ' ; and ' se habere prae exiguitate sua ad modum puncti in circulo.' So Cicero, *Somn. Scip.*, xvi. *fin.* : ' Iam ipsa terra ita mihi parva visa est, ut me imperii nostri, quo quasi punctum eius attingimus, poeniteret.' Seneca, *Nat. Quaest.*, Prol. quoted by Roger Bacon, *Op. Majus*, ii. p. 268 (ed. Bridges): ' Hoc est punctum quod inter tot gentes igne et ferro dividitur ' (cf. ' che ci fa tanto feroci ') . . . ' Punctum est istud in quo navigatis, in quo regnatis, in quo bellatis.' Again, Boeth., *De Cons. Phil.* II. Met. vii. 1–6 :—

> ' Quicunque solam mente praecipiti petit
>   Summumque credit gloriam ;
> Late patentes aetheris cernat plagas,
>   Arctumque terrarum situm :
> Brevem replere non valentis ambitum,
>   Pudebit aucti nominis.'

Finally, Milton, *Par. Lost*, viii. 17 :—

> ' this earth, a spot, a grain,
> An atom, with the firmament compared.'

and l. 23 :—

> ' This opacous earth, this punctual spot.'

was travelling beneath my feet a sign and more distant from me.'

The result of this is to indicate the position of the sun clearly enough, but that of Dante himself only approximately. As to the former, the limit of darkness on the east was about the coast of Phoenicia. Consequently it was about sunset at Jerusalem, and it would follow that (according to Dante's system of geography explained elsewhere [1]) it was about noon at Cadiz, or the Pillars of Hercules, and therefore the sun would be on the meridian about 90° west of Jerusalem. Hence the limit of darkness on the west would be upon the Atlantic Ocean about another 90° west of the Pillars of Hercules, where the sun would be just rising. But Dante says that these east and west limits of day-light did not correspond with his limits of vision, since he was 'a sign and more distant from the sun.' The sun being in Aries, and Dante in Gemini, the intervening sign of Taurus (i. e. 30° *plus* the number of degrees still remaining to be traversed by the sun within the sign of Aries at the supposed date of the vision) would account for the 'sign and more' of distance. But there might be something to add for the position of Dante within the sign of Gemini. All he says is that he was 'dentro da esso' (xxii. 111). He may have been, as some have supposed, at the central point; or, as others, at the first point of that sign or constellation. Then again, the number of degrees which the sun had advanced in Aries will depend on the date assumed for the commencement of the vision; and that, as all know, is a very much disputed point, varying in fact from March 14 to April 8. Besides this, some maintain that Dante had regard to the true astronomical position of the sun, who owing to the precession of the equinoxes would not even enter Aries [2] till c. April 12; others hold

---

[1] See Essay II. on Geography, pp. 123, 129.

[2] I purposely avoid using the terms 'sign' or 'constellation' here, as I have been censured for confusing them. I may have used them indiscriminately sometimes, but, so far as I am dealing with Dante and not speaking with strict astronomical propriety, I do not admit that I should be wrong. I do not believe that Dante used the terms with strict accuracy. Nor am I alone in this. Prof. Rizzacasa d'Orgogna, *L'Aiuola*, p. 3, says the same ; and Arci, *Cronografia*, p. 25, writes that, while we cannot for a moment suspect that Dante was not aware of the difference, yet, 'dobbiamo affermare che i *segni* e *costellazioni* nel

that he followed the popular view which would associate the entrance of the sun into Aries with March 21.

With all these elements of uncertainty we cannot pretend to define the number of degrees involved in ' un segno e più.' But to fix our thoughts, and to enable us to exhibit the main conditions by a diagram, let us suppose the distance to be 45°. The *principles* both of the difficulties and of their proposed solutions will be the same with any figure intermediate between 30° and 60°, though the expression ' un segno e più' would naturally imply a figure distinctly short of 60°.

In that case, looking at Position II in the Diagram overleaf, Dante's limits of vision (i. e. 90° east and west) would be, theoretically, 45° east of Jerusalem, and 45° west of Gades. But, the sun being just setting at Jerusalem, his limits of vision eastwards would be limited practically to about the longitude of Jerusalem, or, as he puts it, the coast of Phoenicia, which is much the same ; while westwards it would extend over the Atlantic Ocean c. 45° westwards of the ' Pillars of Hercules ' or Gades, the sunlight itself extending yet another 45° or thereabouts beyond this westward limit of Dante's vision.

I may here insert a word as to the interpretation of ' presso ' (in l. 83). It may mean ' nearly to,' or ' hard by.' In the former case it would seem most naturally to mean ' a little short of.' But then there seems no obvious reason for this qualifying term. If it could bear the meaning of ' a little beyond,' then it might possibly refer to the longitude of Jerusalem being a little further east than that of the coast of Phoenicia. Many translators render it ' hard by.' I have not seen this commented on, but it may perhaps refer to the proximity of the eastern limits of his actual vision (45°) comparatively with that on the western (90°).

So far, then, I think there is no special difficulty except that attaching to the obscure expression about ' clima ' in l. 81 which will be explained presently. But when we come to correlate this passage with that in Canto xxii, which Dante's

linguaggio dantesco correspondano perfettamente.' Even Professor Angelitti, my chief critic in this respect, says, ' Si deve riconoscere che Dante fa un poco di confusione tra costellazioni e segni' (*Sulla data*, &c., p. 40). In *Par.* xiii. 13, ' segni' is distinctly equivalent to ' costellazioni.' Comp. *Par.* xxii. 110.

* * *

66   STUDIES IN DANTE

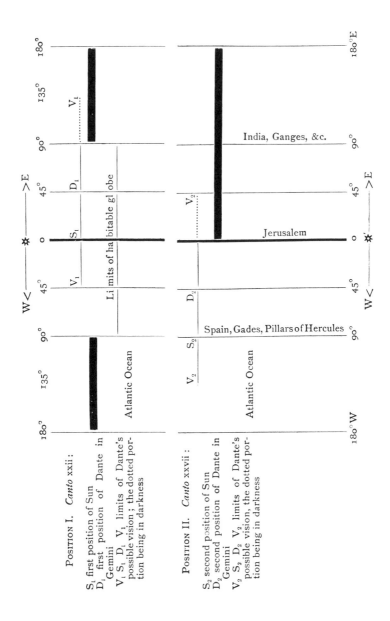

POSITION I. *Canto* xxii :

S₁ first position of Sun
D₁ first position of Dante in Gemini
V₁ S₁ D₁ V₁ limits of Dante's possible vision; the dotted portion being in darkness

POSITION II. *Canto* xxvii :

S₂ second position of Sun
D₂ second position of Dante in Gemini
V₂ S₂ D₂ V₂ limits of Dante's possible vision, the dotted portion being in darkness

language in l. 79 compels us to do, the comparison seems at first sight to involve an impossible situation : for l. 153 of that Canto,

'Tutta m' apparve dai colli alle foci,'

seems to imply, and is generally understood to imply, that the whole inhabited world was visible at once, and this would require that the sun should be on the meridian of Jerusalem, its supposed central point. Hence we appear to have this dilemma :—(1) If the sun were on the meridian at Jerusalem, the whole earth, being illuminated, would be visible ; but not to Dante, who was 'un segno e più partito' to the eastwards in Gemini. (2) If Gemini were on the meridian at Jerusalem, Dante would have been *in a position* to see all the earth, but, the sun being 'un segno e più partito' to the west, a part of the inhabited earth, being in darkness, would not be visible to Dante, owing to conditions occurring similar to those of the second position in Canto xxvii.

The two principal suggestions to afford an escape from this dilemma (omitting others) are as follows :—

(1) That Dante's position in Canto xxii is a purely imaginary and ideal one, as indeed in some sense it must be, from the orrery-like view of the whole solar system which is there described (so Della Valle, Scartazzini, &c.). In this way we might compare it to the 'ideal' position in our Lord's Temptation, denoted as 'an exceeding high mountain' from which he beheld 'all the kingdoms of the earth in a moment of time.'

(2) Others plainly say that Dante has omitted in Canto xxii to take account of the difference between his own position in Gemini and that of the sun in Aries.

But we cannot accept such solutions, because Dante has expressly called attention to the difference of position and its practical results in Canto xxvii, and further he has invited a comparison of the two passages to enable us to picture to ourselves the relation between the two situations.

I believe the true key to the solution is that quite recently indicated by Professor Rizzacasa d'Orsogna in his monograph entitled ' L'aiuola che ci fa tanto feroci [1].' It consists in giving full weight to an expression which has, as far as I know, hitherto been passed over by commentators on this passage,

' *Volgendom*' io con gli eterni Gemelli.' (xxii. 152.)

This he takes (and, I believe, rightly) to mean that the vision of the whole of this paltry globe from end to end was displayed to him *while he revolved* with the eternal Twins in a very brief period of time, during which he contemplates the movements of the whole solar system, xxii. 139-50.

Thus, referring to Fig. I on the opposite page, $V_1 G_2$ would be beyond the horizon of Dante's vision, while $G_1 V_2$ would be invisible through darkness.

In Fig. II the portion $x_1 G_2$, corresponding with $V_1 G_2$ in the earlier figure, will have come into his view, and so Dante will *during his revolution* (of c. 3 hours) with the Twins have seen the whole of the habitable globe from Gades to Ganges, though a portion of what he saw before will now be invisible through darkness, viz. $x_2 G_1$.

In Fig. III, his position in Canto xxvii, he observes that six hours have passed since he first looked down upon the earth.

I believe this makes all clear, with the exception of the singular expression, which alone now remains to be noticed, by which this six hours' interval is described :—

' Dall' ora ch' io avea guardato prima,
Io vidi mosso me per tutto l' arco
Che fa dal mezzo al fine il primo clima.'

(xxvii. 79–81.)

In other words, the eighth heaven, in which Dante was, had revolved with the motion of the *Primum Mobile* over half the arc described by the first ' clima ' in its daily revolution, i. e. 90°.

The subject of the climata will be found discussed and

---

[1] I do not commit myself to all the details of his explanation, but I think as to this particular point he seems to have 'colto nel segno.' Still less can I acquiesce in the surprising (though I am sure quite unintentional) misrepresentations of some of my positions and arguments on this point in my *Accenni al Tempo*. At the same time I wish to take this opportunity of acknowledging with regret that the view which I then advocated as to the main solution now appears to me to be altogether erroneous.

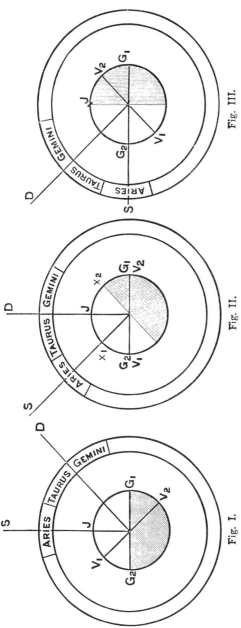

Fig. I.   Fig. II.   Fig. III.

N.B. I do not mean (v. text) to *assume* either that Dante was at the first point of Gemini, or the sun in the centre of Aries. But it was necessary to put them in a diagram in *some* positions more or less fulfilling the conditions, and I have therefore taken these merely for the purpose of illustration. D = position of Dante; S = the sun; G_1 = Ganges, G_2 = Gades; J = Jerusalem; $V_1 V_2$ = the horizon of Dante's vision.

Fig. I is the position in Canto xxii; Fig. III that in Canto xxvii; Fig. II represents the intermediate stage at the point when Dante 'volgendo con gli eterni Gemelli' had seen the whole habitable globe pass under his eyes, as illumined by the sun. On the assumption of 45° between Dante and the sun, this would correspond with a space of three hours; it might be more or less according to the space supposed to be covered by 'un segno e più.'

[These diagrams are borrowed (with some variations) from Rizzacasa d'Orsogna's monograph.]

explained in the following Essay (pp. 130–134), to which reference may be made. It is only necessary here to state that they
were bands or zones of latitude, the limits of which were fixed
by the maximum length of the day, which varies according to
latitude from twelve hours at the equator to six months at the
poles. In the first 'clima' it varied from $12\frac{3}{4}$ hours at its
southern to $13\frac{1}{4}$ at its northern boundary, so that the mean
length would be thirteen hours. It was calculated that the
corresponding limits of latitude would be from $12\frac{5}{6}°$ to $20\frac{1}{2}°$.
If we imagine the heaven to be divided into corresponding
climata or bands [1], and Dante to be on the ecliptic in Gemini,
he would be within the *primo clima*, and he consequently
describes himself as moving with it.

Mr. Tozer has suggested in his recently published English
commentary that *tutta* may be taken to mean 'in all its
details' rather than 'in all its extent,' and thus the dilemma
above mentioned would not arise. The latter and usual
translation appears to me to give much more force to the
passage, though the former might be possible as a means of
escape from a grave difficulty, if none other were available.
But the explanation now offered appears to me to give a sufficiently clear and consistent explanation of the two passages.

There is one other point to be briefly noticed. It has been
thought that Dante had a special reason for fixing his position
at about longitude 45° west of Jerusalem, and departing from
his usual practice of not marking the lapse of time in the
Paradiso. This in his geographical system was the accepted
latitude of Italy, speaking roughly, or probably more precisely
that of Rome, for in Dante's symmetrical system of geography
Rome was the centre of the western half of the world, or, as
we might perhaps say, of the Christian world, as Jerusalem was
that of the whole world. See, for example, *Purg.* ii. 1–9 and
xxvii. 1–6 [2]. Now it is to be observed that the first part of this
Canto contains the tremendous denunciation by St. Peter of

---

[1] The zones of the climata, though terrestrial in origin and purpose, may be
supposed to be 'projected' on the heavens, like the equator or the poles of the
earth.

[2] *Time References*, pp. 70, 72. *Accenni al Tempo*, pp. 76, 79.

the abuses of the Papal Court. As soon as this is concluded, Beatrice bids Dante look down upon the earth and see what point he has reached (xxvii. 77, 78). Then follows the passage which we have been explaining. If Rome were found to be lying directly beneath their feet, there would certainly be an obvious fitness that this terrible condemnation should be uttered by St. Peter while standing over Rome itself, even as David saw the destroying Angel of the Lord 'with a drawn sword in his hand stretched out over Jerusalem [1].' Thus St. Peter and those who heard him might be said

> 'Guardar Roma sì come suo speglio.'

There is a passage of some obscurity in reference to the southerly setting of the autumnal sun in *Purg.* xviii. 79 *seqq.* Dante has referred to the effect of the gibbous moon [2] in quenching the light of the feebler stars, and he describes her position thus :—

> ' E correa contra il ciel per quelle strade
> Che il sole infiamma allor che quel da Roma
> Tra i Sardi e i Corsi il vede quando cade.'

The expression 'contra il ciel' obviously refers to the moon's 'proper motion' from west to east (contrary to the diurnal motion of the *Primum Mobile* from east to west) which has been sufficiently explained *supra*, p. 6. As this retardation may be taken at an average of 50 minutes of time or 13° of space in 24 hours [3], it would amount on the fourth night after the full moon (as I take it now to be [4]) to about 50°. Now, if the sun were fairly well advanced in Aries [5], the

---

[1] 1 Chron. xxi. 16.

[2]   'Fatta com' un secchione che tutto arda.' (l. 78.)
       Shaped like a bucket that were all aglow.

[3] *V. supra*, p. 10, and quotations from Alfraganus and B. Latini given *infra*, p. 85 *n.*

[4] For this see *Time References*, or *Accenni*, &c. But even if this be (as some suppose) the fifth night after the Plenilunium, the description might still hold, for, besides all the elements of vagueness noticed presently in the text, we have no data as to the time of full moon nearer than some time on Thursday night.

[5] The day being supposed to be about three weeks after the Equinox. I purposely avoid making too definite assumptions where there is still so much dispute as to the data. Besides, in the present case, there is no need for any such precision when Dante's language is extremely vague.

moon, when full[1], being in a corresponding position in Libra, a retardation of 50° would carry her some few degrees into Sagittarius.   But we are chiefly concerned at present with the curious *solar* datum by which Dante indicates (roughly enough) the position of the moon[2].   What he says (in effect) is that the moon had through her own proper motion arrived at that region of the sky ('per quelle strade') where the sun is when he sets at Rome in the line of the straits of Bonifacio, between Corsica and Sardinia, i. e. somewhat to the south of west. Obviously this is a very vague indication, for the data do not correspond with any *visible* phenomenon, since the islands of Corsica and Sardinia cannot of course be seen from Rome. The direction might perhaps be more or less inferred from the inspection of a map (and these were very rough and inaccurate in those days); and, after that, it might be found from astronomical tables, or from an armillary sphere, in what position in the zodiac the sun would be when the sunset lay in that direction.   Or a person (and perhaps Dante himself) may have empirically noticed at Rome the time of the year in which such a sunset occurred, and argued from that as to the position of the sun in the zodiac. In that case, such a popular conception of the association of the sun with the zodiacal signs or constellations as has been explained *supra*, p. 54 *n.*, would be assumed as a basis. It will be remembered also that the sun's position in the zodiac is a matter of inference and not of direct vision[3] (*v. supra*, p. 50, *n.* 2). I think it is most probable that Dante in giving this indication may have had in his mind the description in Orosius of the position of Corsica and Sardinia :—[Sardinia] 'habet ab *oriente et borea* Tyrrhenicum mare quod spectat *ad portum urbis*

---

[1] As it was on the previous Thursday, see *Inf.* xx. 127 ; *Purg.* xxiii. 119.

[2] For the difficulties involved in the expression of l. 76—'La luna quasi a mezza notte tarda'—as an indication of the hour, see *Time References*, pp. 101–4, or *Accenni al Tempo*, pp. 110-13. As the former work is now out of print, I may briefly state that it is disputed whether this refers to the actual moon *rise*. I have given reasons for supposing that it is not so, but that this is only a poetical way of saying that the hour was approaching midnight, and the moon was quenching the light of the stars.

[3] Hence the effects of Precession would not be recognizable by 'the man in the street.'

Romae[1].' This would imply a line about south-west, or west-south-west, from Rome. Such a distinct southing of the sunset would be observable from a month or so after the autumn equinox up to the winter solstice, but we might take it to be (in the absence of more precise indications) about November. So that Dante's statement comes in effect to something like this : 'the moon on that night was about where the sun is in November.' As the sun enters Sagittarius (popularly speaking) shortly after the middle of November, his position would approximately correspond with that of the moon on the night in question, this also, as we have seen, being probably a little beyond the east limit of Sagittarius. This, it may be observed, agrees exactly with her position on the previous evening, when the brilliant stars in Scorpio are described as gems on the forehead of the Lunar Dawn. This, at any rate, I believe to be the true interpretation of the much disputed passage in *Purg.* ix. *init.*, as will be seen a few pages later.

The *southerly* setting of the autumnal sun referred to in the last passage suggests a few words on another (also combining points of astronomy and geography) in which according to one, and probably the better, interpretation Dante seems to refer to its *northerly* setting in summer. See *Par.* xii. 49–52 :—

> 'Non molto lungi al percoter dell' onde,
>   Dietro alle quali, per la lunga foga,
>   Lo sol talvolta ad ogni uom si nasconde.'

Dante is here describing the position of Calahorra, the birthplace of S. Dominic. It is situated in the extreme east of Old Castile, and about seventy or eighty miles nearly due south of S. Sebastian. Within what limits of accuracy Dante knew of its position may well be doubted, but it may perhaps be presumed that he knew that it was very much nearer the Bay of Biscay than the Western Atlantic, ' beyond,' as he would describe it, ' the Pillars of Hercules.' On this supposition the passage would be explained to mean—'Not very far from the beating of the waves' [viz. those of the Bay of

---

[1] *Adv. Pag.* I. ii. 102.

Biscay], behind which by reason of his long course [i. e. in the
long days of summer] the sun sometimes conceals himself from
every man [i. e. sets in the ocean, which was supposed to
occupy the whole western hemisphere of our globe, as well as
the southern half of the eastern hemisphere, and hence it was
'mondo senza gente']. The phenomenon would, of course,
be invisible from Calahorra, as that of the sunset described in
the last passage would be from Rome, but the direction
indicated would be equally intelligible and correct. The
other interpretation supposes Dante merely to mean that
Calahorra is in Spain generally, since the setting of sun,
moon, and planets is often associated with Spain, under the
names of Gades, Sibilia, Ibero [1], &c. In that case, *talvolta*
will be taken to mean 'from time to time,' and, in fact, 'daily,'
to which there is no intrinsic objection [2] ; and *lunga foga* to
refer to the length of his ordinary daily course, as in *Ps.* xviii.
7 : 'A summo caelo egressio eius ; et occursus eius usque ad
summum eius.' The former interpretation seems to me pre-
ferable, as giving a more definite and precise sense (1) to
talvolta, (2) to *lunga foga*, and (3) to the description of the
position of Calahorra.

We now pass on to consider references to the Moon and
her motions.

There are two very difficult passages involving references to
the moon's position in the zodiac, and in both cases, as it
happens, to that part of it which is in the region of Scorpio,

---

[1] e. g. *Inf.* xx. 126 ; *Purg.* xxvii. 3 ; and similarly Morocco in *Purg.*
iv. 139.

[2] *Talvolta* occurs again in a somewhat similar passage, descriptive of the
rising sun, in *Par.* xi. 51, and there also its meaning is open to doubt. The
appearance in the world of S. Francis is likened to the rising of another sun
'Come fa questo *talvolta* di Gange.' Here the majority of commentators, ancient
and modern, seem to explain *talvolta* as 'in the summer' (v. Scart. *h. l.*), when
the sun rises with the greatest splendour; which would certainly add point to
the comparison. I do not, however, remember any passage in which Dante
associates sunrise from the Ganges with any special season of the year.
Perhaps here it may not refer to any definite season, but rather to the phenomenon of the sun appearing to rise straight out of the waters of the river, which,
like his rising or setting in the sea, would be at any time a more brilliant sight
than if he rose behind land. Thus the appearance in the world of S. Francis
would be compared to the rising of the sun under the most brilliant conditions.

though in neither is that sign specifically mentioned. The former of these is the celebrated passage in *Purg.* ix. 1–9 :—

> La concubina di Titone antico
> Già s' imbiancava al balco d' oriente,
> Fuor delle braccia del suo dolce amico :
> Di gemme la sua fronte era lucente,
> Poste in figura del freddo animale
> Che con la coda percote la gente :
> E la notte de' passi, con che sale,
> Fatti avea due nel loco ov' eravamo,
> E il terzo già chinava in giuso l' ale [1].'

This is a veritable *crux interpretum*, and probably no passage in the *Divina Commedia*, except perhaps that which relates to the mysterious personage Matelda in *Purg.* xxviii to xxxiii, has given rise to so much discussion. Referring to Scartazzini's lengthy note at the end of the Canto, we shall see that the literature of this passage might almost be described as a small library. Moreover, Scartazzini, in the paragraph headed *Risultato*, regards the difficulties as all but insoluble. I must say, if I may do so without presumption, that these difficulties appear to me to have been very much exaggerated, and that the whole passage comes out clearly enough by the application of the common-sense principle which I have so often insisted upon, viz. that Dante, when giving indications of time by references to astronomical data, does so in such popular language and terms as would be generally understood by his readers, and that he does not take account of scientific corrections of such popular views, whether he may have had access to them or not.

Now, as is generally admitted by those who have written upon this passage, there are three main points to be determined, one in each *terzina* ; but for the purpose of our discussion it will be found convenient to take them in the reverse order.

1. What are the '*passi con che la notte sale*'? (l. 7).

---

[1] I venture to reprint here (in substance) the discussion of this passage in my little work on *Time References in the Divina Commedia*, since this, having been published in a very small number of copies, is now out of print. The astronomy of Dante would be very imperfectly treated if a discussion of this extremely difficult passage were omitted.

2. What is the '*freddo animale, Che con la coda percote la gente*'? (ll. 5, 6).

3. Is the '*concubina di Titone antico*' (in l. 1) the *solar* or the *lunar* Aurora? (It should be added that a quite modern interpretation of Antonelli, adopted by Scartazzini, involving a change of reading in l. 1, denies either Aurora to be referred to. This will be noticed presently.)

I. First, then, what are the *passi con che la notte sale*?

I venture to think that any one, apart from the context, would at once reply that 'the steps with which night ascends' seem most obviously and naturally to describe the six hours of the first half of the night, or the hours before midnight. This would appear still more certain to any one familiar with the *Convito* (IV. xxiii.), where Dante, after comparing human life to an arch culminating at 35 years, and consisting of ' uno salire e uno scendere,' proceeds to apply the same metaphor to the hours of the day (ll. 129 *seqq.*). Noon is described as the 'colmo del dì' (l. 107), and by parity of reasoning midnight would be the 'colmo della notte,' the summit of the night, when 'salire' ends and 'scendere' begins [1]. I think, then, that we can scarcely have any doubt that the 'passi con che la notte sale' are the hours from six p.m. to midnight [2], and consequently that the precise time indicated by the words which follow, viz. that two of these steps were already made, and the third was now beginning to droop its wings (the metaphors, it must be admitted, are a little mixed), would be shortly after 8.30 p.m. or between 8.30 and nine [3]. As Benvenuto quite clearly puts it—' Iam

[1] See *infra*, p. 105 *n.* In further illustration we might add *Par.* xxvi. 139-42, where Adam's time in Paradise is stated to have been six hours, viz. from 6 a.m. to noon, so that his expulsion occurred in the first hour of the *decline* of the day, the hour which follows the sixth hour, when the sun 'muta quadra.' Compare the expression 'inclinare meridiem' in Horace, *Carm.* III. xxviii. 5.

[2] The naturalness of the metaphor may be illustrated by its independent use by Milton, who thus describes the hour of 9 p.m. :—

　　　'Now had night measured with her shadowy cone
　　　　Half way uphill this vast sublunar vault.' *Par. Lost,* iv. 776-7.

As the sun sinks lower beneath the horizon till midnight, so correspondingly the point of the conical shadow cast by the earth rises, or goes 'uphill' (*sale*). For the expression 'shadowy cone,' *vide supra,* p. 30 *n.*

[3] We may compare with this a passage in the first sonnet of the *Vita Nuova,*

fecerat (*sc.* nox) duas horas . . . et tertia hora noctis iam
finiebatur.'

I ought to notice in passing the other explanations suggested for *passi*.

1. The *watches* of the night. To this I should object (a)
the graphic word *sale* loses all force if applied indifferently to
the four watches: (β) the hour indicated would be about
two a.m., which suits neither solar nor lunar Aurora: (γ) it
would not be an appropriate hour for the first coming on of
sleep (see ll. 10, 11) after the very fatiguing day which Dante
has passed through ever since the early dawn in *Purg.* i. 13 *seqq.*
We might also, though it is scarcely necessary, quote the
analogous cases of the two following nights. On the next
night Dante was overwhelmed with drowsiness in any case
some time before midnight, though sleep was dispelled by the
restless activity of the spirits expiating *accidia* (see xviii.
76–90, and the discussion of the passage *supra*, p. 71). On
the night following he laid him down to sleep very soon after
sunset (at an earlier hour than this), and *before* the darkness
of night had come fully on (see xxvii. 70–5), and while some
amount of daylight still remained (ll. 88–92). (δ) We should
remember, finally, the impossibility of making any progress
in Purgatory after nightfall, which is more than once insisted
upon by Dante (e. g. *Purg.* vi. 52–7 ; vii. 43–60; xvii. 62–3 ;
xxvii. 74, 75), and that the last reference to time before this,
in viii. 49, describes the coming on of darkness ; i. e. seven
hours or so before the hour now supposed.

2. The signs of the zodiac have been thought to be indicated by *passi*. But (a) what definite idea can be attached
in that case to the expression (and it is clearly meant to be
a very definite one) 'the signs with which the night *ascends*' ?
(β) What would *fare passi* exactly signify in that relation ?

in which Dante is describing the hour following this, viz. when it was nearly
10 p.m. :—

'Già eran quasi ch' atterzate l' ore
Del tempo che ogni stella è più lucente.'

In other words, the hours of the night were almost one-third past. As to his
meaning there can be no doubt, for it is stated in plain prose just before (ll. 60–5)
'trovai che l'ora . . . era stata la quarta della notte ; sì che . . . ella fu la prima
ora delle nove ultime ore della notte.'

(γ) I might add that those who adopt this view differ (it may be said both metaphorically and literally) *toto caelo* as to the signs of the zodiac supposed to be thus indicated.

As to the expression in l. 8, 'nel loco ov' eravamo,' it is no doubt to be explained in reference to such passages as *Purg.* ii. 8, where nearly the same words occur ('Là dov' io era') : or, again, xv. 6, 'Vespero là, e qui mezza notte era,' where 'là' and 'qui' mean Purgatory and Italy respectively [1]. Similarly in other passages Dante recognizes that the time when indicated by hours, or by reference to the position of the sun or of the moon, is a variable term depending on the longitude of the place. This is definitely stated in *Purg.* xxxiii. 104, 105 :—

> 'Teneva il sole il cerchio di merigge,
> Che qua e là, come gli aspetti, fassi.'

II. We proceed next to inquire, What is the *freddo animale che con la coda percote la gente* ?

Granting, as seems most natural, that some sign of the zodiac is referred to, one may again ask, apart from any reference to the interpretation of the passage, to which of these signs does such a description seem most appropriate? Would not any one at once say, the Scorpion? It is the only one whose tail is conspicuously an object of terror ; and besides, there are two passages in Ovid which may have suggested this description of the Scorpion to Dante [2] :—

'Scorpius exibit, caudaque minabitur unca ;' (*Metam.* xv. 371.)

> 'Elatae metuendus acumine caudae
> Scorpio.'   (*Fasti*, iv. 163, 164.)

Indeed, as far as I know, no one has even thought of suggesting any other of the signs of the zodiac except Pisces, which, though it would correspond with the solar Aurora [3], and though it would suit the epithet *freddo*, is at once excluded by three considerations : (*a*) the singular, 'freddo animale,'

---

[1] So in *Par.* i. 43 *là* = the southern hemisphere and *qua* the northern.

[2] On Dante's familiarity with Ovid, and with the *Metamorphoses* in particular, see *Studies*, I. pp. 206 *seqq.*

[3] *V. supra*, pp. 57, 61.

would be rather out of place [1] : (β) there are no conspicuous stars in that sign [2], so that the beautiful description in l. 4,

'Di gemme la sua fronte era lucente,'

becomes unmeaning : (γ) the reference to the formidable tail in l. 6 would be simply ridiculous.

It should be added that the constellation *Cetus*, or the Whale, has been suggested by some commentators. This, however, is not a sign of the zodiac, and it is most probable that Dante would have referred to these (as we have already seen in numerous cases) for either his solar or lunar data. In any case, it should be observed that Cetus (which is not far from Pisces) could only refer to the solar and not the lunar Aurora.

One objection remains to be dealt with. It has been urged that *freddo* is an inappropriate epithet for Scorpio, especially in view of Virgil's 'ardens Scorpio [3].' I would reply—(a) Virgil's epithet refers to the appearance of the constellation rather than the nature of the animal. In Dante the reverse appears to be the case. Also the epithet 'ardens,' as I believe is generally agreed, describes not heat, but the 'burning and shining light' of the brilliant stars in that constellation, notably of Antares. If so, its meaning corresponds with the feature described by Dante in l. 4. (β) Even supposing Dante to have been thinking of the constellation rather than the animal, the epithet *freddo* might be justified (as Philalethes has suggested) by a reference to its association with the months of October and November in the sun's annual course [4].

But if, as is more probable, he is referring to the scorpion itself, the epithet *freddo* can be justified by several lines of association between it and coldness. First, it is an invertebrate and cold-blooded animal ; next, its *habitat* is in cold and shady places ; and further, its venom produces cold. As Brunetto Latini says when speaking of poisonous serpents : 'Tutti i veneni sono freddi.' Also I have found in the *Coltivazione* of Alamanni the two following passages where

---

[1] Though it might be contended that the singular, 'celeste lasca,' is used of this constellation in *Purg.* xxxii. 54.

[2] See *Purg.* i. 21 and *supra*, p. 57.   [3] *Georg.* i. 35.   [4] See *supra*, p. 73.

the epithet is applied to Scorpio, both to the constellation and the animal :—

    'Quando al *freddo* Scorpion Delio ritorna.'   (*B.* vi, l. 281.)

And again,

    'Il *frigido* scorpion, l'audace serpe.' (l. 1089.)

I think, therefore, we may now lay it down quite confidently that ' Scorpio ' is the constellation here described as being on the horizon ; for it, and it alone, combines the three points mentioned : (1) a brilliant group of stars ; (2) the suitability of the epithet *freddo* ; (3) a formidable tail.

III. We come lastly to the question raised by the first *terzina*. Does Dante refer to the solar or the lunar Aurora in the mysterious expression ' La concubina di Titone antico ' ? Both views have been vigorously contended for. As before, I might say that, apart from its ultimate bearing on the general interpretation of the passage, the singular and indeed unique expression ' *concubina* di Titone '—the solar Aurora being, according to the universal language of mythology, described as the *wife* of Tithonus—would lead us to suppose that Dante had a special reason for adopting the unusual term *concubina* here[1], and that the word might not unnaturally express the sort of secondary position or inferiority of the lunar as compared with the solar Aurora.

It seems to me that this would be a perfectly legitimate expansion of the mythological idea upon the same lines, and also that it would be an original and ingenious touch very much in Dante's manner. It is absurd to object, as Scartazzini[2]

[1] We might add to this the choice of the somewhat suspicious term *amico* in l. 3. This consideration is well put by Scartazzini (p. 154): ' Invece di chiamare la bella Aurora *moglie* o *consorte*, ei la chiama *concubina* di Titone ; invece di dire costui *marito*, ei lo dice *amico* dell' Aurora.' *Amico* and *amica* are thus commonly used by Boccaccio. We may perhaps compare *Inf.* xxx. 38, 39 :

    ' Di Mirra scellerata, che divenne

       Al padre, fuor del dritto amore, amica.'

Petrarch (doubtless in imitation of this passage) calls the dawn ' la bianca amica di Titone' (*Morte*, ii. l. 5). Finally, we may illustrate this use from Dante's language in *Conv.* II. xv. 175, where he is quoting *Canticles* vi. 7, 8 : ' Sessanta sono le regine, e ottanta l' *amiche* concubine.'

[2] Scartazzini's virtuous indignation can only be described as preposterous when he stigmatizes this conception as a ' lordura,' and as being a ' sozza pittura,' from which we are compelled ' svolgere con nausea e con ribrezzo gli occhi ! '

and others have done, that Dante would be '*falsifying* mythology.' It would rather be a reasonable *modification* or *ad-
aptation* of it. We should then, I think, be prepared to admit
at the outset that, other considerations apart, the peculiar
language of Dante would rather lead us to expect that, if any
Aurora be in question, it would probably be the lunar rather
than the solar.

But the question is to be mainly settled on the ground of
the better suitability of one or the other of these interpretations to the passage, when viewed in connexion with other related passages giving data of time. From this point of view
I assert most unhesitatingly that this is the case with the lunar
Aurora. In the first place, following the usual popular computation, and assuming that we are right in determining this
to be the evening of Easter Sunday, April 10, the third
night after the full moon, then moonrise would occur about
nine p.m. or soon after[1], and the phenomenon of the lunar
Aurora about half an hour before. Further, allowing the
same daily retrogradation for the moon of about 13° of
space, which is equivalent to about fifty minutes of time, she
would have fallen back either from the first point of Libra, or
from whatever point in that sign we might rather take as the
terminus a quo of the full Moon, say, about 40°. That would
obviously bring her into Scorpio, and probably somewhere
about the middle of that constellation. It will be also remembered that the bright band of stars, with Antares among
them, are those that rise first. So that I think we have all
the various details of Dante's description fulfilled in the
minutest particulars. And if I may paraphrase in plain prose
the first few lines of the Canto, I should read them thus:—

'The Aurora before moonrise was lighting up the eastern
sky (ll. 1–3) ; the brilliant stars of the constellation Scorpio
were on the horizon (ll. 4–6) ; and, finally, it was shortly
after 8.30 p.m. (ll. 7–9).'

---

[1] There is here as always a considerable margin of uncertainty, as we do not
know the time of the full moon more nearly than that it was *some* time on the
previous Thursday night,
  'E già iernotte fu la luna tonda' (*Inf.* xx. 127).
The same statement is repeated in *Purg.* xxiii. 119.

* * *

Let us next point out how entirely this harmonizes with the other data of time in this part of the poem. In viii. 1 it was just the hour of sunset. In viii. 49 the air was growing dark, say from seven to 7.30. Then occurs the incident of the serpent driven away by the angel guards (ll. 95 *seqq.*), and the conversation with Conrad Malaspina, &c. The present passage then follows, indicating an hour or more later, when Dante, weary with 'the burden of the flesh' (l. 10), lies down to sleep. It will be found that the position of the moon on the following night, which is given in another passage of some obscurity in xviii. 79 (already discussed *supra*, pp. 71–73), is consistent with that here described.

It remains to point out briefly that the solar Aurora, which some have thought to be indicated by the description of Dante's dream at dawn, immediately following in l. 13 [1], is quite unsuitable to the details of the passage before us.

(*a*) It implies that Dante and his companions remained awake all night till nearly daybreak, and leaves a gap of nine or ten hours unaccounted for since the last Canto, where see l. 49. (*β*) It is inconsistent with *Purg.* vii. 43 *seqq.* and other passages, as has been pointed out *supra*, p. 77. (*γ*) The brilliancy of the stars (l. 4) would be quenched by the light of the *solar* dawn, as is beautifully described by Dante himself in *Par.* xxx. 4–9 [2]. (*δ*) The term *concubina*, as applied to Aurora, the *wife* of Tithonus, would be meaningless and even offensive. (*ε*) There would in fact be no such brilliant stars at all, since Pisces would be the sign preceding sunrise, as Dante implies in no less than three different passages (see *supra*, p. 61).

Still less worthy of consideration is the singular modification of this view that has been suggested, viz. that Dante is referring to the solar Aurora in *Italy*, in contrast with the

---

[1] It is noticeable that on the next night but one the description of Dante's falling asleep soon after sunset, and that of the dream at the following dawn, come similarly in immediate conjunction. See xxvii. 88–93, and 94 *seqq.*

[2] Compare Virg. *Aen.* iii. 521 :

'Iamque rubescebat stellis Aurora fugatis,'

or. as Tacitus says of the brief Arctic night, the glow remaining between sunset and dawn ' sidera hebetat,' *Germ.* c. xlv.

nocturnal phenomena of ll. 7–9 in Purgatory, 'nel loco ov' eravamo.' It is argued with misplaced ingenuity that, if it were $2\frac{1}{2}$ hours after nightfall in Purgatory, it would be $2\frac{1}{2}$ hours after sunrise in Jerusalem [1], and consequently in Italy, 45° of longitude west of Jerusalem (according to Dante's system of geography), there would be three hours' difference of time [2], so that it would be half an hour before sunrise. But, apart from the force still remaining of some of the above objections, it would surely be preposterous to suppose that all this brilliant description refers to an absent and invisible phenomenon.

Without attempting an examination of several other views that have been maintained, the extraordinary interpretation suggested in recent years, first, I believe, by Antonelli [3], and championed by Scartazzini with his usual vehemence, must be briefly noticed. This view involves a change of the text in l. 1, reading *Titan* (i.e. the sun) instead of *Titone* (i.e. Tithonus [4]). The following are the main outlines of the theory in question :—

1. Neither solar nor lunar Aurora is referred to in the word *concubina*, but ' La concubina di Titan ' is Tethys, the wife of Oceanus, and is in fact equivalent to ' onda marina.' The statement of the whole passage amounts to this, that the ocean waves towards the east were illuminated by light, probably from the rising moon, but at any rate from some source *other than the sun* (for thus strangely Scartazzini would interpret the words in l. 3!).

2. The *freddo animale* is not the Scorpion, or indeed any other constellation specifically, but only certain stars, among which there might possibly be some of those in Scorpio ' disposte in forma di serpe,' the serpent being known as ' frigidus anguis.'

---

[1] See passages collected *supra*, p. 50, *n.* 2.

[2] Compare *Purg.* iii. 25, and xv. 6, where this difference of time is recognized.

[3] *Studi speciali* (Florence, 1871) ; and an article ' *Sulle dottrine astronomiche della Divina Commedia*' contained in the collection entitled *Dante e il suo Secolo*.

[4] This reading is found in the great Vatican MS. (Witte's ' B '), but has little (if any other) authority that I am aware of.

3. Scartazzini interprets *passi* of the hours of the night, just as I have done, so that his final conclusion is the same, viz. that the hour was towards nine p.m.

One scarcely knows where to begin in enumerating the objections arising against such an interpretation in every single line of the original passage, at least in the first two *terzine*.

l. 1. Scartazzini, as we have seen (p. 80 *n*.), severely censures Dante for foully falsifying mythology in describing the lunar Aurora as 'concubina di Titone.' What shall we say to his own 'falsification' of it in attributing to Tethys, the lawful wife of Oceanus, the position of 'mistress' of the sun? The lunar Aurora had at any rate no other attachment, or any connubial responsibilities, that we are aware of.

l. 2. The word *balco*, i. e. gallery or balcony, implies some elevation, and clearly indicates some phenomenon *in the sky*, not on the 'suol marino,' as Dante calls it (*Purg.* ii. 15[1]), and would lose all significance if applied to light down on the waves. Scartazzini very inadequately paraphrases it by *lembo*.

l. 3. The interpretation of Scartazzini that the words mean (as above) 'illuminated by light other than that of her lover, the sun,' needs no refutation. For, considerations of language apart, who can doubt that *fuor delle braccia* represents the idea of Homer (*Il.* xi. 1),

ἐκ λεχέων παρ' ἀγαυοῦ Τιθωνοῖο,

or, as Dante may have known it in the words of Virgil (*Georg.* i. 447),

'Tithoni croceum linquens Aurora cubile'?

l. 4. This interpretation takes no notice of *fronte*, which as the 'front' or 'forehead' of the dawn [2] speaks for itself; but what would be the point of it in reference to the ocean wave?

ll. 5, 6. What are these stars 'poste in forma di serpe'? Are there any such as would convey any definite idea to a reader of the passage? If not, why should it be worth while to mention that there were stars in the neighbourhood arranged in this form?

---

[1] Compare Milton's 'ocean floor.'

[2] So Milton speaking of the day-star says that it
'Flames in the forehead of the morning sky' (*Lycidas*).

My apology for this very lengthy digression must be the
importance of the passage in view of the extraordinary
amount of controversial literature to which it has given rise;
and my conviction that, in spite of this, it really presents no
serious difficulty.

Returning to the subject of the Moon and her motions,
little more need be said, for though her position and aspect
are often referred to instead of that of the sun (invariably in the
Inferno, and occasionally in the *Purgatorio*) to indicate time,
yet there is nothing which involves any astronomical theories
going beyond popular and familiar knowledge of her apparent
position in the heavens in reference to the sun. This is
a point on which I should wish to insist strongly, as I have
already done in my little work on the *Time References*, &c.
I mean that it is to obvious phenomena and to popular and
familiar knowledge, such as would be intelligible to readers
of average intelligence, and not to esoteric astronomical calculations of the moon's position and motions, that we must
refer in explanation of such allusions in Dante's poem [1].
I mean, for example, that when Dante speaks of the position
of the moon so many nights after full, he would presuppose
the popular conception that the moon rises some fifty minutes
or an hour later on an average each night, though any one
may see on reference to an almanac how very far the facts are
from corresponding with this *average* amount [2].

An important question bearing upon Dante's references to
the moon's position arises from the difference between the
'real' moon and the 'calendar' moon. The determination
of the moon's motion became a burning ecclesiastical question [3] with a view to the appointment of Easter, which, in the

---

[1] Thus, in *Inf.* xx. 125 (the moon being about full) moon-setting is used to indicate
sunrise, and in xxix. 10 'la luna è sotto i nostri piedi' means approximately noon.

[2] *V. supra*, p. 71. As Alfraganus (c. xiii.) says, after an elaborate account of
the five circular motions of the moon, the general result is, 'Quam ob causam
epicycli centrum videtur transire in zodiaco gradus 13° et minuta prope 11, qui
est Lunae *motus medius*.' This, according to the explanation given *supra*,
represents c. 53 minutes of time. So again, Brunetto Latini in *Trésor*, I. pt. 2,
c. 120, [La lune] 's'esloigne dou soleil chascun jor xiii degrez po s'en faut.'

[3] Compare the case of the Roman Calendar which was in the hands of the
Pontifices (*infra*, pp. 92, 96).

western Church at any rate, was fixed to fall on the Sunday after the day of the first full moon after the vernal equinox [1]. Hence it became necessary to determine by authority both the exact time of the equinox and that of the full moon, since a very slight variation of a few hours, or even minutes, in the calculation of these dates would sometimes make the difference of about a month in the time of Easter. But the lunar motions are extremely complicated, so that it was further necessary to adopt some 'mean' and not 'real' motions of the moon. For this purpose lunar cycles were employed, the most celebrated of which was the Metonic cycle, to which the so-called 'Golden Numbers' in our calendar refer. It is evident then that the moon's position as determined by these 'average' and 'rule of thumb' calculations would often differ considerably from her real position. Thus there was a difference sometimes of two or even three days between the 'real' and 'calendar' dates for full or new moon. As a matter of fact, in the year of Dante's Vision, 1300, there was a difference of two days, the 'real' full moon being on April 5, and the 'calendar' full moon on April 7 [2]. Further, as this represents a difference in her position at any given time of c. 26° of space, or nearly two hours of time, one of the most hotly disputed points in the interpretation of Dante's lunar references in the *Inferno* and *Purgatorio* is whether they are to be understood as made to the 'calendar' or 'real' moon of that year. I have discussed this point at considerable length in my *Time References in the Divina Commedia* [3]. But both on

---

[1] The Jewish passover being on the fourteenth day of the first month (see Exod. xii. 2-6), and those months being lunar, this day would represent the full moon of the first month. The year being commonly held to begin at the equinox, and it being also arranged that Easter Day must fall on a Sunday, the rule above given was a rough approximation to the old 'Quartodeciman' rule.

[2] The year 1301 (which some writers have maintained to be the year of Dante's vision, see *infra*, Essay III) affords a still more striking illustration of this anomaly, as I have pointed out in my *Time References*, p. 37 *n*. The *Calendar* full moon in that year was on Monday, March 27, and Easter was consequently kept on the following Sunday, April 2. But the *real* full moon was three days earlier, viz. on Friday, March 24. Hence, if regard had been paid to this, Easter should have been observed on March 26.

[3] The discussion of this point involves a minute examination of a number of passages which could not be repeated here.

a priori and *a posteriori* grounds I have not the smallest doubt that Dante refers (as his readers would naturally assume) to the *calendar* moon.

There is one point in reference to the moon on which Dante evidently spent a good deal of thought, viz. the markings on her surface. In *Conv.* II. xiv. 72 *seqq.* these are explained as being due to the different density of different parts of her body, the ' rarità ' of which in some places is such that the sun's light is not arrested (' terminatur ' [1]) by them, but a certain amount of it is absorbed [2], and consequently such parts of the surface appear less bright than others. This may have come from Ristoro d' Arezzo, or from Averroes, *De Substantia Orbis*, c. 2 [3]. This view is elaborately refuted in *Par.* ii. by arguments put into the mouth of Beatrice. The whole passage is so extremely difficult and obscure that the following analysis of the argument may be acceptable :—

(i) ll. 64–72. In the eighth heaven (that of the fixed stars) ' one star differeth from another star in glory ' ; one is brighter, another less bright, just as are the different parts of the moon's surface. Yet no one supposes a mere *quantitative* difference in the influence of the stars [4] ; there is also a difference of *quality* and of *character*. This is again insisted on in *Quaestio*, § 21, where there are many other striking points of resemblance with *Par.* ii. [5]. Dante there says of the eighth heaven that ' per organa *diversa* virtutes *diversas* ' (influit), and he adds that if any one does not admit this he is ' extra limitem philosophiae.' Now, if the difference of degrees of light in the moon were simply due to ' raro e denso,' the same should be the case also with the similar difference among the stars. If so, their

---

[1] This is a common expression in the *Convito* for light that is reflected back from a mirror, or other reflecting surface. It is common also in Ristoro d'Arezzo.

[2] ' Imbibitur,' as Albertus Magnus says. See quotations given *supra*, p. 45 *n.*

[3] Ristoro on this subject will be found quoted at length in *Studies*, II. p. 362. It was also commonly believed to have been the opinion of Aristotle (though really that of Averroes), and, if so, Dante may have thought, ' che più savio di te fe' già errante ' (*Purg.* xxv. 63).

[4] It must be remembered that the *rays of light* were the medium of stellar influences. See *infra*, p. 89, *n.* 2.

[5] See *Studies*, II. p. 341.

influences would be uniform in *character* (as is that of the moon), and only different in *degree* from one another. But this, as we have seen, is admittedly not the case.

(ii) ll. 73–78. But next (Dante seems to say) let us look at this argument from 'raro e denso' a little more closely. It may be understood in either of two ways :—

Either (*a*) the 'rare" parts go through the whole body of the moon, and so most of the light passes right through ; in that case the light is lost by *Refraction* : or (β) if the 'rare' parts do not go through, but are backed sooner or later by a dense part which arrests and reflects back the light, this would imply a *depression* in the moon's substance before the reflecting part is reached, so that the reflecting surface in those parts would be further removed from us, and consequently would send back less light. In that case the light is lost by *diminished Reflection*.

Next (ll. 79–105), both these suppositions are shown to be untenable : (*a*) in ll. 79–82, by the obvious consideration that in that case when the sun is behind the moon, as in a total eclipse, his light would shine through to us in this direction, which is not the case ; while (β) is refuted, in ll. 82–105, by an experiment which the diagram opposite will explain.

M_1, M_2, M_3 are three equal mirrors, L is the source of light (l. 101). D is the position of Dante, equally removed from M_1 and M_2, but at a greater distance from M_3. He states that it will be found by actual experiment (ll. 94–6) that the amount of light received back from all three mirrors will be equal, it being unaffected by the *distance* of the reflecting surface. Hence the supposed depressions in the surface of the moon would not cause the loss of light which is to be accounted for.

Such is, at any rate, Dante's argument. I have not been able to discover a source from which he may have derived this matter-of-fact experiment so strangely embodied in his poem.

Dante then appeals again to the analogy of the eighth heaven as pointing to the true solution. All the influence, and the very existence, of every celestial body depends on the communication to it of the virtue of the *Primum Mobile*[1]. That single influence—of which *light* is both the symbol and the medium[2]—is exhibited in different results according to the different receptive capacity of the objects upon which it strikes[3]. With each it combines always in such different manners as to produce the best possible result of which the conditions admit[4]. Hence it is that in the eighth heaven some stars are brighter than others; and that in the first heaven some parts of the moon are brighter than others. The difficulties in detail which are involved in this argument have been dealt with *supra* (pp. 18 *seqq.*), as they concern the relations of the several heavens rather than the particular case of the moon.

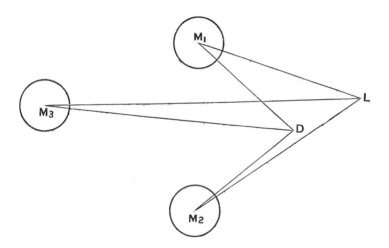

<hr />

[1] This would be illustrated by *Conv.* II. xv. 132–57, where the disastrous results, supposing the motion of the *Primum Mobile* to be arrested, are strikingly set forth : *v. supra*, pp. 16–18.

[2] A familiar thought with Dante. See especially *Conv.* II. vii. 90 ; III. xiv. 32 ; IV. xx. 73 ; *Epist.* X. xx. l. 378 ; xxi. l. 402 ; xxv. l. 466 ; xxvi. l. 489 ; *Par.* vii. 74 ; xix. 90 ; xxix. 29, and other passages.

[3] Another familiar thought. See especially *Par.* xxxi. 22, 23 ; *Conv.* III. ii. 20–49 ; vi. 57 ; vii. 11 *seqq.* ; xiv. 14 *seqq.* ; IV. xxi. 68 *seqq.* ; xxiii. 46. Compare also *Par.* i. 129 ; iv. 35, 36 ; vii. 70–5 ; xiii. 67 *seqq.*, and many other places.

[4] 'Ciascuno effetto, in quanto effetto è, riceve la similitudine della sua cagione, quanto è più possibile di ritenere' (*Conv.* IV. xxiii. 47-9). Compare *Par.* viii. 133 5, quoted *supra* (p. 20, *n.* 1).

Dante again refers to this subject in *Par.* xxii. 139–41, when from the height of the eighth heaven in Gemini he sees the whole of the solar system at one glance. The appearance of the moon is thus described :—

> 'Vidi la figlia di Latona incensa
> Senza quell' ombra che mi fu cagione
> Per che già la credetti rara e densa.'

Dante therefore supposed that only that face of the moon which is always turned towards the earth exhibits this mark of imperfection. This would be explained by the belief that the moon, being intermediate to the earth (dark) and the stars (light), must partake of the nature of both [1]. So also Ristoro d'Arezzo, as quoted in *Studies*, II. p. 362. In this way Pliny accounts for the 'maculae lunae' which we have been discussing :—' Maculas enim non aliud esse quam terrae raptas cum umore sordes' (*N. H.* ii. 9 *fin.*).

It is interesting to inquire *why* Dante attached so much importance to the refutation of the view to which he had committed himself before, and which was the commonly received view in his time. It was generally attributed to Aristotle, though it was not due to him, but to his commentator Averroes. Possibly Dante thought it seemed contrary to the belief in the absolute *perfection* of the heavenly bodies, as it is stated by Aquinas, *Summa* III, Suppl. Q. xcv. A. 5 'Corpora caelestia secundum sui naturam incorruptibilia sunt *et secundum totum et secundum partes.*' Milton, in fact, implies such imperfection when he refers to these darker parts of the moon as

'Vapours not yet into her substance turned [2].' (*Par. Lost*, v. 419.)

---

[1] See this stated as a general principle, and applied to human nature, by Dante in *Mon.* III. xvi. 30 : 'Si ergo homo medium quoddam est corruptibilium et incorruptibilium, *quum omne medium sapiat naturam extremorum*, necesse est hominem sapere utramque naturam.' Compare Aquinas, *Summa*, I. cii. 1. r_1 : 'luna est magis terrae affinis inter omnia corpora coelestia ; unde et tenebras quasdam maculosas habet, quasi accedens ad opacitatem.'

[2] Elsewhere (viii. 145) he curiously infers from this the habitability of the moon :—

> 'Her spots thou seest
> Are clouds, and clouds may rain, and rain produce
> Fruits in her softened soil, for some to eat
> Allotted there.'

The references just given to Ristoro d'Arezzo and to Pliny point to the same inference.

If it be objected that some imperfection in the receptive capacity of portions of the moon is still implied even on the explanation given by Beatrice, this is to some extent true. But Dante would, I think, meet it in this way. In ll. 133 *seqq.* he illustrates the case before us by the way in which the one soul (ψυχή) or life combining with different parts of our 'dust' produces now the eye, now the ear, now the hand. Some of these organs may well be regarded as superior to others, but the result in each case is the best possible. Just as St. Paul argues in 1 *Cor.* xii : 'If the whole body were an eye, where were the hearing? If the whole were hearing, where were the smelling?' In the same way different heavenly bodies, or different parts of the same body (as the moon), receive the greatest amount of divine influence of which each is capable, so that the best possible result is attained in each case.

We have now expounded the theory of 'planetary' motions as it was received by Dante, and I have endeavoured to explain all the passages in the works of Dante which occur to me as presenting any difficulty in relation to this department of astronomy. We now pass on to

III. The Measurement of Time.

This was naturally one of the earliest and most important of the practical applications of astronomical science. We will take first the computation of the length of the *year*, leading to the formation of the calendar.

It is to be observed at the outset that both the Greeks and the Romans regarded the regulation of the calendar as a religious rather than a scientific question [1], and consequently as being an exclusively priestly prerogative. The origin of this, no

---

[1] So in early Christian times the determination of the moon's motions was largely an ecclesiastical question, with a view to the determination of Easter (*vide supra*, p. 86).

doubt, was that certain religious observances were essentially connected with special seasons, and it appeared intolerable that these should be controlled or altered by secular hands. By this means, however, the priests acquired and wielded great political influence, of which both Greek and Latin classical authors afford numerous examples. ' They exercised their power neither scientifically nor honestly. They are stated to have falsified the time in order to favour or to spite particular magistrates, or farmers of the public revenue, by unduly lengthening or shortening the term of their office or contract '[1].

The confusion caused in the times and seasons for religious rites owing to the great inaccuracy of the calendar is treated with characteristic humour by Aristophanes in the *Nubes*, ll. 607 *seqq.*[2] The moon sends down a message to the Athenians by the clouds. She recounts her benefits to them, especially in saving them the cost of torchlights when they go out at night. Yet, she says, the calendar, which ought to follow her days and phases, is in such confusion that it makes the gods extremely angry, because the observance of their sacred days has got all wrong. When they expect a feast, they return home hungry; when the Athenians ought to be sacrificing, they are busy in the law courts ; on days when the gods (who of course observe the correct time) are fasting in memory of departed heroes, the Athenians are making merry, &c.

Returning to the question of the formation of the calendar, we find that the most primitive calendars depended on the moon rather than on the sun. This might be expected, because her periods are marked by visible changes comparatively easy of observation[3]. There is nothing to correspond with this when the sun is beginning a fresh revolution. At the

---

[1] From Lewis, *Astronomy*, &c., p. 236. The primitive year of 355 days necessitated frequent intercalations. The arbitrary treatment of this process alone afforded great facilities for the practices described in the text.

[2] Also referred to by Lewis, *op. cit.*, p. 235.

[3] Thus, *auct.* Alfraganus, c. 1, the first day of each month began 'a prima Lunae visione,' and he adds that, as that occurs about sunset, hence 'the evening and the morning' constitute a 'civil day.' For the important bearing of this on *V. N.* § 30 (*lect.* 'Arabia') see *Studies*, II. p. 123.

same time, it was obvious that the year, with its recurring seasons, must essentially depend upon the revolution of the sun, and so some multiple [1] of the lunar periods must be taken corresponding as nearly as possible with a complete solar revolution. The first thing therefore was to determine the length of the lunar period, or, as it is commonly called, a 'lunation.' And here it is specially important to recall the distinction, already explained, between a 'synodical' and a 'sidereal' revolution in reference to the term 'lunation,' since it can be understood in either of these senses. It will be remembered that a 'sidereal' revolution, as applied to the moon, will represent the time which she takes to go exactly once round her orbit in reference to the stars. But a synodical revolution will represent the time when she is again *in the same position relatively to the earth and the sun*; in other words, the time from one new or full moon to another new or full moon.

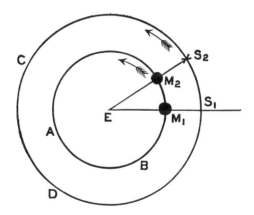

Thus, in the above diagram, if E be the earth, and M_1 and S_1 the position of their conjunction (i.e. of new moon), when the

---

[1] Even this was not possible with any exactness, so that, as Sir G. C. Lewis says, 'a sort of compromise' had to be made between the sun and the moon, the essence of the system being that the year should be formed of the integer number of lunar months which approximated most nearly to the solar year, and the difference made up by intercalation (*op. cit.* p. 117).

moon comes round to the same point in her orbit again, that will represent a sidereal lunation. But when she does so, it will be then a month later, and consequently she will not find the sun where she left him, but he also will have moved on about $\frac{1}{12}$ of his annual orbit, so that when the moon again arrives at M_1 there will not be a new moon, nor will this occur till the moon is once more in a line (or, speaking technically, ' in conjunction ') with the sun [1], viz. at M_2. It is not till that point is reached that she will have completed a synodical revolution, or a synodical lunation.

The distinction of these two periods is interesting as explaining the two kinds of months with which we are all familiar—viz. the lunar month of 28 days and the calendar month of 30 or 31 days [2]. The former approximately represents the moon's *sidereal* or *periodic* revolution in her own orbit, which is exactly 27 d. 7 h. 43 m., and this is roughly taken as 28 days ; and the latter her *synodical* revolution, which is exactly 29 d. 12 h. 44 m., and is similarly taken as 30 days. Now the latter would give about $354\frac{1}{3}$ days for the lunar year of 12 months ; but, as this was about 11 days short of the solar year, it was common to adopt a sort of compromise and take the year at 360 days. Sometimes, however, it was taken more exactly at 354 [3] or 355 days, and some-

---

[1] Not of course necessarily in a direct line *in the same plane*, since when that further condition is fulfilled an eclipse occurs.

[2] Sir G. C. Lewis, *op. cit.*, p. 21, notes the curious fact that the period of child-bearing (280 days) was described by the ancients as ten months, in reference to lunar months, but by the moderns as nine months, since calendar months are now more familiar. The latter would spoil an original piece of symbolism excogitated by Tertullian that the ten months period has a connexion with the Decalogue (!) (*ib.* p. 22 *n.*).

[3] e. g. by the Arabians, *auct.* Alfraganus, c. i., and by Solon, *auct.* Lewis, p. 114. A still more 'abnormal' year is that traditionally attributed to Romulus (*ib.* p. 34), viz. : a year of ten months or 304 days (four of the ten having thirty-one days), the inconvenience of which, in reference to the seasons, must have been almost incredible. I have met with an allusion to this in the following curious statement by Sir John Mandeville (supposed to have died c. 1370). In his *Travels* (p. 77, ed. 1866) he asserts that our Lord died at the age of thirty-three years and three months, but that David was quite correct notwithstanding in prophesying that he should be forty years upon earth, in the words 'Quadraginta annos proximus fui generationi huic' (quoting thus, Ps. xciv. 10), because David referred to the old year of ten months, the other two months having been added later by 'Gayus, that was Emperor of Rome.'

times even at the nearest round number of 350 days. From the first-mentioned of these numbers (360 days) arose the universally adopted practice of dividing the complete circle into 360°. We must not, however, pursue this subject further than as leading up to the partial reformation of the calendar by Julius Caesar, since this contains the key to the explanation of one or two passages of some interest and difficulty in Dante. The most important is this: in *Par.* xxvii. 121 *seqq.* Dante is denouncing the terrible corruption that is in the world through ' cupidigia,' a subject to which he often reverts. Yet he says there are signs and hopes of coming deliverance, and this is indicated in the remarkable statement that this change will come ' before January passes wholly out of winter [1] owing to the hundredth part (of a day) that is neglected in the world below,'

> ' Ma prima che gennaio tutto si sverni
>   Per la centesma ch' è laggiù negletta,
>   Ruggiran,' &c. (ll. 142–4.)

This refers to the fact that, owing to a seemingly small error in the assumed length of the year in the Julian Calendar, the true equinox had in Dante's time fallen back to about March 12. He here anticipates the time when the continued operation of this accumulating error would throw the equinox back even as far as December, in which case January would be ' entirely unwintered ' (*tutto svernato*), and would become one of the months of spring. Now, it is a very striking illustration of this passage, though it is one which I do not remember to have seen noticed, that when Julius Caesar under-took the reformation of the calendar this very result had

---

[1] The word ' svernare ' in this sense seems to have been coined by Dante and to be a ἅπαξ λεγόμενον in this passage. Its sense elsewhere has been explained *supra* (p. 54 *n.*) Dante is fond of words thus formed, e. g. ' sdonneare ' (*V. N.* xii. l. 115), ' smagare ' and ' dismagare,' ' slegare,' ' sviare,' &c., &c. Mr. Lowell (*Latest Essays*, pp. 107, 108) has pointed out several words that were coined by Milton with dis-. He quotes ' disgospel,' ' disworship,' ' dis-alliege,' and ' disesteem,' the last of which, at any rate, has survived. Mr. Lowell himself seems to be similarly responsible for ' disnatured,' and ' disleaved.' The last-named is exactly like ' sfogliare,' for which see *Purg.* xxiii. 58 :—
> ' Però mi di', per Dio, che sì vi sfoglia.'

actually taken place, though *in an opposite direction* to that contemplated by Dante—i.e. it had become an autumn month. This I will now briefly explain.

The Roman year (with which we are concerned at present) was taken at 355 days, i.e. about twelve 'sidereal' or 'periodic' lunations. The enormous annual error of ten days or so was supposed to be compensated for by the pontiffs, who inter-calated varying periods from time to time in the manner which has been already described. But, to say nothing of the intolerable inconvenience that must have been caused by such a practice, we are informed that in spite of this priestly assiduity the calendar had come to be about three months wrong in the time of Julius Caesar, so that the spring equinox had moved *forward* into June, and the autumn equinox into December. Hence the season of spring began in June, and that of autumn in December, winter in March, and summer in September [1]. Thus January was no longer a winter but an autumn month. It had passed entirely out of winter. It was 'tutto svernato.' Now Julius Caesar, in his capacity of Ponti-fex Maximus, corrected this error, and guarded against its recurrence by taking the year at $365\frac{1}{4}$ days, and introducing the leap-year arrangement with which we are all familiar. But he slightly over-corrected the error, and the year was now a little *too long* by 11^m 12^s. This error in the length of the Julian year is probably what Dante refers to in the 'centesma negletta,' since it may be taken roughly as $\frac{1}{100}$th part of a day. It is really between $\frac{1}{128}$ and $\frac{1}{129}$.

But it may well be doubted whether Dante was aware of the true length of the year with such accuracy. It seems most probable that he would accept some authority then current, such as Alfraganus or Albategnius. I cannot find any statement of this kind in the former, but the latter gives [2]

---

[1] One or two classical passages have been cited which curiously illustrate this. Thus, in Caesar, *Bell. Civ.* iii. 6, after the siege of Salonae, commencing in January, had been carried on for a considerable time unsuccessfully, it was raised, and *then* it is said, 'iam hiems *appropinquabat*'; and again, after a further lapse of time, in c. 13 we read 'Multi iam menses transierant et hiems iam *praecipitaverat*.'

[2] *Auct.* Angelitti, *Sull' Anno della Visione*, &c., p. 15.

the length of the year as 365 days 5 hours 46 min. 24 sec. If then Dante took this to be the true length of the year, it would be found to differ about $13\frac{1}{2}$ minutes from the length of the Julian year, and this difference amounts to about $\frac{1}{106}$ of a day. Hence the 'centesma' would be very nearly exact. The result of this was that now the equinoxes began slowly to fall *back* in the year, just as they had formerly rapidly moved *forward* at the rate of more than five days in the year. The accumulated error, which in Dante's time amounted to about nine days, had reached ten when Gregory XIII, in 1582 (also in his capacity as 'Pontifex Maximus'), corrected it. It had come to be eleven days when the Gregorian calendar, or 'New Style,' was at last accepted in England in 1752.

The period of time required for the result imagined by Dante, i. e. for the equinox to fall back at the rate of about eleven minutes a year until it reached December, involving a difference of between seventy and eighty days—would be enormous, in fact, almost 8000 years, so that its introduction here is at first sight a little surprising. It is, however, clearly a rhetorical figure, alike in principle, though converse in character, to that which is familiarly known as 'litotes.' Similarly Dante himself uses 1000 years in the passage already referred to in *Purg.* xi. 106, and so also does Petrarch in *Trionfo d' Amore*, i. 81,

> 'Fiati cosa piana
> Anzi mill' anni.'

We ourselves sometimes employ such an idiom in conversation, in reference both to time and distance[1].

The 'centesma negletta' noticed by Dante was not overlooked in the Gregorian reformation of the calendar. It was remedied by dropping a leap-year in the centenary year ('centesimo anno,' *Par.* ix. 40) three times in each 400 years. The recent omission in the year 1900 was a case in point. The present year being 11 min. 12 sec. too long, the

---

[1] Dante has possibly himself here imitated Boethius, *Cons. Phil.* II. Pros. viii. c. *med.* (quoted in *Studies*, I. p. 287). Similar expressions occur again in *Purg.* xiv. 65, and *Conv.* IV. xi. 81. We may also compare Ps. lxxxix. (xc) 4, and 2 Pet. iii. 8.

* * *

error will be found to accumulate to 18⅔ hours in a century, and consequently to nearly seventy-five hours in 400 years. The thrice-omitted leap-year removes seventy-two hours, so that the error of less than three hours in 400 years remains practically infinitesimal. Roger Bacon had urged the reform of the calendar upon Clement IV, advising him to drop four leap-years in 500 years. This would have over-corrected the error by about a similar amount.

It is stated by Narrien [1] that the extraordinary genius of Hipparchus enabled him to determine the length of the tropical year as being 365·24655 days, which involves an error of only 6^m 13^s too much. Further, that he actually made the suggestion (far too much in advance of his age to obtain attention) that the intercalation of a day in every four years should be further rectified by its omission once in 300 years.

From the astronomical measurements of the *year* we pass to those of the *day*. It is to be observed that in one passage Dante shows that he was aware of the difference in length between a 'sidereal' and a 'solar' day. This is the same difference as that between a *periodic* and a *synodical* revolution already explained, and it is in fact only a particular application of that distinction, like that which has been noted between lunar and calendar months. A sidereal day (= 'periodic') is the exact time which any star takes (speaking according to appearances) to go round the earth, i. e. the exact time which the earth takes to revolve once upon its axis in reference to the stars. But since, in the case of the sun, the earth has in the meanwhile moved on a day in her orbit going from west to east (or, as the older astronomers would say, the sun has meanwhile moved on a day in his annual course round the ecliptic from west to east), the earth will, so to speak, take a little longer, or have to revolve a little further round on her axis (also from west to east), before the sun comes up with the same point in her again, or before any given point in the earth comes round to the same position in reference to the sun. This would not apply to the fixed stars, which have no such orbital revolution, or which are at such an

[1] *Op. cit.* p. 227.

infinite distance that the earth's orbital motion does not affect their apparent position (i. e., technically, they have no parallax).

The following familiar illustration will probably make this quite clear. Let us imagine two men to start round a course together in the same direction, one on a horse or bicycle, and the other on foot. When the rider has come round to the starting-point he would have completed an ordinary 'lap,' corresponding to a 'sidereal' revolution or day. But it will evidently take him a little longer to come again alongside of the pedestrian who has moved on meanwhile. Now if (speaking in the language of Dante) the rider represents the sun's daily revolution due to the motion of the *Primum Mobile*, and the walker represents the daily amount of the sun's movement in his annual orbit due to the revolution of his own heaven—or, to put it in modern language, if the rider represents the earth's revolution on its axis and the walker its revolution in its orbit—then the time of the return of the rider to the starting-point will correspond to a sidereal day, and the time of his overtaking the walker will correspond to a solar day. Thus in the diagram, p. 93, M_1ABM_1 will represent the completion of one lap round the course by the rider, or 'a sidereal day.' But as meanwhile the walker has advanced from S_1 to S_2, the space M_1ABM_2 must be traversed by the rider before he overtakes the walker, and similarly the earth must revolve a little further on her axis before any given point on her surface comes up into the same position as regards the sun ; before, for example, the sun again reaches the meridian of that place, which will mark the completion of a solar day. This therefore will be represented by M_1ABM_2. The solar day is evidently thus a little longer than the sidereal day. Another result is this. It is clear that by the time the walker has come round to the starting-point again, if we suppose the rider to have overtaken him (say) x times, the rider will have gone round the course $x + 1$ times. So when we employed the diagram to illustrate the motions of the moon and the sun, we saw that thirteen lunar months corresponded with twelve calendar months. Similarly in regard to these two kinds of days, by the time the earth has gone completely

round her orbit, i. e. in one year, a whole sidereal day will
have been gained, or, in other words, there will be one solar day
less in the year than there will be sidereal days (the solar days
being those with which we are naturally familiar). Hence it
is that any one who travels round the world in a westerly
direction (i. e. from east to west) loses one day in his reckoning
by the time that he has completed the circuit. He has, so to
speak, counteracted one whole revolution of the earth on its
axis (west to east) by himself going round that axis in a contrary direction (east to west), so that *for him* in that time the
earth has practically revolved once less round her axis than
if he had remained still.

The result is, in fact, that, as a solar day is 24 hours, so
a sidereal day is 23 hours $56^m\ 5^s$, very nearly, i. e. about four
minutes shorter. Now recurring to what has been said about
the revolution of the *Primum Mobile*, i. e. the revolution
which accounts for the diurnal motion of the heavens, it is
clear that this must correspond not with a 'solar' but with
a 'sidereal' day. Accordingly we find Dante clearly stating
in *Conv.* II. iii. 45 that the revolution of this ninth heaven
'is completed almost in 24 hours, that is, in 23 hours and 14
parts out of 15 of another hour, setting it down roughly.'
Now $23\frac{14}{15}$ hours = 23 hours 56^m. Thus the 'rough' calculation apologetically adduced by Dante was within 5^s of the
exact amount.

But the most interesting practical application of the
measures of the length of the day in the Ptolemaic system is
derived from the observation of the length of the longest day
at different places, which leads at any rate to a rough determination of terrestrial latitudes [1]. We have already seen how
Dante recognized that the equable day of the equator never
exceeded twelve hours, while at the poles it reached six
months. Consequently in going northwards from the equator
to the pole the maximum length of the day would gradually
pass through every stage from twelve hours to six months,

---

[1] This seems to have been the earliest method employed for the purpose, as
by Pytheas of Massilia, c. 330 B. C. (see Tozer, *Ancient Geography*, p. 160), and
again by Hipparchus (*ib.* p. 176).

and as this is entirely dependent on the latitude of the place, it would afford a rough measurement of it. The application of the method indicated was limited to the (supposed) habitable globe, since, as Strabo declares, anything beyond those limits has no interest for geographers. That habitable space was thought to be contained entirely within the northern hemisphere, and to be limited to $180°$ in longitude and about $30°$ in latitude, viz. c. $20\frac{1}{2}°$ to $50\frac{1}{2}°$. This space was divided into seven 'climata' or zones which were defined by the maximum length of the summer day, each 'clima' covering a space within which the mean length of the day was increased by half an hour. Thus in the first 'clima' the day varied from $12\frac{3}{4}$ hours at the southern limit to $13\frac{1}{4}$ at the northern limit, the mean length being thirteen hours: and this 'clima' commenced in the south at what was thought to be the southern limit of habitability, about $12°$, i. e. 600 or 700 miles north of the equator[1]. In the second 'clima' the mean length of the day was $13\frac{1}{2}$, and so on to the seventh, when it was 16 hours. Beyond that it was not thought worth while to proceed, though some Scythians (see *De Mon.* I. xiv. 43) were found further north.

Now the two chief passages in Dante on which this explanation bears are (1) the exceedingly difficult one in *Par.* xxvii. 79–87, which has been already discussed *supra*, pp. 48 *seqq.*; (2) that in *Conv.* III. vi. 23 *seqq.*, where Dante makes the singular statement that, assuming the day and night together to consist of twenty-four equal hours, sometimes the day has fifteen hours and the night nine, and sometimes the night has sixteen hours and the day eight. Now this is very curious indeed, for we naturally ask : (1) Why does Dante, who, as we have seen, was aware of the prolongation of the day and night to six months, stop at the limits of fifteen or sixteen hours ? And (2) Why does he give a different length for the maximum day and the maximum night, since clearly, if he is speaking of the same place, or of the same latitude, such a difference could not exist ? The only explanation that I can suggest

---

[1] This being a matter of geography rather than astronomy will be found more fully explained in the following Essay.

as to the former of these questions is that Dante was probably speaking of the limits of his own personal experience.   If so, and if we further inquire what are the latitudes corresponding to the differing phenomena of daylight here described, the result is certainly curious and significant.   The first condition, i. e. when the longest day is sixteen hours and the shortest night eight, corresponds with the latitude of Paris or there-abouts.   The second condition, where the longest day is fifteen hours and the shortest night nine hours (or, as Dante puts it, *vice versa*), corresponds with the latitude of Rome or thereabouts.   Now these are just about the northern and southern limits of the travels of Dante, of which we seem to have something like authentic information.   At any rate this passage, so interpreted, seems to give some support to the belief that he had travelled sufficiently far north to have had actual experience of the conditions here described, viz. a day or a night sixteen hours long.   It seems difficult other-wise to suggest any explanation for the figures here selected. It may be added that our English longest day is about 16½ hours.   The difference, however, is too small on which to found an argument for or against Dante's supposed visit to England, the positive evidence for which is extremely slender.

The passage just quoted conducts us to the last point to be noted in connexion with the measurement of time, viz. the length of the *hour*.   Dante is continuing, in the passage last commented on, the illustration of the same sentence of the Canzone which led to the discussion of the solar motions in ch. v., which has been explained at length *supra*, pp. 45–50. As he there spoke of the ' hour' in which the sun shone upon his lady, he now declares :—

' *Wherefore* it must be known that the " hour " is taken in two different ways by astronomers ; one is that they make of the day and of the night twenty-four hours, i. e. twelve of the day and twelve of the night, whether the day be long or short. And these hours themselves become short or long in the day and in the night, in proportion as the day and night increase and diminish.   And these are the hours employed by the

Church when she says Prime, Tierce, Sext, and None, and they are called " temporal hours " ' (*Conv.* III. vi. 12–22).

Thus the length of an hour of the day in summer would be longer than in the winter : e. g. in England a midsummer hour would be about 1 hour 23 min., and a midwinter hour about 37 min. At night, of course, these conditions would be reversed.

Dante next explains the other method by which the hours were equal in length, and consequently a variable number was assigned to the day and to the night, except at the equinox. These were called ' equal hours ' [1]. This strange and, as it seems to us, very inconvenient distinction of hours was commonly employed both in ancient and mediaeval astronomy. The Greeks and Romans employed both methods, and the system of equal hours does not appear to have been adopted among the Greeks till after the time of Alexander [2]. The earlier Arabian astronomers retained the use of temporal hours [3], and both methods are explained by Alfraganus (c. xi.). I believe that the use of these irregular and 'temporal' hours still prevails in Turkey.

It is hard for us to realize the constant difficulties and strange shifts to which people were put before the invention of clocks, which was not until the twelfth century A. D., while their use seems to have been extremely rare until well into the thirteenth, and they were far from common even in the time of Dante. The passage in *Par.* x. 139–44, in which he refers to an ' orologio ' in this sense, is well known. In monasteries the hour was ascertained at night by a rude

---

[1] They are also sometimes called 'equinoctial' hours, because their length (as Dante goes on to explain) is the same as that of the 'temporal' hours on the equator, or equinoctial line. Strabo calls them ὧραι ἰσημεριναί.

[2] Lewis, *op. cit.* p. 178. He also refers to Aristoph. *Eccl.*, 651, 652, where an invitation to dinner is given in terms of the length of the shadow of the gnomon. A passage is quoted from Menander, where a typical fool (a sort of classical Calandrino), who received an invitation to come to dinner 'when the shadow was twelve feet long,' is represented as mistaking this to mean the shadow due to the moon, consequently arriving about sunrise with apologies for being, as he feared, rather late !

[3] Lewis, *op. cit.* p. 242. Among others by Albategnius, c. 900 A.D., who has been already mentioned, *supra*, p. 96.

observation of the stars, or by the gradual burning of a candle, or sometimes, when it could be afforded, by a clepsydra or water-clock. A monk (*significator horarum*) was appointed for the special duty of observing the time, and S. Peter Damian[1] recommends him on dark nights, when the stars cannot be seen, to repeat several Psalms, a known quantity of which will empirically represent a certain lapse of time. This may throw light on a quasi-astronomical passage in Brunetto Latini, in which the Arctic day is unscientifically described as being so short as hardly to allow time to sing a mass! It is curious to find an old writer[2], even after the invention of clocks, giving elaborate directions for remedying their inconvenient regularity, and for making them mark longer or shorter hours according to the season! These 'temporal' hours were the result of dependence upon the sundial[3]. The period of daylight, whether long or short, was divided into twelve equal periods or ' hours,' and tables were constructed giving the length of the shadow of the gnomon of the sundial at each of these hours. The first sundial, and consequently the first recognition of hours, is said to have been introduced at Rome in 263 B. C. The dial in question was taken from Catana in the First Punic War, and, as it was constructed for the latitude of Sicily, it was inaccurate at Rome. Yet 1co years are said to have elapsed before this error was corrected[4]! Before this date we do not hear of hours, but only sunrise, noon, and sunset[5]. Sir G. C. Lewis quotes a fragment of Plautus (c. 220), preserved by Aulus Gellius[6], giving us a curious glimpse into these primitive and pre-

---

[1] Quoted by Lewis, *op. cit.* p. 244.   [2] Bernardus Monachus, *ib.* 243.

[3] Still one would have thought that 'equal' hours would win their way by the support of the clepsydra or water-clock.

[4] Lewis, p. 182. So also Pliny, *N. H.* VII. lx. 214.

[5] The language of Ps. lv. 18:—' In the evening and morning and at noon-day will I pray '—recognizes the same three primitive divisions of the day, the order in which they are mentioned reminding us that the day began at sunset.

[6] See Pliny, *N. H.* VII. lx. 212, from which it appears that even the recognition of ' mid-day ' was a later refinement. ' Duodecim tabulis ortus tantum et occasus nominantur : post aliquot annos adiectus est et meridies, accenso consulum id pronuntiante, cum a curia inter rostra et Graecostasin prospexisset solem . . . sed hoc serenis tantum diebus usque ad primum Punicum bellum.'

orarian days. He introduces a slave complaining of the new-fangled introduction of sundials and hours, because his meals were now made to depend upon the sun, whereas, when he was a boy, he used to eat when he was hungry! Is it not indeed surprising to think of the advances made in astronomy by the ancient Chaldeans, Egyptians, and Greeks, in the absence of any better conditions for recording the lapse of time? It seems almost incredible that such accuracy can have been obtained in the determination of the planetary orbits, and above all that such a minute inequality as the precession of the equinoxes should have been detected in the second century before Christ.

There is one other passage (*Conv.* IV. xxiii. 129 *seqq.*) in which Dante speaks of these 'temporal' hours, and again it is in reference to the offices of the Church. He is pointing out that, as there are four 'ages' in human life[1]—childhood, youth, mature age, and old age—so there are, corresponding to these, four seasons in the year, and also four divisions in the day, beginning at the first, third, sixth, and ninth hours respectively. The Church, he adds, uses the 'temporal' hours in the sense previously explained, and so regulates her offices by the position of the sun, leaving a longer or shorter interval between them. But besides this, having regard to the sixth hour, or the hour of noon, being the most perfect and noble of the hours[2], she makes all her offices approach this as much

[1] The context a little above (l. 65) contains the well-known passage in which our life is compared to an arch, the summit and most perfect point of which is reached at thirty-five. That is the 'mezzo del cammin di nostra vita,' after which we begin to 'go downhill.' Hence, argues Dante, our Lord died in His thirty-fourth year, that His divinity might not reach the point of decline (*stare in discrescere*). He proceeds further to argue that for the same reason it was (as S. Luke says) about the sixth hour when He died, that being 'il colmo del dì,' before the day began to decline. This is a curious misquotation of S. Luke, whose narrative in fact implies (as those of S. Matthew and S. Mark distinctly state) that our Lord's death was at about the ninth hour.

[2] Hence Dante appropriately represents himself as entering Paradise at noon, the hour of consummation and perfection (see *Purg.* xxxiii. 103, 104, and *Par.* i. 43); Ante-Purgatory, Purgatory itself, and the Earthly Paradise at dawn, the hour of hope and aspiration (see *Purg.* i. 19 *seqq.*; ix. 13 *seqq.*; xxvii. 109 *seqq.* and 133. The same symbolism is implied also in *Inf.* i. 16–18). In contrast with these Hell is entered at nightfall, the hour of darkness and despair (see *Inf.* ii. 1–6).

as possible. Hence, Tierce is not said at the *beginning* but at the *end* of the first division of the day ; but the offices of the third and fourth divisions are said at the beginning of each. Then (after explaining ' mezza terza,' ' mezza nona,' &c.) he adds, ' Therefore let every one know that " None " should be sounded at the beginning of the seventh hour of the day,' i. e. at twelve o'clock, or, as we in consequence call it, 'noon,' though the word in its derivation applies not to the sixth hour but to the ninth.

I will conclude with two brief remarks :—(1) In whatever direction we sound the depths of Dante's wonderful knowledge and culture, we gain the same impression that it is as profound as it is varied and extensive. In theology, in scholastic philosophy, in metaphysical, moral, and physical science, and in classical literature, if judged by the standard even of a contemporary specialist in each, he will not be found wanting. (2) From this we understand why Dante is often found to be difficult to understand. To adopt a distinction made by Coleridge, he may be ' hard,' but he is seldom, if indeed ever, ' obscure.' In other words, the difficulty lies in the subject rather than in the writer. For surely no writer ever had more entirely clear ideas on every subject on which he speaks. They are as sharp in outline as if they were graven on a rock with a pen of iron. And not only this, but he very often displays a power of luminous exposition and apt illustration which is scarcely less exceptional.

P.S.—Since this Essay was in type, my friend, Dr. Rambaut, Radcliffe Observer at Oxford, besides kindly revising the proof-sheets, has shown me an article which he contributed to ' The Scientific Proceedings of the Royal Dublin Society ' in May, 1889. He therein describes an arrangement in some Japanese clocks similar to that which I have mentioned on p. 104 *med.* The face of the clock is not a dial, but a kind of pillar, on which the ' equal ' hours would be shown by a descending index. There are vertical columns belonging to each month, and these are crossed by a series of curves, like ' isobar ' lines, starting from equidistant points on the left-hand border which would correspond with the Spring Equinox. By this means the clock is enabled to register the varying 'temporal' hours at different seasons, in the latitude for which it is constructed.

SUPPLEMENTARY NOTE ON *Conv.* III. v. 154.

(v. *supra*, p. 49.)

THIS passage involves a difficult piece of textual criticism, since the text in all the MSS. is so corrupt as to be quite unintelligible. Before therefore attempting to explain it, we must endeavour to recover, if possible, the true reading. I have discussed this point in the *Bullettino della Società Dantesca Italiana*, N. S. vol. ix, fasc. 5–6, p. 131.

The following is an abbreviation of the note in question.

Dante is describing the maximum altitude of the Sun at the North Pole at the Summer Solstice. Now, as the Sun is then at the Tropic of Cancer, his altitude must obviously be $23\frac{1}{2}°$, since the Equator is the horizon of the Pole. The difficulty lies in the fact that Dante does not directly mention this figure (which he knew quite well, see l. 139), but, instead of doing so, gives merely a rough illustration of the Sun's height, saying that it is about as much ('quasi tanto quanto') as it is under the conditions presented to us in such confusion in the MSS.

Now the text in twenty-three MSS. which I have examined is as follows:—

'lo suo montare è a Maria quasi tanto quanto esso monta a noi

$\left\{ \begin{array}{l} \text{nella mezza terra,} \\ \text{alla mezza terra,} \\ \text{nel mezzo della terra,} \end{array} \right\}$ che è del giorno e della†mezza†notte eguale.'

It was long ago suggested by Dionisi (*Anedd.* iv. p. 76) that we should read 'mezza *terza*' for 'mezza *terra.*' This is an expression found in Dante (*Inf.* xxxiv. 96, and *Conv.* IV. xxiii. 153), meaning 7.30 a.m., since *Terza* is 9 a.m. It is not found here, as far as I know, in any MS.; yet any one familiar with MSS. will be aware (1) that *terza* (i.e. *terça* or even *terça*) and *terra* are very easily confused; and (2) that the phrase *mezza terza*, being comparatively rare, would be sure to be mistaken by many copyists for *mezza terra*. But unfortunately the conjecture of Dionisi gives no sense to the passage [1]. For the Sun 'with us' (wherever that might be) never rises to the height required at 7.30 a.m., *except at the Equator*, as to which, after Dionisi's alteration, nothing is said in the text. I am convinced therefore that *both* the expressions *mezza terra* and *mezza terza* are required; and I should now propose to read the passage thus:—

'lo suo montare è a Maria quasi tanto quanto esso monta a noi nella mezza terra [*or* nel mezzo della terra] alla mezza terza, ch' è del giorno e della

---

[1] I had to adopt it, *faute de mieux*, in the Oxford Text in 1894, but I propose now to introduce the emendation proposed above.

notte eguale,' i. e. 'the sun's altitude at the North Pole [at the summer solstice] is roughly that which we should find at the Equator, at 7.30 a. m. at the time of the Equinox.'

Certainly, if we read the text thus, the meaning is perfectly clear. Three conditions are implied : (1) the spectator is at the Equator ; (2) the hour is 7.30 a. m. ; (3) the season is the Equinox.

Now Dante describes a few lines below very graphically the appearance of the Sun's revolution at the Equator on the day of the Equinox. It is a vertical revolution like that of a wheel (not, as when seen from the Pole, a horizontal revolution like that of a millstone[1]), of which only one half is visible to the spectator, i.e. 180°. Consequently, at noon, the Sun's altitude is 90°, and at 7.30 a. m. it is $\frac{90°}{4}$, i. e. $22\frac{1}{2}$°. Thus we have a very good rough illustration of the Sun's altitude at the North Pole at the summer solstice, that being exactly $23\frac{1}{2}$°. The narrow limit of error, being only 1°, is far less than could possibly be detected by the eye. Observe, finally, how natural are the steps by which the proposed text, if original, would become corrupted into its present form. These are the stages :—

1. quanto esso monta a noi nel mezzo della terra [*or* nella mezza terra] alla mezza terza ch' è, &c.

2. quanto esso monta a noi nel mezzo della terra [*or* nella mezza terra] alla mezza terra ch' è, &c.

Next would follow the omission of one of these superfluous descriptions of the same thing, which were naturally suspected of having arisen from a ' conflate ' reading ; and we should then have

3. quanto esso monta a noi nel mezzo della terra [*or* nella mezza terra] ch' è, &c.

as in the MSS. at present[2].

I ought to say a word as to the superfluous word *mezza* before ' notte.' I have found it, so far, in all MSS., but it makes no sense, and I suspect that it represents the second *mezza* of the original text gone astray. It seemed natural to attach it to ' notte' to match ' mezzo giorno.'

---

[1] See ll. 147 and 176.

[2] The MSS. vary between ' nel mezzo della terra,' ' nella mezza terra,' and ' alla mezza terra.'

II. THE GEOGRAPHY OF DANTE [1]

DANTE has sometimes been unreasonably credited by injudicious admirers with the anticipation of modern discoveries in physical science, such as the theory of gravitation [2] and even the circulation of the blood! But no less unreasonably has he often been censured for so-called errors in history and geography, such as in his day could only have been avoided by a prescience no less remarkable than that with which he has been falsely credited in the case of physical science. A writer cannot be blamed if, being fully abreast of the knowledge available in his day [3], he does not rise beyond it, especially in a subject on which he has bestowed no special study, and wherein he has had no opportunities of personal investigation.

Let us first endeavour to ascertain that environment of general knowledge (or ignorance) in which Dante lived in respect of the subject of geography, and to set down briefly the authors most likely to have found a place in his geographical library.

It is obvious that the broad principles and outlines of the contemporary geography would be so generally familiar that no special sources of information need be sought for them. But in matters of detail we find Dante occasionally making direct quotations from authorities on geographical subjects, and sometimes also displaying reminiscences, more or less obvious, of passages in such authors, when they are not directly quoted. If we can in this way determine the authorities generally employed by a writer who, like Dante, deals with geography incidentally only and not as a specialist, we obtain a clue to the opinions which he probably held on points other than those to which he has occasion specifically to refer.

[1] Delivered as a Lecture in the Sala Dante, Or San Michele, Florence, Easter, 1900.

[2] For this see *Studies*, II. pp. 321–3.

[3] And let it not be forgotten that 'the knowledge of the day' was represented by the grotesque Hereford *Mappa Mundi*, and the fabulous romancings of Sir John Mandeville.

The following seem to me the most important of such authorities.

1. His so-called ' Master,' Brunetto Latini, who in Book III of his *Trésor*, or *Tesoro*, has a short but comprehensive section relating to geography under the title of *Mappa Mundi*. This work, it will be remembered, is that which Dante represents Brunetto as commending to his notice in *Inf.* xv. 119:—

> ' Siati raccomandato il mio Tesoro
> Nel quale io vivo ancora.'

This perhaps may be taken as a hint that Dante valued and studied that encyclopaedia of contemporary science. This geographical section contains several details (often erroneous enough) which find place also in Dante, and is a mere compilation, and often a careless one, from Solinus [1] (c. 230 A. D.), who was himself in his turn a mere compiler of a very unintelligent kind. He has been sometimes called ' Pliny's ape,' though he never has the grace to mention the name of the author on whom he so largely bestowed what has been sometimes called the sincerest form of flattery. To Solinus are due most of the travellers' tales in so-called geographical works from the fourth to the fourteenth centuries [2].

2. Another writer very familiar to Dante, and often quoted by him (especially on historical subjects), is Orosius. The first book of his *Historiae* is mainly geographical, and this was the chief authority on the subject of geography for many generations. It is expressly quoted by Dante, *Mon.* II. iii. 87, as an authority for the limits of Africa ; and there is a still more important appeal to Orosius in the disputed, but, as I firmly believe, genuine work, entitled *Quaestio de Aqua et Terra*, § 19, as determining the limits of the habitable portion of the globe. In the previous Essay [3] I have suggested that a passage in *Orosius* may have supplied the line of direction indicated between Rome and the Straits of Bonifacio in *Purg.* xviii. 81.

---

[1] See especially an article by Dr. Toynbee on ' B. Latini's obligations to Solinus,' in *Romania*, vol. xxiii, pp. 62–72.

[2] Beazley, *Geography*, p. 247. In illustration of this, the Hereford map (c. 1300) among others is said to be little more than a reproduction of Solinus.

[3] *Supra*, p. 72.

3. I have also pointed out elsewhere how familiar Dante was with the *Elementa Astronomica* of Alfraganus, and how this certainly seems to have been the chief source of his remarkably minute astronomical knowledge. That treatise contains four chapters (6–9) entirely devoted to geography. We find in these notably a full account of the divisions of 'climata,' or zones of latitude, to which we shall refer later, as well as other details which figure in the well-known astronomico-geographical chapter, *Conv.* III. v [1].

4. Isidore, who quotes Solinus about 200 times [2], was also an author probably known to Dante [3], since he was very widely read at that time. I do not think he is ever directly quoted by him, but he is honoured with a place beside Aquinas, Albertus Magnus, Richard of S. Victor, and others, in one of the garlands of beatified Doctors in the heaven of the sun. He was therefore probably (as each of the others mentioned was certainly) an author known and valued by Dante. The assignment of a place in heaven is perhaps a very practical acknowledgement of literary obligation.

5. Albertus Magnus, who is (as just noted) similarly honoured by Dante, was a writer to whom he is very largely indebted on a great variety of subjects, though his obligations to him are rather scantily acknowledged, according to our modern ideas [4]. Among his numerous and voluminous works we may specially notice, in connexion with our present subject, the treatise *De Natura Locorum*, and particularly Tract. III, entitled *Cosmographia*.

6. Are we to add Roger Bacon? There are no doubt many close resemblances with Dante to be found in his *Geographia*, but they are mostly of the nature of common property. There is one remarkable point of contrast, in that, while Dante regarded the southern hemisphere as being entirely covered with water ('mondo senza gente'), Roger Bacon argues for its habitability, and even for there being more dry land and less water there than in the northern hemi-

---

[1] Explained in the previous Essay, pp. 46-50.   [2] Beazley, *op. cit.* p. 252.
[3] See Toynbee, *Dante Dictionary*, s.v. *Tifeo*; and *Studies*, I. p. 304.
[4] As pointed out by Dr. Toynbee, *Dante Studies and Researches*, pp. 38 *seqq.*

sphere[1]. This is explained as being due to the sun's heat being greater there because of the sun's perigee ('oppositum augis') occurring on that side of the equator[2], and hence there would be more dry land.

It is remarkable that Dante never mentions Roger Bacon. He can hardly have been ignorant of his fame, especially if, as there seems good reason to believe, Dante visited Paris and in some way studied at the University there. I say nothing as to the vague tradition of his having visited Oxford also. But more than this, it has been contended by the late Dean Plumptre that there is considerable evidence of Dante's acquaintance not only with the fame but also with the works of Bacon. In a paper in the *Contemporary Review* for December 1881 several passages of very unequal weight, and none altogether conclusive[3], are adduced in support of this. A further question suggests itself: if Dante was not ignorant of Bacon but ignored him, what was the reason? An interesting speculation is that of Dr. Liddon in his delightful essay on 'Dante and the Franciscans[4],' that Roger Bacon as well as Duns Scotus and Alexander of Hales (Doctor Irrefragabilis) were passed over by Dante when so many Franciscans of less note were glorified, because he held the same opinion of Britain that the Jews had of Galilee. 'Is it that the Italian in Dante . . . cannot understand how Normans and Saxons, who had come from remote Britain, should challenge comparison with men of Latin blood like St. Thomas and St. Bonaventure?'

It is only natural that such authors as those I have mentioned, rather than their more famous predecessors, such as Strabo, Pliny, Ptolemy, Solinus, on whom they all relied for the greater part of their information, should be the sources from which Dante and his contemporaries drew their ideas on geography. This was partly because they were the more recent 'authorities,' if such a term could be applied to those in whom there is so little that is original: and partly also

---

[1] See further *infra*, p. 117.

[2] *Geographia*, vol. i. pp. 293, 4. For 'auge' see *Studies*, II. p. 373. Also p. 340.

[3] I say this because they include subjects on which (as in the case of geography) there seem to be other authorities equally available.

[4] In the volume of *Essays and Addresses*.

because Strabo and Ptolemy would be 'sealed books' until Latin translations were made. This in the case of Ptolemy was not done till 1405, though Arabian versions and epitomes of Ptolemy (notably that of Alfraganus) were Latinized very much earlier, and in this way many of his opinions and conclusions came to be generally known ; but, even so, his influence was slight and transient, and very many of the errors corrected in his writings continued for long ages to hold the field[1].

The science of geography, fully as much as that of astronomy, was strangled by the misplaced attentions of theologians. The observation of facts was checked or overborne by appeals to the language of Scripture, often fantastically misunderstood or misapplied. Certain fundamental principles of geography (like that of the central position of the earth in the sister science of astronomy) were thought to be irrevocably settled by revelation. Further inquiry was in such matters superfluous or even impious, in the face of an authority to which even the evidence of the senses must, if necessary, be subordinated. A good illustration of this may be found in the very title of the work of Cosmas Indicopleustes (c. middle of sixth century), viz. *Christian Topography*[2]. This indicates the author's purpose ' to work out a scheme of the visible world from the teachings of the invisible contained in the Jewish and Christian Scriptures,' in short 'a religious system of geography' (Beazley, *Geography*, pp. 192, 245, 273, &c.).

I will select the following as the most conspicuous features in which Dante's system of geography differs from that standard of knowledge which has long since become familiar to ourselves. These points will be illustrated in succession from his own writings :—

I. The Ocean surrounding the whole earth, which lay upon it like a vast island.

II. The limitation of 'the dry land' to the northern hemisphere.

III. The limits of latitude and longitude of the habitable earth, and the general form assigned to it.

[1] See Tozer's *Ancient Geography*, p. 367, for a long list of such survivals.
[2] 'Topographia Christiana, sive Christianorum opinio de Mundo.'

* * *

IV. The relative size of the three Continents.

V. The size of the Mediterranean Sea.

VI. The central position of Jerusalem.

VII. The methods of computing latitude and longitude.

VIII. The site of the Terrestrial Paradise.

At the end of this article will be found a map of the world according to the conception of Strabo, which has been reproduced by the kind permission of Mr. Tozer from his volume of *Selections from Strabo.*

This map may be taken as exhibiting very well the *general* geographical ideas prevalent in Dante's time ; i. e. such points as are included in I to VI of the above divisions. No attention need be paid to the *details* (e. g. such as the nature of the Caspian or many of the local names) which are not mentioned by Dante.

I. The earth, or 'dry land,' was from the earliest times supposed to be entirely surrounded by water, i. e. by the 'Oceanus,' ' Mare Oceanum,' or the 'Ocean River' of Homeric geography[1]. In reference to a spectator *ab extra*, we might say of the general appearance of the dry land, as Homer says of the distant aspect of an island,

$$\epsilon\text{ἴσατο δ' ὡς ὅτε ῥινὸν ἐν ἠεροειδέϊ πόντῳ}^2.$$

This is the ' exterior Oceanus atque ignotum mare ' of Tacitus (*Germ.* c. 17). The same writer (c. 45), after describing the Arctic Sea, adds : ' Illuc usque tantum natura,' ' the world, or nature, extends only as far as this '[3]. Similarly we read in Seneca, *Suasor. Lib.*, *sub init.* : ' Ita est rerum natura ; post omnia Oceanus ; post Oceanum, nihil.' Lucan uses a phrase like that of Tacitus when he calls Oceanus ' exterius mare[4],' and similarly Isidore calls it 'extremum mare ' (*Nat. Rer.* c. 44 ; cf. also c. 48). Orosius begins his geographical sketch by stating the traditional view that the whole world was ' oceani limbo circumsaeptum[5].' The same idea will be

---

[1] *Iliad*, xiv. 245 ποταμοῖο ῥέεθρα 'Ωκεανοῦ. Cf. ἀψόρροος 'Ωκεανός, *Iliad*, xviii. 399, and elsewhere. Cf. also *Iliad*, xxi. 195-7.　　　　　[2] *Od.* v. 281.

[3] Compare ' natura ' as used by Seneca in the passage quoted p. 118 *n*.

[4] *Phars.* x. 37.

[5] Comp. *Epist.* VIII. xi. 182, where one might almost suspect that Dante, in reminiscence of this expression, may possibly have written 'undique Oceani limbo *circumsaepta* ' rather than *circumspecta*.

found in Cicero (*Somn. Scip.* § 20), Pliny (*N. H.* ii. 68), Strabo (ἡ οἰκουμένη γῆ περίρρυτος οὖσα, II. v. 18), and other authors, too commonly to need further illustration.

Coming nearer to Dante's own time, Brunetto Latini lays this down as the first and most fundamental fact of geographical science both in the *Trésor*[1] and in the *Tesoretto*[2]. Then again, finally, the same is found in Ristoro d'Arezzo, *Comp. Mund.* vi. 2 *fin.* : 'avemo l'acqua attorno attorno la terra . . . e tali sono e tali che 'l chiamano mare Oceano.' He says this is accounted for by portions of the earth having emerged from the water which naturally overlay it everywhere. ('Naturally' is explained by the problem discussed in the ' *Quaestio de Aqua et Terra*,' v. *infra*, p. 116.)

Coming now to Dante himself, he states or implies the same general theory as to the circumambient Ocean several times, e. g. :—

In *Par.* ix. 84 it is ' quel mar che la terra inghirlanda.'

In *Conv.* III. v. (ll. 82, 93, &c.), that very important and difficult chapter which has been explained in the previous Essay (pp. 46–50), we recognize it in the ' mare Oceano ' which is described as underlying the north and south poles of the heaven, so that a stone dropped from either of them would fall upon its surface (*dosso*).

In *Mon.* I. xi. 83 the dominion of the Emperor is bounded only by the ocean (' sua iurisdictio terminatur Oceano solum '), which cannot be said of any other rulers. In other words, it embraces the whole world.

In *Epist.* VII. iii. 58 the true boundaries of the Roman

---

[1] e. g. in *Trésor*, Lib. I, c. 122 we read—' Terre est ceinte et environnée de mer . . . Et sachiez que ce est la grant mer qui est apelée Oceane, de quoi sont estraites toutes les autres qui sont parmi les terres diverses, et sont aussi come braz de celi, dont cil qui vient par Espaigne en Ytaille et en Grece est graindres que li autres . . . et est apelée Miterreinne.' I quote this passage specially from its resemblance to *Par.* ix. 82 and 84 :

' La maggior valle in che l'acqua si spanda,

. . . .

Fuor di quel mar che la terra inghirlanda.'

Fuor di I take certainly to mean ' except ' ; but it is sometimes translated ' issuing from,' in which case the resemblance between the two passages would be closer still. Similar statements will be found in *Trésor*, B. I, cc. 106 and 125.

[2] See xi. 141 *seqq.*

Empire are described in similar language. With this we may
compare *Epist.* VIII. xi. 182, which has been referred to *supra*,
p. 114 *n.*

Finally, the same theory is expressed twice in the *Quaestio*,
viz. viii. l. 6, and xv. l. 6. In the latter passage, 'Amphitrite
ipsa,' in contrast with 'maria mediterranea,' represents the
Universal Ocean. The expression 'Amphitrite,' as thus used,
is very common in Albertus Magnus, who occasionally uses
Amphitrix as the nominative [1].

This universal belief was thought to be amply justified from
Scripture : e. g. from 1 *Pet.* iii. 5, where we read of 'the earth
standing out of the water and in the water'; or *Ps.* xxiv.
1, 2, 'The earth is the Lord's,' &c., for He 'hath founded it
upon the seas and prepared it upon the floods'; or again,
Gen. i. 9, where on the third day the waters under the
heaven were all gathered together in one place, and the dry
land was commanded to appear—i. e. to emerge from the
'natural' position of that element beneath that of water. But
the *modus operandi* of this elevation—which was 'fuor di sua
natura[2],' in view of the common belief that the 'proprio loco[3]'
of earth was below that of water—was a standing puzzle to
the mediaeval mind, and a fruitful subject of discussion and
speculation. The problem in the time of Dante 'indeterminata
restabat[4],' and he, if, as I believe, we may regard him as the
author of the *Quaestio de Aqua et Terra*, claims to have finally
settled it in that treatise.

II. The most conspicuous feature of mediaeval geography
in respect of the distribution of Land and Water on the surface
of the globe was the limitation of the land—the 'dry land' or
'arida' of the book of Genesis (i. 9), the 'gran secca' of
Inf. xxxiv. 113, and the 'terra detecta' of Dante's prose works

---

[1] See *Studies*, II. p. 347 *n.*

[2] So Dante describes the converse process of fire falling downwards in the
case of lightning, *Par.* xxiii. 42.

[3] See *Conv.* III. iii. 9 *seqq.*

[4] In illustration of this, see authorities referred to in *Studies*, II. pp. 367 *seqq.*
To those may now be added Andalò di Negro (whom Boccaccio styles
'praeceptor meus') in a passage cited by Messrs. Wicksteed and Gardner, *Dante
and Giovanni del Virgilio*, p. 107 *n.*

—entirely to the northern hemisphere[1], and its restriction, even within that hemisphere, as we shall see later, to comparatively narrow limits both of latitude and longitude. This common ancient belief respecting the uninhabitability of the southern hemisphere is curiously illustrated by the fact that in some of the old Egyptian zodiacs, or star-maps, the figures representing the southern constellations are said to be depicted in boats[2]. That belief, originating at first doubtless in ignorance and want of exploration, became a sort of article of faith with the Christian Fathers[3], who held the notion of antipodes to be unscriptural. That it was held so to be, depended chiefly on an inference from another proposition generally accepted or assumed, viz. that the tropical ocean was absolutely impassable from extreme heat, and consequently that, if there were any inhabitants of the southern

---

[1] Herodotus, assuming the impossibility of there being ' Hypernotians,' argues on grounds of symmetry that there cannot (as is generally believed) be 'Hyperboreans' (IV. 36). The view mentioned in the text will also be found in Strabo, II. v. 14, 15 (Tozer, *Selections*, pp. 81-3) ; Pliny, *N. H.* VI. xxx. 194 ; Alb. Magnus, *De Caelo et Mundo*, II. i. 5 (p. 86) 'pars habitabilis non est nisi quarta habitabilis septentrionalis hemisphaerii superioris.' On the other hand Cicero, *Somn. Scip.* § 20, describes the south temperate zone as inhabited, adding :—' australis ille, in quo qui insistunt adversa vobis urgent vestigia, nihil ad vestrum genus.' See also Roger Bacon quoted *supra*, p. 111. Bede too held that there was there a habitable, but uninhabited, temperate zone. This reservation is probably due to the belief in antipodes being thought unscriptural (Beazley, *Geography*, p. 371). Then again Albertus Magnus in another work (*De Nat. Loc.* I. c. xii) argues that, since similar climatic conditions exist in the southern hemisphere, it probably has land and 'climata' similar to those in the north, and consequently the common belief in its being overspread with water is erroneous. (He does not say that it is actually inhabited, *v. supra*.) Averroes is quoted by Ristoro d' Arezzo, *Comp. Mond.* Dist. viii. c. 12 (p. 146), as arguing that the southern hemisphere was probably inhabited as much as the northern, for otherwise the sun would traverse those parts in vain. But Ristoro maintains that in that case there should be as great an abundance of stars in that hemisphere also, in order to account for the elevation of the land ; but this is not the case, and so the common belief is probably true.

[2] See Narrien, *Astronomy*, p. 25.

[3] Notably Lactantius and S. Augustine (e. g. *C. D.* xvi. 9) ; and, some centuries later, Vincent de Beauvais : but S. Basil and S. Ambrose, who were followed by Isidore in the sixth century, held that the question of antipodes was not thus closed (Beazley, *op. cit.* p. 283). The dogmatic pronouncement of Cosmas is characteristic : 'The blasphemous theory of antipodes makes Christ to be a liar and His word not in us. For how could we exercise the power which He gave us of treading on serpents and scorpions when walking reversed' ? (*ibid.* p. 294).

hemisphere at all, they could not possibly be descended from Adam, but would have required a separate act and centre of creation [1]. Dante has a curious outburst on this subject in *Conv.* IV. xv, where he says that not only Christians but also Plato would reject such a notion, and that Aristotle would laugh heartily (*forte riderebbe*) at the idea that there could be more than a single origin for mankind, as there might be for horses and asses ; for (Dante proceeds) 'if Aristotle will excuse the expression, one may well call those asses who can think any such thing as this'! The uninhabitability of the southern hemisphere, whether it be land or water, is distinctly argued on these grounds by S. Augustine, *De Civ. Dei*, xvi. c. 9. We are not therefore surprised to find this common belief shared by Dante. It is not only distinctly stated in the *Quaestio*, but it appears also in the splendid episode of the voyage of Ulysses in *Inf.* xxvi. We are told of his mad flight (*folle volo*) beyond the pillars of Hercules, first westwards and then southwards. For this, see l. 124, 'volta nostra poppa nel mattino' (i. e. first sailing west), and then (ll. 126, 127) always bearing to the left (i. e. south) till all the southern stars were seen and those of our northern heavens disappeared. And so he came to the 'mondo senza gente' (l. 117). Several of the details of Dante's description in this narrative may be illustrated by some of the facts mentioned by Mr. Beazley in his work on Henry the Navigator. The Arabs—from whom the Christian world borrowed most of their geographical ideas even as the Arabs borrowed theirs largely from the Greeks— were adventurous enough in their explorations of the *eastern* seas, allured by the pursuit and profit of commerce. But they had a strange horror of the Atlantic, 'the green sea of darkness,' and they imparted much of this paralyzing cowardice to Christian nations [2]. It was said that a man who should em-

---

[1] Another objection based on the inaccessibility of the antipodes was that they would be entirely beyond the reach of the appointed means of salvation. In reference to this, appeal was made to Ps. xix. 4, as applied by S. Paul in Rom. x. 18.

[2] See Beazley, *op. cit.* p. 14. It is curious to compare with this a passage from the work of Seneca lately quoted (*Suasor. Lib.*, *sub init.*) respecting the sea beyond the pillars of Hercules :—'Stat immotum mare, et *quasi deficientis in suo fine naturae* pigra moles, novae et terribiles figurae, magna etiam Oceano

bark on such a voyage was so clearly mad that he ought to be deprived of civil rights. Dante's description of the voyage of Ulysses as ' folle volo' in *Inf.* xxvi. 125, or again 'folle varco' in *Par.* xxvii. 82, seems like an echo of this. Moreover, it was said that 'whirlpools always destroy such an adventurer.' This, it will be remembered, is precisely the fate which Dante assigns to Ulysses (see *Inf.* xxvi. 136-142).

It is perhaps worth mentioning that there were in fact some exploring expeditions about Dante's time which took this direction, and which were never heard of again. In particular, a well-known Genoese expedition started between 1280 and 1290, of which we are told that in 1312 nothing had ever been heard. Some of these tragic stories, and perhaps this very one, may have impressed Dante, and suggested his working them up round the central figure of Ulysses, the typical ocean-wanderer of all time. The southern hemisphere then was entirely, in Dante's belief, covered with water, with the solitary exception of the Mountain of Purgatory, the denizens of which were indeed no longer of this earth. Dante (in *Inf.* xxxiv) indulges in a curious speculation as to the cause of this contrast between the northern and southern hemispheres, which, as far as I know, is original. Lucifer, projected from heaven, fell on the southern hemisphere, and the land that was formerly there, in fear of him, covered itself with the sea as with a veil, and came into our hemisphere (*Inf.* xxxiv. ll. 121-124). Next—and this theory Dante cautiously introduces with a ' perhaps ' (*forse*)—when Lucifer was at last fixed at the centre of the world, in order to avoid him, the earth that was there fled away, and, leaving a hollow space, rushed up so as to form the solitary Mountain of Purgatory in the southern hemisphere (ll. 124-6). Thus the earth in both directions, as it were,

portenta, quae profunda ista vastitas nutrit, confusa lux alta caligine, et interceptus tenebris dies, ipsum vero grave et devium mare, et aut nulla aut ignota sidera.' (The words italicized curiously resemble *Quaestio*, xxi. l. 50.) It was also supposed that there were openings into Hell at unknown spots in the Atlantic. The terror among his sailors was one of the main obstacles which Columbus had to contend with. In a mediaeval text-book of science it is asserted that the reason the sun is so red towards sunset is 'because he looketh down upon hell.' (From White's *Warfare of Science with Theology*, i. p. 97.)

shrunk from contact with Lucifer. *Northwards* there extended the conical pit of Hell; *southwards* the dungeon-like
passage, 'natural burella' (*Inf.* xxxiv. 98), the materials of
which went to form, in the manner described, the Mountain of
Purgatory. And in regard to this perforation of the globe
from north to south Lucifer himself is described in the same
passage as ' il vermo reo che tutto il mondo fora.'

III. Next as to the general shape or appearance presented
by the habitable earth, and the limits of latitude and longitude
within which it was comprised. In respect of *longitude* it
was a common belief of the ancient world that the οἰκουμένη
was all included within the space of 180°[1]. There were
indeed some differences of opinion, but such was the view
of Ptolemy, and that is the limit recognized by Alfraganus[2],
with whose work, as we have seen elsewhere, Dante was
certainly well acquainted. Alfraganus further states that
180° = 10,200 miles (a degree being 56⅔ miles), this making
the whole circumference of the globe to be 20,400 miles.
These are just the figures adopted by Dante, for in *Conv.*
III. v. he states that Rome is 2700 miles from the North
Pole and 7500 from the South Pole, which gives 10,200
miles for the semi-circumference of the globe, it being assumed
to be spherical, and not, as we now know it to be, an oblate
spheroid.

As to the limits of *latitude* within which the ' dry land ' is
comprised they are stated by Alfraganus to lie between the
Equator and the Arctic Circle, the latitude of which is 66⅓,
and consequently to extend over 3764 miles ; but of this space
only about three-fifths was habitable by man[3]. Such, I doubt
not, would be Dante's belief. This indeed is set down quite
clearly in the *Quaestio*, and even those who may be unwilling to
accept that work as genuine need not hesitate to admit that
Dante's own views are accurately expressed in the important

[1] So Roger Bacon, *Geographia* (i. p. 290), quoting Ptolemy: 'habitatio nota
non est nisi in quarta terrae, scilicet in qua habitamus ; cuius longitudo est ab
oriente in occidens, et est medietas equinoctialis [i. e. 180°] ; et eius latitudo
est ab equinoctiali in polum, et est quarta coluri ' [i. e. 90°].

[2] *Elem. Astr.* chapters vi and viii.

[3] See Table of the Climata, *infra*, p. 132.

§ 19, where we read as follows :—' As is commonly held by all, this habitable earth extends in longitude from Gades, which lies on the western boundaries of Hercules, as far as the mouths of the Ganges, as Orosius states. That longitude is such that at the equinox the sun is setting for those who are at one of these boundaries, when it is rising for those who are at the other.' This obviously involves a difference of 180° in longitude [1], or the half-circumference of the globe, as the passage goes on to state [2]. In the matter of *latitude* (it proceeds), 'following the same authorities as before, it extends from those whose zenith is the equinoctial line [in other words, from the equator] to those whose zenith is a circle described from [or, as we should express it, 'through'] the pole of the zodiac round the pole of the earth as a centre [i. e. in fact the Arctic Circle]. That pole of the zodiac is distant from the pole of the earth [i. e. of the equator] about 23° [a distance equal to the latitude of the highest point of the ecliptic] and so the extent in respect of *latitude* is about 67°, and not more, as any one can see at a glance.' Then notice this conclusion :—' So it is evident that the "emergent earth," or dry land, must have the appearance of a half-moon or thereabouts, because that figure results from this amount of latitude and longitude, as is apparent.' The writer adds that 'this must be obvious even to women'! I cannot help thinking that he may have been somewhat influenced in attributing this semilunar appearance to the dry land by the ordinary representation of world-maps in the form of a circle or semicircle, whereby in the upper parts the degrees of longitude are unduly contracted, and in latitude the forms of the lands are distorted by foreshortening, errors now remedied by the method known as Mercator's Projection. The writer may have been unconsciously so influenced, I think, since the half-moon figure does not necessarily result from the actual data of latitude and longitude on which he professes to base it. I do not of course

---

[1] Compare *Par.* ix. 85–7, where the difference of 90° is expressed by saying that it is noon at one end when it is sunrise or sunset at the other.

[2] Some passages in Dante bearing upon this limitation of longitude to 180° will be found collected in *Studies*, II. pp. 342, 343.

mean that his actual knowledge was on the low level of that of a landsman (of whom I have read somewhere), who supposed the great peril of an Atlantic voyage to be the risk that the captain might not succeed in hitting the critical point of contact of the two hemispheres, in which case no one could tell what might become of the ship. Still I think that the above comparison of the half-moon owes something to the popular representation in question.

It is not impossible that this notion of the semilunar aspect of the emergent earth as it lay on the bosom of the circumambient element of water may have been derived from the treatise of Ristoro d'Arezzo already referred to. In *Comp. Mundi*, VI. xi. *fin.* we read :—'Ed avemo la terra scoperta come è la figura della luna, quando noi la veggemo mezza.' There is a passage in Aristotle, *Meteor.* II. v. (362 a, 12–30)[1], which may have suggested the argument in the *Quaestio, l. c.* (though there is nothing in Aristotle about the semilunar figure), where it is urged that the habitable earth cannot present 'figuram circularem,' because in that case 'longitudo et latitudo non differrent in distantia terminorum.' Similarly Aristotle, in the passage referred to, laughs at those who represent the οἰκουμένη as 'κυκλοτερής,' since its length (in longitude) is greater than its breadth (in latitude) in more than the proportion of five to three. These limits are absolutely fixed, in the former case by the sea boundaries, and in the latter by conditions of heat and cold. At the same time he admits the possibility of land existing, though inaccessible to us, under analogous conditions in the southern hemisphere.

Another familiar comparison is that of Strabo, who describes the οἰκουμένη as 'χλαμυδοειδής' or 'mantle-shaped' (II. v. 14)[2], the Greek 'chlamys' being an oblong garment about twice as long as it was broad. Strabo further adds that we must imagine a sort of parallelogram within which the mantle-shaped outline is described. This, I suppose, would be intended to contain the land-surrounding Ocean in a sort of frame.

---

[1] This probable reference was overlooked in my Essay on the *Quaestio* in *Studies*, Series II.

[2] From Tozer's *Extracts from Strabo*, p. 81.

Orosius (I. ii. *init.*) describes the general aspect of the 'dry land' by the curious epithet 'triquadrum,' which is no doubt the same as 'triquetrum' or triangular[1].

One or two illustrations may be added here as to the recognition of these two extreme limits, *i.e.* the Ganges, and the Pillars of Hercules. Juvenal has made us familiar with them in the first two lines of the well-known tenth Satire :—

> 'Omnibus in terris quae sunt a Gadibus, usque
> Auroram et Gangen.'

Dante mentions them in the opening lines of *Purg.* ii. and again in xxvii ; in the latter case declaring quite clearly that it was sunrise in Jerusalem, midnight in Spain, noon on the Ganges, and, consequently, sunset in Purgatory, thus, as it were, 'boxing the compass.' Orosius, I. ii. 13, states explicitly that the mouths of the Ganges are in the Eastern Ocean, 'in the middle of the eastern front of Asia' ('Asiae ad mediam frontem orientis'). So also Roger Bacon, *Mor. Phil.* Part III. c. 4 (ii, p. 268): 'Quod enim ab ultimis Hispaniae usque ad Indos iacet paucissimorum dierum spatium est, si navem suavis ferat ventus.' This is to prove that this earth—

> 'L'aiuola che ci fa tanto feroci'—

is a mere 'punctum' compared with the vast space of the Universe.

As to the Pillars of Hercules—to which Dante generally refers under some such poetical synonym as Spain, Gades, Seville, the Ebro, or Morocco—he states in *Inf.* xxvi. 108, 109 (in the Ulysses legend already quoted) that they were set up by Hercules in order to warn men that they should proceed no further[2].

Some Latin writers are said to have pointed out that another warning against the spirit of presumptuous adventure

---

[1] Ducange gives two examples of 'triquadrum' in mediaeval writers, one in prose and one in poetry, and in both cases it is an epithet of 'orbis.'

[2] Tacitus, after a rather sceptical sneer at the Hercules legend, admits that it has had a deterrent effect upon exploration—'Mox nemo tentavit, sanctiusque ac reverentius visum de actis deorum credere quam scire,' *Germ.* c. xxxiv.

was afforded by the significant name of Cape Non [1] (a little way south on the coast of Barbary), so called because from it there was no return [2]. Brunetto Latini gravely informs us that 'after the death of Hercules' people ventured beyond the limits which he had imposed, and colonized a fair and rich country, which a comparison of two passages in the *Trésor* and *Tesoretto* [3] shows to be no other than Britain. It is to be noted, however, that when Dante and others speak of Gades or Gade they do not refer to the town of Gades or Cadiz, but to an island, or rather islands, called 'Gades insulae,' supposed to lie directly in the mouth of the straits, upon which the Pillars of Hercules were erected. The islands on which the *town* Gades was situated, well outside the Pillars of Hercules, have been, so to speak, moved up by popular imagination into the straits. One old author says—'Hercules fortissimas turres construxit quas Gades appellavit [4].' So also says Brunetto Latini in *Trésor*, I. part iv. c. 124 (p. 168, ed. Chabaille): 'où sont les ii isles Gades et les colonnes Hercules.' Orosius speaks of the 'Gades insulae' where the Pillars of Hercules are visited (I. ii. 7), and in the old Hereford Map, and others, two islands called Gades may be seen blocking the entrance to the Mediterranean. Further I have seen it stated that the mouth of the Ganges is sometimes called the Eastern Gades, or the Gades of Alexander in contrast with the Gades of Hercules [5].

IV. Dante no doubt shared the generally prevailing belief as to the relative size of the three Continents, that Asia (in which Egypt was regularly included [6]) was equal in size to Europe and Africa together. This is found, for

---

[1] Now called 'Nun.'

[2] Beazley, *Henry the Navigator*, p. 112 *n.*, where 'Latini' should apparently be 'Latin authors,' or something like that. No such statement is found in Brunetto Latini.

[3] *Tesoretto*, xi. 117–36 compared with *Trésor*, I. pt. iv. c. 124.

[4] *Hispaniae Chorographia*, quoted in Mr. Phillott's essay on the Hereford *Mappa Mundi*, p. 113.

[5] This is derived from Beazley, *Henry the Navigator*, p. 9, but no authorities are there quoted for this use.

[6] See Herodotus, iv. 41; B. Latini, *Trésor*, I. pt. iv. c. 123; Orosius, I. ii. 38.

example, in S. Augustine[1], Orosius[2], Isidore[3], Rabanus
Maurus[4] (all mentioned by Dante), as well as in the works
of his own contemporaries, Brunetto Latini[5] and Giovanni
Villani[6]. As usual, a good *a priori* reason was found for this
proportion in the fact that Asia was the inheritance of Shem,
the first-born of Noah, who consequently had 'a double portion'
allotted to him[7]. It is curious to contrast with this the
argument of S. Epiphanius (fourth century) that the three
continents must be equal in size, because they were the portions of the three equally favoured sons of Noah[8].

Herodotus, unhampered by considerations of the relative
dignity of the sons of Noah, but firmly possessed by the
notion of geographical symmetry (*vide* iv. 36, quoted *supra*,
p. 117 *n.*), makes Europe (at least in longitude) equal to Asia
and 'Libya' together (iv. 42 and 45).

I may here perhaps notice a curious expression employed
by Dante in one of his Epistles (vii. 3), where he describes
Europe as 'tricornis,' i. e. triangular, or three-cornered. It is
difficult to see the propriety of this epithet, but the explanation seems to be that it is simply borrowed (like much else)
from Albertus Magnus (*De Nat. Locorum*, Dist. III, c. 7),
who explains somewhat apologetically that the triangle
is spherical rather than plane, and that its angles are
rather blunt. But a more curious point is this: that the
description following in Albertus Magnus of these three
angular points does not correspond with those of Europe at
all, but rather with those of Spain. I was for a long time
unable to explain this, but I found at last that the passage
is simply copied by Albertus almost *totidem verbis* from

---

[1] *C. D.* XVI. xvii.   [2] I. ii. 2.
[3] *De Nat. Rer.* c. 48 (quoting 'beatissimus Augustinus').
[4] *De Univ.* XII. ii.
[5] *Trésor*, I. pt. iv. c. 122.
[6] *Cron.* i. 3.
[7] Gervase of Tilbury, *Otia Imp.*, Dec. II. § 2. Also Fazio degli Uberti, *Dittamondo*, I. vi. :—

  'Sem ebbe nome il primo, e 'l suo dimoro
   In Asia fu, e quella parte tenne
   Ch' è grande per le due, e ricca d'oro.'

[8] Beazley, *Geography*, p. 316.

Orosius, I. ii. 69–72, where it stands as a description, not of Europe, but of the Spanish Peninsula! A remarkable instance of most unintelligent plagiarism!

The relative positions of the three continents will be seen, both from authors quoted in the notes on the previous page, and also from the diagrams given by B. Latini and others, to be this: that Asia occupied the whole eastern half of the habitable world, Europe and Africa the northern and southern divisions respectively of the other half.

V. This symmetrical division of the western half of the οἰκουμένη, or habitable world, into the approximately equal continents of Europe and Africa by the inlet of the Mediterranean Sea, was a prominent feature of the geography of Dante and his contemporaries. This sea was therefore supposed to extend over 90° of longitude [1]. This is distinctly, though somewhat enigmatically, stated in a well-known and very difficult passage in *Par.* ix. 85–7. Dante there says: 'Between its opposing [2] shores it extends so far eastwards ('contra il sole') that it makes its meridian where before was its horizon.' That is to say, if one could be suddenly transported from one end of the Mediterranean to the other, the sun which was on the horizon at its west end would be found to be on the meridian at its eastern boundary. So that if the sun were rising, for instance, at the Pillars of Hercules, it would be noon at Jerusalem, at the other end (approximately) of the same inland sea. The length thus assigned to the Mediterranean being more than twice the true amount, it becomes extremely difficult, in attempting to construct a map, to conjecture how to distribute the error among countries the shape and proportions of which are now so familiar to us as those which surround that well-known sea.

The same interval of 90°, or six hours of time, between

---

[1] This is clearly seen, for example, in the Hereford *Mappa Mundi* executed by a contemporary of Dante.

[2] The word used is 'discordanti.' This means more than merely 'opposite.' One shore was Europe, the other Africa; one Christian, the other Mussulman; and, earlier still, one Roman, the other Carthaginian. Dante had probably in mind the words 'littora littoribus contraria' in the comprehensive imprecation of the dying Dido, *Aen.* iv. 628.

Gades and Jerusalem is implied by *Purg.* xxvii. 1–3, where it is said to be sunrise in Jerusalem when it is midnight in Spain ('cadendo Ibero sotto l'alta Libra ').

VI. Another cardinal point in Dante's geography, as in that of most other mediaeval writers, was the central position of Jerusalem. For this no doubt *a priori* reasons in abundance would be forthcoming. But it seemed to be settled by Scriptural authority also. For in *Ezek.* v. 5 we read : 'Haec dicit Dominus Deus : Ista est Ierusalem ; in medio gentium posui eam, et in circuitu eius terras.' So argue S. Jerome and others following him.

It may be mentioned in passing that Boccaccio cautiously observes that 'in medio,' or 'in mezzo,' in this passage must be taken to mean vaguely 'in the midst,' and not 'in the middle,' of the earth, since the latter would not be true [1]. Sir John Mandeville also quotes, as Scripture proof, *Ps.* lxxiii. 12, which reads in the Vulgate : ' Deus . . . operatus est salutem in medio terrae ' (the E. V. is entirely different here, viz. *Ps.* lxxiv. 13).

Mr. Beazley mentions that in 1102 an English traveller Sœwulf records having seen at Jerusalem, at the head of the Church of the Holy Sepulchre, 'the "umbilicus terrae," now called "compas," which Christ measured with his own hands, "working salvation in the midst of the earth," as the Psalms say '[2]! The first mention of this central pillar casting no shadow at midday at the summer solstice is found in Arculf, c. 680. He also quotes the authority of *Ps.* lxxiii. 12 as accounting for this fact [3].

Mandeville (p. 183, ed. 1866) gives not only Scriptural but also experimental proof of the central position of Jerusalem, viz. that at midday at the equinox, 'whan it is Equenoxium,' an upright spear will cast no shadow.

It is curious to find the same experimental proof alleged by Gervase of Tilbury to show that Jacob's Well, upon which our Lord sat, is the precise central point of the earth [4]. As

---

[1] *Comento*, Lez. V. (p. 166).
[2] Beazley, *Henry the Navigator*, p. 83.
[3] *ibid.* p. 133.
[4] *Otia Imp.*, Dec. 1, § 10 *fin.*

the Christian writers made Jerusalem, so the Arabian geographers made Mecca, the centre of the earth[1], chiefly no
doubt on similar *a priori* considerations, which, however,
would be reinforced by the greater extent of their actual
explorations southwards.   It will be observed that not only
in *longitude* was Jerusalem central between the Pillars of
Hercules and the Ganges, but its position in *latitude* also
was approximately central in regard to the οἰκουμένη.   This
extended, as we have seen, between 66° and 67°.   Now the
latitude of Jerusalem being in fact about 32°—I do not know
how near to this contemporary knowledge may have come—
it was about the centre in latitude as well as longitude of the
habitable earth.   Another noticeable point in this symmetrical
geography was that Dante regarded Rome as central between
Jerusalem and the Pillars of Hercules, i. e. 45° west of Jerusalem.
Two passages will suffice to illustrate and establish this.
(1) See *Purg.* xv. 1–6.   This is one of those many curious
passages in the *Purgatorio* in which Dante gives the synchronous
hours at different places, and sometimes several different places,
on the earth's surface[2].   There were three hours of daylight
left in Purgatory, i. e. it was evening *there* (*vespero là*), and
here, i. e. in Italy where Dante was writing, it was midnight
(*qui mezza notte era*).   It will easily be seen that, as 15° of
longitude are equivalent to an interval of one hour in time,
so this difference of nine hours of time between Italy and
Purgatory represents 135° of longitude.   Hence, if Italy was
135° east of Purgatory, it was 180°−135°, i.e. 45°, west of
Jerusalem, which was the antipodes of Purgatory.   (2) The
other passage is like this, viz. *Purg.* iii. 25.   Here Virgil says
it was now 'vespero' in Italy where his body is buried.   We
know from the previous Canto (see l. 55) that it was then
shortly after sunrise in Purgatory.   Consequently, by exactly
the same calculation as before, it would be between 3 and 4 p.m.
in Italy, i. e. there would be the same difference of 9 hours
in time.   Dante himself explains 'vespero' to be the period
from 3 to 6 p.m. in *Conv.* IV. xxiii. 130 *seqq.*

[1] Similarly the Greeks considered Delphi to be the 'umbilicus terrae.'
[2] See Table II, p. 177.

Thus, for Dante, as Jerusalem was the centre of the inhabited world, so Rome was the centre of the western or Christian world, as I have observed in the previous Essay.

VII. I must next explain the methods adopted by Dante and his contemporaries for expressing differences of latitude and longitude, referring to some passages in his works where these methods are recognized.

As to longitude, then, as now, it admitted, *in principle* at least, of easy calculation from the differences in time between different places. But, in the absence of accurate means of determining such differences of time, it became *practically* a matter of extreme difficulty in early days. As the sun has (speaking popularly, and according to appearances) to traverse the 360° of the earth's circumference in 24 hours, he will traverse 15° in one hour. Consequently, if it could be shown that he rose or set, or reached the meridian, one hour later at some given place than at another, the former place would be 15° in longitude west of the latter. We have seen how frequently Dante employs this method in regard to the chief landmarks on the earth's surface[1]. He applies it rather in those cases conversely, i. e. assuming the amount of difference in longitude, he infers the difference of time. But once, viz. in *Par.* ix. 91, 92, we find the direct method employed, when Dante, wishing to fix the position of Marseilles, says that the sun rises and sets there nearly at the same time (though it does not appear how this was ascertained) as at Buggea, i. e. Bougie, in North Africa. In other words, Marseilles has nearly the same longitude as Bougie. This must often have appeared to his readers as rather a curious case of *ignotum per ignotius*, as one would suppose that Marseilles must have been much better known than Bougie. Indeed I almost wondered how Dante would have heard of the latter place at all. It is only just mentioned by B. Latini as one of the towns marking the boundaries of a part of North Africa[2].

---

[1] Besides the two passages lately quoted we may add *Purg.* ii. 1-9, iv. 138, 139, xxvii. 1-6.

[2] Cf. *Trésor*, I. c. 125 'Et sachiez que toute Aufrique commence sor la mer Oceane as Columnes Hercule, et de iluec s'en retorne vers Tunes et vers Bougie et vers la cité de Septis [i. e. Ceuta] tot contre Sardaigne.'

* * *

Mr. Tozer has, however, kindly given me a reference to Réclus' *Nouvelle Géographie Universelle*, vol. xi, p. 440.   It there appears that Bougie was formerly a very famous place.   It was the capital of the Vandal kingdom before Carthage was taken ; and again the capital under the Beni Hammad dynasty, c. 1100.   It is said about that time to have had 20,000 houses, and to have been a kind of Mecca in those parts.   Further, from c. 1100 it was for some three centuries a great commercial centre having a very important trade with Pisa, Genoa, Amalfi, Catalonia, Marseilles, &c.   Among various exports its wax candles were specially valued, hence the name ' bougie' from its Arabic name Bedjaïa.   (In Roman times it was called ' Salsae.')   It was at the height of its importance c. 1300, when it came under the protection of the kings of Aragon, as against other rival towns on the coast.   The way in which it is mentioned by Dante seems thus fully accounted for.

So much then as to the determination of longitude.   The determination of latitude was also a matter of difficulty, in default of good instruments for measuring angles and altitudes. The method commonly adopted is explained by Strabo, Pliny, Ptolemy, and others, and in particular by the Arabian epitomizer of Ptolemy, Alfraganus, to whom, as we have several times noticed, Dante was doubtless indebted for much information on astronomical and geographical details.   This method was to ascertain the length of the longest day of the year at any place, and as this simply depends on its distance from the equator, in other words, on its latitude, the latitude was thence determined.   This method seems to have been first systematically applied by Hipparchus [1], who divided the habitable quadrant of the earth into 90 sections of 700 stadia each.   He also noted the changes in the position (or altitudes) of the stars corresponding to these terrestrial divisions [2].   (This is important, as showing how the term *climata* might be trans-

---

[1] Though it is recognized by Pytheas and Eratosthenes (Tozer, *Geography*, pp. 160, 174, 176).

[2] The words of Strabo are : ἀνέγραψε . . . τὰς γιγνομένας ἐν τοῖς οὐρανίοις διαφορὰς καθ᾿ ἕκαστον τῆς γῆς τόπον (II. v. 34).

ferred from terrestrial to celestial measurements, for which see previous Essay, p. 70 *n*.) Then he laid down in these divisions the names of places whose latitude had been determined by the observation of the length of the longest day there. [See Tozer's *Ancient Geography*, p. 176.]

I suppose I may take it as being generally known that on the equator the day and night are always equal, i. e. twelve hours each. Hence it is often called the 'equinoctial line.' Also that at the poles the longest day lasts for six months. This was familiar to Dante, for he mentions it in *Conv.* III. v. 169. There is a curious passage in Pliny where he states that in Britain [1] the long summer days of seventeen hours give the certain promise, which reason compels us to believe, that still nearer the pole the day must last continuously for six months [2]. Brunetto Latini expresses the same fact very quaintly from the opposite point of view of the long duration of night, when he says that in the extreme north the day sometimes only lasts 'un sol petit, que à poine i pourroit on messe chanter '— it is so very brief that one would hardly be able to say a Mass [3]! Consequently, in the intermediate tracts between the equator and the poles the longest days would be of intermediate duration between the extreme limits of twelve hours and six months. And the ancient geographers generally divided that space—or, to speak more accurately, that portion of it which, being inhabited by known races or nations, alone gave practical interest to such divisions—into seven zones or 'climata.' Each 'clima,' going northwards, included such a space that the mean length of the longest day was half-an-hour longer than that of the longest day in the previous 'clima' to the south.

The following Table will exhibit this system at a glance.

---

[1] *N. H.* II. § 186. We may compare with this Juv. ii. 161 :
'minima contentos nocte Britannos.'

[2] Herodotus (iv. 25) mentions a report that there are people at the north of Scythia who sleep for six months in the year. A curious *Fallacia Accidentis*, as though night and sleep were interchangeable terms !

[3] *Trésor*, I. pt. iii. c. 115.

The seven Climata according to Alfraganus.

	Length of the day.	Mean length.	Degrees of Latitude.	Total width in latitude.	Width in miles.
1.	$12\frac{3}{4}$ to $13\frac{1}{4}$ hrs.	13 hrs.	$12\frac{5}{6}$ to $20\frac{1}{4}$	$7°\frac{2}{3}$	440
2.	$13\frac{1}{4}$,, $13\frac{3}{4}$,,	$13\frac{1}{2}$,,	$20\frac{1}{4}$,, $27\frac{1}{2}$	$7°$	400
3.	$13\frac{3}{4}$,, $14\frac{1}{4}$,,	14 ,,	$27\frac{1}{2}$,, $33\frac{2}{3}$	$6°\frac{1}{8}$	350
4.	$14\frac{1}{4}$,, $14\frac{3}{4}$,,	$14\frac{1}{2}$,,	$33\frac{2}{3}$,, 39	$5°\frac{1}{3}$	300
5.	$14\frac{3}{4}$,, $15\frac{1}{4}$,,	15 ,,	39 ,, 43	$4°\frac{1}{2}$	255
6.	$15\frac{1}{4}$,, $15\frac{3}{4}$,,	$15\frac{1}{2}$,,	$43\frac{1}{2}$,, $47\frac{1}{4}$	$3°\frac{3}{4}$	210
7.	$15\frac{3}{4}$,, $16\frac{1}{4}$,,	16 ,,	$47\frac{1}{4}$,, $50\frac{1}{2}$	$3°\frac{1}{4}$	185
	Total $3\frac{1}{2}$ hrs. diff.			c. $38°$	2140 m.

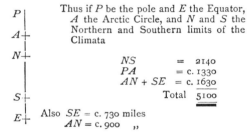

$$
\begin{aligned}
NS &= 2140 \\
PA &= c.\ 1330 \\
AN + SE &= c.\ 1630 \\
\text{Total} &\underline{\ \ 5100}
\end{aligned}
$$

Thus if P be the pole and E the Equator, A the Arctic Circle, and N and S the Northern and Southern limits of the Climata

Also SE = c. 730 miles
AN = c. 900 ,,

This was the supposed length of the quadrant of the circumference of the earth, see *Conv.* III. v. 101–105, and Alfraganus, *Elem. Astr.* c. viii. *AE*, which = c. 3770 miles, would represent the extent in latitude of the 'terra scoperta' or 'the earth standing out of the water,' according to the limits described in the *Quaestio*, § 19.

I will call attention to two points:—

(1) The first 'clima' does not begin at the equator but at $12\frac{5}{6}°$ away from it, i. e., according to the ideas of Alfraganus [1], about 730 miles north of the equator where the day has already attained a maximum length of $12\frac{3}{4}$ hours. The reason for this is that south of that limit the earth was thought to be practically almost uninhabited. The only inhabitants suspected were the half-mythical Garamantes, who,

[1] A degree being, according to Alfraganus, $56\frac{2}{3}$ miles. See *Elem. Astr.* c. viii. Ptolemy's mile was, I believe, about 1617 English yards.

as Dante says in *Conv.* III. v, wear scarcely any clothing, and were visited by Cato when flying from the tyranny of Caesar. Again in *De Mon.* I. xiv he says that the Garamantes live under the equator, having constant equality of day and night, and suffering from such excessive heat that they cannot endure any clothing. The tract beyond the first 'clima' southwards, according to Alfraganus, 'mari cingitur, neque multa habitatione constat' (c. viii).

(2) We should next observe that the seventh and last clima stops considerably short of the Arctic circle, to which the 'terra detecta' was supposed to extend. It falls short of it by about 900 miles, the tract beyond that being again, as Alfraganus (*l. c.*) says, scantily inhabited, 'paucas nobis cognitas civitates habet.' And so also Dante, in the passage of the *De Mon.* just quoted, speaks of the Scythians, 'extra septimum clima viventes,' as suffering extreme inequality of days and nights, and oppressed with almost intolerable cold. Thus the division of climata for the purposes of latitude was not carried beyond the limits supposed to be fairly habitable and therefore of practical interest. Strabo states this *totidem verbis* :—τοῖς δὲ γεωγραφοῦσιν οὔτε τῶν ἔξω τῆς καθ᾽ ἡμᾶς οἰκουμένης φροντιστέον· and again a little later :—ὁ γεωγράφος ἐπισκοπεῖ ταύτην μόνον τὴν καθ᾽ ἡμᾶς οἰκουμένην (II. v. 34). It is a little humiliating to find that the northern limit of the climata $(50\frac{1}{2}°)$ included not much more than the southern part of Cornwall. We Britons were, like the Scythians, 'extra septimum clima viventes,' and thus as 'outer barbarians' were apparently scarcely worthy of the notice of the geographers. They treated us in fact as

'penitus toto divisos orbe Britannos.'

It is perhaps hardly necessary to observe that, the number of miles in a degree being only $56\frac{2}{3}$ according to Alfraganus, this caused the various dimensions in the above Table to be considerably underestimated [1]. Thus the equatorial circumference of the earth is about 4500 miles more than was then

---

[1] This had some important practical consequences, as will appear in the next section.

supposed. As a concluding illustration of the method just
explained of computing latitudes, it may be mentioned that
Strabo (II. v. 14) proves that the ' Sacrum Promontorium,' or
Cape St. Vincent, is in the same latitude as the island of
Rhodes, because the longest day in each case is of the same
duration, viz. $14\frac{1}{2}$ hours [1].

There is a well-known passage of extreme difficulty in
which Dante speaks of the 'primo clima,' *Par.* xxvii. 81.
This has been dealt with in the foregoing Essay, since the
problem involved is astronomical rather than geographical [2].

VIII. Opinions as to the site of the Terrestrial Paradise
may seem at first sight a strange subject to include in an
essay on Geography. But in the Middle Ages this was
treated in all seriousness as a geographical problem. The
Terrestrial Paradise not only appears regularly in maps, but
its position is described by many writers, nor did it occur to
any one to doubt its continued existence any more than that
of India or Britain, and other such seldom visited localities.
Among other authors who speak definitely as to its position
we may mention Isidore, Gervase of Tilbury, Brunetto Latini,
Sir John Mandeville, &c. Mandeville may be specially mentioned, for, living as he did after Dante (he is said to have
died 1372), his credulous romancing may afford some idea as
to the level of current knowledge in the fourteenth century.
He states that he fully intended to visit Paradise when on
his travels [3], but he says: ' It is fer bezonde; and that for-
thinkethe me [i.e. is a matter of regret to me]; and also I was
not worthi:' but he reports a very minute description of it,
which he had ' herd seye of wyse men.' Professor Bartoli
mentions that even the island of the vision of St. Brandan
was marked upon maps, that it was once formally ceded by

---

[1] See Strabo, II. v. 14 in Tozer's *Selections*, p. 83.   [2] *Supra*, pp. 62–70.

[3] Chap. 30. It is fair to notice that Sir John Mandeville's name is now
generally supposed to be as fictitious as his narrative. But, whoever was the
author of the work, its date was something like that implied in the text. The
author professes to have commenced his journey on Michaelmas Day, 1322, and
to have written his book in the year of grace 1356. It was immensely popular,
and was translated from French, in which it was originally composed, into
English, Latin, Italian, and several other languages.

Portugal to the kingdom of Castile, and that as late as 1721 a Spanish expedition was organized to discover and explore this unknown acquisition!

Indeed the situation not only of the Earthly Paradise but also that of Hell and Purgatory were treated as matters of geographical, or at least cosmographical, science, as e. g. in the *Image du Monde* of Gautier de Metz, c. 1245, not so long before the time of Dante. But, surprising to relate, so late as 1620 (!) an Italian quasi-scientific writer [1] on these subjects confidently describes the site of Hell and Purgatory as within the earth: and he thinks it necessary gravely to anticipate the objection arising from the inadequacy of the space in view of the large and ever increasing number of the denizens of Hell. He replies that the souls of the damned have no right to expect to have as much room as the blessed saints in Paradise! [2]

The topography of the underworld [3] was almost as seriously discussed, and as dogmatically mapped out, as that of the οἰκουμένη itself. Thus even Aquinas [4] determines confidently the relative positions of the different ' receptacula' of souls after death, viz. Limbus Patrum, Purgatory, Limbus Puerorum, and Infernus.

But to return to the Earthly Paradise. It was generally thought to be in the extreme east. The mention of the Euphrates and Tigris in connexion with the Garden of Eden in Gen. ii has probably caused the great majority of writers to assign to it this position [5]. Brunetto Latini describes it as

---

[1] By name, Rosaccio. This comes from Wright's *S. Patrick's Purgatory*, p. 100.

[2] Another astonishing illustration of this popular notion as to the vast numbers of the lost I have met with in the *Annales Novesienses* (Neuss) in Martène et Durand, *Vett. Scriptt. et Monumentorum Collectio*, Tom. iv. p. 564 b. Shortly after the death of S. Bernard, a holy monk, who died at the same time, appeared in a vision to a certain bishop, and informed him that in the same hour that he and the saint died 30,000 persons had passed out of this life. Of all these (says the speaker) S. Bernard alone '*una mecum* ad caelos avolavit ; tres alii ad Purgatorium missi sunt ; ceteri omnes per sententiam iusti iudicis condemnati ad infernum perpetuo cruciandi descenderunt'!

[3] As Professor Bartoli says : 'L' Inferno diventa nel concetto medievale un capitolo di geografia.'

[4] *Summa*, III. Suppl. lxix. 4–6.

[5] There is also a *var. lect.* in Gen. ii. 8 which states this explicitly. Where

being in India, which was a general term for that part of the globe, and was in fact supposed to form its extreme eastern boundary, with the mouth of the Ganges about its centre [1]. Brunetto makes 'Paradisus' the eastern boundary of Asia, as the Alexandrian branch of the Nile forms its western boundary.

But whatever geographical reasons may have first determined its locality, S. Thomas Aquinas and others have no difficulty in finding good *a priori* reasons for it; that being the noblest part of the earth [2], and most near to the supposed abode of God Himself. Hence it is that one of the spirits in the valley of the kings, when he rises to repeat the prayer of the beautiful Compline Hymn, raises his hands and turns his eyes towards the east :—

'Ficcando gli occhi verso l'Oriente [3]'.

Hence, too, the practice of turning to the east at the recital of the Creed, and also that of burying the dead with their faces eastward, that they may at the Resurrection at once greet their returning Lord.

The notion expounded by Dante that the Earthly Paradise was situated in the southern hemisphere on the summit of the Mountain of Purgatory [4] (Purgatory thus also being upon

the Vulgate reads 'paradisum voluptatis a principio,' S. Aug. (*Gen. ad Lit.* viii. 6) quotes the passage 'Paradisum in deliciis (hoc est in Eden) *ad orientem.*' Even the expression 'a principio' was sometimes explained = 'ab oriente,' i. e. from where the world begins.

[1] Thus Orosius, I. ii. 13 'Asia ad mediam frontem orientis habet in oceano Eoo ostia fluminis Gangis.' We have seen how this conception of the Ganges is prominent in Dante. (*Supra*, p. 123.)

[2] 'In nobilissimo loco totius terrae,' to which he adds that the east is the right side of the earth, 'dextera caeli' (quoting Aristotle for this), and that is 'nobilior sinistra.' *Summa*, I. cii. 1, r.

[3] *Purg.* viii. 11. So also the Apocalyptic Vision comes from the east (*Purg.* xxix), and again departs towards the east (*Purg.* xxxii).

[4] But the idea of its great altitude, beyond the reach of all atmospheric disturbances, so as to be fit for the secure abode of man (see *Par.* i. 57; *Purg.* xxviii. 78, and especially 91–102), is commonly found in other writers. Indeed it was said by some to be so high as to reach even to the orbit of the moon, e.g. in *Summa*, I. cii. 1, where Aquinas (quoting Bede, who says 'pertingit usque ad lunarem circulum ') maintains that this is not literally true, but 'secundum similitudinem' implying 'perpetua aeris temperies.' Peter Lombard affirms it without this reservation, *Sentt.* II. xvii. 5; adding that it was therefore not

the earth and not, as was generally held, beneath its surface) is, I think, entirely unique[1]. Nor do I suppose that Dante adopted it as a serious geographical theory, but from considerations of poetical fitness. It will be remembered that Dante, in spite of the geographical difficulty, notes that he thought he saw in the Earthly Paradise the common source of Euphrates and Tigris (*Purg.* xxxiii. 112)[2]. With Christian writers this idea of a common origin for these two rivers was probably derived from the form of expression in Gen. ii. 10 'fluvius egrediebatur de loco voluptatis ... qui inde dividitur in quattuor capita'; i. e. '*a river* went forth,' &c. S. Augustine further identifies the other two rivers, Geon or Gihon with the Nile, and Phison with the Ganges; and the same identification is found before him in Josephus, and also in other writers[3]. The difficulty in assigning a common origin to four such distinct rivers is got over by S. Augustine by supposing them to flow underground to the spot where they first come to the surface, and where they are therefore supposed by us to rise. And this solution would probably have sufficed for Dante if pressed on the subject of his assigning the sources of Euphrates and Tigris to a mountain in the southern hemisphere. Some mediaeval writers go further still, and suppose *all* the rivers on the earth to have likewise a common source in 'the fount of Paradise.' So, among others, says Mandeville. This idea also probably originated from the supposed authoritative statement of Gen. i. 9: 'Congregentur aquae, quae sub caelo sunt, *in locum unum.*' It is a curious

reached by the water of the Flood. It should be remembered that, according to Dante, Aquinas, and mediaeval belief generally, atmospheric disturbances were thought to be caused by diabolic agency, by the 'Prince of the power of the air.' Comp. *Purg.* v. 114; *Summa*, II'. lxxx. 2, r *med.*, &c.

[1] Gervase of Tilbury (*Ot. Imp.* I. x.) says that it lay beyond the torrid zone, and therefore in a position inaccessible to man. This might possibly, by inference or implication, be thought to indicate the southern hemisphere. S. Thomas Aquinas also refers to its inaccessibility owing to barriers of mountains or seas or torrid regions. *Summa*, I. cii. 1, r 3.

[2] His words are 'Veder mi parve,' probably because the streams which he observed turn out afterwards to be Eunoe and Lethe.

[3] e. g. among mediaeval geographers, Cosmas, Isidore, Rabanus Maurus, Gervase of Tilbury, B. Latini, Mandeville, &c. See references given in my *Time References*, pp. 123, 124; *Accenni al Tempo*, pp. 141, 142.

illustration of the deep-rooted character of this belief, that so enlightened and adventurous an explorer as Columbus is said, when he encountered the flood of the river Orinoco, to have thought that it could be none other than the fount of Paradise. But it must be borne in mind that Columbus started in the hope, not of discovering a western continent, but of finding a new route to the eastern continent. This both he and others, happily misled by two errors of Ptolemy, believed to be much less distant than it is in fact. For Ptolemy over-estimated the distance from the Fortunate Islands (Canaries) to China across the οἰκουμένη, i.e. going eastwards, by about 50°, so that the distance going westwards by sea was consequently underestimated by a similar amount. And besides this, Ptolemy underestimated the *whole* circumference of the earth by about one-sixth. These erroneous beliefs fortunately encouraged Columbus, by reducing the apparent magnitude of his undertaking[1].

Before we leave this subject, it should be observed that the belief in a common origin for the Euphrates and Tigris was

---

[1] The knowledge of Columbus would not of course be derived direct from Ptolemy, but from the *Imago Mundi* of Petrus Alliacus, Cardinal d'Ailly, who died 1425. Columbus in a letter written to Ferdinand and Isabella, in order to persuade them of the feasibility of his undertaking, quotes from a copy of this work, which still exists in the library at Seville with annotations by his own hand. The curious point is that the paragraph in question is simply borrowed without acknowledgement from Roger Bacon's *Geographia.* Humboldt observes that this fortunate blunder of the *Imago Mundi* (or, as we should now rather say, of Roger Bacon) had more to do with the discovery of America than the correspondence of the learned and scientific Italian astronomer, Toscanelli. (From J. H. Bridges' note to Bacon's *Geographia*, vol. i. p. 290.) Roger Bacon fortifies the opinion there expressed as to the short distance between the west of Spain and the east of India by references to the authority of Aristotle, Seneca, and Pliny. Cardinal d'Ailly appeals to the Apocryphal 4th book of Esdras, vi. 42, where it is stated that on the third day God caused the waters to be gathered together upon the *seventh* part of the world, and the dry land to occupy the other six-sevenths. This 'seventh part' is emphasized by repetition in vv. 47, 50, and 52. Hence the Cardinal argued that, as we know pretty well the extent of the dry land, the extent of the ocean, whose proportions were thus laid down by divine authority, must be very much smaller than was originally supposed (A. D. White, *Warfare*, &c., p. 111). This afforded comfort, or at least a comforting argument, to Columbus. Indeed, a letter of his is said to be extant in which he acknowledges his indebtedness to this mistake in Esdras (*ib.* p. 112 *n.*).

not confined to Christian writers. Thus it is found in Lucan, *Phars.* iii. 256-9 :—

> 'Quaque caput rapido tollit cum Tigride magnus
> Euphrates, quos non diversis fontibus edit
> Persis, et incertum, tellus si misceat amnes,
> Quod potius sit nomen aquis.'

Further, both Isidore [1] and B. Latini [2] (no doubt copying Isidore) state this on the authority of a fragment of Sallust, who asserts, 'Tigrim et Euphratem uno fonte manare in Armenia.' Again, Dante may have found this in Boethius [3], whose language very much resembles that of *Purg.* xxxiii. 112 :—

> 'Tigris et Euphrates uno se fonte resolvunt,
> Et mox abiunctis dissociantur aquis.'

Mr. Tozer (*Geography*, p. 271) points out that in a certain sense this common belief may be true. The head waters of the Tigris are in a marsh above Bitlis. In the same marsh rises the highest tributary of Xenophon's 'Teleboas,' which itself flows into the eastern branch of the Euphrates. Also this marsh, being on the pass between Kurdistan and Armenia, was an important line of communication in all ages.

Having now dealt with the eight main divisions of the subject which were suggested, I will briefly call attention to two or three minor points which tend to throw some light on special passages in Dante which deal with geography or topography.

(i) I note first his habit of using geographical or ethnical terms anachronistically. In one passage at least the neglect to notice this has caused a difficulty. In *Par.* vi. 49 Dante speaks of the overthrow of the Arabs who followed Hannibal. The explanation is that in Dante's time the region about Carthage and Tunis was occupied by the Arabs. It did not come under the Turks till much later. So 'Arabs' here is simply an anachronism for Carthaginians. This may be illustrated by the curious description in *Conv.* IV. v. 161 of the capture of the Capitol by the Gauls, as 'the seizure of the

[1] *Etym.* B. xiii. § 10.　[2] *Tresor*, I. pt. iv. c. 123.　[3] *De Cons.* V. Met. i.

Campidoglio by the French.' So in *Inf.* i. 68 Dante makes
Virgil describe his parents as Lombards (which Voltaire
compares to describing Homer as a Turk!). There is an
important false reading in the majority of modern editions
(though it is found in very few MSS. and in *none* of the old
commentators) at *Inf.* xxviii. 10, *Romani* instead of *Troiani*.
The latter term is applied to the Romans at the time of the
Second Punic War, since Rome had its origin from Troy.
(Compare *Ep.* V. iv. 52, *Conv.* IV. iv. 103, and v. 48, &c.).
Many similar instances might be given. This consideration
may save Dante sometimes from a false imputation of inaccuracy, or even from a tampering with his text.

(ii) Next I will call attention to Dante's habit of describing
towns or countries allusively by the names of their rivers.
This being to us frequently a description ' per ignotius ' is a
severe exercise in geography. This practice of Dante was
noted and illustrated by Mr. Gladstone in his paper on the
supposed visit of the poet to Oxford ; the principal passage in
that relation being *Inf.* xii. 120, where Dante describes the
respect paid to the heart of the murdered Prince Henry
' in sul Tamigi,' i. e. at Westminster. Thus the triumphant
progress of Cæsar in *Par.* vi. 58–60 is marked out by the
six rivers, the Var, the Rhine, the Isère, the Saône, the
Seine, and the Rhone. Among many other places, Paris,
Florence, Lucca, Bologna, Faenza, Imola, Cesena[1] (the last
three together in *Inf.* xxvii. 49–52), Vicenza (*Inf.* xv. 113),
Treviso (*Par.* ix. 44), are allusively described by the names of
their rivers. This point, however, is one rather of topography
than geography proper.

---

[1] In the case of Cesena, I was particularly struck, on the occasion of a recent
visit, with the very graphic description of Dante in *Inf.* xxvii. 52–4 :—

> ' E quella a cui il Savio bagna il fianco,
>   Così com' ella sie' tra il piano e il monte,
>   Tra tirannia si vive e stato franco.'

The town lies on a gentle slope which is the first rising ground from the
boundless plain northwards. Other higher hills stand behind the town, leading
up to the main Apennine range in the background. The Savio runs round
the base of the slope on which the town stands, and so ' bagna il fianco.'
The profile view, so to speak, of Cesena from the west, shows very strikingly
' com' ella sie' tra il piano e il monte.'

(iii) There is at least one case in which Dante has been commonly thought to have fallen into a geographical error from the confusion of two places with the same name, just as the legends and attributes of different but synonymous saints are sometimes confused. The name of Babylon was given to Old Cairo in Egypt, as well as to the great city on the Euphrates. The word Babylonia may be seen on the Hereford Map marked in Egypt. Sir J. Mandeville notices the distinction between the two places. B. Latini has a chapter headed 'Dou regne de Babiloine et de Egypte,' which begins—' Li regnes de Babiloine est contés sor celui des Assiriens et des Egyptiens [1],' and he then proceeds to give the history of Nebuchadnezzar (*Trésor*, I. pt. i. c. 27). Elsewhere he describes Babylon as on the Euphrates ; and in another place he says, ' En Egipte est la cité de Babiloine et dou Caire et Alixandre,' &c. (I. pt. iv. c. 123). But when Dante describes the empire of Semiramis by the words—

'Tenne la terra che il Soldan corregge,' (*Inf.* v. 60.)

we must either suppose that he has confused the Babylon of Semiramis with that in Egypt, or else (as Benvenuto suggests) that he believed the empire of Semiramis to have extended to Egypt. The first passage above cited from B. Latini might perhaps seem to support the latter view, but it is not very clear. Dante is hardly likely to have committed the huge historical blunder which the former explanation would involve, and he has in fact implied his belief in the great extent of the empire of Semiramis just before in l. 54—

'Fu imperatrice di molte favelle.'

At the same time it would surely be strange to identify her empire, in the brief description of l. 60, by such an outlying portion as Egypt rather than by its centre and seat of government.

Dr. Toynbee [2] has made the ingenious and interesting suggestion that a similar confusion of the two Babylons may explain the curious statement of Dante, which has long been

---

[1] Indeed there were two Babylons even in Egypt itself, according to Prof. Sundby, *Brunetto Latini*, p. 104.

[2] *Dante Studies and Researches*, p. 292.

a puzzle, that Alexander the Great died in Egypt. This occurs in *Mon.* II. ix, where it is still more strangely made on the authority of Livy. That at any rate is an error. But since in this same context Dante quotes Lucan to prove that Alexander's *tomb* was in Egypt, and since the fact of his *death* at Babylon was a matter of general notoriety (e.g. from Orosius and others), it seems quite probable that Dante may have put these two things together and supposed that Alexander's *death* occurred at the Babylon in Egypt instead of the Babylon in Assyria.

In conclusion, if it be thought that one who, like Dante, was preceded by such men as Rubruquis, Marco Polo, and Roger Bacon, might have risen to a higher standard of geographical knowledge, it must be remembered that actual discoveries, when made and announced, were very slow indeed in finding their way into ordinary maps. Thus the insular character of the Caspian [1], which was discovered by Rubruquis in 1253, and confirmed by Marco Polo c. 1275, is not recognized in any of the numerous maps now extant for considerably more than half a century later. Many discoveries in geography were no doubt (as I have already hinted) smothered by the general belief that most of its fundamental facts had been already irrevocably determined by Scriptural or patristic authority. Professional map-makers in the Middle Ages did not aim at embodying new (or, as they would probably consider them, new-fangled) ideas in geography. The success and acceptance of their efforts would probably depend on the greater completeness of detail, or the superior artistic skill, with which the familiar traditional opinions were reproduced, these being derived most commonly, as we have noted, from Orosius. Thus the author of the celebrated Hereford Map copies blunders of Orosius even about the British Isles, when the means of correction were both ready to hand and patent to

---

[1] Herodotus rightly regarded it as an inland sea (i. 203); and so also did Aristotle (*Meteor.* II. i. 10); but Alexander the Great was in error, supposing it to be connected either with the Euxine or the Eastern Ocean. The false view prevailed for more than four centuries, till it was corrected by Ptolemy. The correction, however, passed unheeded for more than another 1000 years. (From Tozer's *Geography*, &c.)

any person of average intelligence. We may notice also the co-existence of the singularly accurate ' Portolani,' or nautical charts of the Mediterranean, with fantastically incorrect contemporary maps [1]. This is only one of the many illustrations of the observation of Condorcet that men retain the prejudices of their childhood, age, or country, long after they have recognized the truths necessary to destroy them.

What has been here said of the cartographers is equally true of geographical writers also. B. Latini, for example, often copies the statements of Solinus [2] even on points where they might have been corrected by the most easily accessible knowledge. Some idea of the general level of geographical information in Dante's time may be gathered from the fact that the elaborate but grotesquely absurd Hereford Map, to which I have so often referred, is determined by experts to have been executed between 1275 and 1313, at a date therefore corresponding precisely with the period of Dante's prime. Also that most credulous of romancing travellers, Sir John Mandeville (or whatever his true name may have been), was fully a generation later than Dante. Nor let us forget that these were both, in some sense, geographical specialists, which Dante was not, but rather, from this point of view, one of the general public.

Finally, Dante's great poem, at any rate, would not have been the place for advancing the newest lights on geographical science, even if its author were acquainted with them. Nor does it appear that in the *Convito* he had any special occasion for showing intimate acquaintance (if he possessed it) with the science of Geography, as is the case with the sister science of Astronomy. On this, as we have seen, he manifests an interest and displays a knowledge altogether exceptional [3].

---

[1] See Beazley, *Henry the Navigator*, p. 121.

[2] See Dr. Toynbee's article on B. Latini and Solinus in *Romania*, already referred to *supra*, p. 110 *n*.

[3] I hope it will be also remembered that neither am I a geographical specialist. I have not attempted to treat the subject of mediaeval geography in itself, but only so far as was needed to throw light upon Dante's allusions to the subject.

III. THE DATE ASSUMED BY DANTE FOR THE VISION OF THE *DIVINA COMMEDIA* [1]

WAS the year assumed by Dante for the Vision of the *Divina Commedia* 1300 or 1301—the beginning of the new century in the popular imagination, or in actual fact ? The last few years have witnessed the revival of a controversy which seemed to have been finally closed in favour of 1300—a date which is still maintained by the great majority of writers ancient and modern. The controversy has recently been reopened by some Italian scholars with very great wealth of learning and minute investigation, both historical and astronomical; and the date 1301 has again received the adherence of some whose names cannot fail to carry weight. The recent occurrence of the 600th anniversary of the epoch has naturally awakened interest in the question, especially as that anniversary marks the close of a century in which the revival of the study of Dante, both at home and abroad, has been nothing less than phenomenal.

The point at issue may, at first sight, seem trivial and unimportant, and so perhaps intrinsically it is. But its chief interest lies not so much in the actual result as in the nature of the controversy itself, in the arguments upon which it depends, and the light which the possibility of such arguments throws on the mind and methods of the author; also, we may add, in the connexion which the date may have with the incidents and experiences of his own life.

First of all, it may be taken as generally known that Dante assumes a definite day in a definite year for the commencement of his Vision or Journey. He feigns that he entered the Inferno at nightfall on Good Friday, in a year which he describes as a 'centesimo anno,' which was also the central year

[1] Reprinted (with additions) from the *Quarterly Review* for July, 1901.

(*mezzo cammino*) of his own life ; and this, as we learn from the *Convito*, would mean his thirty-fifth year (IV. xxiii. 89 *seqq.*).

Next, this assumed date he never forgets. This is admitted on all hands. No one is represented as dead who was living at that date, or *vice versa*. No event that happened after that date is referred to unless under the guise of prophecy, with an exception, easily explained, which will be noticed presently. One or two illustrations of this may be given. The Emperor, Henry VII, died in 1313, before the *Paradiso* was written. Yet Dante refers to his becoming Emperor (1308) in the language of prophecy. See *Par.* xxx. 136: 'l'alma che *fia* giù agosta.' A typically bad reading is found here, *fu già*. This was evidently due to some dull copyist who was not aware of Dante's practice, and was unfortunately troubled with 'a little knowledge' of chronology. Similarly, two lines below, the descent of Henry into Italy (1310) is spoken of as still future (*verrà*). In *Purg.* viii. 121 Dante declares that he has never yet been in the territories of the Malaspina family, but prophesies that before seven years are past he will receive their hospitable protection. This occurred in 1306. Hence it is that we have the materials for judging (1) as to the year *assumed* for the Vision, and (2) as to the date of the *actual composition* of different parts of the poem, some portions of which can thus be shown to have been un-finished till within three or four years (or even less) of the author's death. This may be called the *historical* branch of the argument. The other branch is the *astronomical* one. Dante frequently refers to the position of the sun, moon, and planets, for indications of time. Now the positions of the moon and planets would be different at the corresponding periods of 1300 and 1301, and these can be ascertained ex-actly by computation. Here, then, we have quite another class of data bearing on the question. But whether Dante's astronomical references are to be understood popularly, or whether they are to be tested by rigid scientific calculations, is a preliminary and fundamental point which has itself given rise to the keenest controversy. It will be discussed later.

We will first deal with the *historical* argument. Un-

* * *

fortunately, the application of the apparently simple test of drawing the line between history and prophecy is beset with such numerous difficulties in detail that many of the passages in question have been claimed on both sides in the controversy. But before we expound some of these it should be observed that the apparently precise data already mentioned as furnished by Dante for the commencement of his Vision have been understood in different senses. We have seen that one of those data is the Good Friday of the year in question. Now that day occurred on April 8 in 1300, and on March 31 in 1301. The latter date being wholly inconsistent with Dante's frequent references to the age and position of the moon, the advocates of 1301 [1] have recourse to the traditional date of March 25 as being that of our Lord's crucifixion [2], and so imagine Dante to have entered Hell on March 25, 1301, which might therefore be described as a sort of 'ideal' Good Friday. Among the early commentators, Boccaccio alone adopts this view [3]. It should be observed in passing that the 'ideal' Good Friday, March 25, would in 1300 be as hopelessly inconsistent with the lunar references above mentioned as is the actual Good Friday, March 31, in 1301.

But Dante also gives another datum by referring the commencement of his Vision to the spring equinox. Though such references are not so definite as to bind us to the precise day of the equinox, it is curious that the early commentators seem to have paid most attention to this datum; and the majority of them place the commencement about 'mezzo Marzo [4],' that being the period to which the true equinox was

[1] As notably Professor Angelitti, one of the most recent, and certainly the most scientifically learned, of all who have written on this subject.

[2] Cyril of Alexandria says, 'Eodem die conceptus est in utero Christus et mortuus in cruce' (*auct.* Pasquini, *Princip. Alleg.*, p. 257). Dionisi also claims the authority of Tertullian, Lactantius, Augustine, Chrysostom, and others for this tradition.

[3] He says in Lez. ii (p. 112): 'egli nella presente fantasia entrò a dì xxv di Marzo.' This statement is repeated in Lez. vi (p. 178).

[4] This view finds, I believe, no advocates now, and in any case it does not concern us at present, except as contributing a possible element of confusion in the designation of the year; since in the case of those whose year began on March 25 an event occurring 'in mezzo Marzo' would belong to a different year from one that occurred on or after March 25.

believed to have receded in the time of Dante owing to the error in the Julian Calendar, and the 'centesma ch' è laggiù negletta' (*Par.* xxvii. 143). Contemporary documents usually give March 15 as the date of the equinox, though, as a matter of fact, the exact day was March 12.

But though the early commentators are at variance as to the *day*, they seem to be almost agreed as to the *year* being 1300. At any rate, none explicitly adopt 1301, though some doubt has been thrown upon the evidence in two cases ; and Boccaccio is inconsistent with himself, giving 1301 in one passage, and 1300 in two others[1]. In spite, however, of the largely preponderant acceptance of the date 1300 by both ancient and modern commentators, it must not be supposed that this represents the sum of individual conviction based upon evidence, or that the subject is by any means so clear as such a consensus might seem to imply.

Now in regard to the year we must be on our guard at the outset against several sources of confusion by which the discussion is embarrassed. There is first the well-known difficulty arising from the different days taken for the commencement of the year. Besides the present method (to which the expression 'Anni a Circumcisione' is sometimes applied), there were two others more usually in vogue in the Middle Ages. In one, the year commenced on December 25, the traditional birthday of our Lord ('Anni a Nativitate'), and in the other, on March 25, the date of the Annunciation or Incarnation

---

[1] The actual facts stand thus. The date 1300 is distinctly given by Jacopo della Lana, Pietro di Dante, the Ottimo, and Benvenuto. It is true the Ottimo is claimed by Grion for 1301 on the strength of inferences drawn from some of the statements in his Commentary ; but in the central and crucial passage, *Inf.* xxi. 112, the author explicitly states 1300 to be the year. Boccaccio also does so on two occasions, viz. when commenting on *Inf.* i. 1 and on vi. 69. In a third place (iii. 60), it is true, he gives the date 1301, stating that this will appear from *Inf.* xxi. 112. In this passage (iii. 60) the date is quite immaterial to the context in which it occurs. As to *Inf.* xxi. 112, Boccaccio's commentary unfortunately breaks off in Canto xvii, so that we cannot be sure whether in the case before us 1301 may be a casual error or a copyist's blunder, or whether Boccaccio would have maintained this date if he had come to the decisive passage in Canto xxi. Jacopo di Dante gives the date 1299, but the chronological inferences in the context are so confused that it looks as if he also intended 1300. In any case he could not possibly mean 1301.

('Anni ab Incarnatione'). The former of these (December 25),
was called the Roman use, and the latter the Florentine or
Pisan use. Hence arises an obvious confusion in respect of
the date of events occurring in the first three months of each
year. This difficulty is familiar to all students of history.
For instance, in Giovanni Villani, who naturally follows the
Florentine use, we sometimes find the election of a pope in
January or February in succession to one who is described
as dying apparently some months later in the same year.
Thus Villani states that Honorius IV died in April 1287, and
that his successor, Nicholas IV, was elected in February 1287
(our 1288).

But the confusion does not end here, since those who commenced their year from the Incarnation, or March 25, differed
as to whether the numeration of years should start from the
March 25 before our Lord's birth, i. e. the actual day of the
Incarnation, or from the March 25 following, i. e. the first
anniversary occurring during our Lord's lifetime. The former
method was called the Pisan use, and was advocated by the
well-known chronologer, Dionysius Exiguus, in the sixth
century, and also by Bede. The latter is known as the
Florentine use, and was much more commonly adopted, it
being followed also in some provinces of France, and generally
in Spain, Germany, and England. In this case the year 1
would begin on the first anniversary of the Incarnation, i. e. on
March 25 following our Lord's birth[1], when He would be
considered to be one year old. This was the method adopted
by Clavius, who assisted at the Gregorian reformation of the
calendar, and by his younger contemporary, Petavius.

Now let us observe the practical differences which follow
when these systems are brought into comparison with our
method of reckoning. In this, the year 1 is supposed to
begin on January 1 following, not preceding, the birthday of
our Lord, with which actual day the New Year was intended

---

[1] The period between the Incarnation and this date is actually described
by Clavius as the year o. This designation is defended as chronologically
correct by Bishop Butcher in his learned work on *The Ecclesiastical Calendar*,
p. 21.

approximately to coincide. Our New Year's Day, in other words, precedes the Florentine by about three months. Consequently, as the Florentine year 1301 begins on our March 25 of the same year, the last nine months of our year would be described by the same figure on both systems, while the first three months of our 1301 would on the Florentine system belong to the previous year, 1300. Conversely, on the Pisan system, according to which our Lord was born on December 25 of the year 1, the year 1301 would begin on our March 25, 1300, and so the first three months of our year 1300 would correspond with the Pisan in the figure of the year, while the last nine months would belong to the Pisan year 1301 [1]. It will be observed how this difficulty especially besets the declarations of those who, like the majority of the early commentators, place the commencement of the Vision at the critical period of 'mezzo Marzo.'

Let us further make this plain as regards the Florentine use by one or two examples. The battle of Benevento, in which Manfred fell, took place according to our reckoning on February 26, 1266. It is described by Villani as occurring on February 26, 1265. A still better example is given by Professor Angelitti from the letter of Gregory XIII, promulgating the reform of the calendar. The date of the letter is February 24 (vi° Cal. Mart.), 'Anno Incarnationis Dominicae, 1581'; and that of the affixing of the seal a week later, on March 1, is given as 'Anno a Nativitate D. N. Jesu Christi, 1582.' Here we see the contrast, within a few lines, of the

---

[1] The following table will show these differences at a glance :—

Modern.	Florentine.	Pisan.
Jan.–Mar. 25, 1300 .	1299	1300
Mar. 25–Dec. 1300 .	1300	1301
Jan.–Mar. 25, 1301 .	1300	1301
Mar. 25–Dec. 1301 .	1301	1302

dates on the Florentine and Roman systems respectively, the latter practically corresponding with our own.

It is interesting now to inquire which of the above systems of computation, Roman or Florentine, Dante seems to have employed. I think probably the Roman, i. e. beginning the year *a Nativitate*, or on December 25, this being the reckoning officially adopted by the Church, or, as the words run in the Jubilee Bull of Boniface VIII : 'Annos Domini secundum ritum Romanae Ecclesiae.'

The following considerations bear upon the point. (1) If we admit the genuineness of the 'Quaestio de Aqua et Terra,' including the colophon, the question is decided at once, for the subscription, in which the date is given, runs thus : 'Anno a Nativitate D. N. Jesu Christi, 1320.' It is added that the discussion was on January 20, and that that day was Sunday. This was the case according to our reckoning, or the Roman reckoning. But January 20, 1320, according to the Florentine use, was not a Sunday. Angelitti points out another interesting inference from the fact that it is also there stated that the glorious birth of our Saviour, as well as His resurrection, took place on a Sunday. Mathematical calculations show that this would be the case if the Christmas Day of our Lord's birth were considered to be in the year 1, and not in the year 0[1]. Hence probably Dante did not adopt the Florentine use, at any rate. (2) In *Inf.* xxiv. 1–3, the presence of the sun in Aquarius, i. e. January–February (according to popular estimation), is described as ' in parte del *giovinetto* anno.' In the Florentine use it would be just the end of the year. (3) The passage in *Par.* xvi. 34, in which Cacciaguida treats the Annunciation as a sort of *terminus a quo* of all chronology, cannot be adduced (as it has been by Fraticelli and others) to prove that Dante himself reckoned years *ab Incarnatione*, for the words occur in the mouth of the ancient Florentine Cacciaguida, who would naturally reckon thus ; nor, indeed, in any case, would the actual language of the passage bear the weight of any such inference.

---

[1] Angelitti, *Sulla data*, &c., p. 18, 'questa notizia . . . mostra che Dante faceva cambiare col 1° Gennaio il numero che denota l' anno.'

But there is yet another source of confusion in regard to the year, which must not be overlooked. When a writer mentions a definite number of years, are they *anni compiuti* or *anni correnti*? In other words, is the last and incomplete year reckoned in or not? We are met by this difficulty perpetually, and it just makes the difference of one year, which is precisely the difference between the dates under discussion, 1300 or 1301. Here are two obvious illustrations. Our Lord was generally believed by mediaeval writers to have died on March 25, thirty-four years after the date of the Incarnation, or, as we should say, at the age of thirty-three years and three months from His birth. But His age is sometimes stated as thirty-three and sometimes as thirty-four, though the same thing is meant. So again, when Dante (in *Purg.* xxxii. 2) speaks of his longing to see Beatrice as ' decenne sete,' ' a ten years' thirst,' if the date was 1300, it would be actually nine and three-quarter years, if 1301, then ten and three-quarters. The former seems obviously more probable, though both views are tenable.

Bearing in mind all these sources of confusion and ambiguity, let us next turn to a few of the passages that are quoted as bearing on the controversy [1]. There is, in the first place, the passage which stands out prominently as the very keystone of the problem, viz. *Inf.* xxi. 112–14 :—

> ' Ier, più oltre cinqu' ore che quest' otta,
> Mille dugento con sessanta sei
> Anni compiè, che qui la via fu rotta [2].'

[1] The questions and the inferences involved in some of these are too complicated for discussion in such an Essay as this. The passages, also, are too numerous for complete citation. Thus, Angelitti brings between twenty and thirty into the controversy. Another recent critic (Solerti) enumerates twenty, and comes to the general conclusion that eight are in favour of 1300, three in favour of 1301, and nine are doubtful, though in many cases pointing rather to 1300.

[2] It may be noted that there is a monstrous variant here, which consists in the insertion of *uno* after dugento :—

> ' Mille dugent' uno con sessanta sei.'

This, to begin with, will not scan, and on several other grounds is most obviously a false reading and clumsy correction. But it is so far interesting that the variant is of great antiquity, and is recognized by some of the very early commentators. Thus it bears witness to the difficulty that was soon

'Yesterday, five hours later than this hour, completed 1266 years, since here the way was broken [1].'

Here Dante appears, and evidently intends, to fix the year, the day, and the hour, of that part of his journey with the utmost possible precision of language ; but the day and year are still matters of the keenest dispute. Since Dante says, in *Conv.* IV. xxiii, that our Lord willed to die in the thirty-fourth year of His age, the natural consequence would be that we should add thirty-four to the number 1266 here given, and hence infer 1300 to be the year of the Vision. But Professor Angelitti endeavours, even without the help of the variant explained in the note, to wring the year 1301 out of the passage. Assuming that Dante held that our Lord was born on December 25 in the year 1, he claims that He may be said to have died on March 25 in the year 35 (i.e. on the first day of that year), and not on March 25 of the year 34, as commonly held. Hence we are entitled to add 35 to 1266, and so obtain the desired result, 1301. I must say this seems to be a mere arithmetical juggle. What the text states is that 1266 years have elapsed since the death of Christ ; and as that occurred, according to the explicit statement of Dante, in His thirty-fourth year, it would certainly never occur to any ordinary reader who knew that our Lord's age was held to be thirty-three and a quarter, which at most might be described as thirty-four, to take that figure at thirty-five in order to work out the calculation here put into the mouth of Malacoda.

But this is not all. A most extraordinary further question has been raised as to the interpretation of this passage. Professor Angelitti has instituted an extremely elaborate

felt in working out the computations given by Dante, owing probably to some of the causes of confusion in methods of reckoning already noted. Possibly the object may have been to bring out the date 1301 instead of 1300. Some of the advocates of 1301 have caught at this reading, and have attempted to meet the obvious objections to it, sometimes by claiming it to be the *difficilior lectio!* (this indeed it is, but certainly not in the proper sense of that well-known critical principle)—sometimes by suggesting that 'Mille' should be scanned as a monosyllable !

[1] This refers to the earthquake at the moment of Christ's death (Matt. xxvii, 51). Comp. *Inf.* xii. 37-45.

discussion extending over several pages [1] to determine whether Dante, in the mouth of Malacoda, is referring to sidereal, tropical, or Julian years [2]. It is assumed that he would (with his usual care in such details) place himself in the position of the speaker. Hence it is gravely inquired whether Malacoda, whose superior knowledge would make him aware of the error of the Julian Calendar, would have been likely to have committed himself to its erroneous data ; or whether he would not more probably have spoken 'with mathematical precision.' In this case then, he might have adopted either sidereal or tropical years [3]. The latter system might, perhaps, prove ' più simpatico a Malacoda,' as being more likely to be misleading : 'il quale aveva certamente interesse che il mondo cammini sempre storto ! [4] ' The want of humour implied by such a discussion is, if possible, surpassed when a similar question is raised in reference to ' Adamo, e sue prime osservazioni astronomiche [5].' As the figure involved in the case of Adam (see *Par.* xxvi. 118–23) amounts to over 5000 years [6] the resulting difference will be considerable (p. 37). Here, however, Professor Angelitti considers that the question can be answered with full confidence. Adam could not have adopted *Julian* years since they were not introduced till shortly before the birth of Christ : nor *tropical* years, because ' il babbo Adamo ' could not have been aware of the precession of the equinoxes. Hence he can only have spoken in reference to *sidereal* years ! Surely this is solemn trifling with the language of poetry. Dante was, of course, as we know from the *Convito*, perfectly acquainted with these chronological distinctions. It is inconceivable that in his poem he should have vexed his soul or those of his readers with such pedantic details [7].

---

[1] *Sulla data*, &c., pp. 30 *seqq.*   [2] *vide supra*, p. 11.

[3] The difference between the three systems would in 1266 years lie between nine and thirteen days. Angelitti, *op. cit.* p. 31.

[4] *op. cit.* p. 31.   [5] *op. cit.* pp. 37, 38.

[6] As to the chronology followed by Dante, see *supra*, p. 22.

[7] I wish to add that in spite of such passages as those above criticized I have a profound admiration for the scientific attainments of Professor Angelitti, as well as for the services which he has rendered through them to the study of Dante.

There is, however, another way in which some of the above arguments for 1301 appear to me entirely to miss the point at issue. Our inquiry is whether Dante intended his Vision to be associated with the year commonly known as 1300, or that commonly known as 1301. The identity of either year would be easily determined by some well-known historical event in each, such, for instance, as the First Jubilee, in 1300, or Dante's Priorate in that year ; or in 1301, the coming of Charles of Valois to Florence, marking ' the beginning of its destruction,' as Dante expresses it in *Conv.* II. xiv. 1. 176. Our main point then would be to determine whether the Vision were associated with the year of some such well-known event, however the year itself might be designated ; not whether Dante considered that the year commonly known as 1300 would be more correctly (on scientific or chronological grounds) described as 1301. The two questions seem to be quite distinct, and the latter does not really concern the present issue. The dividing line between history and prophecy is the ultimate test of this, by whatever figure the year may be designated.

Following the same principle of taking Dante's words in their natural sense in regard to the question raised on p. 146, we should consider that the anniversary of the death of Christ would be certainly understood by Dante's readers to be that day with which every one was familiar, viz. Good Friday according to the calendar of the Church ; and that few, if any, would ever think (even if they knew it) of the fixed date of March 25, excogitated by certain ecclesiastical writers. Unless Dante employed language ' to conceal his thoughts,' surely his chronological, and (as we shall contend later) his astronomical references also, must be understood in such a sense as would naturally occur to an ordinarily instructed and intelligent reader.

I will now call attention to a few of the other more important passages which are commonly adduced on the *historical* side of the controversy, taking first those which are claimed with most confidence by the advocates of 1300.

A passage generally thought strongly to support 1300,

if not to be almost conclusive for it, is the episode of Casella in *Purg.* ii. 91–9. Among the spirits landed on the shore of Purgatory that morning by the angel is the soul of Dante's friend Casella. Dante expresses surprise that Casella has lost so much time in coming thither (l. 93) [1]. Casella explains that, when the angel is taking on board his daily freight of souls, ' one is taken and another left,' according to what is apparently an entirely arbitrary exercise of his will, though no doubt with strict justice (ll. 94–7). Casella himself has been frequently rejected (' più volte,' l. 96). But when he returned again this time (l. 100) he found that for three months past the angel's demeanour had entirely changed, and all were received without any difficulty, ' con tutta pace' (l. 99). The generally accepted and natural explanation is this, that the kindlier manner of the angel was due to the proclamation by Boniface VIII of the First Jubilee, which was to take effect from Christmas 1299, i.e. the first day of the Roman year 1300 [2]. This would be about three months previously, whatever exact day may be taken as that of the commencement of Dante's journey.

To this Angelitti raises the objection (which he considers fatal) that there is nothing in the Bull conveying any benefit to those already dead ; and it is implied by l. 96 (' Più volte m' ha negato esto passaggio '), as well as by l. 93 (mentioned above), that Casella had died some time before Christmas 1299. For an alternative explanation, he appeals very ingeniously to a further Bull of Boniface dated Christmas Day 1300, i.e. the commencement of 1301 in Roman usage, conveying the benefits of the Jubilee to any who through death or accidental delay in travelling had not been able to complete the prescribed number of days of religious services, ' numero dierum taxato nondum decurso [3].' He assumes that Casella was in this position, and that he died in the course of the year 1300, and consequently was rejected

---

[1] Reading *ora*, not *terra*, in l. 93.

[2] On the interesting point involved in Dante's recognition of even the *antedated* efficacy of the Indulgence, see *Studies*, II. p. 67.

[3] This period was thirty days for Romans, and fifteen days for outsiders.

by the angel until the supplementary Bull of Boniface was promulgated at Christmas 1300, three months previously to Easter 1301 [1].

Now, it is doubtless true that there is nothing in the original Bull of Boniface conveying any benefit to one already dead ; but, if we are to be bound by such rigid conditions of its applicability as this, let us be consistent in our strictness.   In that case, let it be observed, no benefit corresponding to that which Casella here describes is promised in it to any one at all. In the first place, it was to help people out of Purgatory, not into it [2].   Then, again, the scene imagined here is evidently reproduced from Virgil (see *Aeneid* vi. 313-30), like many other subordinate features or details in the *Divina Commedia.* No such impediment to salvation or purgation as this Virgilian incident (nor, indeed, even the existence of any such a place as Ante-Purgatory at all) is found in the teaching of the Church or in the belief of Christians.   The conditions, looked at thus strictly (as Angelitti would demand), are not such as would be affected by the terms of the Indulgence at all.   I believe Dante merely means that the promulgation of the Jubilee brought about during that *anno santo* a general disposition of benignity and clemency to mankind—observe (ll. 98, 99) [3] that since three months the angel had received graciously *all* who came—it inaugurated a period of general ' good-will towards men,' and of easier conditions for humanity at large.   Thus the demeanour of the *ufficiali celestiali*, in

---

[1] I may observe in passing that a difficulty has been raised which applies equally to both dates, viz. why had Casella waited three months before experiencing the benefit in question?   It appears to me that Dante has still in his mind the picture he has derived from Virgil.   The spirits thus rejected are compelled to wander about *elsewhere* until the propitious moment for their acceptance arrives.   Virgil says, 'Centum errant annos,' and, though Dante does not adopt this detail, a similar wandering, though of shorter duration, is implied by ll. 100, 101.   When, after several previous rejections, Casella made another return that morning, he found all was changed, and probably was then informed of the new condition of things.   But, whatever may be the explanation of the difficulty, it does not affect the question now before us, as it obviously applies equally to either year.

[2] See *Studies*, II. pp. 50-52.

[3]   ' Veramente da tre mesi egli ha tolto
             Chi ha voluto entrar con tutta pace.'

their several spheres of operation, was made more favourable thereby,

> 'So hallowed and so gracious was the time.'

How else should we account for the *unrestricted* character of the angel's welcome (l. 99)? Those affected by the concession in the supplementary Bull must have been comparatively very few. Unfortunately, the actual date of Casella's death, like that of many other subordinate incidents in the *Divina Commedia* which would serve as *instantiae crucis* in this controversy, cannot now be ascertained.

The passage in *Inf.* x. 111, on the death of Guido Cavalcanti, seems even more conclusive. Dante requests Farinata to reassure Cavalcanti by informing him that his son Guido is still living :—

> 'Che il suo nato è co' vivi ancor congiunto.'

As Guido died in August, 1300, and was buried at Santa Reparata in Florence on the twenty-ninth day of that month, this statement was true at Easter, 1300, but would not be true at Easter, 1301. One answer attempted to this is that the declaration of Dante is 'a pious fraud' in order to spare the feelings of the afflicted father! It is further suggested that the words are intentionally ambiguous, and that Dante meant to save his credit for truthfulness by using an expression capable of meaning 'present in the memory and affections of those living' (*coi vivi ancor congiunto*)! This is surely 'θέσιν διαφυλάττειν' with a vengeance. The peculiar form of words may be explained, if any explanation be needed, by the fact that Guido was in hopelessly broken health, and was in fact 'a dying man' at this time. Other critics have been reduced to the suggestion that Dante has made a mistake as to the date of the death of one who was his 'primo amico.'

Another statement which seems to be almost decisive for 1300 is that put into the mouth of Cacciaguida respecting the age of Can Grande, viz. that he is then only nine years old :—

> 'pur nove anni
> Son queste ruote intorno di lui torte.' (*Par.* xvii. 80, 81.)

An old chronicle (*Chronicon Veronense*, c. 1378) states the day of his birth to have been March 9, 1291 [1]. If that evidence be accepted, the question is practically settled. Some have adopted the desperate evasion of supposing Dante to be referring not to our years, but to those of the planet Mars, in which he was then situated! Others suggest that for ' March ' we should read ' May,' on the strength of a poem (dated, it is true, 1328) which describes the astrological conditions of Can Grande's birth in a manner said to suit better that time of the year. Angelitti, again, states that the *Chronicon* in question is so full of chronological blunders that its authority is worthless. Still, the fact remains that the one positive and definite statement that has come down to us, and which so far ' holds the field,' distinctly requires the acceptance of the date 1300.

Again in *Purg.* viii. 133 *seqq.*, Corrado Malaspina refers prophetically to his family's hospitable reception of Dante in the Lunigiana, and he says that it will take place before seven spring-times have come round. As this visit took place in 1306, the statement is precisely accurate in 1300. If the date of the words being spoken were supposed to be 1301, it would not indeed be untrue, but it seems almost certain that, in a formal prophecy of this kind, *six* and not *seven* would have been the number given.

I cannot but think that considerable, if not crucial, importance must be attached to the expression ' questo centesim' anno ' in *Par.* ix. 40. ' This centenary year ' is surely an expression much more naturally applied to 1300 than to 1301, apart from the consideration of the technical question of its belonging to the new or to the old century. The very term itself, ' centesimo anno,' occurs in reference to the year 1300 in the language of Boniface's proclamation. The Jubilee was to be held ' in anno millesimo trecentesimo . . . et in quolibet *anno centesimo* secuturo.' And again, the supplementary Bull of Christmas 1300 already referred to is dated ' in die

---

[1] It should be stated that the chronicler appears always to use the Roman reckoning, in which this date corresponds with the modern notation.

natalis Domini, fine videlicet *centesimi* (*sc.* anni) qui fuit mille-
simus trecentesimus.'

We must now turn to the passages most confidently relied
on by the advocates of 1301. Far the most important is
Purg. viii. 73–81, where the second marriage of the widow of
Nino de' Visconti is referred to. This, according to Angelitti,
would at Easter 1300 be 'an irreparable anachronism,' since
that marriage is known to have taken place on June 24, 1300.
Recourse has been had to some unworthy subterfuges here to
save the date 1300, like those we have noted above on the
other side. But it surely seems a perfectly fair answer to say
that Dante does not state that the second marriage is already
celebrated, but only that the widow has been very much too
hasty in putting off her widow's weeds. Note the exact
language of ll. 74, 75 :—

> ' Poscia che trasmutò le bianche bende,
>   Le quai convien che misera ancor brami.'

This sign of mourning would naturally be abandoned as soon
as the intended marriage was arranged or announced, and that
may well have been some weeks or even months before it was
actually celebrated, especially under the circumstances of
indecent haste here alleged. As a matter of fact, Nino de'
Visconti died in 1296, and the *shorter* interval allowed by
1300 would add point to his complaint.

Another passage on which Grion lays some stress is *Inf.*
xviii. 28, where Dante refers to the barrier run along the
bridge of S. Angelo to divide the crowds of those going to or
returning from St. Peter's. Grion thinks that this affords a
strong argument for 1301, since the Jubilee was not actually
proclaimed till February 22, 1300. But if Dante were in
Rome in the spring of 1300 (as has been thought probable) he
might have witnessed this about Easter, when the *esercito
molto* would be at its height. And further, he does not say
that he witnessed it, though it may perhaps be thought a fairly
natural inference that he did so. I think that it may also be
argued that the Perfect Definite ' hanno tolto ' and the following Presents ' hanno ' and ' vanno ' seem to be more naturally

used if the incident were still going on at the (assumed) time
of writing, than when it was a thing of the past, even though
very recently past—in other words, to suggest 1300 rather
than 1301.

There is an important question of principle involved in the
argument in favour of the year 1301 which is thought to be
derived from the passage just cited. It is evidently implied
that an event referred to in any way as having already happened
must necessarily have been anterior to the assumed date of the
Vision. But we must emphatically protest against the notion
that the assumption of a fixed date, and the careful separation
of past and future events in reference to it, should preclude
Dante from making use, *in the way of illustration, simile,
or comparison*, of events that occurred later. This is quite
different from allowing himself, or any of the characters whom
he introduces, to refer, *as speakers*, to such occurrences.
Though Dante as a speaker never does this, Dante as a
narrative poet is not thus hampered. It would have been
sheer pedantry in him to accept such a restriction; and he
did not accept it [1].

Thus he draws a comparison from the ' Slavini di Marco '
in *Inf*. xii. 5, which probably did not occur till June 20, 1309 [2].
Again, in *Inf*. xix. 19, he refers to his having rescued a boy
from drowning by breaking one of the receptacles in the
baptismal font in S. Giovanni. Grion says, on the authority
of Jacopo di Dante, that this occurred in April 1301, and
argues hence against the date 1300. But Dante himself adds,
' it was a few years ago,' ' ancor non è molt' anni,' which
shows that he does so as Dante the narrative poet. The
passage, therefore, cannot bear in any case on the assumed
date as between 1300 and 1301, as it is not more suitable to
one than to the other.

Another pedantic assumption of like nature may be briefly

---

[1] We find a similar distinction observed by Milton. As Professor Raleigh
observes : ' It is plain that, although almost all the characters of the poem are
precluded from making allusion to the events of human history, the poet himself
is free ; and he uses his freedom throughout.'

[2] Some writers, however, suppose an earlier landslip in the ninth century to
be referred to.

noticed for rejection, viz., that any *opinion* expressed by Dante in the *Commedia* must have been held by him at the assumed date of the Vision. Consequently, when a view maintained in the *Convito* is repudiated in the *Paradiso*, as, e. g., the cause of the *macchie lunari* (*Par.* ii), or the order of the Angelic Hierarchies (*Par.* xxviii), while we may reasonably infer that Trattato II of *Convito* was written before the *composition* of the *Paradiso*, we certainly are not justified in arguing (with Fraticelli) that it was written before 1300 (or 1301).

We need not perhaps discuss other less conclusive passages of this kind that have been adduced on either side of the controversy. We will pass on now to another class, viz. those in which the inference depends on the question whether a given number of years includes one incomplete year or not. For instance, does 'ten years' stand for nine and a fraction or ten and a fraction? No certain rule can be insisted on. But generally we might be guided by the magnitude of the fraction over, and we should then naturally adopt the interpretation which most nearly approximates to the round number given. Under this head, besides the inference to be drawn in favour of 1300 from the expression *decenne sete* already referred to (*supra*, p. 151), we may appeal to the datum given in *Inf.* i. 1, by the words 'Nel mezzo del cammin di nostra vita.' It has been said that this may as well describe the year thirty-five to thirty-six as that from thirty-four to thirty-five. But if Dante was born in May 1265, at Easter 1300 his age would be thirty-four years and about ten months, and this is surely much more near the *mezzo cammin* of thirty-five than would be the age of thirty-five and ten months at Easter 1301. Besides, in *Conv.* IV. xxiii. 93, Dante says that the perfection of human life, the summit of its arch (=*mezzo cammino*), is reached 'nel trentacinquesimo anno,' in the thirty-fifth year, i. e. between thirty-four and thirty-five; and that Christ willed to die in His thirty-fourth year so that His Divinity might not 'stare in discrescere,' which certainly seems to imply that this 'discrescere' would begin as soon as the thirty-fifth year was reached. It can scarcely admit

* * *

of a doubt that if Dante were born in 1265 he would describe
the year 1300, during which he reached and passed thirty-five
about the month of May, as marking the *mezzo cammin* of
his life.

Another passage, too vague however to lead to a definite
conclusion, is that in which Dante expresses his surprise to
find (as he feigns) Boniface VIII already in Hell, because in
that case the presage had deceived him by 'several years'—

'Da *parecchi* anni mi mentì lo scritto' (*Inf.* xix. 54).

This period would be 3½ years in 1300 and 2½ in 1301. Again,
the former amount strikes one as more suitable to the expression 'parecchi anni,' but no certain inference can be drawn.

On the other hand, and on similar principles, we should
admit that *Purg.* xxiii. 78—where it is stated that five years
have not yet passed since the death of Dante's wife's cousin,
Forese Donati [1]—seems rather better to suit 1301, since the
choice lies between about 3¾ years and 4¾ years. Perhaps
five is taken as a sort of round number, as we speak of 'five
or ten years'; but, as in the other passages already quoted,
no certain conclusion can be claimed on either side. The
same may be said of *Purg.* xviii. 121, where Alberto della
Scala is described as 'having one foot in the grave.' This,
while quite compatible with either date, would more vividly
correspond with the five months provided by 1301 than with
seventeen months in 1300. But, as he is said to have been an
extremely old man, the expression would be quite suitable in
either case.

There is another interesting department of this controversy
which I am compelled to dismiss with little more than a passing allusion. I mean the numerous passages which contain
formal prophecies, more or less oracular, of future events,
such, for example, as the prophecies of Ciacco in *Inf.* vi. 65
('verranno al sangue,' &c.), and the event that should follow
that bloodshed 'infra tre soli'; or, again, that of Farinata
respecting the calamities that should befall Dante before fifty

---

[1] The death of Forese has recently been discovered by Professor Isidoro del
Lungo, from the Registers of the Church of Sta Reparata, to have occurred on
July 28, 1296.

lunations (*Inf.* x. 79). We could not make any use of such passages without embarking upon an elaborate and exhaustive discussion of the various interpretations that have been suggested for them. The advocates of either date can generally suggest some event which is more or less compatible with the oracular and allusive language generally affected by prophecy. The same style was adopted by Dante, though he was 'prophesying after the event.'

There is, however, one interesting feature of this part of the subject which should not be entirely passed over. It is a consideration which still further complicates the practical difficulty of employing such prophetical passages in argument. I refer to the use that has been made on both sides of the well-known *dictum* as to the limits of the prescience of the lost which is found in *Inf.* x. 100–8[1]. Farinata is there made to declare that, whereas they are able to discern dimly the distant future, yet that when events are close at hand, or are taking place, a veil is drawn over them, and so the lost know nothing of passing human affairs. This principle has been applied to the question before us. It is objected that, on the assumption of one year or the other as the current date, the interval between the prophecy and its fulfilment is so short that the event would fall within the limits of that shadow by which the prevision of the future is obscured.

But before the argument can be thus applied at least three preliminary points have to be settled. (1) Does this limitation apply only to the Circle of the Materialists and Epicureans,

> 'Che l'anima col corpo morta fanno,'

(by one of whom this statement is made), or is it applicable to the other Circles of Hell also? What is, in short, the meaning of 'noi' here? Both views have been held and maintained. And if, as I believe, the latter view is (speaking generally) the correct one, then a further question arises: (2) Does it necessarily apply to the Circles *before*, as well as to those *after*, that in which the principle is enounced? According to a very early tradition the first seven Cantos were written at a con-

---

[1] On this and other points in this context, see further, *Studies*, II. pp. 170-2.

siderably earlier period than the others, the work being for
some reason interrupted and laid aside.   To this the opening
words of Canto viii have been thought to refer—' Io dico
seguitando,' &c.   Several indications in the way of internal
evidence supporting this tradition have been pointed out ; the
most striking of these being the very different scale upon
which the earlier and later Circles of Hell are treated.   Five
out of the nine Circles are already disposed of at the end
of the seventh Canto, and, as the first two Cantos are introductory, we may say that they have only five Cantos allotted
to them.   If then there were such a break in the composition,
it is not improbable that this limitation may have been an
afterthought.   Also it may have commended itself to Dante
from the opportunity which it afforded him of introducing
contemporary events into his poem.   Unless some such
limitation were observed, Dante could not consistently inform
the spirits of such events, since they would be aware of them
as of other things future.   Nor could they inform him, because
he had just come from the earth himself.   Though this argument has been employed in the controversy in respect of
prophecies occurring both in the earlier and later Cantos, it so
happens that the most important of these on which it bears
is the prophecy of Ciacco occurring in Canto vii.   To this, at any
rate, supposing the principle were excogitated by Dante later,
it would not be applicable.   But the ground is not clear yet,
for we must still further determine (3) what are the precise
limits indicated by the vague words, ' Quando *s'appressano.*'

Amidst so many elements of uncertainty it is scarcely
possible to construct any practical arguments.   I will content
myself therefore with recording the fact that even this rather
hopeless ' stone has not been left unturned ' in this controversy.

The results in respect of the ' historical ' aspect of the
question may now be summed up thus.   There seems to
be only one passage, that relating to the second marriage of
the widow of Nino de' Visconti, which is even claimed as entirely conclusive by the advocates of 1301.   We have seen that
it does not support any such positive inference, and that it
may be quite well interpreted consistently with either date.

On the other hand, there are three or four passages pointing very strongly to 1300, which seem only adaptable to 1301 by somewhat forced and unnatural explanations. Finally, there is a considerable number of intermediate passages on which opinions may fairly differ, but in a majority of these the assumption of the date 1300 appears to afford the more natural and obvious explanation. I do not therefore feel any hesitation, so far as this side of the investigation is concerned, in holding firmly to the generally received date, 1300.

We now turn to the astronomical side of the argument. To this Angelitti attaches supreme importance, regarding the conclusion based upon it in favour of 1301 as an ' impregnable rock,' although professing himself also satisfied that it does not conflict with the historical evidence. But here we have at the outset to determine a question of principle, vital to the whole discussion which follows.

It is maintained by Angelitti that every astronomical allusion or statement in the *Divina Commedia* is to be tested and interpreted by the most rigid application of mathematical calculations. For this purpose he has constructed very complete and elaborate tables of ' Ephemerides ' for sun, moon, and planets during the spring of the years 1300 and 1301. Testing Dante's references by these, and especially by those relating to the planets, he comes to the conclusion that such references correspond precisely with the positions of the planets in 1301, and do not at all correspond with their positions in 1300. This result would be no doubt very striking, one might almost say very startling, if established. We shall see, however, that it is very much overstated, and in some points even misstated, though of course not intentionally. But before coming to this we must traverse the fundamental assumption upon which the whole superstructure of this argument rests.

The view which I have always maintained, and that which is the central principle of the work which I published some years ago, *Time References in the Divina Commedia*, is that, whatever may have been Dante's skill and knowledge in astronomy (and from the *Convito* we know it to have been very considerable), in the *Divina Commedia* he is not composing a scientific work for astronomical specialists, but a poem for general readers of average culture and intelligence [1]. In that case, surely, minute calculations in degrees and minutes and seconds of the position of sun, moon, and planets at a particular epoch are out of place and superfluous. Dante would have gained nothing by taking account of such details, which could only be ascertained by himself or his readers by recourse to elaborate astronomical tables, even supposing such tables to have been then generally accessible. Rather, we should maintain, he counts upon—to use a familiar phrase —'astronomy without mathematics,' i. e. a general and intelligent knowledge of fundamental astronomical facts and phenomena. These he employs very skilfully and artistically to add reality and vividness to his narrative, just as he uses also the familiar details of geography and even of local topography.

But, apart from the question of intelligibility [2], due weight must be given to another important consideration. In the interpretation of a poem we must not demand scientific exactness at the cost of poetical fitness. Here is a definite example. In *Inferno* xxxiv Dante represents himself as having passed into the southern hemisphere, where the whole action of the *Cantica* of the *Purgatorio* takes place. Are we therefore to insist (as Prof. Angelitti and others maintain) that Dante supposed himself to have entered Purgatory and the Earthly Paradise *at the autumn equinox*, the season of waning days and the decay of nature? This would be, to use an expression of his own, 'massimamente inconveniente' from a poetical point of view. I do not for a moment suppose Dante would feel bound, as a poet, to take account of this logical inference from his data. Further, I maintain that such a 'poetic licence' would be entirely legitimate. It would exemplify the conditions so admirably laid down by Aristotle in the *Poetics* (c. xxiv): προαιρεῖσθαι δεῖ ἀδύνατα εἰκότα μᾶλλον ἢ δυνατὰ ἀπίθανα: or again, τοῖς ἄλλοις ἀγαθοῖς ὁ ποιητὴς ἀφανίζει ἡδύνων τὸ ἄτοπον (*ib.*). The licence which I am supposing— I mean the assumption that it was spring-time there also—

---

[1] *Vide supra*, p. 2.   [2] See illustrations of this, pp. 54 *n.* and 85.

would be exactly an 'ἀδύνατον εἰκός.' The reversal of the seasons in the other hemisphere, though well known to all moderately instructed people, is often not realized, and therefore the omission to take account of it in poetry would not produce any great shock. Thus I doubt not that the reports of the severe cold experienced by our soldiers in South Africa at 'midsummer' came as a gentle surprise to many who had not thought it out before[1]. I fancy too the idea is not uncommon that at the equator the sun is always directly overhead[2]. It is not in religious matters only that there is an important difference between knowing a thing and realizing it.

Let us take first the arguments derived from the position of the Moon in 1300 and 1301. One of the first applications of the principle just maintained is to determine whether, when Dante refers to the new or full moon, he is speaking of those phenomena as calculated by astronomical tables or by the ecclesiastical calendar. In the latter, with a view to the regulation of Easter, the times of new and full moon were determined by the use of some rough cycles (such as that to which our Golden Numbers refer), and the results varied from the truth sometimes as much as two or even three days[3]. In fact, in March and April 1300, there was an error of two days, and in 1301 one of three days, between the real moon and the ecclesiastical. The question is a vital one for the interpretation of the numerous passages in which time is indicated by the rising or setting or general position of the moon, since the above error would involve a difference of nearly two or nearly three hours, in 1300 and 1301 respectively, in the moon's position on any given day.

If it were urged (as an objection against the calendar moon) that the difference of about forty-eight hours in the moon's age would be patent to the eye, and that consequently Dante could not speak of the moon as full two days after it was really so, the answer is obvious. This would no doubt be

---

[1] I was told at the Cape that invalids often specially asked for rooms with a *south* aspect.

[2] Dante of course knew better. See *Conv.* II. v. 185 *seqq.*   [3] *Supra*, p. 86.

a weighty objection if Dante had said, in reference to some
definite historical event occurring at a known day and hour
in Florence or elsewhere, that he observed the full moon in
a certain position. But as the whole scene is fictitious and
imaginary the objection comes to nothing. Yet, imaginary
though it be, these astronomical landmarks, as they would be
naturally and popularly understood, serve to make everything
seem definite and lifelike, just as any other well-selected
features of detail impart an air of reality to a fictitious
narrative.

Now Prof. Angelitti starts with the assumptions (1) that
Dante's journey commenced not on the ecclesiastical Good
Friday of 1301, but on the 'ideal' Good Friday, i.e.
March 25; and (2) that his references are made to the
astronomical, and not to the calendar, moon[1]. Then, as the
astronomical full moon occurred on March 24 and in the
night between March 24 and March 25, Dante could say on
the morning of the 26th :—

' Già iernotte fu la luna tonda ' ;

and the other lunar references are found to give a consistent
scheme when thus interpreted. He then concludes triumphantly that they are wholly inconsistent in reference to the
year 1300. True, if the above assumptions are granted. But,
supposing we assume (1) that Dante's journey commenced on
the actual Good Friday of 1300, i.e. April 8, and (2) that his
references are to the calendar, and not to the astronomical,
moon, it so happens that we have just the same data to deal
with ; for on April 9, 1300, the moon (calendar) had also been
full ' iernotte,' and consequently the other lunar references are
equally intelligible[2].

So far then as concerns Dante's references to the moon,
I do not for a moment admit that the astronomical argument
tells against 1300, and I maintain further that the pair of
assumptions made in this case are in themselves more natural
and plausible than those made in the other. Very few of
Dante's readers would know anything about any other

---

[1] *Vide supra,* pp. 61, 86, and 146.
[2] See portions of the Calendars for 1300 and 1301 printed *infra,* p. 177.

Good Friday than that which was observed year by year by the authority of the Church. And as to the moon, I can scarcely imagine Dante's having intended by the 'full moon' anything but the full moon of the calendar, which any reader could verify for himself. Probably not one in twenty would know that there was any other full moon possible, and still less would be able to find out anything about it. As a matter of fact, it never occurred to any one to suspect any other view, until the question was raised by Giambullari about 230 years after Dante's death (1554).

Next, as to the argument to be derived from references to the position of the Sun. These do not seem to affect the main issue now before us as to the date assumed for the Vision, nor should we expect them to do so. They do, however, involve some curious problems which bear upon the general question whether Dante's astronomical references are to be interpreted as scientifically correct or as popularly understood. For example, on the latter supposition the sun entered Aries[1] on March 21, Taurus on April 21, and so on of succeeding signs. But, in strict fact, he entered the *sign* Aries on March 12, owing to the error in the Julian Calendar[2]; and the *constellation* Aries on about April 9, owing to the precession of the equinoxes[3]. Yet these astronomical *facts* would not be generally known or easily ascertained, nor could the actual position of the sun in either signs or constellations be at any time recognized by the eye[4]. On these grounds, then, I maintain that the popular interpretation of the sun's relation to the signs of the zodiac is much the more probable.

There is one passage relating to the sun, upon which this question has been definitely raised. The discussion seems to me to have an important bearing upon that of the principle to be applied to Dante's astronomical references generally. In *Inf.* i. 38 Dante says that the sun was rising in company with those stars that surrounded him when he was first created. If we understand this statement in a plain and popular sense, its meaning is perfectly obvious and free from any

---

[1] See on this *supra*, pp. 54 *n.* and 73.
[3] *Supra*, p. 64.
[2] *Vide supra*, p. 95.
[4] *Supra*, p. 50 *n.*

difficulty. It merely amounts to this. It was now the beginning of spring, as it was at the time of the Creation— it being the well-known belief of both mediaeval and classical writers that the world was created in the spring[1]. But, says Angelitti, owing to the precession of the equinoxes there has been a displacement (according to the data accepted by Dante) of more than 60° in the longitude of the stars between the Creation and the year 1300 A.D.[2]. If, therefore, the sun were among the stars of Aries *now*, either he could not have been so at his creation, or else it could not possibly have been about the spring equinox at both those epochs. In fact, if it were spring now, on this supposition the creation of the world would have been in the winter— an alternative gravely discussed by Angelitti—or if, on the other hand, the Creation were in spring, the position thus assigned to the sun would make it to be now summer. But worse still, Angelitti argues from *Convito* IV. v. 54–60, taken in connexion with *Par.* i. 37–42, that the sun was supposed by Dante to be at the first point of Aries at the time of our Lord's Incarnation[3]. If so, it could not be the spring equinox either at Creation or in 1300 if 'the same stars were with the sun' now. The puzzled astronomer is obliged to admit that Dante has fallen into some confusion between signs and constellations[4]. Rather, I should say, he never expects his readers to enter into such technical distinctions, and I would derive from the hopeless confusion which results from doing so another and a forcible argument for understanding such passages in a popular sense.

Next, as to the argument derived from the planets. Only three of these come into the question—Mars, Saturn, and

[1] *Vide supra*, p. 61. We may note in passing how these *a priori* methods of history land their authors in some curious entanglements. Thus some (e.g. Bede, Brunetto Latini, &c.) place the beginning of Creation on March 18 ('il primo dì del secolo,' as Brunetto calls it), in order to bring the Creation of the Sun to March 21. Others consider the 'first day' to be March 20, so as to make the Creation of Adam fall on the 25th, the day of the Annunciation, or the Incarnation of the 'Second Adam.' The Equinox also is, for *a priori* reasons, variously assigned to March 18, 21, or 25.

[2] Comp. *Conv.* II. xv. 113 *seqq.* as explained *supra*, p. 17.

[3] *Sulla data*, &c., p. 41.   [4] *Ibid.* p. 40.

Venus—for it is admitted that there is nothing to be said about Jupiter and Mercury. As to Mars, the argument of Angelitti seems to be extremely weak. As against 1300, it is urged that though Mars would be visible at dawn at Easter, 1300, when he rose about one and a half hours before the sun, yet Dante does not mention him in his famous description of the dawn in *Purg.* i. This is a mere 'argumentum e silentio,' as worthless as that argument generally is, or even more so than usual; for why must Dante needs have appended this mere astronomical fact to his splendid poetical picture? On the other hand, in March–April, 1301 Mars was in Leo. Now, though Saturn is declared to have been in that position (*Par.* xxi. 13), admittedly Dante never states this of Mars. Why, then, may we not now apply the 'argumentum e silentio' again as against the date 1301? Angelitti argues that the presence of Mars in Leo is in fact implied by the expression 'suo Leon,' when Cacciaguida says that at his birth Mars had returned, since the Incarnation, 580 times 'al suo Leon.' But the words obviously need have no such meaning as that which is thus conveniently attributed to them. Indeed, they are generally, and much more naturally, understood to refer to the affinity between the qualities of the Lion and the attributes of the God of War. In any case, the argument, as bearing on the date of the year, is of the flimsiest description.

Next, as to Saturn. In *Par.* xxi. 13–15 the fact that Saturn was in Leo is distinctly stated. But this was equally the case in 1300 and 1301, since Saturn, with his 'year' of about twenty-nine years, takes nearly three of our years to traverse a single sign [1]. Angelitti, however, lays stress on the phrase by which Dante describes the position of Saturn as being 'sotto il petto di Leone.' Now (he argues) 'il petto di Leone' suggests 'Cor Leonis,' the name by which the principal star Regulus is familiarly known. It turns out by calculation that in 1300 Saturn was about 11° distant from that star, in front of it, i.e. eastwards, while in 1301 he was only about 3° distant behind it, i.e. westwards. This is ingenious, no

---

[1] See *Conv.* II. xiv. 227-9.

doubt; but, if we are to be bound by such minutiæ at all, let it be observed that '*petto* di Leone' is not equivalent to '*Cor* Leonis.' Now, if any one will look at a star-map or celestial globe, he will see at once that when Saturn was 10° within the constellation, as he was in March, 1300, he would be much more accurately described as being 'sotto il petto di Leone' than when (as in 1301) he had advanced to the distance of 24°. Also, though then nearer '*Cor* Leonis,' he would have passed beyond it, and also be slightly above it, and so he would no longer be '*sotto* il petto di Leone,' whether *petto* be translated 'breast' or 'heart.' The argument from Saturn, therefore, whatever may be its value, appears to be decidedly in favour of 1300 rather than 1301. The force of this argument will be seen at once from the following diagram:

* *Regulus*	S^0 *Saturn in* 1300
	S^1 ,, ,, 1301

We now come to the stronghold of Angelitti's astronomical case [1], the position of the planet Venus. Every one will remember the lovely picture of the cloudless dawn of 'orient sapphire' at the beginning of the *Purgatorio* which describes how Venus—

'Lo bel pianeta che ad amar conforta' (i. 19) —

was shining so brilliantly as to quench the light of the feeble stars of the constellation Pisces which were in her train. Now, in fact, about Easter, 1300, Venus was not in the sign Pisces at all, but in Taurus, and consequently she was behind

---

[1] 'La pietra angolare della ricerca scientifica dell' anno della visione ' (*op. cit.* p. 62).

and not before the sun, and was, therefore, an evening, and not a morning, star. But at that time in 1301 the conditions described by Dante were exactly fulfilled. If, therefore, Angelitti's initial assumption be admitted, that all astronomical statements in the poem are to be treated as scientifically accurate, *cadit quaestio*, and there is nothing more to be said.

It is quite true that if Dante were describing an actual historical event, and made such an assertion as this, it might then be fairly employed as a test of his accuracy and trustworthiness. If, for instance (as I believe happened during the Crimean war), a letter 'from our own correspondent' described the effect of radiant moonlight on a battlefield when the moon was proved to have been nearly new, the genuineness of the whole narrative would fall under deserved suspicion. But the case is different if even an historical event is professedly made the subject of a poetical composition. Thus, when the author of the well-known poem on 'The Burial of Sir John Moore' adds to the pathos of the scene by the help of ' the struggling moonbeam's misty light,' no reasonable person would think the worse of him because some pedantic critic has objected that on the night of January 16, 1809, the moon was only one day old [1]!

But in the case of this scene in Dante such criticism would be even more unreasonable, seeing that the whole scene is purely imaginary. For Dante never saw the dawn that Easter morning in Purgatory, and if he saw it anywhere else, there is no reason to suppose that the date had for him at the time such a profound significance in reference to his great work as to have impressed all its details upon him so minutely for years afterwards. He is surely but describing an ideally and typically perfect dawn, combining all the features of beauty and splendour naturally or poetically associated with

---

[1] The poet apparently should have taken a lesson from Bottom the Weaver and his company in *Midsummer Night's Dream*, Act III, Scene I :—

Snug. Doth the moon shine that night ?

Bottom. A calendar ! a calendar ! look in the almanac ; find out moonshine, find out moonshine.

such a scene [1]. To say that a poet must verify the position of
Venus at an assumed date before he can put 'the bright and
morning star' into his picture, would surely be (to borrow an
expression of Metastasio) 'confondere il vero col verisimile.'
Supposing we had the weather reports of that period, we
might fear that those who would impose such fetters as these
on the poet's fancy might perhaps discover that on that
Easter morning in 1300 the sky was overcast, while this was
not the case in 1301 !

There is, doubtless, a degree of astronomical accuracy which
Dante would certainly never have disregarded. If Venus
were then a morning star, she would naturally and certainly
be in the sign Pisces. The picture is in this way astronomically exact, and we feel sure that Dante would never, for
either pictorial or poetical effect, have placed the planet in an
impossible position [2]. The liberty he has taken is no more
than that of a painter who should move the position of a tree
or a house in a landscape to improve the composition of
his picture.

But, in spite of the difference in the principles from which
we start, I confess that we should feel seriously shaken if, as
Angelitti triumphantly declares, all the astronomical data of
the poem are precisely suitable ('s' accordano a capello') with
the conditions of 1301, and are totally at variance with those
of 1300. The cumulative force of such an argument would
be very strong, especially if, as Angelitti calculates, the
chances are more than 250,000 to 1 against such a series
of coincidences being reached undesignedly ! But we have
found on examination, first, that the lunar references are quite
as consistent with one year as the other, if different days
be assumed for the commencement of the vision : next, that
the arguments derived from Mars and Saturn come absolutely to nothing—nay, rather, as regards Saturn, that they
even seem to point distinctly the other way. There remains

---

[1] Nor can it be thought inconsistent with this supposition (as has been
suggested) that Dante again alludes to this feature of the dawn in *Purg.* xxvii.
94-6. Having once put it into his picture, he naturally 'sticks to it.'

[2] *Vide supra*, p. 58, on a comparison with Milton in this.

in fact only one astronomical difficulty (if, indeed, it be a difficulty at all) against 1300, and that single point is the position of the planet Venus. That, no doubt, would be crucial if we are to interpret a highly poetical passage with rigid scientific accuracy ; but it loses all its force unless that assumption be granted ; and, in any case, the *cumulative* force of the astronomical argument has entirely disappeared, since we have shown that Venus is the only heavenly body whose position would favour 1301.

Another class of arguments must not be overlooked, viz. that there seem to be several special reasons for the selection of the year 1300 by Dante. (1) It was the year naturally and popularly associated with a new century, as we have lately discovered by experience, since the nineteenth-century public needed a good deal of educating out of this notion [1]. (2) It was the year of the Great Jubilee, the *Anno Santo* ; and we cannot doubt that Boniface designed to mark thus the inauguration of a new era. (3) It was, as we have seen, almost certainly the year of the 'mezzo cammin' of Dante's own life—the year in which he passed the summit of the 'arco di nostra vita.' It was fitting that this should mark the turning-point in his moral and spiritual experience also. (4) It was the year of his fatal Priorate, to which he attributed all the subsequent misfortunes of his life. Lionardo Bruni professes to have seen the letter in which Dante made this statement.

In conclusion, I must again state my conviction that, if we interpret all such passages as those which we have been discussing, whether historical or astronomical, in their plain *prima facie* and (if the term may be ventured on) 'popular' sense, there is really no serious difficulty whatever in explaining every thing throughout consistently with the assumption of the year 1300, and, I would also add, with the initial date of the Good Friday of that year, April 8. When Dante speaks of Good Friday and Easter (whatever be the year), we

---

[1] Heine followed the popular view, since, having been born on the night between December 31, 1799 and January 1, 1800, he claimed to be considered 'one of the first men of the nineteenth century.'

should naturally suppose him to mean those days as commonly observed, and as familiar to all Christian people. And when he refers to the Moon and her phases, or to the equinox, &c., it seems to me to be equally natural that he should mean these and similar terms as they would be ascertained by his readers from the calendars or manuals in general use. But if we allow ourselves to be entangled in the scientific intricacies of Julian, sidereal, and tropical years (as Angelitti in several places demands)—and this, too, in combination with the varying uses of Rome, Florence, Pisa, &c., especially in reference to a period of the year admittedly close to the critical periods of Easter and the equinox—then we can more or less plausibly make out of the materials almost anything we please, within the narrow limits of the rival dates under discussion.

And when, further, we find that not only the data of astronomical statements and chronological computations may be thus variously understood and applied, but that even seemingly plain allusions to historical events yield themselves so readily to the manipulation of rival theorists, we feel almost inclined to take leave of the question in despair, with the cynical admission that 'there is nothing more deceptive than figures, except facts'!

P.S.—I am glad to find that Prof. D'Ovidio, in his recently published volume of *Studi*, strongly maintains the view which has been here advocated. I recognize this the more gladly because in a later Essay I am reluctantly compelled to differ very emphatically from that distinguished scholar.

TABLE I.

Calendars of 1300 and 1301.

March.		1300.	March.		1301.
21	M	SPRING EQUINOX	21	T	SPRING EQUINOX
22	T	New Moon (Real)	22	W	
23	W		23	TH	
24	TH	New Moon (Calendar)	24	F	Full Moon (Real)
25	F	*Annunciation*	25	S	*Annunciation*
26	S		26	☉	*Palm Sunday*
27	☉	*Passion Sunday*	27	M	Full Moon (Calendar)
28	M		28	T	
29	T		29	W	
30	W		30	TH	
31	TH		31	F	*Good Friday*
April.			*April.*		
1	F		1	S	*Easter Eve*
2	S		2	☉	*EASTER DAY*
3	☉	*Palm Sunday*	3	M	
4	M		4	T	
5	T	Full Moon (Real. 3 a.m.)	5	W	
6	W		6	TH	
7	TH	Full Moon (Calendar)	7	F	
8	F	*Good Friday*	8	S	
9	S	*Easter Eve*	9	☉	
10	☉	*EASTER DAY*	10	M	

TABLE II.

The following Table (reprinted from my *Time References, &c.*) will show at a glance the synchronous hours at different places according to Dante's system of geography (*v. supra*, pp. 128, 146, 167, 168):—

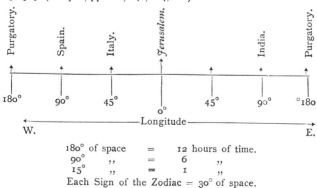

180° of space	=	12 hours of time.
90° ,,	=	6 ,,
15° ,,	=	1 ,,

Each Sign of the Zodiac = 30° of space.

* * *

IV. SYMBOLISM AND PROPHECY IN
PURG. xxviii–xxxiii

PART I.   THE APOCALYPTIC VISION.
  II.   THE REPROACHES OF BEATRICE.
  III.   THE DXV PROPHECY.

PART I.

THE visions and prophecies contained in the last six Cantos of the *Purgatorio*, which I shall endeavour to explain in this Essay, involve confessedly some of the most difficult, if not quite the most difficult, problems of interpretation in the whole of the *Divina Commedia*.   As Professor Earle has observed, 'the whole section is obscure by reason of its continuously symbolic nature.'   We have to keep as it were our eyes and our ears open at every turn lest we may miss at any moment

'la dottrina che s' asconde
Sotto il velame degli versi strani.'

At the outset, I will point out that the scenes with which we have to deal fall under four main divisions :—

1. An allegorical Procession of the Church Militant, as she comes, so to speak, to meet the penitent sinner (typified by Dante) with her divine mysteries, scriptures, teaching, ecclesiastical authority, and means of grace (Cantos xxix. to xxx. 33).

2. An episode personal to Dante himself, which interrupts the further development of this Apocalyptic Vision ; viz. the Reproaches of Beatrice for his backsliding since her death. This is followed by his bitter penitence and confession, and this again by his complete forgiveness, and her reconciliation with him (Canto xxx. 34 to end of Canto xxxi).

3. The resumption of the Apocalyptic Vision, setting forth in a series of *tableaux* the principal vicissitudes of the Church's

history in the past, and the troubles impending over her in the near future—future, that is, to 1300, the assumed date of the Vision (Canto xxxii).

4. A confident prophecy of speedy deliverance and of a special divinely-sent champion who should restore both the fallen Church and the fallen Empire (Canto xxxiii).

It may be well for the sake of readers not thoroughly familiar with the plan of the *Purgatorio* to explain briefly the position occupied by these last six Cantos in the scheme of the poem.

At the end of the twenty-seventh Canto, Virgil, in a singularly beautiful and justly celebrated passage, takes his leave of Dante as his guide. Dante has been conducted through all the seven Terraces of the Mountain of Purgatory, and all of the 'marks on his forehead,' representing the effects of the Seven Deadly Sins, have been successively wiped out. Henceforth, as Virgil says, he may fearlessly follow the guidance of his restored and purified will, which can no longer lead him astray. Thus having regained, as in a figure, the primaeval innocence of our first Parents before the Fall, he enters into the Earthly Paradise. This is conceived by Dante as occupying a sort of table-land on the summit of the Mountain of Purgatory. It affords the opportunity for some of the sweetest and most perfect descriptions of natural scenery to be found in all poetry. At the beginning of Canto xxviii, we find Dante wandering leisurely at his will through this 'Paradise of delights.' He soon comes upon a gently flowing stream of surpassing clearness which is afterwards explained to be the rivulet of Lethe, by which even the *remembrance* of all evil is washed away, just as its guilty stain had already been removed by the purgatorial sufferings of the Mountain below. On the opposite side he sees a maiden alone, 'gathering flowers in a flowery land' (xxviii. 40). She turns out to be the guardian of the Earthly Paradise, just as Cato had been of the lower regions of the Mountain. It is only in xxxiii. 119, when her name is once casually mentioned by Beatrice as Matelda, that we gain any hint as to her identity. So little however does this help us, that the

name has given rise to one of the most interminable and
voluminous controversies of the whole *Divina Commedia*.
I do not propose to enter upon this here[1]. About a dozen
different theories have been held as to her identification, and
there is another large branch of the controversy dealing with
the further question, what does she symbolize?

My own opinion after much study of the dispute is that
the view most generally accepted both by ancient and modern
Commentators is correct, viz. that she is the Countess Matilda,
the friend and ally of Hildebrand. And, further, that she
is chosen as a symbol of the Active Life, forming, as it is
generally held, together with Beatrice as representing the
Contemplative Life[2], a pair of symbols, such as we find
repeated—though perhaps with a difference, as Mr. Ruskin
maintains—in Leah and Rachel in these Cantos, and in
Martha and Mary elsewhere, as in *Conv.* IV. xvii.

Dante had not wandered far alongside of this stream of
Lethe, going up the stream and accompanied step by step
by Matelda on the other bank[3], when he is startled by a
dazzling brightness and the sweet sound of singing (xxix. 34)
coming from the East, i. e. the special abode of God (*v. supra*,
p. 136). On its nearer approach, a wonderful vision discloses
itself, forming an allegorical representation of the Church
Militant. The interpretation of most of the details of this
part of the Vision is fairly obvious, and need not detain us
long. The procession is headed by seven golden Candlesticks, or rather by one Candlestick with seven branches like
that of the Jewish Temple. This is implied by the expression
'bello arnese' and the singular verb in l. 52 (comp. *Exod.*
xxv. 31 *seqq.*). The seven 'Candelabri' (l. 50) are afterwards
described as the standards of the advancing army (l. 79). It
is added that the flames of these seven Candles streamed out
like pennons behind them, further than the eye could reach,

---

[1] An analysis of the principal views with a brief discussion of the question
will be found *infra*, pp. 210-216.

[2] See further on this, Supplementary Note I (pp. 210-212).

[3]   'Allor si mosse contra il fiume, andando
                  Su per la riva, ed io pari di lei,
                  Picciol passo con picciol seguitando.' *Purg.* xxix. 7-9.

overshadowing the whole procession which followed (see xxix. 73–81). The allegorical significance of this will be apparent if we observe that the sevenfold Candlestick doubtless represents the 'seven Spirits of God [1]'; or, better perhaps, the Holy Spirit in His sevenfold operations; while the seven streamers indicate these operations or gifts [2] themselves, as proceeding from the Spirit. To the diffusion and the influence of these in the Church no limit can be set. Hence—

> 'Questi ostendali dietro eran maggiori
> Che la mia vista.' (xxix. 79, 80.)

These streamers of light varied in colour as the rainbow, or the lunar halo—

> 'tutte in quei colori
> Onde fa l' arco il sole, e Delia il cinto.' (ll. 77, 78.)

Beneath them, as beneath an overarching sky ('Sotto così bel ciel,' l. 82), the whole army moved, with its various figures symbolizing the Books of the Old and New Testaments. Thus signifying, that from the earliest days 'holy men of old spake as they were moved by the Holy Ghost'; and that 'every member of the Church in his vocation and ministry' acts both after the guidance, and also under the overshadowing influence, of the Spirit's operations [3].

[1] See *Rev.* i. 4; iv. 5, &c.

[2] The 'seven gifts of the Spirit' are distinguished and enumerated by Dante in *Conv.* IV. xxi. 108–112, following, as he says, the prophet Isaiah. The passage referred to is *Is.* xi. 2, 3. It is to be observed that the 'seven gifts' come out more clearly in the Vulgate than in E. V. But as the 'Seven Spirits' are in reality 'one and the selfsame Spirit,' so the 'seven gifts' are 'one gift,' since 'Charity' is the root of them all. See *Summa*, II[1]. lxviii. 5, r 'Sicut virtutes morales connectuntur sibi invicem in Prudentia [= φρόνησις in *Nic. Eth.* vi. 13], ita dona Spiritus Sancti connectuntur sibi invicem in Charitate: ita scilicet quod qui charitatem habet, omnia dona Spiritus Sancti habet, quorum nullum sine charitate haberi potest.' Comp. *Q.* lxv. *A.* 1, r. Dante also connects them all with 'Carità,' but by a somewhat different process, in *Conv.* IV. xxi. 105 *seqq.*

[3] It should be noted that several other explanations have been suggested for the seven Candlesticks. Thus Pietro di Dante offers a long list of alternatives such as (besides that given in the text)—the Seven orders of the Ministry; or 'the seven particular Churches of the Universal Roman Church,' as in Rev. i–iii; or the seven Articles of the Creed relating to the humanity of Christ, while the seven streamers of light denote seven other Articles relating to His Divinity. Buti suggests the seven Sacraments, to which Scartazzini objects that these were *after* Christ, whereas the gifts of the Spirit were in some sense in the Old Testament dispensation also, as the order of the Vision implies.

By the presence of every colour of the rainbow [1] we have symbolized the 'diversities of gifts,' just as the fact that 'all these worketh one and the selfsame Spirit' is signified by the seven 'Candelabri' forming one object, as already pointed out.

In line 81 we are told that the distance between the two outside of these streamers of light, was, as Dante estimated, ten paces. This figure is sometimes explained merely as indicating a 'perfect number.' I think it is more probable that it has reference to the Ten Commandments. All gifts of the Spirit include and bring about the fulfilment of the law, since (as we have seen), they all have Love as their common root, and 'love,' as S. Paul says, 'is the fulfilling of the law' (see *Rom.* xiii. 8–10). Some would compare with this the 'decimo passo' of Beatrice in xxxiii. 17, though I myself think (as will be seen later) that the interpretation there is quite different.

The Army itself, following these its standards, falls into three divisions:—(1) Vanguard ; (2) Centre ; (3) Rearguard.

(1) ll. 61–87. The Vanguard consists of allegorical figures representing the Books of the Old Testament. These are twenty-four elders clothed in white raiment, see l. 65, and compare *Rev.* iv. 4, from which the imagery is evidently borrowed. We need not here stop to examine the various devices of grouping by which the Old Testament Books are brought by different writers to the precise number of twenty-four [2].

(2) ll. 88–132. The *centre* of the Army. Here we find the Triumphal Car of the Church immediately flanked by the three

---

[1] The rainbow hues are also a feature in the Visions both of Ezekiel and S. John. See *Ezek.* i. 28, and *Rev.* iv. 3, and x. 1.

[2] The idea of associating the twenty-four Books of the Old Testament with 'the twenty-four elders' was probably derived by Dante from S. Jerome's 'Prologus Galeatus' to the LXX. We know that he was acquainted with these *Praefationes* from *Par.* vii. 3, and *Conv.* IV. v. 143 (see *Studies*, I. p. 60). Jerome makes twenty-two books thus: of Moses five books, of the Prophets, eight ; of Hagiographa, nine. Some, he adds, include Ruth and Cinoth (Lamentations) among the Hagiographa, 'et per hos esse priscae Legis libros viginti quatuor, quos sub numero viginti quatuor Seniorum Apocalypsis Ioannis inducit adorantes Agnum.' The Apocryphal Books are not included.

Evangelical Virtues on the right (l. 121) and the four Cardinal Virtues on the left (l. 130), and accompanied by the 'four Beasts' of the Apocalypse, and of the vision of Ezekiel, evidently symbolizing the four Gospels. These seem to have been placed at the four corners of the Car. This appears from the language of l. 106, 'Lo spazio *dentro a lor quattro* contenne Un carro,' 'The space between those four contained a car.' Compare 'they four,' 'ipsorum quattuor' in *Ezek.* i. 10. The Chariot is on two wheels, which have been very variously explained; but, perhaps on the whole, they most probably denote the Old Testament and New Testament, or rather perhaps the two Covenants corresponding to them. Yoked to the Chariot is a Gryphon or Griffin, i. e. a creature with the head and neck of an Eagle and the body of a Lion. This animal is generally supposed to represent Christ in His double nature, though the interpretation has been of late fiercely disputed.

I will not interrupt the general interpretation by a discussion of this thorny question here, but I propose to return to it later on, and to justify my conclusion that the common interpretation is most certainly the correct one.

(3) The third division, or the *rearguard* of the Army, consists of seven figures evidently representing the remaining Books of the New Testament in seven groups. (1) The Acts, under a figure easily recognizable as S. Luke (l. 136); (2) the Pauline Epistles—including of course 'Hebrews'— represented by S. Paul (l. 139); (3, 4, 5, 6) the Catholic Epistles, treated as four, since they had four different authors, viz. SS. James, Peter, John, and Jude. They are described as 'in umile paruta' (l. 142) 'of humble aspect' as being shorter than most of the previous books; (7) the Apocalypse, represented by an old man 'fallen into a trance but having his eyes open,' for so we may paraphrase l. 144 :—

'. . . dormendo, con la faccia arguta.'

Let us now notice the elaborate and beautiful symbolism of the colours assigned to these various mystical figures. Professor Earle has drawn special attention to it [1]. It will, of

---

[1] See *Introduction*, p. xl.

course, be remembered that white is the recognized colour to symbolize faith ; green, hope ; and red, charity or love. All the figures alike were clothed in white garments, partly as it is the colour in which the Saints are always represented in the Book of Revelation, and also as it symbolizes Faith, which is common to them all alike (see especially ll. 65 and 145 taken together). But note carefully the distinction in their crowns. The twenty-four elders representing the Old Testament Books have also crowns of white lilies (l. 84), for 'these all died in Faith, not having received the promises.' The four living creatures representing the Evangelists are crowned with green leaves, the colour of Hope (l. 93). They represent 'the bringing in of a better Hope' ; and their main purpose is to make known to us 'Christ who is our hope.' Finally, the seven figures representing the later Books of the New Testament, though still clothed in white, are crowned with a perfect thicket (*brolo* [1]) of roses and other red flowers, so that 'at a little distance one might have sworn that their heads were all on fire' (ll. 145–150). In this is clearly sym- bolized the supreme Evangelical Virtue of Charity or Love. So again, ll. 121–126, the three maidens on the right of the Car symbolizing the three Evangelical Virtues are clothed in these three colours, one as red as fire, the second green as an emerald, and the third as white as newly fallen snow. Here we recognize obviously Charity, Hope, and Faith. But further, there is, as it appears to me, a very beautiful piece of symbolism, the point of which is often missed, in the colour of 'purple' with which the four Cardinal Virtues on the left of the Car are clothed (see l. 131). The very lame explana- tion of this commonly given is, that purple is the regal or imperial colour which is assigned to the Cardinal Virtues, because they govern and regulate human conduct (κύριαι τοῦ βίου). I believe the explanation to be something very different and much more significant. It could be shown by a great many illustrations that 'purple' in Dante's time was the name given to deep red. In fact purple is always an admix- ture of red and blue, and so may range from deep red to

---

[1] See Supplementary Note on 'brolo,' *infra*, p. 216.

violet. In our modern usage the blue generally predominates, but in mediaeval and in classical times the red largely predominated ; and thus the term was commonly applied to what we should call 'lake,' or even to 'crimson,' or 'carmine.'

Thus 'purple' is found as an epithet of roses, poppies, blood, and even of the blush upon a maiden's cheek! It is applied so commonly to 'the *roseate* hues of early dawn' that 'purpureus' is almost an 'epitheton ornans' of the Dawn [1]. Even 'scarlet' itself is sometimes interchanged with 'purple.' The 'scarlet robe' of mockery in S. Matthew is a 'purple robe' in S. Mark and S. John. A comparison of two passages in the *Convito* and *V. N.*[2] shows that Dante describes the same phenomenon as *purpureo* in one place and *rubicondo* in the other.

But to return to the text. These four figures then representing the Cardinal Virtues were clothed not in pure red, but in a mixed colour, of which red was the foundation and chief ingredient. If so, is not the meaning this—and a beautiful piece of symbolism I think it is—that even in the Cardinal Virtues, Charity or Love must be the prevailing feature? It must form their foundation, though it is only to be found pure and unalloyed in the crowning Virtue of the Gospel. This view receives a strong confirmation from the teaching of S. Thomas in the *Summa*. He says (II [1]. lxv. 2) that the Moral or Cardinal Virtues, up to a limit 'qui non excedit facultatem naturalem hominis, possunt per opera humana

---

[1] e. g. Ovid, *Met.* ii. 112 :—

> '*rutilo* patefecit ab ortu
> *Purpureas* Aurora fores, et plena *rosarum*
> Atria.'

In *Met.* vi. 46 a blushing maiden is thus described :—

> 'Ut solet aer
> *Purpureus* fieri cum primum Aurora movetur,
> Et breve post tempus candescere solis ab ortu.'

It is interesting to compare these two stages of colour in the dawn with the three recognized by Dante in *Purg.* ii. 7-9 :—

> 'Sì che le bianche e le vermiglie guance,
> Là dove io era, della bella Aurora
> Per troppa etate divenivan rance.'

Here the dawn is pale before sunrise, then red, and finally orange.

[2] *Conv.* III. ix. 135, and *V. N.* § xl. 33. These and several more illustrative passages will be found collected in a Supplementary Note, p. 218.

acquiri, et sic acquisitae sine charitate esse possunt,' but, in their highest degree, and as inspired by God's help, ' huius-modi virtutes morales sine charitate esse non possunt,' and again (*ad fin.*),' prudentia dependet a charitate . . . et per consequens omnes virtutes morales infusae ' (*sc.* a Deo). Compare 1 *Cor.* xiii. 1–3. Such I believe to be the symbolism involved in Dante's choice of ' purple ' robes for these four emblematical figures.

As I have mentioned S. Thomas, I will point out one or two other points on which Dante seems to have been indebted to him in his description of these two groups of Virtues. Of the group on the right we are told (ll. 127–130) that sometimes Faith takes the lead and sometimes Charity, but it is not said that Hope ever does so. As Cary paraphrases it—' Faith may be produced by Charity, or Charity by Faith, but the inducements to Hope must arise from one or the other of these.' This idea again may have come direct from Aquinas [1]. The same may be said of a similar statement made as to the relations of the group of the Cardinal Virtues on the left, that the same one always takes the lead, viz. ' Prudentia.' That is said almost in as many words in the *Summa*, though doubtless Dante might have derived the thought, as S. Thomas himself did, from Aristotle [2].

There is another point to be noticed respecting the symbolism of colour here. When Beatrice, as the type of Theology or Divine Revelation, descends on to the Car (xxx. 31–33) all the three colours are represented in her clothing ; but, as Professor Earle has remarked, green, the colour of hope, is

---

[1] See II². xvii. 7, r ' Fides absolute praecedit spem.' We cannot *hope* for anything (he proceeds) unless we *believe* it to be possible. Again, in Art. 8, r_1 ' In via generationis spes est prior charitate. (i.e. secundum quem [ordinem] imperfectum prius est perfecto) . . . Sed secundum ordinem perfectionis charitas est prior naturaliter.' And again, ' Spes et omnis motus appetitivus ex amore provenit aliquo, quo scilicet aliquis amat bonum expectatum ' (*ib.* r_2). See further II¹. xl. 7.

[2] See II¹. lxv. 1 ' nulla virtus moralis potest sine prudentia haberi . . . similiter etiam prudentia non potest haberi nisi habeantur virtutes morales '; and again, *ib.* r_4 ' Ea ad quae inclinant virtutes morales, se habent ad prudentiam sicut principia.' See also *Conv.* IV. xvii. 76–84 where Dante, following Aristotle, shows ' Prudenza' to be the Intellectual quality common to all Moral Virtues.

most prominent, since it occurs twice, viz. in her mantle and also in her crown [1]. We may note further that when her unveiled eyes are at last revealed to Dante (in xxxi. 116) they are described as ' emeralds ' ; the force of the symbolism overpowering other considerations [2], or, as Dante would say, the ' literal and fictitious ' sense is here swallowed up in the ' allegorical and true [3].' And this association of Hope with Beatrice is further illustrated by *Par.* xxxi. 79, when Dante addresses her as

'O Donna, in cui la mia *speranza* vige.'

I think it is worth remarking that though Beatrice appears in the *Vita Nuova* sometimes in white and sometimes in red [4], she is never (unless I am mistaken) associated with green. This is suitable to a work in which the tone throughout is one of disappointment and even despair.

This will suffice to explain the general features of this first part of the Vision. Well worthy of remark is the very great prominence here given by Dante to Holy Scripture in the economy of the Church, which seems to be altogether ' founded upon the Apostles and Prophets.' This is entirely in accordance with the profound reverence for the supreme authority and dignity of Holy Scripture exhibited by Dante both in the *Divina Commedia* and in his other writings. I have shown by many quotations in my second volume of *Studies* [5] that scarcely any ' Protestant' could go further than Dante in the language which he uses in regard to the Bible.

The next Canto (xxx) opens with the descent of Beatrice from Heaven greeted by clouds of angels with songs of welcome [6] and the scattering of flowers. She takes her stand

---

[1] *Introduction*, &c., pp. lix, lx.

[2] At the same time (as Longfellow points out in his note, *h. l.*) green eyes, ' ojuelos verdes,' are extolled by Spanish poets. Also my friend Mr. Vernon quotes Shakespeare, *Romeo and Juliet*, Act III, Scene 5 :—

'an eagle, madam,
Hath not so green, so quick, so fair an eye
As Paris hath.'

[3] See *Conv.* II. xiii. 1–3, and 61–65.

[4] e.g. *white* in §§ iii. 6 ; xxiii. 52 and 65 ; *red* in §§ ii. 15-17 ; iii. 38 ; xl. 5, 6.

[5] pp. 34–37.

[6] I do not myself doubt, though I am aware that it is a disputed point, that

upon the Car of the Church as the central figure of the whole scene. The symbolism of Beatrice both here and elsewhere (as in the case of several other of Dante's principal symbols, as well as those of other writers sacred and profane who adopt this method of teaching) is complex, and can scarcely be given in a single word, since different aspects of such symbols come into prominence at different times. Thus Beatrice often symbolizes Theology, not as a scientific system, but rather in its aspect of Revelation, or Revealed Truth. Further, as the Church is the 'keeper and witness' of Revelation which is guarded and dispensed by Ecclesiastical Authority, that embodiment of Authority is sometimes represented by Beatrice. Following on from this to a still more definite and concrete symbol, she sometimes stands, as in some parts of the Vision now under consideration, as the representative of the ideal Papacy, which guides and governs humanity on its spiritual side as the Empire does on its temporal side, according to the theory expounded and defended by Dante in the *De Monarchia* (see on this *Studies*, II. pp. 13–34).

The question *how* Beatrice came to occupy so exalted a place in Dante's system of symbolism will best be considered under the second division of our subject, viz. the personal Episode of the 'Reproaches of Beatrice.' That is introduced in the poem at the point we have now reached, and occupies from xxx. 34 to the end of xxxi. After that, the development of the Apocalyptic Vision is resumed. I propose to continue here without a break the consideration of that subject, reserving to a separate division of this Essay the discussion of the personal episode in question.

Turning then now to Canto xxxii. l. 13, Dante's attention is directed to a new movement of the Celestial Army, which had halted [1] since the moment of the descent of Beatrice at the beginning of Canto xxx (see especially ll. 1–9). The

the greeting 'Benedictus qui venis' is addressed to Beatrice. It would have been scarcely possible to distort such very familiar words by adapting the gender to their present application.

[1] Observe that another Apocalyptic feature is that the close of that stage in the Vision is marked by the sound of thunder. See xxix. 152 and compare *Rev.* vi. 1 ; xvi. 18, and many other passages.

Vision so far has set forth in a figure the growth and constitution of the Church from the dawn of Revelation to the close of the Canon of Scripture. From this point we have depicted in a series of *tableaux* the principal episodes of her subsequent history up to Dante's own times, ending with the catastrophe of the Avignon captivity. After that, her future deliverance is set forth in the confident tones of a prophecy that was destined to remain unfulfilled.

First then (xxxii. 16) the Chariot turns to the right, which, besides the common symbolism of that direction in the *Divina Commedia*, may also mean that it rests mainly on the wheel representing probably the New Testament or the New Covenant. It will be remembered that it first came from the east, and moved westwards (see xxix. ll. 12, 34). It now proceeds through the north, eastwards (xxxii. 18). As it came forth from God, so it now returns towards God. The vanguard naturally wheeled round first, and afterwards when this movement was completed[1], the pole of the chariot itself turned round, drawn by the Gryphon, ' without moving a feather ' (ll. 22–27); this probably to indicate that in Christ there is ' no variableness nor shadow of turning[2].' Matelda, Statius, and Dante followed beside the right wheel (ll. 28–30); and so they traversed the deserted forest of Paradise till they came to the Tree of Knowledge ' in the midst of the Garden ' (ll. 31–36). The lower branches were utterly stripped and bare, but its foliage spread out more and more towards the top which rose to an inaccessible height. The name of Adam is uttered in reproach by the whole company; while the Gryphon is blessed in like manner for abstaining from injuring it (ll. 37–45). It is added, in evident recollection of *Ezek.* iii. 1–3 and *Rev.* x. 9, 10, that it is sweet to the taste, but bitter afterwards to the belly. (The symbolism of the Tree generally will be discussed presently.) The Gryphon replies in effect, and (as I should say) with a very obvious reference to the words of Christ in *Matt.* iii. 15,

---

[1] A reminiscence perhaps of Dante's soldiering days. Compare *Inf.* xxi. 94–96 ; xxii. 1–12.

[2] Or, as Dean Plumptre suggests, that when the Church is guided by Christ there is perfect tranquillity.

' Thus it becometh us to fulfil all righteousness.' This reference has, I know, been disputed [1], but it seems to me very
clear, especially when we note how closely ' omnem iustitiam '
in the Vulgate corresponds with ' ogni giusto ' here. Similarly I have no doubt that ' quanto è giusto ' in *Purg.* xxiv.
154 represents ' iustitiam ' in the fourth Beatitude (*Matt.* v.
6). Next the Gryphon draws out the pole from the Chariot
and binds it to the Tree, from the wood of which, as Dante
adds, it was originally made [2].

'E quel di lei a lei lasciò legato.' (l. 51.)

This would seem to be the appropriate place to deal with
the question of the symbolism of the Gryphon, and to give
my reasons for adhering, as I do most unhesitatingly, to the
commonly accepted view that it is a figure of Christ. This
opinion has lately been subjected to a very powerful attack
by Professor Earle, with whom I regret in this or any matter
to find myself in disagreement. I wish here to avoid, as far
as possible, direct controversy, and to aim at establishing my
own opinion without attacking, more than is absolutely
necessary, those of others.

1. The language of xxxi. 81 seems to me almost con-

---

[1] Professor Earle lays the greatest emphasis on the absurdity and utter
unreasonableness of supposing this text to be referred to. But it is surely not
a little remarkable that on the one other occasion on which Dante quotes this
text it is precisely in this application. Dante argues that Christ would not
have submitted Himself to the authority of the Empire by being born at the
moment when His enrolment under the 'Census' was the result, if the authority
of the Empire had been unjust, since it became Him ' to fulfil all righteousness.'
Now the Tree here which the Gryphon is blessed for having respect to, as we
shall see directly, is certainly in one aspect a symbol of the Empire. But after
all it is by no means *necessary* that we should assume the text to be referred to.
For the Empire itself might surely be called by Dante 'il seme d' ogni giusto,'
i. e. the seed, source, origin, or fount of all right and justice upon the earth.
Seed is the particular metaphor chosen here, as being most akin to the symbol
of the Tree. But let any one read *De Mon.* I. xi. and he will see how 'iustitia'
(or ' ogni giusto ') is associated by Dante with the idea of the Empire as of
necessity. In that case the meaning would be that by the abstention of Christ
and His Church from meddling with the 'things of Caesar,' the Empire as the
source of all 'iustitia' is safeguarded. Comp. *Mon.* III. xv. and xvi.

[2] Some account of this legend will be found in a supplementary note,
infra, p. 219.

clusive. To whom or to what else could these words be applied :—

> ' Ch' è sola una persona in due nature ' ?

It is quite theological in its precision, and with it we may compare *Par.* xiii. 26, 27 :—

> ' Ma tre Persone in divina natura
> Ed in una persona essa e l' umana.'

2. The combination of the two highest types of animal nature, the eagle, of those that ' move in the open firmament of heaven,' and the lion, of those that walk upon the earth, is very suitable to represent the divine and human natures respectively [1]. Compare 2 *Sam.* i. 23 *fin.*

3. The symbolism of the colours in this mystic animal is equally appropriate. See xxix. 113, 114. The Eagle, or divine part, had ' its feathers like gold.' In the Lion, or human part, white and scarlet were mingled, the colours, that is, that symbolize Faith (or Trust) and Love.

Professor Earle objects that ' Faith ' cannot be attributed to Christ. Perhaps not in any narrow or technical theological sense, but in its grand primitive meaning of *Trust*, so prominent in the Epistles to the Romans and Hebrews and in the New Testament generally, nothing could be more appropriate to the human nature of Christ, or to Christ as Man upon the Earth. Most truly, though in mockery, was it said, ' He trusted in God.' At the moment of His capture, when He was most apparently helpless and deserted, He declared that God would at once, if He asked for it, give Him ' more than twelve legions of angels.' Did He not solemnly and confidently thank God, for the sake of those who stood by, for hearing Him in the matter of the resurrection of Lazarus, *before* that stupendous miracle occurred, and *before* there was any indication of its likelihood ? But surely

---

[1] The comparison of our Lord to a Lion is not uncommon, the idea being probably suggested by ' the Lion of the tribe of Judah ' in *Rev.* v. 5 ; that to an Eagle is less frequent, but it is found in Ambrose, *Serm.* xlvii. in a strangely fanciful exposition of *Prov.* xxx. 19, 20 (ed. Migne, xvii. p. 701). Also Isidore in *Orig.* VII. ii. 43, 44, states that Christ is compared to (among several other creatures) the Lion, ' pro regno et fortitudine ' ; and the Eagle, ' propter quod post resurrectionem ad astra remeavit.'

one need not labour further so obvious a point that Trust in God, as well as Love, is a characteristic of the human nature of Christ.

4. These colours of the Gryphon are generally thought to have reference, besides the propriety of symbolism already claimed, to those by which the Bridegroom is described in *Cant.* v. 10, 11: ‘My beloved is white and ruddy, the chiefest among ten thousand. His head is as the most fine gold.’ If this were in Dante’s thoughts, there can at any rate be no doubt as to his acceptance of the common identification of the Bridegroom (who is thus described) with Christ. See *Mon.* III. iii. 79, where *Cant.* i. 3 is quoted: ‘Hoc est quod dicit Ecclesia, loquens ad Sponsum: Trahe me post te,’ language which corresponds exactly with the definite imagery of the present passage. Or again see *Conv.* II. vi. 34, where *Cant.* viii. 5 is quoted with the same explicit application to ‘Santa Chiesa,’ ‘la sua Sposa e Secretaria’ (*sua* referring to ‘nostro Salvatore’ in l. 26).

5. Next observe the significance of the following statements. The eyes of Beatrice were always fixed steadfastly on the Gryphon (xxxi. 120). When Dante looked upon the eyes of Beatrice all that he could see was the image of the Gryphon reflected like the sun in a mirror, and sometimes the divine and sometimes the human actions were thus presented, itself remaining the while impassive and unchanged (ll. 121–126). Remembering that the *eyes* either of Theology or Philosophy represent their *demonstrations*, as is explained in *Conv.* III. xv. 12 *seqq.* and IV. ii. 145, the meaning of the symbolism in this passage of the *Purgatorio* is too obvious to need explanation. But a striking comment on it may be found in the declaration of *Mon.* III. xv. 14: ‘Forma Ecclesiae nihil aliud est quam vita Christi, tam in dictis quam in factis comprehensa’; and again (l. 48): ‘Formale igitur est Ecclesiae, illud idem dicere, illud idem sentire.’

6. As a friend has pointed out to me, the imagery of Christ as ‘in medio septem candelabrorum’ (*Rev.* i. 13), and as one ‘qui ambulat in medio septem candelabrorum’ (*Rev.* ii. 1), is vividly reproduced here, if the Gryphon be Christ. See

xxix. 50, and 73 *seqq.*; also 109–111, where his uplifted wings are represented as rising between the drawn-out flames of the seven Candlesticks.

7. If the usual interpretation of xxxii. 48 as being equivalent to 'Thus it becometh us to fulfil all righteousness' be accepted, as I have already contended that it should be[1], I should see in it another argument for identifying the speaker with Christ. As the interpretation is disputed, I will lay no stress upon it; but it should be noted that, if the line be explained otherwise, no adverse argument arises.

8. Finally, I should like very pointedly to ask this question: If the Gryphon be not Christ, is it at all conceivable that Christ should be entirely omitted and ignored in this elaborate symbolical representation of the Church which He founded, and of which He is 'the chief corner-stone'?

Though desiring, as I have said, to avoid controversy as far as possible, I feel bound to deal with two further objections raised by Professor Earle beyond those already incidentally noticed, lest I should be thought to evade or ignore them.

i. In the passage referred to *supra*, under '5,' viz. *Purg.* xxxi. 121 *seqq.*, it will be observed that I paraphrased the words

'Or con uni or con altri reggimenti'

by 'sometimes the divine and sometimes the human *actions* were thus presented.' Professor Earle maintains that *reggimenti* must mean 'governments' or something like that[2], and points to *Purg.* xvi. 128, where it undoubtedly bears that meaning. It is true that his arguments are principally directed against the common translation of the word by 'natures,' in favour of which I have nothing to say. But as to the rendering 'actions,' let Dante be his own interpreter. In *Conv.* III. vii. 97 *seqq.* Dante describes the operations proper to 'a reasonable soul' as being specially speech (*parlare*), and also such acts (*atti*) as are usually termed 'reggimenti e portamenti,' i.e. *conduct* or *deportment*; and he goes on to state

[1] *Supra*, p. 190.   [2] *Introduction*, &c., p. lxxxix.

* * *

that man alone among animals speaks, and is capable of 'reggimenti e atti' which are called 'rational.' He proceeds further to show that no objection to this can be taken from the talking of magpies or parrots, or the apparently rational acts of monkeys, &c. His words are: 'Se alcuno volesse dire . . . che alcuna bestia fa *atti, ovvero reggimenti.*' To this he replies that it is not true in these cases, 'che parlino, *nè che abbiano reggimenti,* perocchè non hanno ragione[1].' From all this it is perfectly clear that he uses *reggimenti* as equivalent to 'rational actions,' or as we might perhaps say in one word, 'conduct.'

Thus we may say that when Christ performed miracles, or forgave sins, these are *reggimenti* belonging to His divine nature; and that when He endured pain, want, sorrow, weariness, we have *reggimenti* belonging to His human nature[2].

It should be added that even the sense in which *reggimenti* is used in *Purg.* xvi. 128, i. e. the kingly and priestly governments, would still be applicable to Christ in this passage, though I feel myself no doubt that the word is here used as in the passage cited from the *Convito.*

Let those who still feel any difficulty in accepting any sense but 'government' note how nearly the word 'conduct' comes to uniting in itself both the senses claimed for *reggimenti.*

ii. The other objection of Professor Earle which I desire to meet is this: that the image of Christ as yoked to the Car and drawing it is a menial and unworthy one. I cannot however see the smallest force in this, seeing that our Lord declared Himself to be among His disciples 'as he that serveth,' and also that the metaphor fitly embodies the ideas of leading and guiding on His part, and of following after Him on the part of the Church. Might not Dante also have in his mind some echo of the familiar words 'Trahe me post

---

[1] See further *V. E.* I. ii. 60-62, where these animals are said to imitate us 'in quantum *sonamus,* sed non in quantum *loquimur.*'

[2] I since find that Pietro di Dante (p. 520) gives precisely similar illustrations of the meaning of these words.

Te,' which he himself declares in the passage already cited from *Mon.* (III. iii. 79) to be spoken by the Church 'loquens ad Sponsum '?

But further let us note that Dante is careful not to represent Christ merely as any beast of draught or burden (as this objection implies), but as an ideal creature combining all the noblest qualities of animal life, those of the eagle and the lion (as we have seen), whereby the supreme dignity of His twofold nature is aptly symbolized.

And, besides all this, surely any teaching by parable, allegory, symbol, or metaphor is open to rather shallow objections of this kind, if the figure be followed out along lines of possible inference or casual association. It is enough if it conveys sufficiently well the main idea for which it is employed. It can never be suitable in every detail and in every aspect.

It is necessary next to say a few words on the very much disputed subject of the symbolism of the Tree, though we are not yet fully in possession of all the materials for working it out.

The Tree of Knowledge in the Garden of Eden was to our first Parents the type and symbol of Obedience—absolute unquestioning Obedience. Of all the trees in the garden they might freely eat, but of this they might not eat, nor even touch it. This seems to be the central thought connected with it by Dante. Hence it fitly provided the wood for the Cross (l. 51), the Cross being, as is generally held, symbolized by the pole attached to the bar of the chariot to which the Gryphon was bound. That the Cross was made from this Tree, the wood of which had been miraculously preserved for it, was a commonly received legend, though the actual form of it varies considerably [1].

The Cross, one need hardly point out, is most fitly associated with the idea of absolute Obedience. 'Christ was obedient unto death, even the death of the Cross.' 'He learned obedience by the things which He suffered.'

Also it will be remembered that the Tree in the Sixth Cornice, by means of whose tempting yet inaccessible fruits

[1] See further Supplementary Note IV, *infra*, p. 219.

the gluttonous are punished, is also expressly said to be an offshoot of this same forbidden Tree:—

> 'Legno è più su che fu morso da Eva
> E questa pianta si levò da esso [1].'

It enforces on them, as the tree itself did on our first Parents, the lesson of abstinence and self-restraint, which they had not learnt or practised in this life.

Next, observe that the form of growth of this tree, as well as that of the Tree in the Garden from which it sprung, is such that its fruit is inaccessible. Compare the description of the first Tree in the Sixth Cornice in *Purg.* xxii. 133–135 and the reasons for its shape, 'Cred' io perchè persona su non vada,' with xxxiii. 64–66 :—

> 'Dorme lo ingegno tuo, se non estima
> Per singular cagione essere eccelsa
> Lei tanto, e sì travolta nella cima.'

But in the second place the Tree evidently also symbolizes in this vision the Empire. In the *De Monarchia* Dante expounds his belief that the Empire was as much a divine institution as the Church; that it was quite as necessary for the guidance and well-being of humanity in things temporal as the Church in things spiritual (see especially III. xvi). It is both the duty and the privilege of all men to submit themselves in unquestioning obedience to the commands of the Empire (see *Mon.* I. viii, ix, xi, xiii) [2].

As the Tree was planted in the midst of the Garden, so is the Empire set up in the midst of the Earth. None may touch or harm or despoil it in any way; the impiety of such an act is an offence against God (see xxxiii. ll. 58, 59). So

---

[1] *Purg.* xxiv. 116, 117.

[2] It is also probable that this second line of symbolism may have been suggested to Dante by the Tree of Nebuchadnezzar's dream, which typified the universality of his dominion, see *Dan.* iv. 11, 'the height thereof reached unto heaven, and the sight thereof to the end of all the earth.' And again, in verse 22, [The Tree] 'is thou, O king ... for thy greatness is grown, and reacheth unto heaven, and thy dominion to the end of the earth.' The overshadowing form of the tree may also recall the idea of verse 12, 'The fruit thereof was much, and it was meat for all, the beasts of the field had shadow under it, the fowls of the heaven dwelt in the boughs thereof, and *all flesh was fed of it*.'

far as Dante has seen in his vision that such despoiling has
already occurred, he is bidden to describe it to men as a
repetition of the Sin of Adam (see ll. 57 and 61–63). Even
the Emperor himself may not despoil or diminish Imperial
rights as Constantine, for instance, did. He is forbidden
'*scindere* Imperium.' See *Mon.* III. x. 35 *seqq.* The presumption of such an action is there likened to the rendering
(*scindere*) of the 'tunica inconsutilis,' or 'seamless robe,' of
Christ. Compare with '*scindere* Imperium,' the words 'che
non *discindi*' in the present passage.

It is from this point of view especially that the Gryphon is
blessed, for not despoiling the Tree[1], though, side by side
with this, we may well see also an allusion to the perfect
obedience of the second Adam in contrast with the disobedience of the first Adam in relation to this same Tree.
It affords the key to many difficulties if we remember the
double character of the allegory or symbolism, and that not
only in the case before us but in many other similar passages.
Thus the second Adam not only (1) did not repeat the
disobedience of Adam[2], but also (2) respected the Imperial
authority. On the other hand, those who despoil the Empire
may be regarded as repeating the sin of Adam (see xxxiii.
57). So again the bareness of the lower branches and the
abundant foliage at the lofty top of the Tree may symbolize
both the inviolability of the Empire and the inaccessibility
of true knowledge ; as well as, besides, a contrast between the
worthlessness of all lower forms of knowledge and its ever
greater value as it rises towards God and heavenly things.

[1] In illustration of this, which I should take to be the principal line of interpretation here, let us note how repeatedly Dante insists upon this idea. He
argues Christ's unquestioning submission to the Empire and His recognition
of its authority, (1) from the fact that the 'fulness of time' when Christ was
born was just that of the first establishment of the Empire under Augustus ;
see *Mon.* I. xvi. 6–22 ; II. ix. 99–103 ; *Ep.* VIII. ii. 23 ; *Conv.* IV. v. 24 *seqq.* ;
(2) that He allowed Himself to be enrolled as a Roman citizen under the Census ;
see *Mon.* II. xii. 41 ; *Ep.* VII. iii. 64 ; (3) that He submitted Himself to the
authority of Pilate, recognizing that that authority was 'given him from above'
(*John* xix. 11). See *Ep.* V. x. 158 ; *Mon.* II. xiii. 38–49. See also the references to Orosius given in my *Studies*, I. p. 280, and vide *Legenda Aurea*, c. vi.
(p. 40, ed. Graesse).
[2] See *Rom.* v. 19, &c.

When in the passage still before us (xxxii. 49–51) the Gryphon is represented as attaching the pole of the Chariot (or, as we have interpreted it, Christ as attaching His Cross) to the mystic Tree, the allusion is probably to the union at Rome of the supreme seats of the Church and of the Empire; the Church of Peter and the Empire of Caesar being there, as it were, linked together. Coincidently with this happy union, the Tree at once significantly breaks forth with purple blossoms, the imperial colour,

'Men che di rose e più che di viole [1].' (xxxii. l. 58.)

i e. the Empire is invigorated with new life by its symbolized union with Christianity.

There is no point in objecting either (1) that the Empire did not become Christian till much later (Constantine), or (2) that no such renovation of it occurred even then. The passage is symbolical and ideal, as is also the harmony and peace on earth, probably figured by the tranquil and profound sleep into which Dante himself is immediately afterwards lulled by angelic songs of ineffable sweetness (ll. 61–63). By this, I say, is probably typified the peace on earth which the harmonious union of Church and Empire would portend for humanity, according to the teaching and belief of Dante, which is familiar to all readers

---

[1] The meaning of this description has been much disputed. It is not clear what is the quality to which *men* and *più* here refer. The context would seem to imply a reference to the colour of red, which is nowhere explicitly mentioned. If so, the words would describe aptly enough the hue of 'purple' as understood by Dante, in which the ingredient of red was less pure and unmixed than in 'rose-colour' and yet more prominent than in violet. [See the Supplementary Note on 'purple,' *infra*, p. 218.] I am quite at a loss to imagine how most (I believe) both of ancient and modern Commentators have supposed the blood of Christ, and perhaps of the early martyrs, to be indicated. Could Dante, with his wonderful eye for colour, possibly have given such an inappropriate description of the colour of blood! Contrast the language of *Purg.* ix. 101, 102 :—

'Porfido mi parea sì *fiammeggiante*
    Come sangue che fuor di vena spiccia ;'

or of *Inf.* xvii. 62 :—

'Vidine un' altra come sangue *rossa*.'

Mr. Ruskin, thinking mainly no doubt of the aspect of the mystic Tree in which it represents the (Apple?) Tree of the Temptation, is very enthusiastic over the beauty and accuracy of this description of *apple blossom*. 'It certainly (he says) would not be possible in words to come nearer to the *definition* of the exact hue'; and a good deal more to the same effect. (*Mod. Painters*, iii. p. 226.)

of the *De Monarchia*. Being aroused from this sleep by Matelda, he finds that the Gryphon and the mystic procession have disappeared, nor can he at first perceive Beatrice. Matelda points her out to him sitting upon the roots of the tree, and overshadowed by its new foliage (ll. 85–87). In other words, he sees the Church seated at Rome under the protecting shadow of the reinvigorated Empire. Such was at least the ideal purpose of God when Peter set up his throne beside that of Caesar[1]. The special aspect of the complex symbolism of Beatrice[2] that now becomes prominent is that of the Ecclesiastical Authority by which the Church is guided, in other words the ideal Papacy of the *De Monarchia*. She is left as Guardian of the Car, the Church (l. 95); and she is sitting upon the bare ground (l. 94), alone, except for the companionship of the seven Maidens representing the seven Virtues[3]. They have in their hands the lamps which can never be extinguished (l. 99); these representing either the undying light of each several virtue in constant exercise; or the seven gifts of the Spirit before symbolized by the branches of the candlestick; or, perhaps, also the seven Sacraments. We need not insist on any one of these interpretations so as wholly to exclude the others: a mistake which is often made in interpreting parabolic or allegorical teaching, and especially in the case of the latter, where the duplication of the meanings signified is very common[4]. The general meaning at any rate is clear enough. The primitive Church was poor like her Master; her Ruler had no palace or retinue of courtiers; no such were needed beyond the seven primitive and fundamental Virtues, and each 'a burning and a shining light.' Such was the Papacy in the ideal of Dante. What is here set forth in a figure is inculcated and expounded at length in the prose of the *De Monarchia*.

There is another point which may be noted here,

[1] See *Studies*, II. pp. 19, &c.

[2] *V. supra*, p. 188.

[3] There is great doubt as to the meaning of *vera* in this passage, but for our present purpose we need not discuss the point.

[4] As in the well-known instance of the Allegory of the Good Shepherd in S. John x.

though it arises out of an earlier passage, viz. xxxi. 107, 108—

> 'Pria che Beatrice discendesse al mondo
> Fummo ordinate a lei per sue ancelle.'

That is to say, the four Cardinal Virtues had been ordained to be the handmaids of Beatrice before she came down upon the earth.   In other words, before the explicit Revelation of the Gospel, 'God left not himself without witness.'   As 'the Law was our schoolmaster to bring us to Christ,' so for the world at large the practice of the four Cardinal Virtues was a preparation for the higher Christian ideal to be exhibited in the three Evangelical Virtues.   That was the highest standard attainable before Christianity [1], yet by this a man was brought 'not far from the kingdom of God.'   Cato, in Dante's estimate of him, was a palmary instance of this.   See *Purg.* i. 37–39—

> 'Li raggi delle quattro luci sante
> Fregiavan sì la sua faccia di lume,
> Ch' io 'l vedea come il sol fosse davante.'

Compare this with the striking declaration of *Conv.* IV. xxviii. 121–123, 'Quale uomo terreno più degno fu di significare Iddio, che Catone? Certo nullo.'   See also the description of the virtuous heathen in *Purg.* vii. 34–36—

> 'Quivi sto io con quei che le tre sante
> Virtù non si vestiro, e senza vizio
> Conobber l'altre, e seguir tutte e quante.'

(Virgil is the speaker.)   'Here (i. e. in Limbo) I abide with those who were not clothed with the three holy virtues, but faultlessly knew the others and followed them every one.'

---

[1] See Aquinas quoted *supra*, p. 185.   Compare also *Mon.* III. xvi. 55 *seqq.*

Observe further that these four Virtues are represented as bringing Dante to the Eyes of Beatrice, i. e. the practice of these Moral Virtues prepares men to receive the *demonstrations* of Theology, for this is distinctly stated in a similar context to be the significance of the Eyes of Philosophy (*Conv.* III. xv. 11). But the full light that flows from the Eyes of Beatrice can only be enjoyed through the Evangelical Virtues (ll. 109–111).   See also *Mon.* III. xvi. 53-63. Note finally how these four Cardinal or Moral Virtues are associated with Wisdom in *Wisd.* viii. 7 : 'If a man love righteousness, her labours [the fruits of her labours, R.V.] are Virtues, for she teacheth temperance and prudence, justice and fortitude.'

Finally we must not forget the picture, drawn by Dante in *Par.* xix. 73 *seqq.*, of the Indian who had never heard of Christ, but lived a spotless life, as far as man can judge, in respect of moral virtues.

After this, we have set forth in symbol, or in a series of *tableaux,* seven principal calamities which have successively befallen the Church.

I say 'seven' without hesitation, though this number has not always been clearly recognized. For instance, Dr. Döllinger (*Dante as a Prophet,* p. 111) very strangely speaks of ' four' calamities. He does not specify them, and I am unable to identify them. I have never seen it noticed how Dante, with his usual love of symmetry, has distinguished the seven incidents by devoting precisely two *terzine* to each of them, excepting that the last, the concluding and contemporary catastrophe, has a few more lines than the others at the end of the Canto. Here is the list:—(1) ll. 112–117; (2) ll. 118–123; (3) ll. 124–129 ; (4) ll. 130–135; (5) ll. 136–141; (6) ll. 142–147 ; (7) ll. 148 to end.

(1) ll. 112–117 (or if we were to include the introductory simile, ll. 109–117):—

> ' Com' io vidi calar l' uccel di Giove
>   Per l' arbor giù, rompendo della scorza,
>   Non che dei fiori e delle foglie nuove ;
> E ferì il carro di tutta sua forza,
>   Ond' ei piegò, come nave in fortuna,
>   Vinta dall' onda, or da poggia or da orza.'

The first of these calamities is the series of persecutions under the early Emperors, such as Nero, Domitian, &c. It is thus indicated. An eagle, the Imperial Eagle, swoops down through the branches of the Tree, rending its trunk and scattering its leaves and new-grown flowers. It then smites the Chariot with all its force, so that it reels like a storm-tossed ship. Observe that these persecutions are thus represented as disastrous to the Empire itself, so that the fresh flowers of promise that bloomed when the Church was first brought into connexion with it are scattered and lost.

(2) ll. 118–123 :—

> ' Poscia vidi avventarsi nella cuna
> Del trionfal veiculo una volpe,
> Che d' ogni pasto buon parea digiuna.
> Ma riprendendo lei di laide colpe,
> La Donna mia la volse in tanta futa,
> Quanto sofferson l' ossa senza polpe.'

Next, the Car is invaded by a lean and hungry fox. But
Beatrice herself speedily drives it away. This clearly refers
to the early heresies, which were overcome and suppressed
by the authority of the Church herself, and so she purged
herself of them.

In contrast with the assaults of persecution by open enemies
from without, the mischief of heresy is aptly represented by
the fox, for the operations of heretics

> ' Non furon leonine, ma di volpe.'

They claimed not only to be within the Church, but to
represent the truest aspect of her teaching. ' Of your own
selves shall men arise, speaking perverse things.' Note that
it is precisely in reference to such false teachers that Ezekiel
says, ' Thy prophets are like the foxes in the desert' (xiii. 4) [1].
Also, to judge from chronological order, coming, as this does,
after the early persecutions and *before* the Donation of Constantine (which will be found denoted as the third calamity),
the heresy principally indicated is probably Gnosticism [2], as
Scartazzini suggests. He further points out that as the
fox dashed into the very body of the Car from outside, so
Gnosticism had its origin in the heathen philosophy, which
claimed to ex ound by its own principles Christian revelation,
and to possess the key of knowledge for the lack of which
both the Old and New Testaments had been so far entirely
misunderstood.

---

[1] S. Augustine, commenting on *Ps.* lxxx. 9, 10, says ' Vulpes insidiosos
maximeque haereticos significant, dolosos, fraudulentos' (quoted by Scart. *h. l.*).
Also Rabanus Maurus expounds *Matt.* viii. 20 by the words : ' in vulpibus
haereticos, et in volucribus coeli malignos spiritus exprimens.'

[2] Dean Plumptre and others suggest Arianism, but I think that chronological
and other considerations make Gnosticism the more probable reference.

(3) ll. 124-129:—

> 'Poscia, per indi ond' era pria venuta,
>   L' aquila vidi scender giù nell' arca
>   Del carro, e lasciar lei di sè pennuta.
> E qual esce di cor che si rammarca,
>   Tal voce uscì del cielo, e cotal disse :
>   "O navicella mia, com' mal sei carca ! " '

The third great calamity is the acquisition of temporal possessions through the 'Donation of Constantine.' The eagle descends once more, and leaves the Car covered with *its own feathers.* Note the expression, 'di sè pennuta.' This exactly describes the position maintained by Dante in the *De Mon.* It is of the very 'form' or essence of the Church that she should have no such possessions. They are of the plumage of the eagle. They belong of right to the Emperor alone; he had no power or right to alienate them ; nor had the Church any power or right to receive them [1]. They were as wholly out of place as the feathers and plumage upon the triumphal Car. A bitter cry was heard from heaven upon the consummation of this disastrous event [2] (ll. 127-129).

(4) ll. 130-135 :—

> ' Poi parve a me che la terra s' aprisse
>   Tr' ambo le rote, e vidi uscirne un drago,
>   Che per lo carro su la coda fisse :
> E come vespa che ritragge l' ago,
>   A sè traendo la coda maligna,
>   Trasse del fondo, e gissen vago vago.'

---

[1] Other passages in which Dante pronounces judgement on the Donation of Constantine, are *Inf.* xix. 115 ; *Par.* xx. 56 ; *Mon.* II. xii. 14 ; xiii. 67 ; III. x. 1, 27, 68, 116 ; xiii. 60. See also the discussion of this subject in *Studies,* II. pp. 14-16. It may be added here that in this Dante differs entirely from S. Thomas Aquinas, who in the *De Regimine Principum,* I. xiv ; III. x, xvii, xviii, &c., rests the supremacy of Papal jurisdiction, and the dependence of the Emperor on the Pope, upon the Donation of Constantine, and upon the conferment of the Empire on Charles the Great by the Pope. See Gregorovius, vi. pp. 120, 122. Gregorovius observes that William of Occam (d. 1347) denied, like Dante, the power of Constantine to renounce the inalienable rights of the Empire, and that Marsilius of Padua (d. 1328) in his *Defensor Pacis* went very much further in his limitations of the Papal authority.

[2] It is possible that Dante may have had in his mind a legend, mentioned by Pietro di Dante and others, that at the time when the Donation of Constantine was made a voice was heard from heaven, saying, 'Hodie diffusum est venenum in Ecclesia Dei.'

This fourth calamity or tribulation is more difficult to identify.

From the earth between the wheels of the Car issues a dragon. He fixes his envenomed tail through its floor, and drags away a part of it, and so goes his way.

The imagery is clearly derived from the Apocalypse, ch. xii. The dragon that comes from beneath is probably the devil, ' the old serpent' (*Rev.* xii. 9), who inflicts this injury upon the Church[1]. The carrying away of a part of the floor of the Car (an incident imitated from *Rev.* xii. 3, where the dragon's 'tail drew the third part of the stars of heaven, and did cast them to the earth') seems beyond doubt to represent some great schism by which the Church was rent. Several of the early commentators think the reference is to Mohammedanism at the beginning of the seventh century. This is the view, I believe, most commonly held[2], and is, in my opinion, almost certainly the true one. It may perhaps be objected that this interpretation treats Mohammedanism as a kind of heresy, and one effecting a schism in the Church itself, rather than as an erroneous and rival system external to it. To this I would reply that, however we may now regard it, such a view would be quite in accordance with the position assigned to Mohammed in the *Inferno*, where he figures as the most conspicuous and typical example of the *Schismatics* in the ninth Bolgia of the eighth Circle in the *Inferno* (see Canto xxviii). It should also be remembered that Mohammed professed a deep reverence for Christ ; he held Him to be the greatest of the prophets ; he believed in His birth being miraculous ; and also in His return to earth hereafter to establish peace and to reconcile Islam and Christianity, by restoring the latter from its corruptions (which were already

---

[1] Observe that the word 'Serpent' is the word used for the 'dragon' of this passage when this disaster is again referred to in xxxiii. 34.

[2] See Renan, *Averroes*, p. 304. He there says : 'Il faut se rappeler que Dante n'a vu dans Mahomet que l'auteur d'un schisme, et, dans l'islamisme, qu'une secte arienne.' He further quotes a medieval historian, who says, 'Unde verius *haeretici* quam Sarraceni nominari debent.' So again, Ozanam, *Dante et la Philosophie*, &c., p. 189 : 'Dante considère l'islamisme comme une secte arienne, et Mahomet comme le chef *du plus grand schisme qui ait désolé l'Église.*'

gross enough even in Mohammed's day) to the ideal originally intended by Christ [1].

Thus then I would certainly explain the fourth great calamity of the Church [2].

Other views that have been held are as follows:—Mr. A. J. Butler suggests the Iconoclastic Schism, c. 730, about a century later. Others, like Pietro di Dante, suppose the 'dragon' to represent the demon of cupidity invading the Church, and causing greater disaster to it than any of the ills from which it had previously suffered. Somewhat similarly Dr. Döllinger interprets the 'dragon' to be *Simony* [3]. Others again (as Lombardi and Scartazzini), still more vaguely, interpret the passage as referring to the various corruptions and temptations to evil by which the devil infected the Church. I should object, at any rate, to the three last of these four views: (1) that the explanation is too vague to suit the very definite imagery of actual *disruption*; and (2) that this would not range fitly with the other calamities, as not being a definite historical event.

(5) ll. 136–141:—

> ' Quel che rimase, come di gramigna
> Vivace terra, della piuma, offerta
> Forse con intenzion sana e benigna,
> Si ricoperse, e funne ricoperta
> E l' una e l' altra rota e il temo, in tanto
> Che più tiene un sospir la bocca aperta.'

The fifth vicissitude is a further accession of temporal possessions represented in the additional plumage (*v. supra,* l. 126) by which the whole Car is now entirely smothered and overgrown, wheels and pole and all. This no doubt refers to the Donations of Pepin (A.D. 755), and Charles the Great (A.D. 775), and other similar and rapidly growing accessions of wealth and endowments to the Church. Dante graphically says the change was effected before his eyes

---

[1] See Bosworth Smith's *Mohammed and Mohammedanism*, pp. 182–192.

[2] I do not for a moment suppose (as e. g. Longfellow and others have done) that the 'drago' is Mohammed himself. The devil worked the mischief through him ; or, in the language of Scripture, 'the devil entered into him.'

[3] *Dante as a Prophet*, p. 113.

in less time than the mouth remains open in uttering a sigh (l. 141). These possessions had now become so vast as to alter the whole aspect of the Church, and to bring about a complete transformation of its original character (l. 142). Certainly nothing strikes us more in the whole of mediaeval history in every country of Europe than the keen and perpetual struggle in every grade of the Church to acquire more and more wealth. The constant quarrels of the Popes with the Emperors, and with our own English Kings, were almost invariably due to the exorbitant rapacity of Papal claims for money.

(6) ll. 142–147 :—

> 'Trasformato così il dificio santo
>   Mise fuor teste per le parti sue,
>   Tre sopra il temo, ed una in ciascun canto.
> Le prime eran cornute come bue ;
>   Ma le quattro un sol corno avean per fronte :
>   Simile mostro visto ancor non fue.'

Next follow still further and more hideous distortions of the outward form of the Church. It put forth seven heads, three on its pole and one at each of its corners. The three first had two horns, and each of the others one. Again we recognize the source of this imagery in the Apocalypse, and we remember how Dante has employed it before, though differently, in *Inf.* xix. 109, 110 [1]. The interpretation of Dante's meaning here is extremely difficult. The number of heads and horns is no doubt dictated to him by the passage in the Apocalypse. Further, if with his habit of exact description he went on to specify how the ten horns were placed on the seven heads, they could hardly be otherwise distributed, i. e. three of the heads must have two horns apiece. But I can scarcely doubt that Dante intended some definite mystical meaning besides. The earliest, and still most common, explanation is that he refers to the seven capital or deadly sins, all of which now disfigured the hopelessly corrupted Church. The various attempts to explain why some of these have one horn and some two are not very convincing. If

---

[1] See the discussion of that passage in *Studies*, I. p. 70.

we are to take the reference to the seven deadly sins at all (which, however, I do not accept), it seems to me most natural to suggest that Pride, Envy, and Anger (the three worst sins) have two horns, because they involve sin against one's neighbour as well as against God ; whereas the other four do not necessarily do so. This idea would accord well with Dante's well-known analysis and classification of the seven sins in *Purg.* xvii[1], especially ll. 112–114, and indeed as far as l. 126, in which these first three sins have special guilt in that they imply positive love of evil, and that evil must be not for oneself but for one's neighbour. But I cannot think this common explanation at all satisfactory. Mr. Butler has made the ingenious suggestion, with which I entirely agree, that Dante is probably referring to the seven Electors of the Empire, of whom three, being mitred, might be described as having two horns (Archbishops of Maintz, Trier, and Cöln). He adds that they were originally appointed to be Electors by the Pope (c. 1000 A.D.)[2], and so might be said to spring out of the Church itself. Dante might well think that this new and bold departure in the way of encroachment upon the Imperial Power constituted a further and a very aggravated distortion of the true ideal of the Church. Moreover, in Dante's opinion, the actions and conduct of the Electors deserved reprobation, no less than the vice of their origin. He says of them in *Mon.* III. xvi, that 'nebula cupiditatis obtenebrati, divinae dispensationis faciem non discernunt.' This interpretation then seems to me very probable. It has the great advantage of falling into line with the explanation

---

[1] See this classification explained in *Studies*, II. pp. 204-208.

[2] The following is Villani's account of the matter, and the one therefore that Dante is likely to have followed. In *Cron.* iv. 3 (*init.*) he states that since three Otto's in a direct line had succeeded one another as Emperors, it seemed good (in fear no doubt of the dignity becoming hereditary) to *Pope Sergius IV and to the cardinals and to the princes of Rome*, that the Emperor should be elected by the Germans, they being a powerful people, and also an important arm of Christendom ; and that thenceforth the Empire should pass by the election of the most worthy, subject to the confirmation of the Church if the elected were approved as worthy. The passage goes on to explain that 'per dicreto' seven Electors were named, and their titles follow. Hence Dante might well represent the 'seven heads' as being put forth *by the Church itself.*

of the other calamities in the series, which all refer to some definite and historical event.

This brings the panorama of the Church's history comparatively near to Dante's own time. Henceforth we have depicted contemporary troubles, and notably the Avignon captivity from 1305 onwards. These form the seventh and last of the tribulations here figured.

(7) ll. 148 *seqq.* :—

> 'Sicura quasi rocca in alto monte,
>   Seder sopr' esso una puttana sciolta
>   M' apparve con le ciglia intorno pronte.
> E come perchè non gli fosse tolta,
>   Vidi di costa a lei dritto un gigante,
>   E baciavansi insieme alcuna volta :
> Ma perchè l' occhio cupido e vagante
>   A me rivolse, quél feroce drudo
>   La flagellò dal capo infin le piante.
> Poi di sospetto pieno e d' ira crudo,
>   Disciolse il mostro, e trassel per la selva
>   Tanto, che sol di lei mi fece scudo
> Alla puttana ed alla nuova belva.'

The Church has now become utterly corrupted and distorted beyond all recognition. See l. 147—

> 'Simile mostro visto ancor non fue.'

'A like monster never before was seen.'

The seat in the Car itself is occupied no longer by Beatrice, or the ideal Papacy, but by a wanton and shameless harlot. Dante applies the same metaphor elsewhere to the corruption of the Roman Court, e.g. *Inf.* xix. 4 and *Par.* ix. 142. This imagery once more is borrowed obviously from the Apocalypse. The giant in this passage (xxxii. 152) carries on the metaphor of the kings of the earth who committed fornication with the great whore of the Book of Revelation. This giant figures no doubt chiefly Philip the Fair, but also other earlier representatives of the detested royal house of France. (For this see further *Purg.* xx.) Their friendly intrigues from time to time with different occupants of the Papal throne[1], which are here described as mutual caresses of the

---

[1] e. g. Urban IV, Clement IV, Martin IV, Nicholas IV.

giant and the harlot ('baciavansi insieme,' l. 153), were now replaced by the violent hostility between Philip and Boniface VIII. The gross outrage upon Boniface perpetrated by the myrmidons of Philip, Nogaret and Sciarra, at Anagni (for which see *Purg*. xx. 85 *seqq.*), may well be pointed at in the scourging of the harlot by the giant, her former paramour, in ll. 155, 6. Then, full of jealousy and fury, the giant unbinds the chariot from the tree, and carries it away with the harlot out of sight. This quite evidently represents the removal of the Papal Seat from Rome to Avignon under Clement V in 1305.

I have now endeavoured to explain step by step the two main divisions of this Apocalyptic Vision of the Church Militant, excluding the personal episode of the reproaches of Beatrice in Cantos xxx, xxxi. The first of those divisions, it will be remembered, related to what may be called the organic constitution of the Church, as it was *meant* to be,—'built upon the foundation of the apostles and prophets,' and following Christ as its leader and guide.

The second division sets forth in a series of figurative scenes the actual troublous history of the Church from its first settlement at Rome by S. Peter, under the guidance of Christ (see xxxii. 49–51), to its removal to Avignon in Dante's own time. By this action it may be said to have been completely (though not finally) 'destroyed.' This strong expression is Dante's own. See xxxiii. 34, 35—'Know that the vessel which the Serpent broke "was and is not."' This language again is evidently derived from *Rev.* xvii. 8. In the final division of our subject, in Canto xxxiii, we have no longer *history*, but *prophecy*; a prophecy of the regeneration and restitution of the shattered Church. In this the difficulties of interpretation are still greater, since prediction is naturally more obscure than historical allusion, especially when it is (as was unhappily the case with that of Dante) 'unfulfilled prophecy.'

•••

SUPPLEMENTARY NOTES TO
Essay IV, Part I.

I.   Matelda.

The following is a *résumé* of the principal views that have been held as to this mysterious personage, together with a brief statement of my reasons for holding to the earliest and still most generally received explanation, that she is Matilda, Countess of Tuscany.   This is one of the thorniest problems in the *Divina Commedia*.   Its discussion by Scartazzini occupies twenty-two closely printed pages in small type in his Leipzig edition.   What here follows is to be taken as merely a skeleton outline of the controversy.

There are two main questions :

I. What is her Office, and what does she symbolize ?

II. What historical person (if any) is thus idealized ?

I. (1) As to her *Office*, she appears to be the Guardian of the Earthly Paradise, very much as the highly-idealized Cato is of the realm of Purgatory on the slopes of the mountain below.   In proof of this :—

(*a*) The service which she is directed to perform for Dante, in leading him to bathe in Eunoe, is described as her usual function—

'Menalo ad esso, e *come tu sei usa,*

La tramortita sua virtù ravviva.'   *Purg.* xxxiii. 128, 129.

(*b*) She is (as Miss Rossetti observes) the only permanent inhabitant in the Earthly Paradise.

(*c*) She is not represented (in *Par.* i.) as ascending with Dante and Beatrice to Heaven.

(*d*) If (as is presently shown) she is a symbol of the Active Life in its highest aspect, the office here attributed to her would be most appropriate.   For this see *Mon.* III. xvi. 45 *seqq.*

(2) As to her *symbolical purport*, she seems to represent the Active Life (as above said) in its highest development.

The old-world distinction between the Active and Contemplative Lives occurs frequently in the works of Dante.   See especially *Mon.* I. iv. 5 ; III. xvi. ; *Conv.* II. v. 66–89 ; IV. xxii. 135 *seqq.* ; xvii. 85 *seqq.*   We find in the last passage that it was derived by him, as by many other writers, from Aristotle, and especially from *Nic. Eth.* X. vii [1].

Now it is generally held that there are three pairs of symbols by which Dante figures this antithesis. Leah and Rachel (Old Testament); Martha and Mary (New Testament); Matelda and Beatrice (*Divina Commedia*). As to Leah and Rachel, see *Purg.* xxvii. 97–108.

As to Martha and Mary, see *Conv.* IV. xvii. 94 *seqq.*

It is hardly necessary to add that as regards these two pairs the symbolism is commonly accepted by theologians from very early times [2].

First note the following parallelisms between the second and third pairs.

Leah and Matelda are both introduced as gathering flowers, *Purg.* xxvii. 99 and xxviii. 41.

Rachel and Beatrice are represented more than once as sitting [3] beside one another in Heaven. See *Inf.* ii. 102 and *Par.* xxxii. 8, 9.

Then again, observe that the *hands* are the symbol of activity, as the *eyes* are of contemplation. So the *hands* of Leah are contrasted with the *eyes* of Rachel (*Purg.* xxvii. 97–108); and also the *hands* of Matelda (as implied in *Purg.* xxviii. 41) with the *eyes* of Beatrice (*Purg.* xxvii. 54 ; xxxi. 108, 119, 133; and *Paradiso, passim*). In illustration of this symbolical meaning of *hands*, note the curious use made of it by Dante in *Mon.*

---

[1] See further on this subject, *Studies*, I. pp. 74, 100, 262.

[2] We may specially mention, among writers known and studied by Dante, S. Gregory, S. Augustine, S. Thomas Aquinas, Richard and Hugh of S. Victor, and S. Bernard. For S. Gregory and Aquinas compare *Summa*, II². clxxix. 2 : 'Istae duae vitae significantur per duas uxores Iacob ; activa quidem per Liam, contemplativa vero per Rachelem ; et per duas mulieres quae Dominum hospitio receperunt ; contemplativa quidem per Mariam, activa vero per Martham, ut Gregorius dicit.' Then in II². clxxxi. 1 S. Gregory is again quoted as saying that 'per Liam, quae fuit lippa sed fecunda, significatur vita activa ; quae dum occupatur in opere, minus videt'; and in clxxxii. 2 as pointing out another suitable lesson, viz. that Man can only reach the Contemplative Life through the Active Life, just as Jacob had to accept Leah first, before finding his full satisfaction in Rachel. A curious passage may be quoted from S. Bernard, viz. *In Assumpt. Mariae*, Serm. iii. (Fol. 54, Col. 2 of *Ed. Bened.*)—'Felix domus et beata congregatio est, ubi de Maria Martha conqueritur.' He explains this to mean, when administrators and rulers of the Church are dissatisfied, and in a manner envious of the lot of Mary, which is that of those who follow the Contemplative Life. The converse would be 'indignum et illicitum.' S. Augustine, besides several other references to the subject, says in *de Cons. Evangg.* i. 8 that the contrast between Leah and Rachel is like that between the first three Gospels and that of S. John. Compare *Contra Faustum Man.* B. xxii. c. 52.

[3] In both cases *siede* occurs in reference to Rachel. We note that the very attitude of *sitting* is significant as appropriate to Contemplation. Dante emphasizes this in the case of Mary, in *Conv.* IV. xvii. 104 ; in *Purg.* xxvii. 105 he says of Rachel 'siede tutto il giorno.' Again in *Mon.* I. iv. 9, when contrasting *operandum* and *speculandum*, he says, '*sedendo* et quiescendo prudentia et sapientia ipse (*sc.* homo) perficitur.' Compare S. Augustine, *Hom.* xiv. 'Illa (Lia) operatur; haec (Rachel) requiescit.'

I. xiii. 20–25, where Dante, in order to show that (as he expresses it in *Mon.* II. xii. 38) 'opera persuadentiora sunt quam sermones,' quotes the fact that 'plus persuaderunt manus Iacob quam ve.ba, licet illae falsum, illa verum persuaderent.'

When I say that the pair Matelda and Beatrice represented the *highest type* of the Active and Contemplative Lives respectively I follow the distinction expounded by Mr. Ruskin, *M. P.* iii. 222—'Observe: Leah gathers the flowers to decorate *herself*, and delights in *Her Own* Labour. Rachel sits silent, contemplating herself, and delights in *Her Own* Image'. These are the types of the Unglorified Active and Contemplative Powers of Man. But Beatrice and Matilda are the same powers, Glorified. And how are they Glorified? Leah took delight in her own Labour; but Matilda *in operibus manuum Tuarum—in God's Labour*[2]: Rachel in the sight of her own face, Beatrice in the sight of *God's face*[3].'

---

[1] See *Purg.* xxvii. 101-107 :—

> 'Ch' io mi son Lia, e vo movendo intorno
> Le belle mani a farmi una ghirlanda.
> Per piacermi allo specchio qui m' adorno ;
> Ma mia suora Rachel mai non si smaga
> Dal suo miraglio, e siede tutto giorno.
> Ell' è de' suoi begli occhi veder vaga,
> Com' io dell' adornarmi con le mani.'

[2] See *Purg.* xxviii. 80, where Matelda explains the probable wonder of Dante at her beaming and happy mien by an allusive reference to *Ps.* xci. 5 :—

> 'Ma luce rende il salmo *Delectasti*,
> Che puote disnebbiar vostro intelletto.'

The passage is found to run thus : 'Delectasti me Domine in *factura tua*, et in operibus *manuum tuarum* exsultabo.' On this and similar allusive references on Dante see *Studies*, I. p. 18.

[3] I have thought it better in the text, and also *supra*, p. 180, to follow the commonly received view as to the antithesis between Matelda and Beatrice, which involves the assumption that Beatrice symbolizes the Contemplative Life. But I must confess myself not wholly satisfied with this. For, in *Par.* xxxii, S. Bernard appears to represent the Contemplative Life, and so to him at the last Beatrice herself yields place, when the light even of Revelation is swallowed up in Intuition. It seems rather to me that Virgil and Beatrice, Matilda and Bernard, are the naturally contrasted pairs ; Virgil symbolizing Human Reason without Divine aid, and Beatrice the enlightenment of Divine Revelation. Virgil yields place to Beatrice, and Beatrice in like manner to S. Bernard. So we progress from Reason, through Revelation, to Intuition ; and to these correspond respectively, Proof, Faith, and Sight. Compare the beautiful lines in *Par.* ii. 43-45 :—

> 'Lì si vedrà ciò che tenem per fede,
> Non dimostrato, ma fia per sè noto,
> A guisa del ver primo che l'uom crede.'

Matelda introduces the pilgrim to the Earthly Paradise, Bernard to that which is above. Matelda and Bernard exhibited the contrasted types of Action and Contemplation upon earth at any rate in the same age and country.

II. We now turn to the second question—What historical person (if any) is thus idealized by Dante?

The various theories on this point may be classified thus :—

  (i) The Countess Matilda.

  (ii) Some Matilda from Germany.

    (*a*) The Empress Matilda, wife of the Emperor Henry I.

    (*b*) Matilda of Hackeborn.

    (*c*) Matilda of Magdeburg.

    (*d*) Matilda, daughter of the Emperor Henry I.

  (iii) Some friend or associate of Beatrice.

    (*a*) The 'Donna dello schermo' *Vita Nuova*, § 5.

    (*b*) The friend of Beatrice in *Vita Nuova*, § 8.

    (*c*) The lady mentioned in *Vita Nuova*, § 18.

    (*d*) Primavera or Vanna in *Vita Nuova*, § 24.

    (*e*) The 'Donna Gentile' of the *Vita Nuova* and *Convito.*

  (iv) A purely fictitious symbol, without relation to any real or his-
    torical person.

Since attempting the above classification, I have met with another sug-gestion, viz. that 'Matelda' is Mary Magdalene ! Nothing further probably need be said respecting a theory for which it is difficult to imagine any other origin than the *dira cupido*, which oppresses some modern writers on Dante, of saying something at all hazards which shall be at least entirely original.

i. The Countess Matilda of Tuscany was the well-known friend and supporter of Hildebrand. Her father died when she was six years old. She leaned on the authority of successive Pontiffs for the defence of her insecure rights against the encroachments of the Emperors. Even at the early age of fifteen she is found in arms in support of the Pope, as often later ; yet she always vigorously maintained her own independence. She was twice married, but died childless in 1115, at the age of sixty-nine, leaving to the Church the 'damnosa haereditas' of her territorial possessions.

I would urge the following points in favour of the received view :—

  (1) This is the opinion of the ancient commentators without excep-tion, and it is still held by most of the moderns.

  (2) The name (Matelda) is introduced in xxxiii. 119 as 'speaking for itself.' Possibly this would be accounted for, if she were (like Beatrice) known to Dante ; but she offers a better parallel to Cato, whose office resembles hers, if she be also a character known to mankind generally.

  (3) She would be a suitable type of the Active Life, owing to her splendid energy and vigorous activity in her life of constant conflict.

  (4) Her noble gift to the Church, though, as being the source of the temporary sovereignty of the Papacy, scarcely less disastrous than that of Constantine, was, equally with his,

' offerta
Forse con intenzion sana e benigna ': (<i>Purg.</i> xxxii. 138.)</div>

or, as we read in *Par.* xx. 56, it was—

'Sotto buona intenzion che fe' mal frutto.'

Hence Dante would not hesitate thus highly to exalt her, even as he has exalted Constantine himself, of whom he says in *Par.* xx. 58-60—

'Ora conosce come il mal dedutto
Dal suo bene operar non gli è nocivo,
Avvegna che sia il mondo indi distrutto.'

This thought is repeated in *Mon.* II. xii. 17, where such gifts are described as 'bene data et male possessa'; and in II. xiii. 69, where the 'pia intentio' of Constantine is again recognized.

(5) But further, the enrichment of the Church is *in itself good*, provided the power and opportunities thence arising are put to good use. See *Mon.* III. x. 127 'Poterat et vicarius Dei recipere, *non tamquam possessor*, sed tamquam fructuum pro Ecclesia pro Christi pauperibus dispensator.' Compare *Mon.* II. xii. 4-6; *Par.* xii. 92, and xxii. 82, 83.

(6) If the historical Countess Matilda should be thought to differ considerably from the picture or ideal here presented, we must remember the similar liberty which Dante has taken in other cases: most notably in that of Cato, whose office in the *Purgatorio* (as we have seen) exhibits some points of similarity with that of Matelda. He is transformed almost out of all recognition from the actual Cato of history. It is also noticeable that Dante's treatment of Cato supplies an answer to another objection sometimes made to the Countess Matilda in the present relation, viz. that she was a supporter of the Pope as against the Emperor. Even so was Cato a bitter opponent of Caesar, as Dante several times recognizes, e. g. *Conv.* III. v. 122; *Mon.* II. v. 132-140, and 168-170.

ii. (*a*) Matilda the Empress, d. 968, was wife of Henry I (the Fowler), and mother of Otto the Great. She was noted for her works of charity, but beyond the similarity of name there seems no special fitness in this guess. She has found an advocate in the eminent Dante scholar, Michelangelo Caetani, Duke of Sermoneta [1].

(*b*) This Matilda was a nun of Hackeborn, who left some writings of a mystical character. Her claims are strongly advocated by Lubin, *Studi* (pp. 314-353) and also by Dr. Döllinger.

(1) It is thought that there can be traced many resemblances to her writings in the *Paradiso*. (But it appears that these are mostly such common stock as can be found equally in Bonaventura, Richard and Hugh of S. Victor, and other mystical writers, with whose works Dante was familiar.)

(2) Dr. Döllinger, in *Dante as a Prophet*, says that this Matilda would be an apt personification of the knowledge of divine things in the way of Vision or Intuition, such as might come between Virgil and Beatrice: also that the gathering of flowers might serve to recall the imagery and allegories abounding in her writings. (The former of these

---

[1] '*Matelda nella divina foresta della Commedia.*' Rome, 1857.

reasons does not seem specially appropriate to the position and functions assigned by Dante to Matelda ; while the latter appears extremely fanciful.)

Besides, there seem certain positive *objections* to this theory.

(1) This Matilda, as a mystical nun, could not serve as a symbol of the Active Life, if we are right in so interpreting Dante's purpose.

(2) Dante is not very likely to have become acquainted with her writings. (Lubin says he might have done so in France or Germany, if not in Italy.)

(3) It seems almost certain that this Matilda lived till 1310. If that be so, this objection is at once fatal, though Lubin endeavours to face it [1].

(*c*) Matilda of Magdeburg was also a nun and mystic writer, who died in 1299. The same objections apply as in the last case ; and she was also a person still more obscure.

(*d*) This Matilda is a new claimant who has lately (in 1900) been added to the list by Scherillo [2]. She was daughter of the Emperor Henry I, and sister of Archbishop Bruno of Cologne. She flourished c. 930, and is said to have seen a Vision resembling that of the Earthly Paradise of Dante. But, apart from these slender claims, how would Dante be likely to know of her ; and how would any one else ever guess that so exalted a position was devised for one so little familiar ?

We proceed to Class iii, in which are comprised persons associated with Beatrice.

iii. (*a*) The 'Lady of the Screen' in *Vita Nuova*, §§ 5-7. This person, though advocated by Scartazzini, seems to have no appropriateness either in herself (she being quite obscure) ; or in the character of the transient relation in which Dante stood to her. She finally disappears in § 7.

(*b*) The friend of Beatrice, who is described in *Vita Nuova*, § 8, is strongly supported by Dean Plumptre, and perhaps of the four in this Class she has the best claim. They all have the advantage of forming a suitable pair with Beatrice, just as Leah and Rachel, and also Martha and Mary, form pairs of naturally associated persons.

In favour of this claimant it might be said that (1) she was very dear to Beatrice ; (2) Dante was deeply affected by her death ; (3) when Dante says that 'the Lord of Angels has taken her to his glory' he uses language similar to that which he employs about Beatrice [3] ; (4) she and Beatrice, being 'united in their lives,' might naturally be so in their symbolical union after death. But, on the other hand, we have no evidence of any

---

[1] Scartazzini's objection, that this Matilda, as also the next mentioned, died *aet.* c. 80 comes to nothing, in view of the terms 'Giovane e bella' applied to Leah in *Purg.* xxvii. 97. As Aquinas says—'in aetate iuvenili resurgent omnes': and S. Augustine, *C. D.* xxii. 15, declares that we shall all rise at the age of about thirty, 'in mensuram aetatis plenitudinis Christi' (*Eph.* iv. 13).

[2] *Matelda svelata.* See 'Bullettino della Società Dantesca,' N.S. vol. viii. pp. 85, 86.

[3] See *V. N.*, § viii. 2 and § xxix. 6. Compare also § xliii. 12-17.

fitness in this case for the symbolical purpose in question ; and further, we can scarcely suppose one so unknown to be made Guardian of the Earthly Paradise for all mankind.

(*c*) To the Donna who accosted Dante in § 18 of the *Vita Nuova* (see especially ll. 21, 44) the same objections apply as to (*a*).

(*d*) As to 'Primavera,' or Vanna, in *Vita Nuova*, § 24, the 'lady' of Guido Cavalcanti, and companion of Beatrice, besides the objections in the other cases, what possible reason can there be for giving her the false name of Matelda ?

(*e*) The *Donna Gentile* of *Vita Nuova*, § 36, and *Conv*. II, seems to me entirely out of the question, for (1) she is distinctly identified by Dante with Philosophy (see *Conv*. II. xiii. 37 *seqq*., and xvi. *fin*.), and no one imagines Matelda to represent Philosophy [1], nor does there seem any propriety in her doing so in the Earthly Paradise. (2) She was in a sense a *rival* to Beatrice, and Dante blames himself for his devotion to her after Beatrice's death (see *Conv*. II. ii, &c.). (3) Beatrice's reproaches of Dante in Canto xxx would be sadly out of place in her presence [2] !

iv. Finally the supposition that Matelda is no real person at all, but an allegorical fiction may, I think, be dismissed (though I am surprised to see it supported by Prof. Earle [3]), on these grounds :—

(1) It would be a discordant note, when all the other personages in the *Divina Commedia* are real [4].

(2) I believe that no such airy or baseless symbol is found anywhere in Dante [5].

(3) For what possible reason is she called Matelda ?

In conclusion therefore I maintain that the Countess Matilda, in accordance with the common opinion, still holds the field.

II. The word 'Brolo' in *Purg*. xxix. 147.

[I owe several suggestions in the following note to a communication made by Prof. Earle to the Oxford Dante Society some years ago.]

This interesting word is an ἅπαξ λεγόμενον, not only in Dante, but almost in all literature. The *Gran Diz*. registers only two other examples, one in Doni, and the other in Poliziano, but the latter looks suspiciously like a reminiscence of this passage. 'Bruolo,' however (which is obviously

---

[1] I have since observed that Prof. Earle appears to do so : *Introduction*, &c., p. cxxvii.

[2] This theory has lately been combined with a further identification of the 'Pietra' of the 'Pietra Canzoni' (referred to *infra*, p. 245) with both Matelda and the Donna Gentile. This strange view will be found advocated by S. de Chiara in a monograph entitled '*La Pietra di Dante e la Donna Gentile*,' Caserta, 1888.

[3] *Introduction*, &c., p. cxxviii.   [4] Compare *Studies*, II. p. 141.

[5] See *Studies*, II. pp. 132, 133.

the same word), occurs in the *Dittamondo*, 'far prati e bruoli.'   In this work there are very frequent echoes from the *Divina Commedia*.

The exact meaning of the word is uncertain.   It is generally explained to be 'garden,' partly from the absurd derivation suggested ($\pi\epsilon\rho\iota\beta\acute{o}\lambda\alpha\iota\sigma\nu$), and partly as a guess from its use in this context.   We are left to con-jecture its meaning from words in other languages which it resembles. The result would seem to be that wild or uncultivated thicket or forest is the primary sense of the word.

(1) *Latin*.   Ducange gives instances of *Bruilletum* and *Brogilus* in this sense.   These forms Prof. Earle suggests may have arisen from a Celtic word Latinized, such as *brwg*, which is a 'brake' or forest in Welsh.   I find in Ducange 'lucos quos vulgus " Brogilos " vocat' associated with 'ferarum venatio.'   'Brogilus vallatus' is also found, but it will be seen that the idea of enclosure is added, and is not inherent in the word itself.   Prof. Earle remarks that a hunting-ground, even if not fenced or walled, was asso-ciated with very jealous enclosure or exclusion.   [Note the cruel forestry laws of our early kings.]   Ainsworth also gives the word *Bruilletum* among 'Vocabula in Iure Anglicano municipali occurrentia,' and explains it to be 'a small coppice or wood.'

(2) In *Old French* we find broil, breuil, bril, &c. (Godefroy gives about twelve different forms of the word.)   Also 'broglie' is, I believe, pro-nounced 'broil' in French (as in the title 'Duc de Broglie'[1]).

See *Chanson de Roland*, l. 714 :—

　　　　'Enz en un broill par sum les puis,'

　　i.e. 'Within a wood at the top of the hills.'

I have found somewhere Raymond of Toulouse quoted as describing the song of a nightingale 'per miez lo brol.'   Dante himself, in *Vulg. Eloq*. II. ii. 87, quotes Arnald Daniel—'L'aura amara fa 'ls broils blancutz clarzir.'

(3) In *English* we have several traces of the word in the names of places.   My friend Dean Burgon informed me of two so-called 'Broyles,' near Chichester, the word being applied to 'open scrubby ground.'   These in old charters are called 'Bruillum regis' and 'Bruillum Depemersh.' I myself met with the word 'Broyle' in use in Devonshire, and was told that it meant a thicket *when cut down*, and not when growing.   'Brill,' near Oxford, was a hunting-lodge of Edward the Confessor.   (Cf. *venatio ferarum* quoted *supra*.)   Dr. Johnson mentions some lands in W. Scotland called 'Brolos' (ed. Hill, iii. 126).

---

[1] The word is doubtless connected with 'broglio,' 'imbroglio' (whence our 'embroil'), i. e. an 'entanglement,' as in a thicket.   'Brogliare' in *Par*. xxvi. 97 means something like 'wriggle about.'   As to the 'g,' this letter, often of evane-scent pronunciation like 'y,' is frequently both lost, and also superfluously inserted. In MSS. such words as taio, fiolo, boiente are found on the one hand, and noglia, Troglia, aglia (= aia) on the other.   Compare *raia* in *Purg*. xvi. 142 with *raggia* ; and *ib*. l. 140 I have found *Gaia* written *Gagia* in Venetian MSS.   In some MSS. the initial 'g' is constantly omitted in such words as ià, iù for già, giù, &c.   See, for further illustrations, my *Textual Criticism*, pp. 512, 532, 542.

All seems to point to the sense of 'thicket' as inherent in the word[1]; so that in this passage of the *Purgatorio* I believe Dante's idea is not the brilliant garden-like look of the flowers of which he is speaking (as the passage is often explained), but their bushiness and abundance and thicket-like aspect. The later figures in the procession had a perfect thicket or forest of rosy flowers about their heads. We may compare Virgil's use of *silva* for the luxuriant umbelliferous head of flowers of the 'amellum':—

'Namque uno ingentem tollit de caespite silvam
Aureus ipse.'   (*Georg.* iv. 273.)

III. THE MEANING OF PURPLE IN DANTE, AND ESPECIALLY IN *Purg.* xxix. 131.

I have pointed out in the text how wide a range of colour has been at different times included under the term 'purple.' For the sake of the important piece of symbolism which I believe to be conveyed by the 'purple' garments borne by all the *cardinal* virtues alike in *Purg.* xxix. 131 (as explained above, pp. 184–186), I have brought together here some further proofs and illustrations that 'purple' corresponds with what we should call a 'deep red.'

In addition to the two passages quoted in a note, *loc. cit.*, I may add Virgil's description of the plant 'amellum' ('Aureus ipse'), which has golden flowers but dark leaves. The latter are thus described: 'in foliis . . . violae sublucet purpura nigrae' (*Georg.* iv. 274, 275). Thus 'niger' is the epithet of violet, and 'purpura' describes the dark red by which the violet is qualified. We learn from Pliny[2] that Tyrian purple was of two kinds, 'purple-red' and 'purple-blue,' these being derived from different shells. He says that purple-red is like scarlet viewed obliquely, and that that dye is most precious when it resembles 'curdled blood.' Thus 'scarlet' would be a yellowish-red, and 'purple' a bluish-red; though we have seen that crimson, and even scarlet itself, was sometimes called 'purple' (*v. supra*, p. 185). Delitsch observes that one cause of this was the increasing scarcity in the Middle Ages of the purple dye shell, so that official or regal 'purple' robes became nearly scarlet in hue. He states that where, in the Mosaic law, 'purple fringes' are ordered, the Rabbis made a dispensing ordinance, 'because these could not be provided, since we have no longer any purple blue' (*op. cit.* p. 66). Luther, in his translation of the Bible, freely interchanges 'purple' and 'scarlet.' Again we are familiar with the term 'porphyry' as applied to a *deep red* stone, and Dante himself speaks of 'porfido' as

'sì fiammeggiante,
Come sangue che fuor di vena spiccia.'   (*Purg.* ix. 101, 102.)

Mr. Whitwell has kindly sent me the following illustrations from heraldry:

---

[1] I am told that 'brolo' is still used locally in Sicily meaning 'thicket.'
[2] I owe this and some other references in this note to Delitsch's *Iris*, ch. III.

(1) Heraldic purple has been defined[1] as 'a colour that consisteth of much Red and a small quantity of Black.' (Compare *niger* in *Georg.* iv. 275, quoted above.) (2) Woodward and Burnett say that the lion of Leon, though blazoned 'purpure,' is in no way distinguishable from 'gules.' Dante's own idea of purple may be illustrated by two references : (1) In two places, viz. *Vita Nuova*, § 40, l. 32, and *Conv.* III. ix. 135, he speaks of the discolouration of objects caused by the affection of his eyes from which he suffered shortly after the death of Beatrice. That colour is described as *purpureo* in the former and *rubicondo* in the latter of these passages. (2) Again, in *Conv.* IV. xx. 14, the colour *perso* is said to be one composed of purple and black, with black predominating. This certainly implies a large amount of *red* in 'purple' to make the description intelligible. (3) *Purg.* xxxii. 58 is probably too obscure and of too doubtful interpretation to quote in proof of anything. But if the colour of the flowers that burst forth on the Tree, which symbolizes (*inter alia*) certainly the Empire, is intended to recall 'imperial purple,' the description would be in point here. The colour is indicated as 'men che di rose e più che di viole,' which seems probably to mean less (red) than roses and more than violets.

IV. THE LEGEND OF THE WOOD OF THE CROSS.

The legend that the Cross was made from the wood of the Forbidden Tree in the Garden of Eden seems clearly recognized by allusion in *Purg.* xxxii. 51 : —

'E quel di lei a lei lasciò legato.'

It is difficult, if not impossible, to find any other satisfactory explanation for these words. If it be accepted, it establishes beyond doubt that the pole of the car with the Crossbar symbolizes the Cross.

There is an elaborate monograph by Mussafia, *Sulla leggenda della Croce*, to which I owe some of the following references. It was a legend very widely spread, and is found in France, Spain, Italy, Germany, &c.

Thus the tradition, in one form or another, was so generally familiar that Dante would be safe in referring to it in this passing and allusive manner. The following strange medley is derived from the *Aurea Legenda*, c. lxviii. Seth is said to have planted an offshoot from the Tree of Knowledge on Adam's grave. By the time of Solomon it had grown to a very large tree. This he cut down, and employed either for one of his palaces, or as a bridge to cross a pool. The Queen of Sheba, to whom it was miraculously revealed that the Saviour of the world should one day hang upon this wood, refused to set foot on it, and warned Solomon of the revelation she had received[2]. Solomon, hoping to avert

---

[1] By Guillim, *A display of heraldrie*, ed. 1724.

[2] Pietro Comestore (see *Par.* xii. 134) also associates the Queen of Sheba with the legend. In Gervase of Tilbury, *Ot. Imp.* Dec. III., c. 54 and 105,

such an evil prophecy (just as often in Greek mythology the oracular predictions were sought to be evaded), caused the beam to be buried at a great depth in the earth. At the spot was afterwards dug the Pool of Bethesda whose healing properties were due to the presence of this wood. Shortly before the Passion, the wood came to the surface, and was employed to form the Cross!

The *motif* of all this is obvious. It was deemed appropriate that the instrument of death should also be that of redemption[1]. Compare a similar thought, as recognized in a sober form, by S. Paul in *Rom.* v. 19 and 1 *Cor.* xv. 21. Also we may note the curious comment of Pietro di Dante in *Par.* xxxii. 4, where Mary is described as having healed the wound which Eve inflicted. Hence, says Pietro, she is greeted with 'Ave,' which is 'Eva' reversed.

nearly the whole of the above story is found. There are many variations in the details in different writers. Thus the Sybil often takes the place of the Queen of Sheba in the warning to Solomon (Mussafia, *op. cit* p. 174). Others say that the Queen of Sheba's name was Sybilla! (*ib.* p. 187). Moses and David occasionally play a part in the preservation of the shoot (or sometimes three shoots) of the tree (*ib.* p. 182). [In the Edition quoted this monograph begins at p. 165.]

[1] The same idea is embodied in the classical legend of the power of the spear of Achilles to heal the wound which it had itself inflicted. See *Inf.* xxxi. 4-6.

PART II.

THE REPROACHES OF BEATRICE.

HAVING now followed to its conclusion the Apocalyptic Vision of the Earthly Paradise. I turn back to the personal Episode of the Reproaches of Dante by Beatrice, by which it was interrupted from Canto xxx. 55 to the end of Canto xxxi. Thus the Episode falls between the two main parts of the Vision ; the first of which represents the growth and constitution of the Church from the beginning of Revelation to the close of the Canon of the New Testament; while the second embodies in a series of *tableaux* the principal vicissitudes in its later history.

So much has been written on this subject that it is very difficult to say anything new. But as most of the works upon the controversy are in Italian or German, and many exist only in detached monographs or extracts from Reviews, it may not be amiss to present some account of it to English readers. And, besides this, I wish to advocate the solution which seems to me most nearly to satisfy the puzzling, and often conflicting, data with which we have to deal. At any rate having undertaken the explanation of these concluding Cantos of the *Purgatorio*, I could not avoid the discussion of so striking a portion of them.

At the end of his ' ten years' thirst' (xxxii. 2), when he is kindling already with 'the well-known symptoms of the bygone flame' (xxx. 48), instead of the joyful greeting which he anticipated, Dante meets with an abrupt and startling rebuff. The first word which he hears (xxx. 55) is his own name, mentioned here only throughout the whole poem. It is the prelude to a stern reproof, so stern as to move the compassion of the attendant Angels (ll. 82–84 ; 94–96). Then Beatrice turns her speech to them, as it were justifying her severity. This is not however so much for their sakes, who ' see all things in God,' as for that of Dante, who now stands weeping and downcast on the opposite side of the stream (ll. 103–108). She does not again address him directly until the beginning of the next Canto (xxxi), when she forces him to a full and free confession of his fault with his own mouth. The words in which that formal confession is made are particularly to be noticed, since they may naturally be expected to embody 'the head and front of his offending.' In xxxi. ll. 34–36 we read:—'Things present with their deceptive pleasure turned astray my steps, as soon as your countenance was hidden from me.'

To this we shall return, but we must first trace the scene to its close. The confession is followed by prompt and frank forgiveness. Yet to produce in Dante more profound shame, and thereby more assured strength for the future, Beatrice proceeds to depict the greatness of his fall, and how utterly he was without excuse, in ll. 43–63. At the end, she compels him to lift up his head, and look her full in the face. That glance, though she is not yet unveiled (l. 82), so overpowers him with remorse that he sinks down unconscious. When he recovers his senses, he finds that Matelda has plunged him into the river (i. e. Lethe). After drawing him through it, she presents him to the four Virtues on the left of the Car, i. e. the Cardinal or Moral Virtues, who embrace him, and promise that their more exalted Sisters, the three Virtues on the right, i. e. the Evangelical Virtues, will lead him, as they presently do, face to face with the unveiled Beatrice herself (ll. 88–117).

So much for the scene in outline. We must now point out and bring together those passages in which Beatrice most pointedly describes the nature of Dante's offence. The language of these charges, together with that of Dante's confession, form the problem which we have to solve[1]. She says (xxx. 115) that Dante's youth was full of the highest promise and the greatest capabilities, and that she, while on earth, 'guided him with her eye,' and kept him in the right way (ll. 121–3). But as soon as she died,

'Questi si tolse a me, e diessi altrui.'　(l. 126.)

---

[1] No one familiar with Boeth. *de Cons. Phil.* can fail to be struck with the numerous points of resemblance between this scene and the Reproaches of Philosophy in Lib. I. Pros. ii. Compare Lib. III. Pros. ix. *sub fin.* See also *Studies*, I. p. 286.

'This man took himself from me and gave himself to others (or, to another).' She became ever less dear and less pleasing to him (l. 129). Then note the next words, describing the actual result in the conduct of Dante himself, ll. 130–132—

> 'E volse i passi suoi per via non vera,
> Imagini di ben seguendo false,
> Che nulla promission rendono intera.'

'He turned his steps upon a path that was not true, following deceptive images of good, which to no promise render fulfilment.' At last, in spite of good inspirations procured for him by her prayers (ll. 133–135), he fell so low that nothing would avail for his recovery but the vision of the eternal penalties of sin in those that have finally forsaken God, or as they are described at the beginning of the *Inferno* (iii. 18):—

> 'le genti dolorose,
> Ch' hanno perduto il ben dell' intelletto.'

Whatever then may be the meaning of the desertion of Beatrice, the result is described as 'minding earthly things,' abandoning himself to pleasures that are deceptive and that can never satisfy. Compare with this the language of *Purg.* xvii. 133–5:—

> 'Altro ben è che non fa l' uom felice;
> Non è felicità, non è la buona
> Essenza, d' ogni ben frutto e radice.'

'Another good there is which makes not man happy; it is not happiness, it is not the essential good, of all that is good the fruit and root.' All this, it will be noticed, corresponds exactly with the language of Dante's formal confession already quoted. 'Things present with their deceptive pleasure turned him astray, as soon as Beatrice was removed out of his sight' (xxxi. 34–36). But, next, when Beatrice returns to the charge in l. 43 onwards, we meet with an expression rather more precise, and more difficult to explain. Again, in l. 56, the 'cose fallaci' play the most prominent part; but at last, when reproaching him for the ease with which he had been overcome, and the want of spirit shown in his acquiescence without a struggle in his degradation, there occurs one word which has opened the floodgates of controversy and speculation, and has of itself given an entirely new turn to the discussion. See xxxi. 58–60:—

> 'Non ti dovea gravar le penne in giuso,
>   Ad aspettar più colpi, o pargoletta,
>   O altra vanità con sì breve uso.'

'Thou shouldst not have weighed down thy wings to await further strokes, either young girl, or other vanity of like brief enjoyment.' Even here the brief enjoyment and transitory pleasure of the objects of Dante's pursuit is emphasized once more. The 'pargoletta'—a trivial, or silly girl (note the depreciatory diminutive)—comes in almost casually as a sample, among other things, of the transient and deceptive pleasures by which he was captivated.

Yet out of this has arisen a vast amount of traditional gossip and scandal as to the generally immoral character of Dante's private life. It should be added that at least five or six different theories, some literal, some allegorical, dating too from the earliest Commentators, have been suggested in explanation, or identification of this 'pargoletta.' But I do not propose to follow the controversy into these details. I can only attempt to offer some general explanation of the scene as a whole.

There is an important passage in a later Canto to be taken in connexion with those already cited, where Beatrice censures the aberrations of Dante in language which seems once more to give a new and unexpected colour to her charges. In xxxiii. 82, Dante expresses surprise that the more he strains his mental vision to understand the lofty teaching of Beatrice, the less he seems able to comprehend it. Her answer is this (ll. 85–90):—' It is in order that thou mayst know that school which thou hast followed (Philosophy), and mayst see how (little) its teaching is able to follow my discourse ; and that thou mayst see that your way is as widely removed from the way of God, as is distant from the Earth the heaven that speeds round the highest of all [1] ' (i.e. the *Primum Mobile*).

---

[1] From Mr. Vernon's translation (mainly). Dante has evidently in his mind *Isaiah* lv. 9.

Now as the passage last quoted seemed to point mainly to moral laxity, so this seems to point mainly, if not exclusively, to intellectual error. As the former seemed inconsistent with merely speculative aberrations, so the latter seems inconsistent with merely moral declension. Hence this passage, like the other, has proved the starting-point for much dispute as to the relation between the charge brought in Canto xxxiii with that (or those) brought in Canto xxx. Thus Scrocca maintains that the two charges have no relation to one another, and refer to two entirely distinct faults [1], one of sense, the other of intellect. But surely this second passage has clearly the air of a retrospective and summary reference to the faults already denounced, and, let us add, already pardoned. It has not at all the character of a newly formulated accusation. Scrocca himself admits, 'la seconda accusa *si fa a caso, e non di proposito.*' Its mention is entirely due to a difficulty experienced by Dante, which is thus accounted for by Beatrice (ll. 82–84). It seems clear to me that as the moral aspect of Dante's fall is emphasized in the passage cited from xxxi. 59, so the intellectual aspect is emphasized here; while both are included in the general charge of worldliness of life which we have shown to be so prominent in several passages of Cantos xxx and xxxi. Such errors of both doctrine and practice would be natural incidents or consequents of such a life.

Before proceeding further, I must first lay it down, as the starting-point of all my explanation, that I firmly maintain the real personal existence of Beatrice. I might almost say that I feel scarcely more fully assured of the existence of Dante himself. I do not affirm that she was necessarily Beatrice Portinari, as Boccaccio positively asserts. That is a matter of quite secondary importance, though I do not myself see any sufficient reason for denying it [2]. I consider

---

[1] *Il peccato di Dante*, pp. 39, 40 : ' Due son le accuse di Beatrice al poeta, e due le colpe in costui, diverse per lor natura et distintamente significate.' Again, ' due sono certissimamente.' Again, ' Che le accuse di Beatrice, essendo due, sieno distinte nei due Canti xxx e xxxiii, e *non congiunte nel primo*, mi pare assai dimostrato,' &c.

[2] As to the objection taken from her being a married woman, Gaspary

* * *

those who do not believe in a literal Beatrice (whether Beatrice Portinari or not, as I say, matters little) to be beyond argument, but no less so are those (as it seems to me) who believe in no more than a literal Beatrice. In other words, I regard it as equally essential both to believe in a literal *substratum* for this wonderful creation of Dante [1], and also to admit an allegorizing and idealizing exaltation of that original, which makes it (to our ideas) almost unrecognizable. I would only in passing illustrate this by the similar idealization by Dante of Cato, and, I should add, also of the Countess Matilda, supposing that we are right in identifying her with the mysterious Matelda of the Earthly Paradise. I have given my reasons for this belief concerning Beatrice fully elsewhere [2]. The present bare statement therefore will not I hope be taken as mere dogmatism. It is only a declaration of the point of view from which I approach the subject before us. I will define my position a little more precisely, to guard still further against any misconception on so fundamental a point. I hold that Beatrice was none the less a real person *because* she was thus idealized by Dante beyond the recognition of common eyes. I believe that Dante's affection for Beatrice was no less real and

observes : ' That Dante should have loved and celebrated a married woman can cause but little surprise, in view of the manners of the age : the troubadours always extolled married women, and the Italian poets probably did likewise, though in their case we have no positive testimony. . . . Dante's passion was for the angel, not for the earthly woman, her marriage belonged to her earthly existence, with which the poet was not concerned. We must beware of confounding our age with that of Dante . . . Accordingly we have no valid reason for doubting Boccaccio's statement ' (*op. cit.* p. 232). Further Gaston Paris writes thus of ' Love,' as it was understood by Dante and Guinicelli, in *Romania*, Ann. xii. p. 521 : it was ' amour de tête et non amour de cœur ' ; p. 522 : ' L'idée que l'amour est une vertu, et qu'il excite à toutes les autres, surtout aux vertus sociales, est devenue un principe fondamental ' . . . ' L'amour était un art, une science, et pour avoir le droit de s'en mêler il fallait en posséder les règles.'

[1] As Wordsworth says :—

> ' each airy thought revolved
> Round a substantial centre.' (*Prelude*, B. viii.)

A recent writer says : ' Here as ever Dante dared to draw from life. He did not invent some female figure to embody a divine meaning, he saw the divine meaning embodied in the living woman.'

[2] *Studies*, II. pp. 79-151.

intense, because it was spiritual and refined, or, as it would
sometimes be termed, Platonic. I maintain also that the
incidents recorded by Dante about Beatrice, especially in
the *Vita Nuova*, are, in their main outlines, literally true,
notwithstanding the mystical or allegorical significance which
he attaches to them. I am sure that it would be quite alien
to the mind of Dante to imagine a series of deeply important
events and experiences in his, or any one else's, life as not
having a deeper meaning of this kind. For him 'all things
were double one against the other[1].' No doubt however
these two aspects of life acted and reacted on one another.
Consequently, when I say that the incidents recorded in the
Vita Nuova or *Convito* really occurred, I mean that they
are literally true in *general outline*, though probably not
in all their picturesque and significant details. Such details
were no doubt modified, more or less consciously, when
missing links had to be supplied in the web of mystery and
allegory with which Dante's mind was preoccupied, and to
which he would certainly attribute even a higher degree
of truth[2]. For in a well-known passage of the *Convito*
(II. xiii), he says that, after expounding the literal meaning

[1] The following passage from Dr. Sanday's *Bampton Lectures* (p. 405) seems
to me to express very aptly the point of view of Dante : 'There are subtle
analogies in things. The spiritual world and the material world are "double,
the one against the other." Both proceed from the hand of the same Creator,
and He has impressed similar laws upon them. Hence it is not an illegitimate
process to make use of these analogies, to speak of the spiritual in terms of the
not-spiritual, if by so doing spiritual things are brought home more closely to
the apprehension.' Bede speaks of such analogies as 'pulchra rerum concordia'
and 'mira sacramenti concordia' (ed. Plummer, p. lxi).

[2] Carlyle in justification of such a process, though not in reference to Dante,
writes thus :—
'What if many so-called Facts were little better than a Fiction ; if here we
had no direct Camera Obscura Picture of the (writer's) history but only some
more or less fantastic Adumbration, symbolically, perhaps significantly enough,
shadowing forth the same? . . . What are your historical facts, still more your
biographical? Wilt thou know a Man . . . by stringing together a bead-roll of
what thou namest Facts? The Man is the Spirit he worked in, not what
he did, but what he became' (*Sartor Resartus*, ii. 10). Aristotle's well-known
contrast of the poet and the historian is still worth repeating : τούτῳ διαφέρει,
τῷ τὸν μὲν (sc. ἱστορικὸν) τὰ γενόμενα λέγειν, τὸν δὲ (sc. ποιητὴν) οἷα ἂν γένοιτο.
διὸ καὶ φιλοσοφώτερον καὶ σπουδαιότερον ποίησις ἱστορίας ἐστίν (*Poetics*, c. ix.
§§ 2, 3). So Tennyson used to say, 'Poetry is truer than fact.'

of a passage, he will pass on to its 'allegorical and true' meaning; and in II. xvi. 15, he contrasts the 'vera sentenza' of a verse with the 'sposizione fittizia e letterale.'

Dante then, like all other poets of his day, idealized 'the Lady' whom he had chosen, and whom, by the then current custom of poesy, he was bound so to choose as the central figure of his verse. But, when Dante so idealized the Lady of his choice, it was a halo of religious idealization and spiritual exaltation that he threw around her [1], corresponding to the interests and experiences of his own inner life. In that he was unique among his contemporaries. Finally, the language of metaphor and allegory was to him—almost as truly as to a Hebrew Prophet—the natural and spontaneous mode of expressing his thoughts and feelings. For this also we must make due allowance when interpreting his language into that of the present century. I regard then the purely literal or purely allegorical interpretation as equally erroneous, I might almost say equally inconceivable [2]. Both of the extremists are (as is so commonly the case in the development of theological error also) 'right in what they affirm, and wrong in what they deny.'

The following are, I think, the main theories as to the precise meaning of the indictment of Beatrice.

(1) That Dante literally became forgetful of her and transferred his affections to some one else; some Com-

---

[1] It should not be forgotten, however, that Guido Guinicelli had already struck a somewhat similar note, and there are many occasions on which Dante either quotes or manifestly imitates him. In *Purg.* xxvi he expresses admiration for him, and acknowledges indebtedness to him in no grudging tones. He speaks of him as 'il padre mio, e degli altri miei miglior' (l. 97). See further, ll. 112-114. Among the poems of Guido Guinicelli the beautiful Canzone beginning—

'Al cor gentil ripara sempre Amore'

should be specially noticed. Dante refers to this in *Conv.* IV. xx. 67, and distinctly borrows from it in his Canzone III, and Sonetto X, and in *V. N.* §§ 11 and 26. It is translated by D. G. Rossetti with his usual skill in *Dante and his Circle*, pp. 291-293. See further, on Dante's indebtedness to Guinicelli, Nannucci, *Manuale della Letteratura*, pp. 46-48, and Gaspary's *History of Italian Literature*, translated by Dr. Oelsner, pp. 101-103.

[2] So Beatrice remained 'a woman still to memory and devotion, a disembodied spirit to the ecstasy of thought.' (Lowell, *My Study Windows*, p. 215.)

mcntators going further, and even maintaining that the reference is to his marriage with Gemma Donati !

(2) That Dante abandoned himself to an immoral life, some Commentators again supplying details as to several *liaisons* of this description.

(3) That the meaning is purely allegorical and relates entirely to his devotion to Philosophy instead of Theology ; and further that he went so far in this direction, as to fall into Philosophical error, Religious Scepticism, or Heresy ; or that at least he came to be in sympathy with such views.

(4) Others, finding no proof of any such aberrations in his writings, hold that Dante's devotion to philosophical and secular learning led him merely to general worldliness of life, and indifference to Religion and to Theology which had once and for so long held the supreme place in his affections, but not to any speculative error.

(5) As it is clear that these theories are not mutually exclusive, it may be maintained that the accusation of Beatrice is to some degree a complex one. In other words (as I have already hinted) this general charge of worldliness may have had a double aspect, or a double development. Dante may have combined Religious Scepticism or Religious Indifference with some degree of that frivolity, or even laxity, of life, which prevailed in contemporary society at Florence. If he did so, it would certainly have been (to borrow his own language)

'Conforme al viver del paese.'

This last view, in some form or other, I hold to be the true one.

(1) The first may be rejected confidently and even scornfully.

(*a*) Under any view whatever of the nature of Dante's devotion to Beatrice, the reproach of transferring his affections to another person after her death would be utterly unreasonable.

(*b*) This would be doubly so, and in fact preposterous, if she were Beatrice Portinari, who was certainly the wife of Simone de' Bardi. That question however we leave open.

(*c*) It would be worse still if we suppose the allusion in the line

    'Questi si tolse a me, e diessi altrui[1]'

to refer to Dante's marriage with Gemma Donati, about three or four years (probably) after the death of Beatrice. Scartazzini in fact has distinctly maintained[2] that the Donna Gentile of the *Vita Nuova* and the *Convito* was none other than Gemma Donati.   Others have identified one or both of these with the 'pargoletta.'

(*d*) It involves in any case an utterly false and unworthy notion of the nature of Dante's affection for Beatrice.

(*e*) Above all it miserably degrades Beatrice herself. She becomes nothing but a selfish, fretful, jealous and unreasonable woman, exhibiting a very low type of the 'spretae iniuria formae.'   In fact we may well protest

    'Tantaene animis caelestibus irae !'

(*f*) Finally, how could a personal offence of this kind be treated as a *sin*, and one moreover needing special and severe penitence (see the end of Canto xxx) above and beyond the completed purgation of the seven Deadly Sins by the penance of Purgatory.   What an anticlimax !   How this belittles the whole scene[3] !

But we need not waste further words on a view, which, I imagine, no one would now seriously maintain.

(2) The second view—that Dante abandoned himself to a licentious and immoral life, which has found expression in the famous sentence in the biography of Boccaccio—' In questo altissimo poeta trovò ampissimo luogo la lussuria '—

---

[1] *Purg.* xxx. 126.

[2] *Prolegg.* p. 211 and elsewhere.   At the same time it should be observed that though Scartazzini's opinions were generally very dogmatically expressed, they were also very frequently changed.   Thus, on this very subject, Scrocca points out (*op. cit.* pp. 14 *seqq.*) that at different times Scartazzini maintained Dante's faults to have been (1) chiefly 'amorosi' but combined with intellectual pride, and perhaps also 'miscredenza '; (2) exclusively an inordinate devotion to poetry and philosophy, 'colpa non sensuale ma intellettuale'; (3) the engrossing pursuit of worldly riches, honours, glory, pleasures, &c.

[3] Perhaps I may be allowed to offer as a parallel to this incongruity an old Oxford story of the reprimand of an offender by a high College authority. 'You have not only offended against Almighty God, but, Sir, you have also incurred my serious displeasure ! '

this also may, I think, be briefly dismissed [1]. There is simply no further evidence for such a statement, though other Commentators, like sheep, simply repeat it. It has probably been developed *more Commentatorum* out of the literal interpretation of such passages as this, and others that might be quoted from the *Convito*, especially if the precaution be taken of doing so without regard to the context. Dante there endeavours carefully to guard himself against any such possible inference from his language [2]. How ready and shameless was the inventive faculty of Commentators may be illustrated by their utterly different and inconsistent statements as to the character of Fabbro in *Purg.* xiv. 100, or of Gaia in *Purg.* xvi. 140 [3]. In these and other cases they are obviously merely inventing facts to suit what they suppose to be the meaning of the passage before them. Those who have done the same in regard to the present passage may be dismissed, in the language of Dean Plumptre, as among 'the unclean birds of literature who scent carrion everywhere.'

It is a strong point as against both (1) and (2) that the description of Dante's fault given in *Purg.* xxxiii. 85 *seqq.*, whatever may be its precise meaning, would not be suitable to either of these hypotheses.

(3) The third view that Dante lapsed into sympathy with Scepticism, Freethinking, or Heresy was maintained by Dr. Witte [4] in his first series of *Dante-Forschungen.* Accord-

---

[1] Scrocca (*op. cit.* p. 2) surely goes too far in saying that it is the opinion to which 'consentono, se si tolga lo Scartazzini, gli studiosi tutti del gran poema.'

[2] See *Conv.* I. ii. 117; II. xvi. 19 and 98, and especially III. iii. 95 *seqq.* : 'che questo amore era quello che in quella nobilissima natura [*scil.* mente] nasce, cioè di verità e di virtù, e *per ischiudere ogni falsa opinione di me, per la quale fosse sospicato lo mio amore essere per sensibile dilettazione.*' No words could be more explicit or more emphatic than these.

[3] Thus *Purg.* xiv. 99–102, by a change of punctuation and taking 'quando' interrogatively or otherwise, can be understood so as to imply that Fabbro was either a good or a bad man. Hence Commentators boldly describe him as in fact one or the other, evidently to suit their view of the sense of the passage. The same occurs in reference to Gaia. Some say that her notoriety in vice caused her father's name to be better known than it would have been through his own merits; others that she was such a paragon of virtue that her father thereby gained a yet more honourable fame!

[4] p. 66 *seqq.* See also especially pp. 12, 14, 172, 173.

ing to Scartazzini, Dr. Witte followed in this the footsteps of Dionisi. But it is found much earlier in the *Letture* of Gelli[1]. I have noted in an earlier volume of these *Studies*[2] that there is absolutely no evidence of any such aberration in the writings of Dante. There is (I believe) no trace whatever of any wavering in his belief in the Divine authority of the Church on any matter of doctrine[3].

In regard to this charge or suspicion of heresy in Dante it does not seem that he is always accused of having himself held any definite heretical views, but he has been supposed to have shown some sympathy with heresy, or at least free-thinking, on such loose and vague grounds as these :—(1) his strong denunciations of abuses in the Church. But while such denunciations are naturally a common feature in most heretical systems, it does not prove that any one who employs them is heretical, and there is this important difference that in Dante they are limited to matters of discipline or practice, and they never touch doctrine or the Church's authoritative teaching. (2) The absence of definite condemnation of contemporary heretics in the *Divina Commedia*, the ' eresiarchi ' of Circle VI being chiefly Materialists and ' Epicureans[4].' No doubt this silence of Dante on the subject of heresy is a remarkable fact, but the inference drawn from it as above is by no means a necessary one. It can be quite otherwise explained. For instance as follows :—

i. Most of the heretical sects which were prominent in the

---

[1] *Lettura* 1ᵐᵃ, *Lez.* 4ᵗᵃ, pp. 72, 73 : ' dandosi agli studii di filosofia e delle scienze umane, dove si truovono molte opinioni contrarie dirittamente alla lume della fede, cominciò a poco a poco *a lasciarsi svolgere e tirare al tutto nella lor sentenza di quelle*.'

[2] II. p. 46. Scartazzini maintains the same very emphatically in his *Hand-buch*, p. 233 : ' There is no single dogma of the orthodox faith as then held of which we can show that Dante at any time or in any of his writings either contested the truth or even felt any doubt.' A. J. Butler's *Translation*, p. 234. See also *Prolegg.*, pp. 224, 226. See further *infra*, p. 248.

[3] Note the expression in *Conv.* II. iv. 31, 32 ' Secondo che la santa Chiesa vuole, che non può dire menzogna '; and in vi. 33 ' santa Chiesa ' is described as the ' Sposa e Secretaria [di Dio].'

[4] It is however perhaps worth noting that ' Epicureans ' is a constant name for Heretics in the Talmud (Dean Farrar, *S. Paul*, ii. p. 537 *n.*). On Dante's probable acquaintance with Hebrew literature, see *infra*, pp. 277 *seqq.*

earlier half of the thirteenth century had become insignificant at its close, except the Waldenses [1]. Certainly a very bitter persecutor of the Albigensian heretics at the beginning of the century, Bishop Folco or Folquet, is highly favoured by Dante, since he grants him an exceptionally early admission to Paradise, in spite of his exceptionally vicious life (see *Par.* ix).

ii. (*a*) So far as these sects denounced practical abuses in the Church, and also extolled the Virtue of Poverty, Dante would be in sympathy with them [2], as he was with this feature in the Franciscan System (see *Par.* xi); but (*β*) so far as this feature was combined with speculative error (e. g. the nature of the soul, dualism, &c.), Dante would strongly condemn them. Thus (*a*) would save them from his denunciation, while (*β*) would exclude them from his sympathy. Hence they are severely let alone.

iii. Whenever heresy took the practical form of schism, Dante's condemnation of it is unsparing and severe, but if it do not go beyond speculative opinions held by each man 'in the deep of his heart,' it would not fall within the range of positive sins of act such as are punished in the *Inferno*. Nor would it come under the head of sins expiated in Purgatory, since, by the teaching of the Church, for one who departed hence under her ban for heresy unrepented of, there 'remained no more sacrifice for sin.'

(4) As then the third view fails from the total absence of any evidence in support of it, we pass on to the fourth. This undoubtedly contains a large element of truth, though it may not be quite the whole truth. That Dante did lapse from the high promise of his early life into general worldliness, religious indifference, excessive devotion to secular studies

---

[1] See Tocco, *Quel che non c'è nella Divina Commedia*, o *Dante e l' Eresia* (the alternative titles are significant), pp. 8, 10. Also Mazzoni, in his monograph on the authorship of the mediaeval poem *Il Fiore* (which he thinks may be probably attributed to Dante himself), refers to 'la nessuna o scarsa importanza' assigned in the chroniclers to the Paterine heresies, and 'come se ne perse presto la memoria' when the policy of Boniface VIII opened up much larger questions (*Raccolta di Studi Critici dedicata ad Alessandro d' Ancona*, p. 659. See further *ib.* pp. 684–686).

[2] Comp. *Par.* xi. 58 *seqq.*; xxii. 82–84; *Mon.* III. x. 105–132, &c.

and pursuits (not necessarily in themselves censurable or involving the adoption of speculative error) seems to follow not only from his admissions in the *Convito* but also from some of the expressions in *Purg.* xxx, though it may by no means exhaust their meaning ; and still more from the passage already spoken of (*supra*, p. 224) in Canto xxxiii. Those who think that Dante's faults were entirely of a moral kind (i. e. the second of the views lately enumerated) endeavour to evade the force of that passage by claiming that the word *scuola* is simply equivalent to *compagnia*.   But apart from the facts that the 'dottrina' which it involved is conspicuously censured, and also that the intellectual inability to follow the lofty teaching of Beatrice is the difficulty to be explained, it seems highly improbable that *scuola* could bear so general a meaning.   As Scrocca rightly urges, it always involves some connotation of teaching or discipleship.   This is clearly so in *Inf.* iv. 94, where the 'school' of the poets under their leader Homer is described [1].   But it is so even in *Purg.* xxxii. 79, where those present at the Transfiguration are spoken of as *scuola,* 'one being their Master, even Christ.'

(5) While admitting then the reality, at least as forming part of Beatrice's accusation, of the charge that Dante abandoned theology for philosophy and secular pursuits, I feel bound to admit that though this might be enough to satisfy the description of *Purg.* xxxiii. 85-90, yet it cannot be thought an adequate explanation of some of the expressions which occur in the more formal and detailed indictment of Cantos xxx and xxxi.   I am ready to admit that some degree of moral laxity seems to be also therein implied, though it is by no means necessary to concede that it went very far, and certainly not to any such lengths as many writers, ancient and modern, have imagined.   I say this simply because there is no evidence in fact to establish anything of the sort.   It is at any rate a very subordinate feature or detail in the general charge.

Let us now endeavour, from such data as Dante has given

---

[1] With this we may compare 'the schools of the prophets' and 'scuole dei religiosi' in *Conv.* II. xiii. 47.

us, to reconstruct and to realize the probable course of his life, after the supreme crisis of the loss of Beatrice.

The conditions which led up to it are familiar to all from the *Vita Nuova*, but, as even these have been most variably interpreted[1], it will be well to restate them briefly in the sense in which I receive them. The meaning given to them, whatever it be, is obviously of vital importance for the interpretation of the scene we are now considering.

It is a thrice-told tale how when Dante was about nine years old, Beatrice, who was a few months younger, flashed across his path ; how from that moment a vision of imagined beauty and perfection dawned upon the perfervid imagination of 'the marvellous boy[2]'; how this image impressed itself more and more deeply on his highly sensitive, enthusiastic, poetical nature[3]. Like others in whom the poetic imagination is intense, he idealizes the fleeting image that he has seen, the process being all the more easy because, in the absence of other meetings between them for some years, the growth of the ideal was not checked by being brought into contact with fact. But, as I have already noted, unlike all other poets, Dante does not deck out his ideal with physical beauty and social charms, but rather with 'the ornament of a meek and quiet spirit,' with all the attributes of moral, religious, spiritual perfection, and most prominently with that crowning virtue of humility, which commanded above all others his constant and especial admiration[4]. Such was in *his* case the ennobling effect of

'The consecration and the poet's dream.'

We read (*Vita Nuova*, §§ x, xi) how the thought of her, and still more her presence, as she moved forth 'clothed with humility,' expelled every base or unkind thought and filled him with love and goodwill even to his enemies. It killed

---

[1] For several such interpretations see *Studies*, II, Essay II.

[2] Wordsworth's designation of Chatterton.

[3] He confesses of himself—

'che pur di mia natura
Trasmutabile son per tutte guise!'   (*Par.* v. 98, 99.)

[4] See illustrations of this in *Studies*, II. p. 75.

all vices in him, inspired all virtues [1] (§ x). Such a beneficent influence must surely come direct from above. The type thus conceived of perfect Womanhood, bearing the same ideal relation to Woman as the 'Son of Man' to humanity at large, could be none other than a revelation vouchsafed to him from heaven. Its embodiment might then aptly symbolize for him the Revelation of God. And when Dante came later on to treat his own experiences as typical of that of mankind in general [2], the significance of this symbol also might be enlarged so as to become typical of Divine Revelation to mankind generally [3].

But to return to the career and experience of Dante. After many years of boyhood and youth passed under a strange, abnormal, even unnatural, spiritual tension, a period in which Dante may almost be said to have been 'moving about in worlds not realized,' that dominating presence and influence is taken from him; the ideal whom, or which, he had thus worshipped and adored is lost to him. This again no doubt proved a fresh and very powerful stimulus to the idealizing process. 'When she died (writes Mr. Lowell [4]), Dante's grief . . . filled her room with something fairer than the reality had ever been. There is no idealizer like unavailing regret, all the more if it be a regret of fancy as much as of real feeling.' So, at the age of about twenty-five, Dante finds

---

[1] Very similar sentiments will be found in Guido Guinicelli's Canzone *Al cor gentil*, already referred to *supra*, p. 228 *n.*

[2] I think perhaps this representative character of Dante in the *Divina Commedia* has not always been sufficiently recognized. He himself declares that if his poem is regarded allegorically, 'subiectum est *homo*, prout merendo et demerendo per arbitrii libertatem Iustitiae praemianti aut punienti obnoxius est' (*Ep.* x. § 8). From this point of view it may be worth considering whether for every incident recorded we are bound to find a 'private interpretation'; whether every detail in this present accusation must needs have a direct personal application. May not even such lines as xxx. 130-138 have a wider significance for humanity at large which would find an echo in *Par.* vii. 79-120?

[3] Some of my readers may have met with a Sermon by F. W. Robertson, on 'The Glory of the Virgin Mother,' in which he points out how she has gradually become the type and ideal of the perfection of all the tender and womanly qualities of human nature. The present writer once heard a very striking sermon by Cardinal Manning on the 'Festival of the Assumption,' in which the same thought was admirably developed.

[4] *Among my Books*, ii. p. 67.

himself suddenly and all unprepared, face to face with the prosaic realities of life. What then is likely to have been the probable course both of his inner and his outer life during the nine or ten critical years that followed, until the great re-awakening and recovery at the age of thirty-five, which is delineated in the *Divina Commedia*? So far from religion affording consolation to him in his despair, religion itself seemed to have deserted him. Her 'candlestick' has, as it were, 'been removed out of its place.' He turns for consolation (' dopo alquanto tempo,' as we read in *Conv.* II. xiii) to the philo-sophical treatises of Cicero and Boethius. His mental and intellectual energy finds refuge in philosophy and secular learning. He further admits that such studies, in which he first found consolation, soon began to exercise a fascination over him, and became too absorbing, to the exclusion of higher and spiritual interests. Perhaps even, as in the experience of S. Augustine (see *Conf.* III. v, &c.), admiration for the greater polish and perfection of literary style in the classical authors may have provoked unfavourable comparison with the more homely diction of scriptural or ecclesiastical writers. Dante himself declares (in *Conv.* II. xiii) that though he went to such authors (and primarily Cicero and Boethius) seeking consolation, he found much more than that. ' He found (he says) not only a remedy for his tears, but a revelation of new authors and sciences and books, so that he deemed that Philosophy, the sovereign lady of these authors, sciences, and books, must be something supreme.' In his own words he was like a man who going in search of silver, without intending it, discovers gold. He pictured to himself this Philosophy as a gentle Lady (Donna Gentile) full of com-passion, and he betook himself to places where he could meet her, that is to say, to the schools of the 'religious[1],' and the

---

[1] 'Religiosi' is here used in its technical sense for those who follow the 'religious' life, i. e. monks, so that 'scuole de' religiosi,' side by side with 'dis-putazioni de' filosofi,' will nearly correspond with professed Theologians. The word might perhaps as well be written with a capital letter, as in III. xi. 105, and as it is *h. l.* by Giuliani. Dante uses 'religioni' in the sense of 'the religious orders' in *Conv.* IV. iv. 60. He protests, however, against this restricted use of 'religione' in a striking passage in *Conv.* IV. xxviii. 68–74.

disputations of the philosophers, and in a short time, perhaps about thirty months, her sweetness and the love of her banished and destroyed all other thoughts.

Coincidently with this condition of things there occurred a significant incident in his private life. The dates are fixed for us thus. In *Vita Nuova*, § 35 we are told of something which occurred on the first anniversary of Beatrice's death ; and after that, 'poi per alquanto tempo' (as we read in § 36), the compassionate regard and evident sympathy of a gentle lady ('Gentil Donna') so touched him that his soul came to be more and more attracted to her. The gradual growth of this new and disquieting affection is described in *Conv.* II. ii, and the time of its commencement is given, by a curious astronomical datum [1] in the same chapter, as being September 1291. (This makes the 'alquanto tempo' of *Vita Nuova*, § 36 to represent about three months.) Then the triumph of the new love became complete (as we may fairly gather from *Conv.* II. xiii) in about thirty months, viz. in March 1294, and then was composed the *Canzone*, 'Voi che intendendo il terzo ciel movete.'

He could not fail to be struck with the parallel courses of his inner and outer life. This 'Donna Gentile' became to him a type of Philosophy ; for he thought that he saw in his growing interest in her, and his slackening devotion to Beatrice, a warning and an object-lesson of the change that was going on in his inner life also. For in just the same way he recognized that he was becoming absorbed in secular learning and Philosophy, while his devotion to his first Love, Theology and Religion, was waxing cold [2]. Mingled with the feeling that he had lost his first love, in the spiritual sense, was the feeling that he had done so at this same time in respect of one to whom he felt, as he looked back on the experiences of his *Vita Nuova*, that (as S. Paul says to Philemon) he 'owed his own self besides.' Thus the two streams of his outer and his inner life seemed to be flowing

---

[1] This has been explained *supra*, pp. 39–42.

[2] 'Contrary to his knowledge and better judgment he had chosen Science and Philosophy, to the neglect of Theology and Beatrice' (Earle, *Introd.* p. lxviii).

in parallel courses, and Dante would certainly not doubt that there was a real, though underground, connexion between these two currents.

One thing at least may be confidently affirmed. However we may interpret the affection of Dante for the 'Donna Gentile,' it was at least entirely pure and 'Platonic.' There is no suspicion of any moral default so far. Else could she never have been to him a type of 'divine Philosophy' (*Conv.* III. xii. 100), 'sposa, suora, e figlia dell' Imperadore del Cielo' (*ib.* 115–118); 'la cui propria magione è nel secretissimo della divina Mente' (IV. xxx. 66–68).

After this date, i. e. early in 1294, the curtain drops, and it is not again lifted until the epoch of the great conversion or awakening of the year 1300. What is likely to have been the course of his life in these six unrecorded years? Though we must admit that only

' Dio si sa qual poi sua vita fusi,'

yet we may attempt to trace what its external conditions are likely to have been. The crash, as we have seen, fell upon him when he was little more than twenty-five, when he had barely crossed the 'soglia di sua seconda etade' (*Purg.* xxx. 124). We have learnt how for the first three or four years he seems to have led a more or less secluded life, finding, as many others in sorrow have done, in study and literary pursuits a refuge from distressing thoughts, until such occupations had come to be no longer only a means to an end, but an end in themselves. His marriage probably took place about this time, and perhaps as a natural result, his return to the social and political life of Florence. He became enrolled as member of a guild, viz. that of the 'Medici e Speziali,' which was a precedent condition of exercising political rights. This was probably, in the opinion of Fraticelli, in 1295, when he attained the minimum age for the exercise of such rights, viz. thirty years [1]. The time for dreaming is now past. Theology

---

[1] See Fraticelli, *Vita di Dante*, p. 112, for an account of the MS. in which this entry is found. It is only a late compilation (dated 1446–7) from older documents. The names are alphabetically arranged; they are in Italian and not, as the originals would have been, in Latin ; and it is defective for the years

and philosophy give place to a life of secular activity. Both in society and in politics Dante has now to associate, since he cannot 'go out of the world,' with commonplace and often frivolous companions, both male and female ; often too no doubt, as he says of his later surroundings, even with a ' compagnia malvagia e scempia[1] ' (*Par.* xvii. 62). Dante has now to take his part in public or civic life ; he has in short to fall in with the ordinary surroundings of a young ' Florentine gentleman,' among ' the Christians of the thirteenth century[2].' The daily round of this life we may take to have been of no very exalted type, whether we turn to the romances of Boccaccio, or the chronicles of Villani. In the unhinged and utterly unsettled condition of his whole being so vividly depicted in the *Vita Nuova* and *Convito*, some relief might naturally be found not only in the resources of study but also by plunging with keen vigour into the duties and occupations of common life. What is more natural than to suppose that Dante's high ideal, his impossibly high ideal, of life should deteriorate under such circumstances ? Is it surprising that ' things present ' should gain a sway over him ; that he should ' mind earthly things ' ; that his affections should be set no longer upon ' things above,' but on ' things of the earth ' ? Putting aside for a moment the single word ' pargoletta,' could any picture accord more precisely with the form of the self-accusation of Dante in *Purg.* xxxi. 34–36, ' Things present with their deceptive pleasure turned aside my steps, so soon as your face was hidden from me,' or with the language of the indictment of Beatrice in xxx. 130–132, ' He turned his

1282-97. This will explain a fact which has sometimes caused surprise, viz. that Dante should be entered at that early date as ' poeta Fiorentino.' This is probably an anachronistic description introduced when the Register was modernized.

[1] This is admirably expressed by Professor Earle (*Introduction*, p. cxxxvi) : — Dante was like ' a pilgrim lost in such perplexities as occur only to those who have begun well, and who have kept high aims, moral and intellectual, continually before them. Such a man may lose his way in speculative mazes, theological and philosophical, especially if he be involved in political conflicts, and find himself in a situation where there is no path for an honest man, but wide openings for the unscrupulous—such desperate straits may tempt a high-minded man to renounce effort, lapsing into apathy and torpor.'

[2] *V. N.* § 30.

steps upon a way that was not true, following deceptive images of good, which to no promise render fulfilment ' ?

In both of these no unprejudiced reader can fail to be struck with the reiterated emphasis on 'presenti cose' (xxxi. 34) ; 'falso piacer' (l. 35) ; 'false imagini di ben' (xxx. 131) ; 'cose fallaci' (xxxi. 56) ; 'vanità con sì breve uso ' (l. 60).

In the midst of all this, the one isolated allusion to the 'pargoletta,' touched as with the lightest possible hand, cannot possibly be the gist, the kernel, the keynote, of the whole accusation. It cannot possibly be the main feature in the life which is thus censured at length. Besides, let us note this. If 'the head and front of his offending' were a dissolute or incontinent life, why does it demand a special and separate penance (see *Purg.* xxx. 142–145)? This would naturally have been expiated on the last *Cornice* of Purgatory itself, where in fact Dante does admit that he had to suffer severely in the fire of purification[1]. Possibly as a subordinate incident in that generally worldly life there may be some literal truth in this particular charge, though in the present passage (as I have already noted) this 'pargoletta' seems to be no more than a type or sample of generally trivial, frivolous, fleeting, vain and unworthy objects of pursuit. I do not feel at all concerned to deny that Dante may perhaps have fallen into a somewhat loose and irregular life for a time[2]. If, as suggested, he plunged into the ordinary routine life of Florence he can scarcely have touched so much pitch without some defilement. The moral tone of social life at Florence was deplorably low. Whenever Dante has to refer to sins of incontinence or impurity he never fails to note the enormous numbers of such sinners. But not only the quantity but the quality also of such offenders is as regularly insisted on. They were of the highest rank both in Church

---

[1] So writes Professor Earle : ' We are clearly past the stage at which such an imputation could be in place. After purification in the fire of the seventh Cornice, *that* weakness is no longer to be thought of.'

[2] His admission to Forese Donati in *Purg.* xxiii. 115 (for which see *infra*, p. 244), seems to imply this in some degree, though neither here or elsewhere in Dante's own works is there any specific admission of ' immorality ' in the special sense of the term.

* * *

and State; they were estimable and lovable characters[1];
and it is even in respect of the most degrading forms of that
vice, of which it is 'a shame even to speak,' that both in
Inf. and *Purg.* these expressions are most conspicuously
employed. All this implies that public opinion was very
lenient to them, that (as with regard to slave-holding, cock-
fighting, &c. 100 years ago in England) one did not lose caste
by being notoriously addicted to them. Can we suppose,
or should even the most devoted admirer of Dante need to
suppose, that in such a vortex of temptation he kept himself
wholly pure, at the time when he had lost the restraining
influence of religion, and when all the 'foundations' of his
moral being were 'out of course'? It is surely not unlikely
that there may have been some foundation for the statements
of Boccaccio[2], Benvenuto[3], and even of his own son Pietro[4],

---

[1] The very easy terms on which the dissolute sinners Cunizza and Bishop
Fulk or Folquet have been admitted to Paradise by Dante (see *Par.* ix) have
caused much 'searching of heart.' But too much must not be made of this.
For the last fifteen years of Cunizza's life, which she spent at Florence (c. 1265
to 1280), were conspicuous for works of piety and benevolence. She was much
in the house of the Cavalcanti, and Dante may have known her in her old age,
and have been interested in her through his 'primo amico' Guido Cavalcanti,
who was sixteen years his senior. He would be more impressed with her good
deeds which were known to him personally than with the far-off rumours of her
dissolute youth. Further, he may have wished to present her as an object
lesson of the boundless mercy of God; even as he writes of Manfred :—
    'Orribil furon li peccati miei ;
        Ma la bontà infinita ha sì gran braccia,
        Che prende ciò che si rivolge a lei.' (*Purg.* iii. 121-123.)
He might also have justified himself by such passages of Scripture as *S. Luke*
vii. 47 (the Magdalen) ; *Ezek.* xviii. 21, 22 ; or 1 *Pet.* iv. 1-3 and 8. But the
further question still remains, why is she in Paradise and not Purgatory,
since she had been dead only about twenty years? We can only suggest that
Dante may have been so impressed with her *exceptional* works of piety that he
might apply to her the words of *Wisdom* iv. 13 : 'Consummata in brevi explevit
tempora multa.' The case would be parallel to that of Provenzan Salvani in
Purg. xi. 127-142, though he indeed did not gain Paradise, but only much
advancement in Purgatory. The *principle* (though in an inverse sense) of *Purg.*
xi. 72 would apply. Something of the same kind might perhaps be said of
Folco, who for the last thirty years of his life was a monk and a bishop, although
this in itself would be no sort of guarantee for his good behaviour.

[2] As quoted *supra*, p. 230.

[3] Benvenuto, i. p. 543, describes him as ' Summe amorosus et nimis amator
mulierum.'

[4] Pietro, in reference to the fire of purification from Lust in *Purg.* xxvii,

though the picture may be highly coloured and exaggerated ; nor must we forget the stern reproach addressed to Dante by his 'primo amico' Guido Cavalcanti in the Sonnet beginning ' Io vengo il giorno a te infinite volte' (translated by Rossetti in *Dante and his Circle*, p. 161).

With all this smoke, one cannot but suspect there must have been some fire, but the essential point to insist upon is that, even if this be so, the reproaches of Beatrice relate to the levity, frivolity, yes, even degradation, of such a life in comparison with what had been, and might still have been, and not with unfaithfulness (as the world understands it) to herself ;—unfaithfulness to her indeed, as an ideal, and a guiding influence, but most certainly not as a neglected lover !

We will now turn to the evidence which is thought to bear on this subject in other passages in the works of Dante himself, apart from the untrustworthy gossip of his Commentators.

It is to be premised, first of all, that beyond all doubt his love both for Beatrice and the ' Donna Gentile ' was absolutely pure and spiritual.   Also that in the case of Gentucca [1]

---

says of his father—' Nota auctorem in hoc vitio fuisse multum implicitum, ut nunc ostendit de incendio quod habuit in dicta flamma in reminiscentia conscientiae ' (p. 489).   It is to be observed that Pietro's statements at any rate are not based upon the 'pargoletta' allusion in *Purg.* xxxi. 59.   His comment on this is :—' Ut fuit, cum, dicta theologia relicta, ipse Dantes se dedit pargolettae, id est, poesi, et aliis mundanis scientiis.'   Also the words ' ut nunc ostendit' might raise some suspicion as to the independence of his statement.

[1] D'Ovidio (*Stud,* p. 569) takes precisely the same view that I have advocated elsewhere, viz. that she was 'benefattrice, un ospite gentile.'   In that case Dante's grateful recognition of her would be like the tributes paid elsewhere to the Malaspina (*Purg.* viii), or the Scaligeri (*Par.* xvii).   D'Ovidio adds the weighty consideration that Dante would not be likely to foretell a new amorous lapse, when he is on the point of entering the fire of purification for such sins.   Scherillo makes the suggestion that Dante may have put this into the mouth of Bonagiunta from a knowledge of some special grounds for the speaker's personal interest in Gentucca : ' chi sa quali rapporti di parentela o di amicizia non corressero tra la Gentucca e Bonagiunta ? '   *Alcuni Capitoli,* p. 162.   It is indeed a strange slip on the part of the excellent Benvenuto when he identifies Gentucca with the 'pargoletta' of xxxi. *seqq.* !   ' Ista fuit iuvencula virgo de civitate Lucana cuius amore captus est aliquando post mortem Beatricis ' (iv. p. 231.   Compare also a similar statement on p. 74).   But Dante's relations

(see *Purg.* xxiv. 37–45) there is not the slightest reason to suspect anything dishonourable. For we must not forget that Dante puts in the mouth of Bonagiunta absolutely no more than this :—' A woman is born who is still young and un-married (i. e. in 1300) who will make my much abused city find favour in thine eyes.' 'This honourable and delightful reference (writes Mr. Eliot Norton) to this otherwise unknown maiden has given occasion to much worthless and base com-ment.' We may surely apply to such a case the kindly words of S. Thomas, *Summa*, II ^{2}. lx. 4$_r$ 'ubi non apparet mani-festa indicia de malitia alicuius, debemus eum ut bonum habere, in meliorem partem interpretando quod dubium est.'

But, beyond this, though we have no evidence as to details, there are certain admissions or indications furnished by Dante himself which are brought into the controversy and which have to be taken into account. These fall under three heads :—

(1) The remarkable confession which, in *Purg.* xxiii. 115 *seqq.*, is made by Dante to his wife's cousin Forese Donati (d. 1296), as to the unsatisfactory character of his life during a certain period. 'If thou recall to mind what thou wast with me, and what I was with thee, still will the present memory of it be burdensome.' Whatever that allusion may precisely indicate, it does not follow that it is limited, or that it necessarily at all refers, to the particular sin of gluttony which Forese was then expiating. Dante makes no reference to his having any special dread of punishment for that sin, as he does in some other well-known cases [1]. Forese may have been associated with Dante in other evil ways, the penalty for which both of them might have to expiate elsewhere than in the sixth Cornice.

In any case, Dante adds that his deliverance from that life dates from the conversion which he experienced in the 'selva oscura,' in other words, from that regeneration of his life which he describes as having taken place in the year 1300. Hence, as nothing answering to this admission took place in his

with Gentucca were *future* in 1300 (see *Purg.* xxiv. 43–45) whereas Beatrice (in 1300) is reproaching him with *past* errors.

[1] e. g. Pride chiefly, Envy less severely, and possibly (see what follows) the sin of the last Cornice.

Vita Nuova, the errors in question (whatever they were) must have occurred some time between the death of Beatrice (i. e. 1290) and 1300; which is just the period indicated in these reproaches.

(2) The second piece of evidence is found in the admission that Dante had to suffer severely in the fire of purification for 'Lussuria,' in the seventh Cornice. Not only did he suffer very severely (see *Purg.* xxvii, especially 49–51), but also it has been remarked that this is the *only* case in which he is pointedly made to share in the punishments which he witnessed. It is fair to say that perhaps the physical conditions made it inevitable in this case, as in that of blinding smoke of the third Cornice, since the fire *must* be passed through by any one, in order to reach the upward path on the other side. Also in ll. 10–12, the necessity for this is stated in quite general terms, as though affecting all alike; and Virgil and Statius are in fact subject to the same condition, though they are not described as suffering from it. In relation to the exalted standard of the Beatitude pronounced immediately before—'Beati mundo corde'—such a necessity might well lie on all, for judged by that strict rule we may indeed exclaim with Job, 'What is man that he should be clean?' (*Job* xv. 14). I think therefore that too much may easily be made of this circumstance, still I am ready to admit that in *some* degree, greater or less, it does seem to point to a confession of some offence in this regard.

(3) We come now to the remarkable series of four *Canzoni*, commonly known as the '*Pietra*' *Canzoni*, because in all of them the word, or name, *Pietra* is played upon with most singular and ingenious artifice.

These are *Canzoni* xii and xv and *Sestine* i and ii in the Oxford Dante. The *Sestina* was a highly artificial form of *Canzone*, invented in Provençal by Arnaut Daniel (for whom see *Purg.* xxvi). It was imitated by Dante in Italian in the case of the two *Sestine* in question, both of which are quoted and referred to by Dante himself with evident satisfaction in *Vulg. Eloq.* II. x. and xiii.

Now whether this *Pietra* be a proper name or not, no one

can read these *Canzoni* without feeling that the writer describes
a very intense and very literal love.   Also it was one entirely
unrequited, whence possibly the significant name *Pietra* applied
to its object.   But again there is no evidence whatever of
anything dishonourable or immoral in such an attachment
either in fact or in intention, though there may be of very
undignified weakness.   We have no clue as to its date.   It may
have occurred (for all we know) between the death of Beatrice
and Dante's own marriage : though it is not unthinkable,
remembering the times we are dealing with, that it may have
been even after that.   It strikes me as not a little significant that in the last line of one of these petulant effusions
(Canzone xv), the person thus passionately loved, and whose
coldness is so deeply resented, is actually called 'pargoletta':—

> 'Se in *pargoletta* fia per cuor un marmo.'

May it not be possible that in the employment by Beatrice
of this very word, Dante may (as in *Purg.* xxxi. 75) have
recognized 'il velen dell' argomento'?

Moreover Dante describes his utter prostration and despair
at the stony coldness of this object of his love.   Life is not
worth living, his anguish is 'nigh unto death,' he is beaten
down to the ground.   Can anything better correspond with
the language of that part of Beatrice's indictment which we
are specially now considering? (xxxi. 58–60).   'There should
not have weighed downwards thy wings, to await further
strokes, either young girl or other vanity of like brief enjoyment.'   And even granting that this love were ever so honourable and free from moral stain, what a miserable contrast it
presents in its overpowering intensity with the ennobling and
spiritual devotion that he had once felt towards Beatrice !
What humiliating and abject weakness that one who has
risen so high should be exhibited as a commonplace and
petulant, disappointed lover, a Hercules prostrate at the feet
of Omphale !   Again, I say, there is no direct evidence, even
in this case, of any immorality on the part of Dante, though
there certainly is of just such pitiable weakness as Beatrice
censures in *Purg.* xxxi. 55–63.

We seem then to be at least entitled to claim a verdict of 'not proven' in regard to any definite charge against Dante of sensual passion or of an immoral life. But at the same time I do not at all feel bound to contend that he must have maintained all through life, and among such surroundings as his were, a spotless and saintly self-control. Nor need our admiration for him be so blind as to make us struggle obstinately against the admission that such may have been the case, if the proof were forthcoming. Who thinks of the early life of S. Augustine in prejudice of the saintliness of his maturity? And in Dante's case the most gossiping of commentators have not gone to the length of the revelations of 'the Confessions[1].' His admirers do him an ill service when they insist on his being treated as either intellectually infallible, or morally impeccable. As D'Ancona has admirably put it—'Volendo far di Dante qualche cosa più che un uomo, ne fanno in realtà assai meno che un uomo[2].' Are we to suppose that in the impetuous period of his early manhood, Dante displayed the same stern and ascetic type, which advancing years, broken health, bitter disappointments, hopeless exile, have made so familiar to us? We are too apt to forget the human and domestic side of life, which even great men cannot escape from, and in which (as the phrase is) 'no man is a hero' to those about him. We forget too that the most revered and most venerable of men were once young, and may have had some 'sowing of wild oats,' that they did not spring, like Minerva from the brain of Jupiter, with full equipment of intellect or character; we forget the work of those 'years which bring the philosophic mind' even to the greatest. Our reluctance to imagine and realize the possibility of such a period in Dante's life is mainly due to the fact that in some sense even *before* this period he 'had already attained,' under the very exceptional influence by which his *Vita Nuova* was moulded, though the mould was too soon broken for that premature character to be firmly 'set.'

But granting that there were a literal meaning of some

---

[1] See *Conv.* I. ii. 105-110.   [2] *Discorso*, p. xxxix.

kind to be attached to the charge relating to the 'pargoletta' it is most important once more to observe in what the sting of it lies. Most assuredly not in any petty thought of rivalry or jealousy on the part of Beatrice, but in the utter unworthiness of such an object. What a fall was there from the ennobling ideal which he had formed of Beatrice (see ll. 49 *seqq.*, just above) to the paltry reality of some frivolous girl, whatever may have been the nature of the love inspired by her, especially if it were so violent and uncontrolled as utterly to unman the victim of it, according to the picture given in the 'Pietra' *Canzoni*. It is as if Beatrice would say, 'Look on this picture and on that!' That the same nature could be attracted by both is verily an object-lesson of that 'Corruptio optimi pessima,' which Beatrice has expounded in xxx. 118–120[1]. She displays throughout the whole of this painful scene

> 'quel sembiante
> Che madre fa sopra figliuol deliro' (*Par.* i. 101, 102);

or, as we read in *Purg.* xxx. 79–81,

> 'Così la madre al figlio par superba,
> Com' ella parve a me; per che d' amaro
> Sente il sapor della pietate acerba.'

Comparing now the conclusion at which we have arrived with the other theories that have been mentioned, I would observe that the changes both in Dante's inner and in his outer life appear to me to have been overstated. As to the former, we have evidence of Religious Indifference, but not of Religious Scepticism. As to the latter, we have evidence of a worldly and frivolous, perhaps even to some extent of a dissipated, life[2], but not of an actually immoral life. The evidence in fact for these exaggerated views (as far as the *Purgatorio* is concerned) seems to me to reduce itself almost entirely to a single word in each case: the word 'scuola' in *Purg.* xxxiii. 85 ('scuola ch' hai seguitata'), in the former; and

---

[1] 'But all the more malign and the more wild does the soil become when sown with bad seed and left uncultivated, in proportion as it has more of the good strength of soil.'

[2] See especially *Purg.* xxiii. 115, already referred to on pp. 241, 244.

the word 'pargoletta' in the passage under discussion, in the latter. Religion, as I believe, lost its practical hold upon him after the death of Beatrice. But I hold that there is no evidence that such practical indifference ever passed on to formulated scepticism or heresy [1]. A man may be 'without God in the world,' and yet never 'say in his heart, There is no God': and this is equally true of other less fundamental dogmas than this.

I think then we must admit that Dante had the experience in himself of a sort of 'Classical Renaissance' in which Religion in its practical aspect was almost extinguished ; and though I would not press this parallel so as to include the moral decadence involved in that later movement, yet it is almost inevitable to suppose a very considerable lowering of the exalted moral standard which had been maintained by the spiritual influences overshadowing Dante's early life.

I would now sum up briefly thus: (1) The explanation now offered seems on the one hand not to outrun the evidence we possess, and on the other, to give an adequate and a natural meaning to the whole passage with which we have had to deal in Cantos xxx and xxxi, or rather with this taken in due connexion with the language of Canto xxxiii.

(2) The offence of Dante, thus understood, affords grounds for a special penance over and above that prescribed for the definite forms of flagrant sin in Purgatory itself. For the moral element (using the word 'moral' again here in the

---

[1] Compare Bartoli, *Storia*, &c., vi. p. 23 'Io ammetto che nei rimproveri di Beatrice si allude anche agli studi filosofici, ma non già perchè questi studi fossero *contrari al dogma*, sibbene perchè *allontanavano il Poeta dalla Beatrice celeste*.' Nor does even the often quoted *Purg*. xxxiii. 85–90, necessarily go beyond this, especially if taken in connexion with *Par*. xxix. 85–87:—

> 'Voi non andate giù per un sentiero
> Filosofando ; tanto vi trasporta
> L'amor dell' apparenza e il suo pensiero.'

As an example of a speculation which at least brought Dante on to dangerous ground, we might cite that as to the 'prima materia degli elementi,' whether it was created by God or not (*Conv*. IV. i. 64). In regard to this inquiry he admits that the aspect of Philosophy became less attractive to him. It is interesting to compare with this the confession of Socrates as to the ambitious nature of his youthful speculations, which much resembled this of Dante. See Phaedo, 96 A–C. On 'prima materia,' see further, *Quaestio*, § 18 ; and *Studies*, II. p. 356 *n*.

restricted sense) in his backsliding, so far as it is included in the indictment at all, has been shown to occupy a very subordinate position. Among the seven Sins, the nearest approach to this special fault of wholly 'minding earthly things,' would be found in 'Accidia,' but that is much narrower and more specific in its meaning.

(3) The remedy in *Purg.* xxx. 136-138 (with which passage compare *Purg.* i. 59, 60) is specially appropriate for such a case. The realities of the other world have to be brought vividly home to one who is so entirely absorbed in things present as to have become indifferent to anything beyond.

(4) If it be objected that this explanation falls below the measure of the accusations of Beatrice and of the intense contrition of Dante—that in short ' colpa e duol' are *not* 'd' una misura' (as we read in xxx. 108), three points must be remembered :—(*a*) The self-accusations of a sensitive and contrite spirit with a lofty standard of duty are not to be interpreted by the measure of dull average humanity. They are altogether 'fuor di nostra usanza.' To us they may seem exaggerated, perhaps morbid. Familiar examples of the need for such caution may be found in the language of S. Paul, of Bunyan, of the poet Cowper. Let us remember the words of Dante himself :—

> 'O dignitosa coscienza e netta,
> Come t' è picciol fallo amaro morso!' (*Purg.* iii. 8, 9.)

(*b*) We must make allowance for the different points of view of those times and ours in regard to the paramount supremacy of Theology as a scientific study among all the objects of human knowledge.

The following words of Scartazzini are worth quoting both as to this point and also as showing that the view which he held at one time (1892) agrees in some important features with that for which I have been contending :—

'To the modern man it may seem strange, well-nigh inconceivable, if we express our view that the fault with which Dante reproaches himself was not scepticism, not infidelity, not religious indifference, not any lack of faith, hope or love, but simply that he had neglected divine science, and thrown himself with exclusive enthusiasm into the arms of that which the world offers. So far the poet's own admissions and intimations bring us of necessity, but not a step farther; that philosophy made of him a sceptic or an infidel, is an assumption for which his works afford no support, and which can owe its rise only to the fact that according to modern views the confessions of the great epic require us to look for something more than the mere preference of secular to divine science. The Middle Ages thought otherwise— to them a neglect of theology and of matters of the faith counted as a sin, and not one of the lightest' (Butler's translation of the *Handbuch*, pp. 237, 238).

(*c*) This is not a case of ordinary Worldliness, or mere negative or Laodicean indifference to Religion. It is the backsliding of one who had 'known his Lord's will,' of one who had enjoyed (as he believed) supreme and unique privileges, as is admitted in xxx. 115–123 [1]; it was the relapse of what Wordsworth calls 'a consecrated spirit.'

(5) In thus maintaining the truth of the literal as well as of the allegorical meaning of Dante's relations to Beatrice, one may say with Newton, 'Hypotheses non fingo.' There is nothing postulated beyond the actual range of human experience, though (as I have already admitted) it is a very rare and exceptional experience, just as indeed Dante himself must be allowed to have been exceptional among men of all time. In attributing such an influence to a living woman the experience of Dante finds a parallel in that of Goethe and Shelley, in their youth; and, in a quarter where we should little have expected it, in that of the pious Bishop Ken, in his mature life.

The striking parallels afforded by Goethe and Shelley I have already pointed out, and justified by illustrative quotations in my Essay on Beatrice, in the second volume of these *Studies* (p. 136). The other interesting parallel from the life of Bishop Ken I owe to a note by Dean Plumptre on *Purg.* xxxi. 32 (p. 356). From this I make the following extract:—

---

[1] With which perhaps compare *Inf.* xxvi. 21–24.

'Few writers can be more contrasted with each other than the authors of the *Commedia* and of the Morning and Evening Hymns; and yet, as I read the life of Ken, and especially his Funeral Sermon on Lady Margaret Maynard, the thought comes into my mind that he too had had in her his vision of a Beatrice, whom he loved as a guide and teacher, with no touch of sensual passion, and whose influence was strong to purify and ennoble his whole life. And when she died she became to him as one who had never "known any sin but that of ignorance or infirmity," and who had passed to "the bosom of her Heavenly Bridegroom, where how radiant her crown is, how ecstatic her joy, how high exalted she is in degree of glory, is impossible to be described".' These are Ken's own words. Dean Plumptre proceeds:—'By a curious coincidence, he too turns to the *veni, sponsa de Libano*, to the "Bridegroom's garden, where, when the south wind blows, the several spices and gums, the spikenard and the cinnamon, the frankincense and the myrrh," blend their fragrance, as a parable of the excellences of the "gracious woman" whom he honours.'

PART III.

THE DXV PROPHECY[1].

WE have seen how in the Apocalyptic Vision of Cantos xxix, xxx, and xxxii Dante has displayed in a series of scenes or *tableaux*, first, the constitution of the Christian Church as 'built upon the foundation of the Apostles and Prophets' (Cantos xxix, xxx), and then the vicissitudes of its history from its establishment at Rome to the removal of the Papal seat to Avignon (Canto xxxii). In this concluding Canto (xxxiii) he ventures upon prophecy. That is to say, he embodies in the form of prediction his own confident hopes and aspirations for the future. We can only form conjectures as to the time and manner in which Dante believed that the coming deliverance would be effected, for unhappily his hopes were never realized, so that we have no longer, as before, historical facts to guide us in our interpretation. We cannot say of his prophecy, as he so confidently affirmed elsewhere, 'l' effetto nol nasconde' (*Purg.* vi. 138). Consider how hopelessly for him, quite apart from his own private calamities, 'the times were out of joint.' Rome was 'deserted of both her kings,' the Pope and the Emperor. Dante regarded it as 'formal' or essential in God's providential design, that the seat of both should be established at Rome[2]. Hence, though he would regard both of these divine institutions as equally imperishable, yet both were now in abeyance, both were in a state of suspended animation ; humanity was left without a guide either in things spiritual or in things temporal[3]. Dante himself solemnly pronounces both Papacy and Empire vacant. At the time at which he is supposed to be writing (1300) he held that there was no Pope and no Emperor. As to the Pope, though, as Dante knew to his cost, Boniface was ruling at Rome, and at the summit of his power, he declares by the

---

[1] This last division of the Essay was read as a Paper to the Oxford Dante Society in 1900, and a few copies were then printed for private circulation.

[2] See further *Studies*, II. pp. 13–34, for Dante's theory of the relations of the Papacy and Empire.

[3] See *De Mon.* III. xvi. 75 *seqq.*

mouth of S. Peter in *Par.* xxvii. 22-24 that the throne of the Pope is vacant in the sight of the Son of God :—

> ' il loco mio,
> Il loco mio, il loco mio, che vaca
> Nella presenza del Figliuol di Dio[1].'

He says the same of the Empire in *Conv.* IV. iii. 39, where Frederic II is declared to be the last Emperor, though Rudolph and Adolph and Albert had been elected after him; for none of them had visited Italy or been crowned at Rome[2]. Albert was indeed nominally Emperor in 1300, and we all remember how passionately Dante appeals to him in *Purg.* vi. 97 to come and deliver Italy, though he somewhat bitterly addresses him as ' Alberto *Tedesco.*'

For all that, Dante never for one moment gave way to despair. Faith and hope never deserted him. Both in the Canto now before us and in *Inf.* i. and elsewhere, he expresses his confident faith in a coming Deliverer, and one too that was close at hand. ' E ciò sarà presto,' in the well-known words of Savonarola. As to his hopefulness, surely it was no idle boast, when he makes S. James declare (in *Par.* xxv. 53) that no son of the Church militant has more hopefulness than he, ' hoping indeed (as we may well say) against hope.' This key-note of hope is struck at once at the beginning of this Canto where Beatrice, her face burning with fiery indignation[3], declares, borrowing the words of Christ, ' A little while and ye shall not see me, and again a little while and ye shall see me.' In these words is foreshadowed beyond doubt Dante's belief in a speedy restoration of the Papacy to Rome. Beatrice next walks ten paces forward preceded by the seven Maidens[4], and followed by Dante, Matelda and Statius. She then turns to Dante, and comforts him by ' showing him things that must shortly come to pass.' True, the car representing the Visible Church, sorely injured by the dragon (see xxxii. 130 *seqq.*) and finally carried

---

[1] Chiefly and technically no doubt in consequence of the invalidity of the 'rifiuto' of Celestine, which altogether vitiated the election of his nominal successor.

[2] Other passages in the same sense are *Par.* iii. 120 ; *Purg.* vi. 89 ; *Ep.* vi. ll. 11 *seqq.*

[3] ' Colorata come foco' (l. 9) like S. Peter in *Par.* xxvii. 19 *seqq.*

[4] See xxix. 121-132 ; xxxi. 103-111.

away out of sight (xxxii. 157–160), has now been destroyed ;
(fu, e non è) 'it was, and is not[1]' (l. 35). But God is able to
raise it up again; and he who has the blame for this will soon
discover that God's vengeance is not to be averted by any
idle ceremonies or superstitions (l. 36). Then follows what is
perhaps the most obscure and enigmatical passage in the
whole of the *Divina Commedia*, ll. 37 *seqq.* A coming deliverer
is foretold, he is close at hand, he is sent forth from God, and
both the Empire and the Church will find in him a Saviour.
The vacant Empire will not remain without an heir. The
harlot and the giant[2] will both be slain, and so the Church as
well as the Empire will find deliverance. But while thus
much is clear, the declaration that the number 515 in some
mysterious way represents the coming deliverer is so obscure
that no satisfactory solution of the riddle has been hitherto
suggested. As the construction is a little involved, I will
translate the lines, *Purg.* xxxiii. 37–45 :—

> 'Non sarà tutto tempo senza ereda
> L' aquila che lasciò le penne al carro,
> Per che divenne mostro e poscia preda ;
> Ch' io veggio certamente, e però il narro,
> A darne tempo già stelle propinque,
> Sicure d' ogni intoppo e d' ogni sbarro ;
> Nel quale un cinquecento diece e cinque,
> Messo da Dio, anciderà la fuia
> Con quel gigante che con lei delinque.'

'Not for all time shall be without an heir the Eagle that left
his plumage in the Car[3], whereby it became a monster and
afterwards a prey[4]. For I see with certainty, and therefore
I tell it, stars already near at hand, free from every obstacle
and from every hindrance, to give us a time in which a 515,
sent forth from God, shall slay the harlot[5] with that giant who

---

[1] Again we recognize the language of the Apocalypse, c. xvii. 8.

[2] See xxxii. 148–156.

[3] xxxii. 125, 126; 136–141.   [4] xxxii. 142–160.

[5] It is doubtful whether *fuia* in itself conveys the notion of 'harlot,' though
the term 'puttana' is distinctly applied to her in xxxii. 149 and 160. This
word probably comes from 'furius,' i. e. thievish (or *h. l.* 'the plunderer'), the
'r' being lost as in *paio, staio, buio* (probably) and other words. Compare
fuia in *Inf.* xii. 90.

is joined with her in guilt': i.e. Clement V and Philip IV; or possibly further, the prostituted Papal power and the over-mastering French Monarchy of which these were at the time the representatives. The Papacy, it will be remembered, was removed to Avignon in 1305.

I wish now to establish the three following points:—

    I. That the Deliverer here foretold can be none other than the Emperor Henry VII.

    II. That his name, by a process familiar in the Middle Ages, will actually give the number 515.

    III. That there is abundant reason for believing that this process was known to Dante.

But, first of all, there are two commonly received views respecting this passage on which I wish to say a few words before proceeding further.

1. It seems to be generally accepted as a full and sufficient explanation of the number 515, that as this would be represented in Roman numerals by the letters DXV, which may be transposed into DVX [1], so Dante merely foretells 'a Leader.' I cannot possibly believe this to be the whole solution, though I am far from denying that it may be a part of it, as will be seen later. Can any one suppose that this peculiarly solemn and elaborate prophecy amounts to no more than this, that 'a Leader shall arise'? If so, we may well exclaim with the Chorus to Cassandra in the *Agamemnon*,

προφήτας δ᾽ οὕτινας μαστεύομεν,

'We need no prophets to tell us only this.' Such vagueness is least of all in the manner of Dante, especially in such a moment of lofty enthusiasm. Who can suppose his intense and eager hopes to rest on such an unsubstantial basis, on such

---

[1] As to the transposition of the Latin numerals to make a significant or at least a pronounceable name, we may note that the same process was applied by Victorinus early in the fourth century to the number 666 or DCLXVI, and the meaningless name DICLVX thus formed was treated as the name of the Beast (*Speaker's Commentary*, p. 698). Rossetti, *Spirito Antipapale*, p. 275, supposes not DUX but JUDEX to be the word here indicated. By transposition of the letters he obtains the required number thus:—

Un cinquecento dieci e cinque.
I . D . X . E . V

a vague commonplace as this—'a Leader shall arise'? I feel sure that his hopes, like the anticipations of a Hebrew prophet, were always centred on something much more definite than that, not only on a Leader, but on some one who should be that Leader. He may have had to transfer them (as we know) from one ideal to another, for with him (in the language of Pope),

'Hope builds as fast as knowledge can destroy.'

A. H. Clough has very strikingly described in *The New Sinai* how when 'all men are in expectation' they are apt to see the realization of their hopes in very imperfect ideals. But whether we can identify the name that was in Dante's mind or not, I felt confident that when he used such language as this, some definite person is designated among those on whom at some period or another his supreme hopes were fixed.

Further, if 'Dux' were intended either exclusively or even primarily, why should not Dante have said,

'Un cinquecento cinque e diece,'

since 'diece' would be a much easier rhyme? Thus, in the *Divina Commedia, -ece* occurs in ten *terzine*, and *-inque* in one only, viz. in the present passage.

2. The second point is this. It has sometimes been thought that Dante is here referring to events happening in 1314, and that consequently the date of the composition of this part of the *Purgatorio* is indicated as being somewhat later, and perhaps c. 1315. No doubt 1314 was for Dante an eventful year. It witnessed the deaths both of the first Avignon Pope, Clement V, and of his patron Philip the Fair, the harlot and the giant of this vision (see xxxiii. ll. 44, 45). Thus the two chief obstacles to the restoration of the Papal See to Rome seemed to be removed as it were together. In the same year a new Emperor was elected, Lewis of Bavaria, the imperial throne having been vacant for fourteen months since the death of the ill-fated Henry VII, in whose grave all Dante's hopes seemed to have been buried. Lewis was no doubt, when Henry's son was found impossible, the candidate of the Ghibelline party. But not only was he, in the language of

* * *

Gregorovius (vi. 113), 'dull-witted' and 'intellectually in-significant,' but he was hampered, at any rate all through the remainder of Dante's life, and for some time afterwards, by the opposition of the unsubdued rival Emperor, Frederick of Austria. There was never anything either in the character or the actions of Lewis to inspire any such enthusiasm as this in Dante.

But assuming this to be a ' retrospective prophecy,' it is surely inconceivable that it should bear so little correspondence to its supposed fulfilment. For (1) the deaths of Clement V and Philip IV were in no sense attributable to the hand of any such deliverer, 'messo da Dio' (see ll. 43–45). The death of Clement on April 20 occurred in the ordinary course of nature. That of Philip, on November 29, was the result of an accident when hunting, and this is referred to by Dante himself in *Par*. xix. 120 :—

> ' Quei che morrà di colpo di cotenna.'

If Dante when he wrote the passage before us was aware of these facts, I do not think he could possibly have used this language. I do not of course suppose that Dante expected Henry VII or any other DUX literally to *put to death* either Philip or Clement, but to overthrow or destroy them as rulers. This indeed would have probably been the result of the triumphant establishment of Henry and the seat of the Empire at Rome, as anticipated by Dante. Nor, if we give a wider range to the prediction, can it be said that any great blow was dealt in that year to the powers or causes of which Clement and Philip were the embodiment. I should rather gather from it that the date of composition must have been earlier, as indeed on other grounds I believe it to have been [1]. But (2) further, there was no great or conspicuous leader in 1314, for whom any such heroic career could be anticipated, unless it were possibly Lewis of Bavaria. But he at any rate had

---

[1] It has indeed sometimes been argued that the warning addressed to Philip in ll. 35, 36 seems to imply that he was still living. But this does not follow, since it has reference to the *assumed* date of 1300. The warning to be conveyed to Fra Dolcino in *Inf*. xxviii. 55 is very similar, and it was probably *written* after his actual death in June, 1307.

nothing to do with the deaths of Clement and Philip, and he was not in fact elected Emperor till Oct. 20, 1314, six months after the death of Clement. Nor is he elsewhere alluded to in the works of Dante in any way. Besides, as the Empire had been vacant barely fourteen months when Lewis was elected, the language of l. 37—

'Non sarà *tutto tempo* senza ereda,'

would surely lose all point. This is found in the vacancy (as held by Dante) of nearly sixty years between the death of Frederick II and the election of Henry VII (1250-1308).

As then the events of 1314 cannot be thought to satisfy the terms of this passage regarded as an *ex post facto* prophecy, I can only conclude that we have here to deal with a genuine prediction. In other words, that the passage was written when coming events seemed to cast such very definite shadows before them that Dante, enthusiast as he was, felt secure and confident in predicting the issue[1]. Now we know that there was one period in his life when Dante did feel such confidence, and that the centre of his hopes was the newly elected Emperor Henry of Luxemburg, commonly known as Henry VII, who became Emperor in November, 1308. Thus the Imperial throne, having been vacant (in Dante's opinion) for more than half a century, had at last once more an occupant.

I. Having thus shown these two interpretations or inferences to be unsatisfactory, I will now endeavour to establish the first of my three points (p. 256), by giving several reasons for believing that Henry, and none other, must be the subject of this celebrated prophecy.

1. I do not think that Dante would have been likely to attribute to any one in a less exalted position than that of Emperor the overthrow of the giant and the harlot of his vision, Philip and Clement, or of the French domination and the degraded and subservient, though still very powerful, Papacy. If it be an Emperor, the choice can only lie between Henry and Lewis. But, as I have said, Lewis is nowhere else mentioned,

---

[1] Just as Savonarola prophesied, with better success and to the astonishment of Comines, the expedition of Charles VIII to Italy. Gregorovius, *Rome in the Middle Ages*, vii. p. 433.

or even alluded to, by Dante.   If he were honoured by such a very remarkable prophecy as this, and if he ever held such an exalted place in Dante's hopes, it is scarcely possible that there should be no further trace of it in Dante's writings.   It is true that some other distinguished Ghibelline leaders have been suggested of less than imperial dignity, such as Can Grande, or Uguccione della Faggiuola.   Also in favour of Can Grande (the name most commonly advocated) there might be urged the probable allusion to his name in the mysterious Veltro in *Inf.* i, and also the brilliant future prophesied for him in *Par.* xvii. 76.   But what we read there is far less definite than this, and does not necessarily amount to more than a panegyric of gratitude prompted by Dante's personal obligations to him.   It seems to me to form a closer parallel to the eulogy of the Malaspina family (on similar grounds) in *Purg.* viii. 121-139 than to the language here employed. Then again the Veltro prophecy in *Inf.* i. (supposing that to refer to Can Grande) has a much more limited range.   He is to be the saviour of prostrate Italy, and will purge her cities in succession of the presence of the wolf, whatever be its meaning, or different meanings, in that Canto.   I believe therefore an Emperor to be designated, and *if* an Emperor, *then* certainly Henry VII.

2. But secondly there is a still stronger reason.   This passage, looked at closely, seems distinctly to imply that the coming Deliverer would be an Emperor.   Observe the close connexion in 'Che' in l. 40 with the statement of the previous *terzina*.   It will of course be remembered, as I have already explained, that in Dante's opinion the Empire was now vacant.

We have seen that he did not recognize Rudolph and Adolph and Albert as Emperors at all, since they had not visited Italy, nor been crowned at Rome.   Now Henry was actually on his way thither in 1310 and 1311.   Hence Dante might confidently declare that the Imperial Eagle should not long be without a successor (see l. 37), *because* (l. 40) the stars foretell the speedy advent of one sent forth from God who should work deliverance, &c.   Surely this ' because ' distinctly implies that the Deliverer would himself be the heir of the Eagle, or, in other words, an Emperor.

But (3) next consider side by side with this prophecy the extravagantly enthusiastic language which Dante applies to Henry VII in *Epistles* v, vi, and vii. He is the 'Lord's Anointed'; 'He that was to come[1]'; 'a second son of Jesse[2]'; 'the Lion of the tribe of Judah'; 'another Moses[3]'; in one place, even 'The Lamb of God[4].' He regards him as another Messiah by whom all the woes of the distracted world were to be cured[5]. He says that we may refer to him in a secondary degree 'post Christum' the prophecy of Isaiah in liii. 4, 'He hath borne our griefs and carried our sorrows.' Also two of these *Epistles*, vi and vii, are dated 'in the first year of the advent of Henry ("divi Henrici") to Italy,' as though it were a sort of new 'Anno Domini[6].' But besides this, and much more of the same kind, there are at least two passages bearing a striking resemblance to the language of the prophecy before us, in ll. 44, 45. In *Epist.* v. 2, ll. 32 *seqq.* we read in reference to Henry that 'percutiens malignantes, *in ore gladii perdet eos*, et vineam suam aliis locabit agricolis,' &c. (again, be it observed, transferring to him words of Divine

---

[1] *Ep.* vii. 2, l. 31.

[2] *Ep.* vii. 8, l. 176 reading *altera* ; lect. vulg. *alta.*

[3] Both these in *Ep.* v. 1. In the same *Ep.* § 5 he applies to Henry's advent to Italy the words of Luke xxi. 28, 'lift up your heads, for your redemption draweth nigh.'

[4] In this surprising passage, *Ep.* vii. 2, l. 45, Dante declares that when he prostrated himself at Henry's feet (probably on the occasion of his coronation at Milan on Jan. 6, 1311) his spirit rejoiced in him ('exultavit in te spiritus meus,' evidently borrowing the language of the *Magnificat*), and he said silently within himself, ' Ecce Agnus Dei, ecce qui abstulit peccata mundi.'

[5] It is remarkable that even Clement V at first favoured the expedition of the Emperor Henry to Italy. Dante refers to his 'benediction' in *Epist.* v. § 10 *ad fin.* The Pope (as Gregorovius says, *op. cit.*, vol. vi. p. 27) announced him as a kind of Messiah : 'Exultent . . . sibi subditae nationes . . . quoniam ecce Rex ipsorum pacificus eis veniet mansuetus, ut in eo suo sedens solio maiestatis solo nutu dissipet omne malum, cogitet pacis cogitationes pro subditis.' The date of this was Sept. 1, 1310, just after Henry had announced his intended journey to Italy. Shortly after his coronation at Rome, June 29, 1312, Clement's tone was much changed (Gregorovius, vi. p. 67). Within another year he was threatening excommunication (p. 85).

[6] Compare too the language of *Ep.* vii. 1, ll. 21-24.

application). And again in *Epist.* vii. 8, 1. 178, Henry is exhorted to bestir himself and with his sling and stone to overthrow Goliath, i. e. (as generally explained) Philip IV, the very giant whose imminent death at the hands of the deliverer is here confidently prophesied [1].

4. It is hardly necessary to point out that in regard to no one else does Dante ever use language at all like this.

5. At no time in Dante's life did any person, or any position of events, offer such a near prospect of the realization of his hopes and ideals as came into view (or at any rate into *his* view) on the descent of Henry VII into Italy in the Autumn of 1310, on his way to be crowned at Rome.

6. I may add that I have some time since come to the conclusion, on grounds entirely independent of this passage, and from internal evidence elsewhere, that certain parts of the *Purgatorio* were written about 1309 or 1310 or 1311, and that, so far as we can speak of the *Cantica* generally as bearing a certain date, that is the period to which most of the evidence points [2]. If I am right in my interpretation

---

[1] I must not lay too much stress on this passage, since I cannot regard the words 'this Goliath' as necessarily referring to Philip IV. The allusion may perhaps be to Robert of Naples, or to some other power more actively opposing Henry at that moment.

[2] The chief arguments commonly alleged against so early a date are:—

(1) That in *Purg.* xxxiii. 44, 45 it is implied that Philip and Clement were already dead. But we have seen that this points the other way, since the language of the passage is wholly inapplicable to the manner of their deaths.

(2) The allusion to Gentucca and Dante's visit to Lucca in *Purg.* xxiv. 37--45. As to this, it is argued that Dante could not have gone there till Uguccione della Faggiuola was in power, i. e. not till 1314 or 1315. But Gaspary (Oelsner's *Translation*, p. 275) and Witte (*auct.* Gaspary *l. c.*) dispute this statement as quite unfounded, and suggest that at any time between 1307 and 1310 Dante might quite well have gone to Lucca. I am not aware of any definite allusions whatever in the *Purgatorio* to events after 1310, though there are admittedly some in the *Inferno*.

I think it is a strong argument against supposing the *Purgatorio* to have been written after the death of Henry VII, that it contains no allusion to that crowning calamity of Dante's life in the way of 'prophecy' or foreboding. It may be added that while *Purg.* vi. 100 points to a date after 1308, when Albert was assassinated, so the warning of l. 102, compared with the language of *Ep.* vii. 3 *init.* and 8 *init.*, implies that Henry was still lingering or hesitating. Thus Canto vi at any rate seems to have been written about the same time as the Epistle, i.e. in the autumn of 1310, or the spring of 1311. Probably, I think, the whole *Purgatorio* was written between 1308 and 1312.

of *this* prophecy, that date would receive further strong confirmatory evidence. At any rate it will be observed that if on these or any other grounds it be admitted that Henry VII is the Deliverer here referred to, the date 1314–15 as that of composition is at once and obviously excluded, since Henry VII died in August, 1313.

7. If the ten paces of xxxiii. 16, 17 represent, as is generally supposed, ten years, the *terminus a quo* is most likely to date from 1300, the assumed date of the Vision and of the utterance of this prophecy by Beatrice, and that again would bring us to the date of 1310 (*vide supra*, p. 260 *sub fin.*). Others who think 1314 to be the period referred to, reckon the ten years from the date of the Avignon captivity, 1305.

Everything, therefore, in the way of general considerations of probability seems to me to point very strongly to Henry VII being the Saviour whose coming is here foretold.

II. I now proceed to the second main division of my subject. I am sanguine enough to believe that I have discovered at least a probable solution of the mysterious number 515, and that by this also is designated the name of the same Emperor. I had arrived at the conclusion already expounded, viz. that Henry VII is certainly the person referred to, without any reference to this enigma, and without any thought of attempting a solution of it. I felt confident, however, that it must represent in some way or other *a definite name*, because it is so evidently suggested by the riddle of the number of the Beast in Rev. xiii. 18. This is declared to be 666, and there is added, as a sort of hint to the solution of the problem, to which ὁ ἔχων τὸν νοῦν is invited [1], ἀριθμὸς γὰρ ἀνθρώπου ἐστί—Vulgate: 'Numerus enim hominis est [2]'—

---

[1] The word ψηφισάτω (as Bengel observes) implies making a calculation, or computation.

[2] It ought to be said that in spite of these words the number has been explained by many as giving a chronological date. But I can hardly imagine the words ἀριθμὸς γὰρ ἀνθρώπου ἐστί as having any other meaning than that implied in the text. Yet some maintain the meaning to be 'according to the way men count.' But surely this is superfluous, for how else could any beings count? Alford thinks that this meaning is established by c. xxi. 17, where the *cubit* by which the city was measured is said to be μέτρον ἀνθρώπου. But numbers, unlike cubits, do not depend on human convention. We believe that the

'It is the number of a man.' It seemed therefore to me almost certain that Dante meant this mysterious number similarly to designate *the name of a man*. Besides, the language of his prediction seems to imply the same—'I see . . . a time in which a 515, sent from God, shall slay,' &c.

In reference to the problem in the Apocalypse, I found that various commentators had attempted the solution by the help of numerical values assigned to the letters of the Latin, Greek, or Hebrew alphabets. In fact this seems to have been the generally accepted method from the earliest times. I tried all of these upon various names that have been suggested in the present passage, such as Enrico, Ludovico, Can Grande, &c., both in their Latin and their Italian forms. I confess I thought that Dante was not likely to be acquainted with the numerical values of the Greek and still less of the Hebrew alphabets (though as regards Hebrew I now think very differently), but, whether or no, I could not arrive at any approach to the number by any of these devices. I then found through the kind help of my friend Mr. Cowley, Sub-Librarian of the Bodleian, that there is a very large amount of mediaeval Kabbalistic literature in which this method of

Multiplication Table persists in Heaven and throughout the Universe. We have no reason to feel so sure about the Tables of Weights and Measures.

A chronological interpretation has also sometimes been adopted in reference to the number 515 in Dante. Thus Mr. Butler[1] has made the ingenious, though I think very improbable, suggestion that we are to take the year 799, that of the restoration of the Western Empire in the person of Charles the Great, and add to it 515, and that will give the date 1314 as that in which this glorious regeneration was to take place.

Further Prof. Davidsohn has lately[2] offered an explanation combining the chronological and personal interpretations of the letters DXV. Starting from the coronation of Charlemagne at Christmas 800, the year 515 of the restored Empire would give the date A.D. 1315. He supposes Dante to have written this Canto in 1314 and probably shortly before the election of Lewis, Duke of Bavaria, to the vacant Imperial throne (Oct. 20, 1314), of the probability of which he may have had private information. The new Emperor being 'Dux Bavariae' his title may have given a double significance to the mysterious letters DXV or DVX. This is no doubt an ingenious and interesting suggestion. Still I cannot but think Lewis is excluded from the competition by the considerations alleged on p. 258.

---

[1] In his Translation of the *Purgatorio*, Appendix B, pp. 429 *seqq.*
[2] In the *Bullettino della Società Dantesca Italiana*, N. S. vol. ix. fasc. 5°-6°, pp. 129-131.

interpretation by the numerical value assigned to the *Hebrew* letters is practised. Further, that some of the writers of this class, and certainly the mystical system of interpretation itself, can hardly fail to have been well known to Dante. Of this more in detail presently.

Let us survey the position we have at present reached.

Supposing now these several points to be admitted :—

(1) That the coming Deliverer was an Emperor.

(2) That, if so, he could only be Henry VII.

(3) That the riddle is quite obviously formed on the model of that containing the number of the Beast in the Apocalypse.

(4) That that riddle was almost always interpreted as giving the name of some individual man. (At any rate it was so in any writers at all likely to be accessible to Dante [1].)

(5) That it was thought to do so by the application of numerical values to the letters of his name.

Granting these points, I say, it seems to me to follow almost *necessarily* that the number 515 *must* somehow be made out of the letters of some form of the name of Henry.

Still, however, I could arrive at no satisfactory result by Greek, Latin, or Hebrew letters, till the idea occurred to me that the Emperor Henry is commonly designated by Dante's contemporaries (e. g. G. Villani, Ricordano Malispini, &c.), not as *Enrico* but as *Arrigo*. This is so in the great majority of MSS. examined by me since publishing the *Oxford Dante*, at any rate in the former of the two passages of the *Divina Commedia* where the Emperor's name occurs [2], though I was

---

[1] *V. infra*, pp. 273, 274.

[2] *Par.* xvii. 82 ; xxx. 137. My collations of MSS. seem to show that *Arrigo* is more usually found in the former case and *Enrico* in the latter. I am told by some Italian friends that there is no documentary evidence for the form *Arrico*. But even if none be forthcoming, the possibility or even strong probability of such a form having sometime existed (for the reasons above given) can scarcely be doubted. Further, I cannot imagine, when such an interchange of letters was so extremely common, that Dante would scruple to adopt either form, if he had any special reason or occasion for doing so. In any case I can claim the authority of Gabriele Rossetti, who in the *Spirito Antipapale* (pp. 293, 409) adopts indifferently the forms *Arrigo* and *Arrico*. One may not agree with the use he makes of them in interpretation, but that a native and highly-cultivated Italian treats the form *Arrico* as a perfectly natural one may fairly be pleaded in its favour.

unfortunately misled by Witte's text into printing it 'Enrico.'
Applying the recognized values of the Hebrew letters to the
name *Arrigo*, or *Arrico* (as it might also be written, and as it
surely should originally have been written), the number 515
presented itself at once, granting only one small assumption
as to the value given to the letter *o*. But let me explain
this in detail.

Starting with the word *Arrigo* (or rather in its more
primitive form, as I should suppose, *Arrico*) let us try to
imagine the process by which Dante would be likely to work
out the construction of an enigma of this kind.

As to the spelling of the name, we cannot be quite sure
whether he would write the last syllable as -*co* or -*go*. We
are all familiar with this interchange in the termination of
similar names, e. g. Federico (-go), Alberico (-go), Roderico
(-go), besides common nouns or verbs such as preco, figo,
luogo, amico, segreto, &c., &c. (where *c* and *g* are found
indifferently) ; and so even at the beginnings of words, such
as Gostanza, Gaeta, Gaia, and the well-known family of
Gaetani or Cajetani[1]. In Dante's time, when Italian was
in process of forming itself, the influence of the original
Latin forms would be still strongly felt in orthography.
Indeed the prevalence of such forms in MSS. of the *Divina
Commedia* is one recognized indication of their antiquity.
Dante was therefore most likely to have used the form ending
in -*co*, for this was clearly the original and natural form of
the name, being nearer to the Latin. The change into '*go*'
of this name in particular is a corruption found I believe
in Italian only of all the European languages. The termination of this and similar names is the Teutonic -*reich* or -*rikh*.
The name Henricus or Harricus came into Latin from the
Teutonic ' Heimirich [2],' i. e. ' Home-Ruler ' (of course in quite
a harmless sense), and the ' k,' or tenuis sound, is preserved

---

[1] As a further illustration of this tendency in Italian we may take *ingombro*
from late Latin cumbrus (= cumulus), whence 'encumber.'

[2] See Miss C. Yonge, *History of Christian Names*, 1863. Prof. Earle, however, tells me that the second member of the word is 'rich,' and the whole
meaning, 'rich at home,' or 'rich in domestic possessions.'

in all other languages, e. g. Provençal, Spanish, Portuguese, Dutch, German, Polish, Danish, Swedish, &c.

Next as to the transliteration of the word, and of this guttural sound in particular.

I do not for a moment suppose that Dante transliterated or wrote out the whole word into Hebrew characters. There is no evidence that he could either read or write them, and for the purpose now in view there is no need to suppose it. He would probably take a table of the Hebrew alphabet, with the approximately equivalent Roman letters, and the numerical values corresponding to the several Hebrew letters, exactly as one may find these values set down opposite to them, almost as a matter of course, in any Hebrew grammar that one may take up [1], so thoroughly well known and recognized are these numerical equivalents. Indeed in Hebrew there never was, nor is there even now, any other way of expressing figures or numbers but by the help of the numerical values conventionally assigned to the letters of the alphabet. Hence it is as fundamentally necessary to be acquainted with these values as with the phonetic power of the letters. Greek and Latin are equally devoid of figures, though Latin differs from Greek and Hebrew in utilizing only a few letters for this purpose, not the whole alphabet systematically.

I assume then that Dante would take each of the letters of his word, one by one, and set down the value which he found opposite to it in a list which a Jew friend may have given him, or perhaps, more probably, as he might obtain them, just for the letters he required, orally from a Jew, of which race, as we shall see, there was a considerable and very cultivated body in Italy at that time.

He would thus have five letters to deal with : *a, r, i,* hard *c* (i. e. *k*), and *o.*

As regards the first three there could be no doubt or difficulty. It was quite recognized that *a* = Aleph = 1, *r* = Resh = 200, and *i* = Yod = 10. And any one who knew as much as that Resh = *r* would be equally likely to know that

---

[1] e. g. Gesenius, Nordheimer, Sarchi, Ball, Fitzgerald, merely to notice a few taken from a library shelf at random.

it represented 200, in whatever way either piece of information were obtained.

Next as regards the guttural sound of *k* or hard *c*, the case is almost equally clear. I am informed by Hebrew scholars that beyond all doubt Koph would be its recognized equivalent, though I find in some grammars both Caph and Koph inaccurately transliterated by *k*. Also the value of Koph was certainly 100.

Thus far his total would come to 511, and up to this point everything has gone on perfectly recognized lines. But as regards *o*, a difficulty would present itself. It has no definitely recognized equivalent in the Hebrew alphabet. Let me here interpose an explanation. I am obliged to use the words 'equivalent' and 'corresponding' when comparing Roman and Hebrew letters. This is not of course strictly accurate, and especially as regards the supposed equivalents of the vowels, which do not, properly speaking, exist at all in the Hebrew alphabet. But they are commonly set down as in some general sense 'corresponding' to, or at least having an affinity with, certain Hebrew letters, as any one may see in ordinary Hebrew grammars.

But in the tables, in several grammars that I have consulted, 'o' does not appear at all, though the other four vowels *a, e, i* (or *y*), and *u* (or *v*), are set down as equivalents to the Hebrew letters Aleph, Ain, Yod, and Vau respectively. If then Dante had a list like any of these, or if he asked a Jew friend what Hebrew letter corresponded to 'o' and what was its value, 'the oracle would·be dumb.' The only answer would be, there is no corresponding letter recognized in the Hebrew alphabet. Consequently on this information Dante would be unable to assign a numerical value to 'o.' The probability or reasonableness of this supposition being of vital importance to the interpretation which I am about to suggest, I would ask special attention to the following considerations.

1. There seems no reason whatever to suppose that any table of values that may have been furnished to Dante, or any Jew whom he may have consulted, would have gone beyond the information at the disposal of the much later

writers of Hebrew grammars in the nineteenth century. I
could instance the omission of ' o,' though the other vowels
are included, in several such grammars, among which I may
specially mention the standard work of Gesenius. Let us
remember this also, that Dante was not undertaking a serious
study of Hebrew (of which there is no reason to suppose that
he had any knowledge)[1], but only making such superficial
inquiries about a few letters as might enable him to carry out
the purpose he had in hand.

2. I am not aware of any evidence up to Dante's time of
the application of this Kabbalistic method of interpretation to
languages *outside* Hebrew, as, for instance, to either Greek or
Latin names. A distinguished Hebrew scholar, who has made
a special study of the subject, tells me that he cannot find
any evidence of it. If indeed the science of 'Gematria' (as
it was called) had been so applied, no doubt it would have
necessitated the providing of 'o' with some numerical value,
or quasi-phonetic equivalent. But then 'o' would not be the
only letter that would need to be thus dealt with. *Inter
alia* we might mention θ, ϕ, ξ, and still more the long and
short vowels η and ϵ, ω and o: since their distinction could
not be overlooked without confusing words totally distinct.
A variety of Greek names suggest themselves at once which
could not be treated on this method with Hebrew letters, e. g.
Πάφος, Φθίη, Θέτις, Ξενοφῶν, &c., &c. For though no doubt the
sounds required could be approximately given in Hebrew by
the help of aspirates and vowel points, yet in applying this
method we have to deal only with the plain unpointed
twenty-two letters of the Hebrew alphabet. The Greek
alphabet could of course be easily numerically so applied to
Greek words, and I find it stated by Dean Farrar [2] that they
were sometimes thus treated, and that two words of which
the numerical value thus calculated was the same were called
'isopsephic.' E. g. Demagoras and Λοιμός are described in

---

[1] In *Par.* xii. 80-81, he confesses himself unable to be sure as to the meaning
of the Hebrew name 'Giovanna'—

> 'O madre sua veramente Giovanna,
> Se interpretata val come si dice!'

[2] *The Early Days of Christianity*, p. 468 n.

the Anthology as thus corresponding. Both are in fact equivalent to 420. But the attempt to equate the *Hebrew* letters and their values to the separate letters of either *Greek* or *Latin* alphabets would be beset with so many other difficulties besides that which would apply to 'o,' that we cannot imagine it to have been ever systematically practised, apart from the negative evidence already cited. Dante was therefore, I imagine, conducting a more or less original experiment.

3. It might perhaps be thought that the solution of the Apocalyptic riddle would have called for such an application of the Hebrew letters. This, however, does not appear to be the case. For, if one may trust the note on the passage in the *Speaker's Commentary*, the application of the *Hebrew* letters to its solution appears to date only from the seventeenth century [1]. At any rate there is no trace of this in any writers upon the subject accessible to Dante. Further, as to the particular solution Nero(n) Caesar, which is arrived at by the help of Hebrew letters, I find five or six writers of the *nineteenth century*, each claiming to have been the *first* to suggest it [2]. Hence, as far as *this* problem is concerned, the need for the evaluation of 'o' would not go far back.

4. Observe particularly that I am not for one moment denying that 'o' was sometimes regarded as sharing with 'u' or 'v' the Hebrew 'Vau' as its quasi-equivalent, and by consequence as bearing the value '6.' This is assumed, and I doubt not quite rightly, by those who trace in Nero(n) Caesar the number 666 by the help of Hebrew equivalents. I am only asserting that this equivalence in the case of 'o' is not so obvious or so generally recognized as in that of the other vowels, and that even down to the grammars of the nineteenth century 'o' is actually treated as having no regular corresponding letter in the Hebrew alphabet. All that is necessary for my purpose is that it be admitted that, even as I failed by ordinary means to ascertain this value, so it is not impossible, or even improbable, that Dante may have likewise so failed.

[1] *Op. cit.*, p. 688.   [2] *Ibidem.*

Since the above was written, one of the distinguished Hebrew scholars referred to writes to me : 'I think it *very probable* that Dante would find a difficulty with "o"' . . . 'It is quite possible that he may not have found any letter corresponding to "o," and that he may have gone to work in his own way to assign a numerical value to it.'

Such an admission, on such authority, is all that I want. Nothing more than this is required to justify the suggestion which I wish now to make.

If then Dante were unable to find either that any recognized value existed for 'o,' or that it definitely 'corresponded' with any one of those twenty-two Hebrew letters which had such values assigned to them, it is surely not unreasonable to suppose that he would fall back on his own resources, if he were to complete his riddle. What more natural then (as it appears to me) than that he should give to 'o' the value 4, as being the fourth vowel[1]? If this be admitted, and this (be it observed) is the *only* assumption throughout, we obtain the precise number 515 :—

$$\begin{array}{rr} a = & 1 \\ r = & 200 \\ r = & 200 \\ i = & 10 \\ c \text{ or } k = & 100 \\ o = & \underline{4} \\ & 515 \end{array}$$

The process of thus giving a numerical value to names and words was a thoroughly familiar one in the time of Dante and long before. The chances *against* any given name (especially that of one whom every consideration of probability points to as being almost certainly the person indicated in the context) corresponding thus precisely with a large

---

[1] It is perhaps scarcely worth mentioning in this relation, but in fact a common mediaeval symbol for '4' was ꝗ. I have more than once known this symbol to have been taken for the letter O by persons who were not aware of this, the tails at the base being overlooked or inconspicuous. Reusens, *Éléments de Paléographie*, says that it was used in the thirteenth, fourteenth, and fifteenth centuries.

number like this are simply enormous. Let any one try
with any other name. The process is perfectly easy. For
instance, Dante would be represented by 525. He thus
comes curiously near the fateful number himself! 'Can
Grande' would give 479, Veltro (if 'o' be assumed as 4)
would be 610, Enrico (on the same supposition) 434, and so
on. Scartazzini endeavours, in a most preposterous fashion,
to make the number 515 indicate 'Can Grande,' by the help
of a descriptive title containing a mixture of Latin and
Italian words, and by then selecting out of it most arbitrarily
certain letters and neglecting others. Thus:—*K*an *G*rande
de (*not* della) *S*cala, *S*ignore *de* (*not* di) *V*erona, the letters
in italics being the only ones taken into account! *Inter alia*,
why should the poor prepositions (!) be alone honoured
by being counted in full? But even this is not enough.
He has still to invent—or rather to follow Picci (*Nuovi
Studi*, p. 158) in inventing—a purely arbitrary and imaginary
system of numerical values for the letters of the alphabet,
not Latin, nor Greek, nor Hebrew! This is dignified by
the title of 'l' alfabeto italiano dantesco,' though there is
simply not a particle of evidence for it!

I think it is very probable that Dante, with the true
Kabbalistic instinct, may have been attracted by the significant coincidence that the same number 515 could be spelt
out from the name 'Arrico' with the Hebrew alphabet, and
from the word 'Dux' with the Latin alphabet, a name which
so aptly described his position and office. A Rabbinical
writer would have regarded this as a distinct argument in
favour of his high mission [1]. There would be nothing in this
half so far-fetched as Dante's curious juggling in *V. N.* § 29
with the calendars of Arabia, Syria, and Italy, in order to
secure the presence of the number 9 in the *day*, and in the
month, as well as in the *year* of Beatrice's death, which seems
to have occurred (as I believe I was the first to suggest) on
the inconvenient date of June 8, 1290.

But, whether or no, let it be emphatically observed once
more that I am not supposing Dante to have taken *any*

---

[1] See precisely similar arguments given *infra*, 274 n, and p. 276.

liberty whatever, either for the sake of rhyme, or for the sake of obtaining the significant word DVX, or for any other purpose, with the recognized numerical value of any letter. I am only suggesting that when he came upon a letter which he could not discover to have an equivalent in the Hebrew alphabet, he himself assigned a value to it, and that not arbitrarily, but on quite a rational and intelligible ground.

Finally, it should not be forgotten that we are not dealing with a Scriptural prophecy, but rather with an ornament of poetry. Dante is deliberately constructing for himself a poetical prophecy, upon a well-known prophetic model in Scripture. Further, while on the one hand there is no prudential reason (as was probably the case in the Apocalypse) for disguising the name indicated, so on the other it is of no serious consequence to the writer whether the riddle itself be solved by his readers or not, for there could not be much doubt in the mind of any one regarding the passage with attention, that Henry VII was the Deliverer indicated by it, even if the process of indication could not be discovered [1].

III. It remains to show that this method of interpretation was likely to be familiar to Dante. As to this there cannot, I think, be any possible doubt.

(1) It must surely be admitted that Dante had in his mind the Apocalyptic enigma of the number of the Beast (Rev. xiii. 18), and that he proposed to himself to construct another upon that model.

(2) It follows almost necessarily that he must have been aware of the accepted and traditional method by which its solution was attempted. Indeed how else could he work out the construction of a similar riddle, or expect any of his readers to follow him ?

(3) This method of interpretation of 666 by assigning numerical values to the individual letters of names is found

---

[1] Since writing the above I find a very similar remark by Dean Farrar in reference to the problem of 'the Beast.' 'They [the Fathers] must have known what was *meant* [viz. Nero], even if the exact equinumeration of any words which they could hit upon did not entirely satisfy them. The solution "Lateinos," "Teitan," and even perhaps "Euanthas," might well be thought to point to Nero.' (*Early Days of Christianity*, p. 470.)

* * *

in Irenaeus [1] and his pupil Hippolytus [2]. There we find three names, Euanthas, Lateinos, and Teitan (of which Irenaeus prefers the last), all arrived at by this very method from the values assigned to the letters of the Greek alphabet [3]. Again, S. Thomas Aquinas in his *Expositio Aurea* of the Book of Revelation repeats the solution Teitan ; and adds two others, viz. Antemos (*sic*) = ' contrarius,' and Arnoyme (*sic*) = ' nego,' both of which give the same result. These two are also found in Bede (*Expos. in Apoc.: l. c.*), from whom S. Thomas may probably have derived them. Further, another writer commended by Dante (see *Epist.* x. 28 and *Par.* x. 131), Richard of St. Victor, commenting on Rev. xiii. 18, treats this as the recognized method of interpretation—' computet numerum qui *ex significatione literarum constituitur quibus nomen eius scribitur.*' Further, he likewise gives the curious word ' Antemos,' ' quod " contrarius "significatur,' as a solution. He adds, ' Sunt et alia eius nomina quorum *huiusmodi inter- pretatio* hunc eundem numerum reddit.' (Ed. Rothom. 1648, pp. 649 *b* and 650 *a* [4].)

Thus it is clear that this *method* and *principle* of inter- pretation was perfectly well known, and in fact it seems to be the *only* one generally recognized, though the Greek and not the Hebrew alphabet was the one to which it was applied.

Some later Commentators have used the *Latin* letters, regarding only those letters in a name which have a value among Roman numerals. One curious result is that *Ludo- vicus* has been suggested as a solution of the number of the

---

[1] *Adv. Haer.* v. 30.   [2] *De Christo et Antichristo,* § 50 (ed. Grabe, 1702).

[3] We find Irenaeus in another place (I. xii.) recognizing that the name Ἰησοῦς, similarly treated, will yield the number 888, though denouncing the absurd theories based upon this by the Gnostics. Still more fancifully the author of the Epistle of Barnabas (c. 9) argues that Abraham, in spirit foreseeing Jesus, took and circumcised of his household 318 men (he gets this by combining Gen. xiv. 14 and xvii. 27). He argues that this total is made up of I = 10, H = 8, and T = 300. The first two letters are the initial letters of Ἰησοῦς, and T is a symbol of the Cross ! Another curious use of the number 318 is mentioned by Dean Farrar. This was the number (Gen. xiv. 4) of the armed servants with whom Abraham pursued the five kings. But the name of his steward Eliezer gives 318 numerically. It is therefore argued that he alone was equal to all the rest, in fact ' a host in himself '!

[4] See Supplementary note on these names in Roger Bacon, *infra*, p. 370.

Beast, since, omitting *o* and *s*, the other letters total up to
666! I do not know which of the numerous historical personages bearing that name is imagined to have the honour of
being thus 'foreseen' by S. John! This affords an obvious
answer to the objection which a friend has suggested, why
should not Dante use the Latin numerals in dealing with
a Latin or Italian name? There are only seven letters in
the Latin alphabet that have numerical values. In the case
of the name before us, the only letters that would count in
'Arrico' would be I and C, and in the form 'Arrigo' only
the I. If Dante went beyond Latin he probably would find
it much easier (as we shall see later) to get information about
Hebrew than about Greek. Besides, this process or 'science'
had its origin in Hebrew, and was, certainly in Dante's day,
specially associated with Hebrew.

(4) Next, then, as to his use of the Hebrew letters.

Though these do not seem to have been applied until much
later (viz. 17th century), as we have already seen by the
actual problem in the Apocalypse, their employment in exegesis generally in this precise manner was very familiar, and
indeed of unknown antiquity. From it no doubt arose the
application of the method, in the early Christian writers, to
the Greek and Latin alphabets, and probably also it may
have suggested the construction of the enigma of the number
of the Beast itself.

This process or 'science' was known in the Middle Ages
as 'Gematria,' which is variously explained as a corruption of
γεωμετρία or γραμματεία, more probably the former. There
was a vast amount of Kabbalistic literature, some of which
Dante would probably have known, in which Gematria was
much used. It formed indeed a prominent feature of the
Kabbalistic system, and it is as old as the very beginning of
the Kabbala[1]. Dr. Ginsburg says that the following was one
of the commonest of the Kabbalistic rules of exegesis[2]:—
'Every letter of a word is reduced to its numerical value;
and the word is explained by another of the *same quantity.*'

---

[1] *Speaker's Commentary*, vol. iv. p. 687. Ginsburg on the *Kabbala*, pp. 49, 50.
[2] On *Coheleth*, p. 31.

The most important inferences were thought to follow from such a coincidence in the way of interpretation, moral, mystical, or anagogical[1]. Thus a visionary claiming a divine mission would call attention to the coincidence of the numerical value of his own name with that of some Hebrew prophet[2]. Or, again, it was argued that, because the Hebrew letters of the word Messiah and of the word for Serpent (Nachash) both amounted to 358, therefore the Messiah was designated by 'the seed of the woman who should bruise the serpent's head[3].' Again, since the letters of 'Ha Satan' ('The Accuser') total up to 364, it was argued that on one day in the year his operations were suspended, and his mouth closed, and that day was held to be the Great Day of Atonement[4].

This method could scarcely have been unfamiliar to one so much interested in Biblical exegesis as Dante. Indeed his own processes of interpretation have much in common with Kabbalistic methods, though the direct application of 'Gematria' is not found in his writings.

But there are more definite grounds than this general supposition.

(5) There appeared, just in the prime of Dante's life, the

---

[1] The fourfold interpretation of Scripture so familiar to Dante (*Conv.* ii. 1, &c.) was itself of Rabbinical origin. Ginsburg, *Kabbala*, p. 48 n. *Coheleth*, p. 30.

[2] e. g. Ginsburg, *Kabbala*, p. 114.

[3] From Dean Farrar, who in *The Expositor* for May, 1877 (pp. 362-378), gives an interesting account of Gematria. So, again, in the *Early Days of Christianity*, by the same author, pp. 468 *seqq.* In the former Essay, the method of interpretation explained in the text is happily described as 'an expansion of Scripture interpretation into the number of positive integral solutions of an indeterminate equation' (p. 370). The Christian writers were not slow to learn this absurd lesson. Thus the name ADaM was held to imply that the Messiah should come from Adam through David. Also a Greek writer infers the universal fatherhood of Adam from the fact that the four letters of his name are the initials of East, West, North, and South, i. e. ἀνατολή, δύσις, ἄρκτος, and μεσημβρία(!). From *De Montibus Sina et Zion* (once supposed to be by S. Cyprian). Also by Gematria, the letters A, D, A, M = $1 + 4 + 1 + 40 = 46$, which was the number of years 'the temple was building' (S. John ii. 20), and by the temple is thus symbolized the body of Christ, 'the second Adam.' This is found also in S. Augustine *in Ioann.*, Tract X. § 12; and so is the indication of the four quarters of the globe in Adam's name. It occurs again in *Enarr. in Ps.* xcv. 13.

[4] Farrar, *Early Days of Christianity*, p. 238.

celebrated book Sohar, one of the most important and epoch-making works on the Kabbalistic interpretation of Scripture[1]. It professed to be a revelation vouchsafed by God to a great Rabbi[2] who flourished 70–110 A.D. In point of fact it was the work of one Moses of Leon, a contemporary of Dante, who, when reproached by his wife for palming it off as the work of another age and author, naïvely replied that if he were known to be the author no one would buy it, but under the other name it brought him in a large revenue[3]! From this we may infer that it had a considerable circulation in the author's lifetime[4]. This Moses died in 1305, when Dante was in his fortieth year. One feature of this work is the prominence given in it to the science or method of Gematria[5].

(6) There were several other writers contemporary with Dante, the works of some of whom might be known to him, in which the methods of Gematria were employed and exemplified. Thus, passing over several who wrote in Spain, and limiting our notice to those in Italy, there was (*a*) Abulafia, who published a prophecy at Urbino in 1279[6]; (*b*) Joseph Gikatilla ben Abraham, a disciple of Abulafia[7]. 'The characteristic feature of this School (says Dr. Ginsburg, *Kabbala*, p. 117) is the stress which is laid on the extensive use of the exegetical rules called Gematria[8].'

(7) But there was one very celebrated contemporary Jewish writer in particular with whom there is strong reason to believe (on grounds quite independent of the question now before us) that Dante had acquaintance and even friendship. This was Emanuel ben Salomon, who was born at Rome probably in

---

[1] Ginsburg (*Coheleth*, p. 59) says that it has been aptly called 'the Talmud of the Kabbala.'

[2] viz. Shimeon ben Yoḥai.   [3] Ginsburg, *Kabbala*, p. 90.

[4] This, however, is not a matter of mere inference, as Mr. Cowley informs me that it was certainly the case.

[5] Ginsburg, *Kabbala*, pp. 78 *seqq*.   [6] *Ib.* p. 114.

[7] *Ib.* p. 116.

[8] To these Hebrew writers may be added the celebrated Raymond Lully (1234–1315)—'Doctor Illuminatus.' Dr. Ginsburg (*Kabbala*, p. 118) says of him, 'there is very little doubt that the Kabbalistic method of palming their notions on the text of Scripture by means of Gematria, &c., suggested to him the invention of the *Ars Magna*.'

the very year 1265 which was the year of Dante's birth[1].
He is often known as Emanuele da Roma. He lived at Rome
during the greater part of his life, and was the recognized
head of a considerable literary circle or school of Italian Jews
(many of them poets), which flourished in Rome and other
cities of Middle Italy, c. 1300. They were a numerous and
wealthy body, devoted to learning and culture of all kinds,
and especially to science and to poetry. For some reason
not clearly explained—but probably in connexion with his
unorthodox liberalism and audacious freedom of speech on
religious matters—he was banished, somewhere about his
50th year, and passed the rest of his life (like Dante) in
poverty and exile. Having been settled for many years at
Fermo in the district of Ancona, he died there about 1330.
His teachers were Leone Romano, Hebrew instructor to King
Robert of Sicily, and Judah Siciliano. (I mention these names
to show the prevalence of combined Italian and Hebrew culture at that time.) Emanuel was a physician by profession,
and a most prolific writer on a great variety of subjects,
such as Hebrew Grammar, Exegesis, and especially Kabbala.
His Commentaries (many still only in MS.) extend over nearly
all the books of the O.T.[2], in which we cannot doubt that,
as in the case of all contemporary exegetes, the methods of
Gematria were freely employed. He wrote a large amount
of Hebrew[3] rhymed prose, and poetry formed on the model of
Guittone d'Arezzo[4]. He was the author besides of a large
number of Hebrew novelettes on Italian models[5], by which

---

[1] I am indebted for this information and much that follows to an Article in
the *Jewish Quarterly Review*, vol. iv., Oct. 1891, by Dr. J. Chotzner. Also to
De Rossi, *Dizionario degli Autori Ebrei*, and to a Monograph by Theodor Paur,
Immanuel und Dante, in the third volume of the *Jahrbuch der Deutschen Dante-
Gesellschaft*. See also Dean Plumptre's *Introductory Life of Dante*, pp. lxxv–
lxxvii.

[2] De Rossi, *op. cit.*, pp. 112–114.

[3] Also Italian ; and of this a curious sample is given by Pelaez, *Rime Antiche
Italiane*, in the *Collezione di Opere inedite e rare*, ed. Carducci, vol. iv., pp. 354–
358.

[4] See *Purg.* xxiv. 56 ; xxvi. 124, &c. ; *Jewish Q. R.*, Oct. 1891, p. 73.

[5] One of the jokes of the medico-novelist in one of these tales may be worth
preserving. A patient had been ordered by his doctor to take a certain physic,
and to remain perfectly quiet in his bed until the doctor came the next morning.

great light is thrown on the moral and social condition of
the Italian Jews in the thirteenth and fourteenth centuries[1].
Further he composed in Hebrew verse an imitation of one
of the encyclopaedic Italian *Tesori*, of which we have an
example in that of Brunetto Latini[2]. He also wrote Italian
Sonnets and Canzoni, especially on subjects connected with
love. His fame as a poet spread to France and Spain. His
works are humorous in tone, full of jests, both in and out of
place, often amounting to βωμολοχία in their inappropriate-
ness and coarseness. His sarcasm is keen and bitter, and he
has not inaptly been described as 'the mediaeval Heine.' But
the work of his which has a special interest for us is his Vision
of Hell and Paradise, for, as a Jew, he would naturally not
recognize Purgatory. This was published shortly before his
death, c. 1328, in which, besides the similarity of subject,
Paur finds numerous and unmistakable traces of acquaintance
with the *Divina Commedia*[3]. I will only mention one sample.
On the Gate of Hell he sees the inscription, 'Here is only an
entrance and no exit.' The composition of his 'Vision' came
about thus. At the age of sixty he became anxious about his
future, and he invoked the prophet Daniel, who undertook to
show him his own future place in the spirit world, which he is
assured will be in Paradise[4]. But he begs to be allowed to
visit Hell first, when he sees the inscription above quoted.
Arrived in Heaven, he saw two thrones being prepared side
by side, one for himself, and one for a great friend whom he
had in life, called *Daniel*, who had shown him the paths of

The patient, however, got up in the night and wrote a quantity of poetry, which
he exhibited with pride to the doctor in the morning, at the same time declaring
that his physic had done him no good. 'I am not sure of that,' said the doctor,
'as it seems to have caused the removal from your brain of a good deal of
rubbish.'

[1] *Jewish Q. R.*, Oct. 1891, p. 71.

[2] *Jewish Q. R.* for July, 1895 (by Dr. Gustavo Sacerdote), p. 711. The writer
thinks the original was probably the *Trésor* of Peire (or Pietro) de Corbiac,
c. 1225, which is sometimes believed to have inspired the *Tesoretto* of B. Latini.
(*Ib.* p. 718.)

[3] Dr. Gustavo Sacerdote in the *Jewish Q. R.*, July, 1895, p. 712, goes so far
as to say that it closely follows that original. See also Dean Plumptre's *Life of
Dante*, p. lxxvi.

[4] *Jewish Q. R.*, Oct. 1891, pp. 84 *seqq.*

truth and righteousness, whose mind is still spoken of on earth with great esteem and admiration. His name and his fame will always be held in great honour by posterity. 'You (says his guide) are as far inferior to him as Joshua was to Moses, but you have both striven after truth, you have both been united in friendly activity, so no power shall separate your souls for ever.' (Then he describes at length the splendour of Daniel's throne.) His guide proceeds, 'You see, my son, the work that he has created in the world, full of fame and renown. Equally great and glorious shall be the throne he is to occupy in the world of spirits.' It can hardly be doubted, I think, that Dante is here referred to under the disguise of the name Daniel, as a sort of Hebrew echo of his name. Of whom else in Emanuel's acquaintance could such language be used? Certainly no one of that name can be found at all answering to such a panegyric, nor, surely, apart from the name, any other contemporary writer. May there not also be some significance in the prophet Daniel being selected as his guide in that Vision of Hell and Paradise for which the *Divina Commedia* of Dante provided the model?

But the indications of friendship with Dante go further still. We all know the name of the friend of Dante, Bosone da Gubbio, who composed one of those *Capitoli*, or summaries, which occur so commonly in MSS. of the *Divina Commedia*. It is that which begins—

'Però che sia più frutto e più diletto.'

Now Emanuel was certainly intimate with this Bosone, and they exchanged Sonnets (after the common custom) upon the death of Dante. It so happened that the wife of Emanuel, to whom he was devotedly attached, died in the year 1321, the year of Dante's death. Bosone addressed therefore to Emanuel a Sonnet on the subject of this double calamity. Two lights have lately (he says) been quenched in the world. He then refers to the profound wisdom of one and the fair beauty of the other. 'Therefore let Emanuel the Jew (Manoel Giudeo) weep. Let him weep first for his own private loss; then let him weep for the calamity of this evil world. For never beneath the sun was there a more disastrous year. But (he concludes) I am comforted by the belief that God has assigned to Dante a glorious seat.' (See preceding page.) The answering Sonnet of Emanuel is preserved, but it deals chiefly with the depth of his own sorrow, without any precise reference to Dante.

Then there is another pair of corresponding Sonnets[1], written after the death of Emanuel, the first attributed (but surely quite absurdly) to Cino da Pistoia, the latter in reply, with scarcely more probability, to Bosone.

The first informs Bosone that his friend Manuel, following the error of his sect, has passed into Hell. Still he is not mingled with the common herd, but stands *side by side with Dante*, in the company of the Flatterers, in the plight in which Dante in his book says that he saw Alessio Interminei (see *Inf.* xviii. 122)! Surely Cino da Pistoia could never have written thus respecting 'amicus eius'! In the reply Sonnet, as well as the former, the references to the *Inferno* are extremely obscure and apparently inaccurate (so far as intelligible). However, the author of the reply protests that neither Emanuel nor Dante are in Hell, though he still associates them together in Purgatory. The concluding *terzina* runs thus :—

'Dante and Manoel fulfil their course, where the marrow and the skin are consumed by fire, until the time when the great deliverance comes to them.'

This seems to mean (as Paur observes) that they are in Purgatory, and in the purifying fire of the last Cornice.

But whatever be the authorship of these Sonnets, they are interesting as closely associating Dante and Emanuel, and witnessing thus early to the friendship and intimacy believed to exist between them. They are interesting also as apparently implying a knowledge of the *Divina Commedia* (if we may so call it) of Emanuel, in which he claimed a place for himself, as we have seen, side by side with Dante in Paradise. The first writer seems to be offended at the presumption of this, and in effect says: 'No, your friend Emanuel is not in

---

[1] The two Sonnets are printed by Paur, *op. cit.*, pp. 454, 455.

Paradise, but in Hell, as an unbelieving Jew, in company,
if you will, with Dante, but in the Bolgia of the Flatterers.'
To which the other replies : ' Nay, Jew though he were, he
is assuredly not thus condemned. With Dante he may be,
" in death they are not divided," but both are in the region
of hope, as

" anime sicure
D' aver, quando che sia, di pace stato." '

The writer seems to be pleading for his friend in language
like the touching protest of the Hostess respecting Falstaff :

' Nay, sure he's not in hell : he's in Arthur's bosom, if ever
man went to Arthur's bosom.'

I am afraid this lengthy digression has carried us a long
way from our subject. But I venture to think these proofs
of a probable friendship in Dante's life are sufficiently interesting to justify it, apart from the immediate object for which
they were introduced. This was to show that Dante had
intimate relations with one from whom he could easily have
obtained, and probably did obtain, such information as to
Hebrew words and letters as perhaps this, as well as certain
other well-known passages in the *Divina Commedia*, show to
have been somehow in his possession.   Certainly, then, I say
here is one *definite* source, to say nothing of many others,
from which Dante may well have been acquainted with the
rudiments and principles of the science of Gematria in its
application to *Hebrew* letters. A similar process applied to
the *Greek* alphabet would certainly be familiar to Dante from
writers whose works were undoubtedly known to him, in
connexion with the Apocalyptic enigma.

I conclude with a striking illustration from the writings
of Emanuel himself. He actually employs this method in
making the announcement of his own name at the end of one
of his works [1] :

' My name is 70 and 40, and a *Nun* joined to a *Vau*, and
the ending of my name is " *El*." [2] '

---

[1] From the *Jewish Q. R.*, vol. vii., July 1895, p. 714.

[2] The name is completely spelt out, as the 'a' would not in this case be
represented by a distinct letter in Hebrew.

Thus he spells out his name ' Emanuel,' but instead of saying that the first two letters are Ain and Mem, he says ' gematrically ' that they are 70 and 40.

I wish to submit this suggestion to the consideration of students of Dante. Without pretending to have finally settled a problem of such great difficulty, I venture to think that the solution now proposed, while it does not repudiate the commonly received explanation, adds considerable point and definiteness to it. The two taken together in fact mutually explain and illustrate one another, though I should myself regard the name of Henry as the primary interpretation, and ' DVX ' as at most a subordinate one.

V. THE GENUINENESS OF THE DEDI-CATORY EPISTLE TO CAN GRANDE

(Epistle X in Oxford Dante)

Synopsis

I.

About twenty-five years ago a sort of tidal wave of scepticism, now happily somewhat subsided, threatened to submerge a large number of Dante's works. The high-water mark of this visitation is reached by Dr. Prompt, who had the audacity to publish a work entitled 'Les Œuvres Apocryphes de Dante,' including under that title, the 'Quaestio de Aqua et Terra,' the Eclogues, most emphatically the Epistle to Can Grande, and finally even the *De Monarchia*, the author of which is insultingly described as 'the personage who composed this barbarous and abominable book'! Even more violent language is applied (as we shall see later) to the author of the Epistle to Can Grande. The late Dr. Scartazzini (though not going so far as this) was very prominent

in the sceptical onslaught.   With him, as with others of that
school, the Epistles were the special object of attack.   This
was to be expected, since (1) no doubt some three or four
shameless impostures had come to be commonly included
among them ; (2) they could be attacked in detail, and each
on special internal grounds ; (3) the external evidence for
each individually was, from the nature of the case, very
slender, and nothing like positive or demonstrative evidence,
or indeed anything beyond a general and persistent tradition,
could be produced.

Finally, among the Epistles this 10th Epistle (as it is
commonly reckoned, though sometimes numbered 11) [1] has
been the object of the most determined attack, in proportion
to its pre-eminent interest and supreme importance, if it
be genuine.   Few, if any, of the minor works of Dante are
more worth the effort of salvage.   For, if genuine, it not only
gives us an authoritative exposition by Dante himself of
a portion of his own works ; but, what is even more important, it throws light on the spirit and method by which
he would have us to interpret them generally.   The question
is still fully alive, since the genuineness of the Epistle has
been very keenly both contested and defended during the
last few years especially ; and there is now quite a considerable literature of pamphlets and monographs on the subject.

The Epistle, like all the Epistles of Dante which have

---

[1] The number of Epistles retained by different editors or critics has been
14, 11, 10, 4, or 3.   Out of the 14, there are 3 (written in Italian) purporting
to be addressed to Margaret of Brabant (wife of the Emperor Henry VII) by
the Countess of Battifolle.   There seems to be no better reason for attributing
them to Dante than that they are found in a certain MS. in the middle of some
of the Epistles professing to be written by him.   They have, I believe, now no
supporters, so that 11 may be considered the maximum number.   But of these
one at least is almost universally rejected, viz. one (also in Italian) supposed
to be written to Guido da Polenta, so that the number that have more or less
pretensions to be retained is not more than ten, viz. those printed in the *Oxford
Dante*.   Scartazzini and Bartoli reject all but three or four of these, admitting
only Nos. 6, 7, and 8, which seem to be attested by Villani, and possibly also
No. 5.   The first three or four are so brief and comparatively unimportant
(though I think No. 4 certainly bears marks of genuineness) as to afford no
sufficient material for arguments *pro* or *con*.   But the case of this Epistle X,
both in length and in the character of its contents, is quite different.

any serious pretension to be genuine, is in Latin. That is, in fact, what we should expect. It professes to be a Dedication of the Cantica of the *Paradiso* to Dante's friend and patron Can Grande della Scala. Such a dedication would at any rate be natural and appropriate. Can Grande himself, and also probably his uncle Bartolommeo della Scala, are spoken of in terms of profound gratitude and admiration in a celebrated passage in *Par.* xvii. 70–93. It has often been thought that each of the three *Cantiche* contained laudatory references to Can Grande; viz. as the Veltro in *Inf.* i. and as the 'DVX' in *Purg.* xxxiii, though the interpretation of both these passages, and especially that of the latter, in this sense is very uncertain. As to the plain language of *Par.* xvii there can be no doubt.

It will be well to begin with a short analysis of the contents of the Epistle, as they are probably unfamiliar to the majority of readers.

The first point I would notice is that the Epistle falls into three distinct divisions, so distinct that the unity of the whole has sometimes been impugned on that ground.

I. We have the Epistolary portion, properly so called, that is §§ 1–4, containing the formal Dedication to Can Grande, and also the last two sections in which the Epistolary style is resumed in conclusion.

II. The central portion (§§ 5–16), which has sometimes been styled the 'general doctrinal' part. This contains statements as to the subject, character, purpose, &c. of the *Divina Commedia* generally, and of the *Paradiso* in particular.

III. A detailed exposition of the Prologue to the *Paradiso*, on a plan which the writer hoped some day to carry out for the rest of the Cantica also. What would we not have given to have possessed this! This portion occupies §§ 17–31.

Thus we may briefly describe the three divisions, as Epistolary, Doctrinal, and Expository. Such a plan appears to be quite logical and reasonable, and not (as has been alleged) to indicate 'a stratification of materials,' or 'a patchwork of old and new materials,' as D'Ovidio has described it, adding that the rough joinings of these pieces would strike the eye, even if the writer had not been so clumsy as prosaically to draw our attention to it [1]!

I. As to the first portion, viz. the formal Dedication, in §§ 1–4, we need not in this analysis enter further into the details, though when we come to consider their evidential bearing *pro* and *con* there will be a great deal to be said.

II. Passing on then to the second division, the so-called *Doctrinal* part, we shall find that § 5 contains some curious technicalities—which seem to us superfluous, but which are quite in the manner of Dante and contemporary writers— as to the difference between 'absolute' and 'relative' terms. In the case of 'relative' terms, the knowledge of one is declared to imply the knowledge of the other ; and among examples of such terms are given the words 'whole' and 'part.'

In § 6, we find that the purpose of all this is to justify some explanation of the poem as a *whole* being undertaken by one who professedly intends to expound only one *part* of it, viz. the *Paradiso*. There are next said to be six main points which call for determination in reference to any work, either in whole or in part, viz. its *subject*, its *author*, its *form*, its *purpose*, its *title*, and its *scientific class or description*. Three of these have a different meaning in regard to the *Paradiso* from that which they bear in reference to the *Commedia* as a whole ; in the other three, there is no such difference.

The three which differ, and so have a special sense for the *Paradiso*, are the *subject*, the *form*, and the *title*, and it is proposed to deal first with these.

§ 7. A highly important section follows. But at the outset (says the writer) it must be observed that this work is to be interpreted in more senses than one. It has throughout (1) a literal meaning, and (2) an allegorical and mystical meaning. Then we have repeated the familiar fourfold meanings in which every writing (as Dante says in *Conv.* II. i) both *can* be understood and *ought* to be understood ; i. e. literal, allegorical, moral, and anagogical or spiritual. He adds that the last three are sometimes regarded as sub-divisions of 'allegorical' in a general sense, in contrast with

---

[1] *Studj sulla Divina Commedia*, p. 460.'

' literal,' or 'historical.' These are all illustrated in the present passage from one example, viz. Ps. cxiii. 1: ' When Israel came out of Egypt,' &c. *Allegorically* it means ' our redemption by Christ'; *morally* the conversion of the soul from the misery of sin to a state of grace ; *anagogically* or *spiritually* the passage of the soul from 'the bondage of corruption ' to ' the glorious liberty ' of Heaven.

We turn back after this digression to the six points set out in § 6, and in particular to the three which have a different sense in the *Commedia* generally and in the *Paradiso* specially, viz. the *subject*, the *form*, and the *title*. These are discussed in the next six sections : the first three of them (§§ 8, 9, 10) dealing with the sense in which these three terms are applied to the poem generally; and the last three (§§ 11, 12, 13) with the sense which they bear in reference to the *Paradiso* in particular.

§ 8. First then, § 8 deals with the *subject* of the Poem generally. That is twofold, in accordance with the two main principles of interpretation expounded in the last section. Here we meet with the celebrated and often quoted declaration, which Dante himself has been generally held to have given, as to the literal and allegorical subject of his own Poem. *Literally*, it is ' the state of the soul after death simply understood.' *Allegorically*, the subject is ' Man, accordingly as by merit or demerit, through the exercise of his free will, he becomes amenable to the rewards or punishments of Justice.'

§ 9. Next we pass on to the *form* of the Poem. The form, it is said, may have reference to the form of the *treatise*, or the form of the *treatment* ; ' forma *tractatus*,' or ' forma *tractandi*.'

In the former case it is threefold, relating to the division (1) of the whole Poem into Cantiche ; (2) of these into Cantos ; and (3) of these again into rhymes, or *terzine*. In the latter division (the *forma tractandi*) the methods of treatment are designated by no less than ten epithets, which we need not specify in detail. I will only add that this curious list is found repeated in the Commentaries of Guido da Pisa, Boccaccio, and Buti.

§ 10. The *Title.* As to the title of the work generally, the chief point in this section is the justification of the term 'Comoedia,' on the grounds that the Poem ends happily, and that its language is the ordinary vulgar tongue, which, it is added, even common women use ! ('in qua et mulierculae communicant'). This is not quite as contemptuous as it sounds to us, the main point of the writer being to distinguish the ordinary spoken language from the more honourable and dignified Latin, whose superior claims are set forth at length in *Conv.* I. In reference to the term 'Comoedia,' one point to be remembered is that in Dante's time both Tragedy and Comedy had lost their dramatic character. Poems which were merely narrative and never intended for acting were commonly called by these titles. Thus Dante himself calls the *Aeneid* of Virgil a Tragedy (*Inf.* xx. 113). On this point see further, *infra,* p. 365.

Then follow the three sections (11–13) which expound the modification of these same three terms, *subject, form,* and *title,* when their application is limited to the *Paradiso.*

§ 11. As to the *subject,* it is briefly explained that, having regard to the two definitions of the subject of the Poem in general which are given in § 8, the subject of the *Paradiso* treats *literally* of the state of the souls of the blessed only after death ; and *allegorically* of the rewards only, and not the punishments, of Divine Justice.

§ 12. As to the *form,* and its tripartite division in § 9, it is evident that the two latter only are applicable, viz. that of the Cantica into Cantos, and that of the Cantos into *terzine.*

§ 13. As to the *title,* instead of 'Incipit Comoedia' we must say ' Incipit tertia pars Comoediae,' &c.

We next have three sections (14–16) dealing with the other three terms in which no special meaning is required for the *Paradiso* as contrasted with the Poem generally, viz. the author, the purpose, and the scientific classification of the work. As to the *author* (§ 14) there is nothing more to be said. The *purpose* (§ 15) both of the whole and of the part (i. e. *Paradiso*) is the same, and it is interesting to note what it is here authoritatively declared to be. It is this :—

* * *

'To remove those who are living in this life from a state of misery, and to lead them to a state of happiness.'

§ 16. As to the *class of philosophy or science* to which the Poem belongs both in whole and in part, it follows from what has just been said that it is *Moral* or *Ethical*. In other words it is *practical* throughout, and it is really so even in those places where it seems to be most purely speculative.

III. Here commences the third, or so-called *Expository*, portion of the Epistle.

§ 17. We are now in a position (says the author) to proceed to the literal interpretation of the *Paradiso*. Consequently he proceeds to divide the *Paradiso* into two main parts: (1) the Prologue; and (2) the working out of the subject, or 'pars executiva' as it is termed. This latter part is said to begin at *Par.* i. 37, *Surge ai mortali*. It will be seen presently that the Epistle deals with the former only of these two parts, viz. the Prologue, the other not being reached.

In § 18 we have first another thoroughly characteristic piece of refinement as to the distinction between 'prologue,' 'exordium,' 'prooemium,' and 'prelude,' into the details of which we need not now enter [1]. 'Prologue' is determined to be the correct term to apply in this case. It is then divided into two parts: (a) the announcement of the subject (ll. 1–12); (β) the invocation (ll. 13–36); after which the Prologue ends, and the 'pars executiva' begins.

In § 19 the announcement of the subject in general is justified as fulfilling all the three conditions of a good rhetorical exordium as set forth in the *de Rhetorica* of Cicero. The reader is assured that, *selon les règles*, he will find the subject (1) beneficial or profitable (viz. the joys of Paradise); (2) marvellous (since it treats of the nature of the kingdom of Heaven); (3) possible (since the writer will speak of what dwells in his own memory of that which he has seen). Hence the reader will be made correspondingly (1) well-disposed; (2) attentive; (3) willing to learn. And these are, as Cicero tells us, the three conditions of a good introduction to any subject.

---

[1] On this *v. infra*, p. 326.

In § 20 the literal interpretation begins. This, I may remark, is specially interesting as exhibiting Dante's own idea of the form and character which a Commentary on his poem ought to take. The numerous divisions and subdivisions which follow are so curious, and yet so characteristic of Dante (*v. Convito, passim*), that I have thought it worth while to exhibit them in a tabular form :—

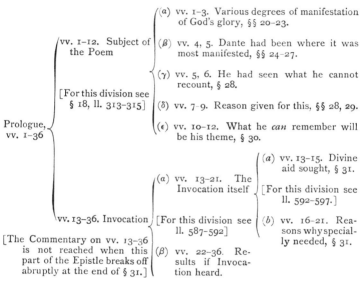

Prologue, vv. 1–36

vv. 1–12. Subject of the Poem
[For this division see § 18, ll. 313–315]

- (α) vv. 1–3. Various degrees of manifestation of God's glory, §§ 20–23.
- (β) vv. 4, 5. Dante had been where it was most manifested, §§ 24–27.
- (γ) vv. 5, 6. He had seen what he cannot recount, § 28.
- (δ) vv. 7–9. Reason given for this, §§ 28, 29.
- (ε) vv. 10–12. What he *can* remember will be his theme, § 30.

vv. 13–36. Invocation
[The Commentary on vv. 13–36 is not reached when this part of the Epistle breaks off abruptly at the end of § 31.]

- (α) vv. 13–21. The Invocation itself
  [For this division see ll. 587–592]
  - (a) vv. 13–15. Divine aid sought, § 31.
    [For this division see ll. 592–597.]
  - (b) vv. 16–21. Reasons why specially needed, § 31.
- (β) vv. 22–36. Results if Invocation heard.

Note. 'vv.' here relates to lines of the *Paradiso* ; 'll.' to the lines of the *Epistle* ; '§§' to its sections.

§§ 20–23 deal with the first *terzina* of the Canto, and the statement therein made that the glory of God is manifested in different degrees in different parts of the universe. The truth of this can be proved both by Reason and by Authority. The former is shown in §§ 20 and 21, and the latter in § 22. In § 20 metaphysical arguments are adduced to prove that God alone can have existence (*esse*) of Himself (*per se*) ; all other creatures or things derive their existence from God, either mediately or immediately. The latter, as we learn elsewhere, would be the case with Heaven (*Par.* vii. 130); with the Angels (*ib.*, and also *Par.* xxix. 16 *seqq.*, *Conv.* III. xiv. 35, &c.) ;

and with the Soul of Man, which is *therefore* immortal (*Par*. vii. 67, 142)[1].

In § 21 similar arguments are adduced to show that the *essentia* no less than the *esse* of all creatures, i. e. their peculiar nature and capacity, 'essentia et virtus' (as it is termed here), must be in like manner derived from God ; their *essentia* (observe) as well as their mere *esse* or existence (ll. 397–399). Hence we conclude that Reason itself shows the Goodness and Wisdom and Power of God to be displayed throughout *all* His works, even as these introductory words of the poem declare. Let it be noted that these three attributes correspond to the three Persons of the Trinity, as they are again recognized in the terrible inscription over the Gate of Hell in *Inf*. iii. 5, 6 ; and also in two important passages of the *Convito* (II. vi. 62–72, and III. xii. 97). So also often in Aquinas, e. g. I. xxxix. 8, r$_3$; xlv. 6, r$_2$, &c.

In § 22 the writer shows that the same truth is supported by Authority as well as by Reason. For this he quotes four passages of Scripture, and also the splendid line of Lucan which is cited as ' scriptura paganorum ' :—

' Iuppiter est quodcunque vides, quocunque moveris.'

In § 23 he refines upon the distinction between the words in *Par*. i. 2, 'penetra' and 'risplende,' the former referring mainly to ' essentia,' and the latter to ' esse,' as these words were used in the previous §§, 20 and 21. He adds that the statement of l. 3, that the Divine influence is manifested ' più e meno ' in different parts of the universe, is too obvious to need further proof.

The next group of §§, viz. 24–30, is concerned with ll. 4–12 of Canto I, which form the remainder of that first division of the Prologue, in which the *subject of the poem* is announced, viz. ll. 1–12 (see § 18). Of these §§ 24–27 are devoted to l. 4 ; §§ 28 and 29 to ll. 5–9 ; and § 30 to ll. 10–12. Each of these groups of lines will be found to contain a separate statement of fact : (1) l. 4, that the author had been caught up to the highest Heaven, the abode of God Himself ; (2) ll. 5–9, that

[1] Comp. Aq. *Summa*, I. xcvii. 1. r.

he had seen things beyond the power of understanding or of speech; and (3) ll. 10-12, that such of these things as *could* be retained by his memory will form the theme of his song.

First then, these four §§, 24-27, explain that the expression in l. 4, 'the Heaven that receives most of the Divine light,' is meant to be equivalent to the tenth Heaven or the Empyrean, § 24; and next, that this description of that Heaven (or *circumlocutio* as he calls it in §§ 26 *fin.* and 28 *init.*) is justified both by Reason (§§ 25 and 26) and by Authority (§ 27); just as the same twofold support was claimed in §§ 20-22 for the statement of the first *terzina* of the Canto.

More in detail, § 24 asserts that by the expression in l. 4 is denoted 'the Empyrean' or the tenth and highest Heaven, the abode of God and of His saints (*v. Conv.* II. iv). This statement, as we shall see, has been most strangely denied by some modern Commentators, who boldly assert that the expression is to be interpreted of Heaven generally, i.e. of all the ten Heavens traversed by Dante in the *Paradiso*, and not of the tenth Heaven specially, and consequently that the forger of the Epistle has betrayed himself by giving a palpably erroneous interpretation of Dante's meaning! I am bound to say that on entirely independent grounds, i.e. from a consideration of the language of many other passages in Dante, the interpretation given by the author of the Epistle appears to me to be beyond all doubt the correct one, but this will be further discussed later on (*v. infra*, pp. 319, 320).

In §§ 25 and 26 it is maintained on two distinct grounds that the Empyrean is correctly described as the Heaven 'which receives the fullest portion of Divine light.' The arguments in question are of a very technical and metaphysical character, which we need not expound further at present, though they afford (as I think) important evidence for the genuineness of the Epistle, when compared with other works of Dante.

In § 27 the conclusion thus reached by 'Reason' is shown to be consonant with the voice of 'Authority.' In support of this, quotations are given from Aristotle, S. Paul, and Ezekiel. I need hardly perhaps remind my readers how thoroughly characteristic of Dante is this combination of appeals to Reason and Authority [1].

Then § 28 passes on to the second of the three statements distinguished above, viz. that of ll. 5–9 of Canto I, that the writer had seen things transcending both human understanding and the power of human speech. The reason or explanation of such an experience first being given, authorities are again quoted to further justify it : viz. S. Paul, S. Matthew, Ezekiel, Richard of St. Victor, S. Bernard, and S. Augustine. This particular appeal to Authority is made because men might perhaps otherwise distrust so sublime a revelation when conveyed by one so unworthy as Dante himself. The authors named are specially significant, because, as a matter of fact, Richard of St. Victor and S. Bernard have been discovered to be the principal sources for many of the dogmatic statements made by Dante on the most mysterious and abstruse subjects in the *Paradiso*, such as the orders and functions of Angels, &c. This again is an indication of authorship, for Dante surely himself knew best the authorities to which he was indebted. For any one else, at any rate, it would imply a very serious amount of investigation [2].

Then § 29 insists on the double deficiency implied by the words 'nè sa, nè può,' in *Par*. i. 6 '*nescit* et *nequit*.' Through ' the greatness of the revelation ' many things have passed out of the mind ; and many other things that are still retained transcend the power of human speech to express. That which remains after these limitations and deductions (§ 30) will form the subject of the work which follows, and will in fact constitute what has been described as the second great division, or *pars executiva*, of the poem.

In § 31 the author passes on to the second division of the Prologue (for which see § 18, l. 313), viz. 'the Invocation.' This, again, is, after his usual fashion, subdivided. It consists of (a) the appeal for Divine aid, ll. 13–21 ; (β) the setting forth of the urgent need for such an appeal, ll. 22–36.

After this, in § 32, the writer suddenly stops, and the Epistolary form is resumed. Such, he says, is the general

---

[1] *v. infra*, p. 325. [2] On this see further, p. 341.

character of the second part of the Prologue ; any further explanation of this in detail he cannot at present undertake. The pressure of private cares and narrow means compel the abandonment of this and other schemes that might bear useful fruit. He hopes, however, that his illustrious patron will remove such impediments.

Finally, in § 33, he observes that the entire explanation of the main body of the poem (*pars executiva*) must likewise for the present be given up. He will only add that it will include the ascent from Heaven to Heaven, with a description of the glorified spirits found in each ; till at last is reached the presence of God Himself, in the vision of Whom all their joy and happiness consists. He is A and O, the beginning and the end, Who is blessed for evermore, world without end.

Now even from this very rapid summary of the plan of the Epistle, any one moderately familiar with the prose works of Dante, especially the *Convito*, the *De Monarchia*, and (as I should myself certainly add) the *Quaestio*, must surely be struck by several general features of resemblance with Dante's style and methods. Among these I might mention the minute divisions and subdivisions [1] ; the elaborate analysis and planning out of the whole subject ; the same cold-blooded dissection, not to say, vivisection, of his own poetry, which is found on almost every page of the *Vita Nuova* and of the *Convito* ; the tendency to diverge at a tangent into metaphysical or scholastic disquisitions and fine-drawn distinctions, often suggested by a single word, and, often too, seeming to our modern notions irrelevant or pedantic ; the enforcement of conclusions by appeals to authority, after they have been established by arguments ; and the intermingling in such appeals of quotations from sacred and profane authors. All these are general characteristics. Many similarities also there seem to be of thought and expression in detail. These will be considered in a later part of the Essay.

---

[1] This process is thus justified by Dante in *Conv.* IV. iii. 16 : 'Però nullo si maravigli se per molte divisioni si procede ; conciossiacosachè grande e alta opera sia per le mani al presente.' The same chapter (ll. 26–36) affords an example of subdivisions exactly like those found in this Epistle.

II

THE INTERNAL EVIDENCE

I think it will be the most convenient plan for the discussion before us if we consider the *internal* evidence first and
the *external* afterwards, since the former comes more closely
into connexion with the analysis which has just been given of
the contents of the Epistle. And under that former head
I will deal first with the adverse arguments which have been
derived from the contents of the Epistle, and afterwards
collect those indications which appear to me to be favourable
to its genuineness.

II. i. THE INTERNAL EVIDENCE ALLEGED TO BE ADVERSE.

The first person, I believe, to raise any doubts was Scolari
in 1819. Since then, and especially in the last decade, many
others have joined in the fray. Among the opponents may
be named Scartazzini, Bartoli, Drs. Prompt and Kraus, and,
quite recently, Prof. D'Ovidio ; and among the supporters,
Giuliani, Witte, Latham, Torraca, D'Alfonso, and Vandelli.
In stating the principal objections, I will follow mainly
D'Ovidio [1], as his attack is both the most recent and the most
exhaustive in detail. It is justly described by Vandelli (p. 6)
as 'il più formidabile e compiuto attacco sinora tentato.'
Though in a controversy one cannot help seeming to 'attack'
one who has championed the opposite side, I wish to speak
with the greatest respect of Prof. D'Ovidio, and to acknowledge the valuable services he has rendered to the study
of Dante. I regret, as will be seen later, the passionate tone
of his Essay. I think his case would have been stronger
if his language had been more temperate. But I wish it
distinctly to be understood that if I have singled out *his*
attack on the Epistle for special criticism it is because it

---

[1] The work referred to is in the vol. of *Studj sulla Divina Commedia*,
pp. 448-485.

is the most comprehensive and complete, and thus the necessity of dealing with other opponents is to a great extent superseded :

'E ciò non fa d' onor poco argomento.'

II. i. (*a*) THE EPISTOLARY PORTION.

Passing over some trifling criticisms of the title, the following objections are raised to the Epistolary or Introductory portion of the document (§§ 1–4).

(1) The address to Can Grande is stigmatized as prolix, fulsome, pompous, and degrading to its author.

(2) The comparison of Dante's visit to those of the Queen of Sheba and of Pallas is audacious and inappropriate.

(3) Certain expressions in the Latinity are peculiar, and unlike the style of Dante.

(4) The treatment of certain subjects or quotations differs from that which is found in the *Convito*.

Now as to the first of these points :—

(1) The censure of the style of the address is purely a matter of opinion, and moreover it involves the judgement of fourteenth-century conventionalities by the standard and fashion of the nineteenth [1]. Not only is the language here paralleled by that employed by Dante himself in a somewhat similar address to Henry VII in Epistle vii [2], but, as Torraca has pointed out, it is quite in accordance with contemporary practice [3]. To have omitted such complimentary language would then have seemed disrespectful, as much so as if we were nowadays to decline an invitation without the conven-

---

[1] But we need not go back beyond the eighteenth century to find abundant examples of this style in dedications, and even in ordinary letters. As to the latter, the letters even of one with so thoroughly proud and independent a spirit as Dr. Johnson may afford an example. As to the former, we have the same great critic's recorded opinion: 'The known style of a dedication is flattery; it professes to flatter' (*Hebrides*, p. 275, Temple ed.). So again Bacon, while protesting, in the *Advancement of Learning* (I. iii. 9), against 'the modern dedication of books and writings as to patrons, seeing that they should have no patrons but truth and reason,' himself fell in with the current fashion with a vengeance in the fulsome dedication of that very same work to King James !

[2] See esp. § 2.   [3] Of this he quotes some examples, p. 7.

tional, even if transparently insincere, 'regret' at being 'unable' to accept it.

Quite of a piece with this is the objection taken to a later passage in § 32 where the author says that he is compelled to abandon this and other works of general utility, ' haec et alia *utilia reipublicae.*' D'Ovidio jeers at this as exhibiting ' poca modestia.' But are we not all familiar with title-pages only a few generations back in which authors described their own works as ' godly,' ' learned,' ' profitable,' ' edifying,' and so forth? Besides, has the objector forgotten that Dante himself introduces his work in the *De Monarchia* in almost identical terms? In I. i. 16 he declares that, lest he should incur the condemnation of 'the talent buried in the earth,' he desires '*publicae utilitati* non modo turgescere, quinimo fructificare.' Not only so, but a similar claim is made also for the *Convito* three or four times. See I. i. 67–86, and IV. i. 35–41 and 73. Again, in *Conv.* I. ii. 115 Dante boldly says that he desires to impart ' teaching that in truth no one else can give ' ; and in l. 127 he promises his readers both ' diletto buono a udire,' and also ' sottile ammaestramento.' Once more in IV. iv. 136 he announces a discussion which will prove ' non senza utilità e diletto grande.' Now looking on to the last section of the Epistle before us we find almost the same words as those from the *Convito*—' multa quaerentur quae *magnam* habent *utilitatem* et *delectationem.*' Surely had the objector remembered these and similar passages he might perhaps have found it better to change his ground, and charge the luckless ' forger ' not with want of modesty, but with plagiarism, as he does elsewhere [1]. It may be noted that this quality of ' utility ' is appropriately claimed for the present work in view of the practical aim—*finis totius et partis*—assigned to it in §§ 15, 16.

But the unfortunate writer who is charged with want of modesty when he claims this merit for his work, is assailed with bitter ridicule [2] when he applies the humble term

---

[1] e. g. in respect of §§ 2, 7.

[2] The following is a characteristic specimen of the controversial methods of Prof. D'Ovidio. If the writer undertook 'a scrivere *a Cane*, nulla lo poteva costringere a scrivere *da cane*'! (p. 457).

munusculum' to the 'Comoediae Canticam sublimem,' in the formal Dedication in § 3. But surely we all know how the conventional language of Dedications (in contrast with that of title-pages noticed above) commonly depreciates the work offered and its author in relation to his patron, who is thus flattered by contrast also. The objection that 'munusculum' is improperly applied to materials for a potential gift is too captious to need further consideration[1].

(2) The objection to the reference to the Queen of Sheba and Pallas is again a mere matter of private opinion, and we cannot fail to note that at any rate the combination of examples from sacred and profane literature accords with the constant practice of Dante.

Besides, as Torraca (p. 10) very well observes, Dante does not compare *himself* to the Queen of Sheba or to Pallas, but his *action* and *purpose* with theirs. In this respect the comparisons are entirely apt. Torraca adds that in like manner Dante in the *Commedia* compares his feelings and experiences with those of Phaeton, Icarus, or Glaucus, not himself with them. Here is another objection based upon this same allusion. D'Ovidio declares that there is a flat contradiction between the statement of *Conv.* I. iii and iv, viz. that (in effect) 'minuit praesentia famam,' whether that fame be good or evil[2], and that of § 1 of the Epistle that Dante could not believe the great things that he heard of Can Grande until he saw with his own eyes, and that then he found that they were not only true, but even less than the truth. What conceivable inconsistency is there between asserting the general tendency to be as stated in the *Convito* and the particular fact to be as stated in the Epistle[3]? It would

---

[1] *Op. cit.* p. 455.

[2] See especially the last words of c. iii: 'Apertamente adunque veder può chi vuole che la immagine per sola fama generata sempre è più ampia, quale che essa sia, che non è la cosa immaginata nel vero stato.'

[3] Perhaps one may venture on a homely illustration of this. During Dr. Johnson's tour in Scotland Boswell records that he offered him some veal which he thought would refute the common prejudice that veal in Scotland was not good. 'Sir (was the characteristic reply), what is commonly thought, I should take to be true.' (This is quite Aristotelian in its gravity!) '*Your* veal may be

be about as reasonable to argue that because experience verifies the generalization of Dante in the *Convito, l.c.* and the quotation of Claudian above which embodies it, as well as the statement of our Lord that 'a prophet has no honour in his own country,' *therefore* the story of the Queen of Sheba must be false, since the report about Solomon *ought* to have exceeded the reality! Further to argue, as D'Ovidio does[1], that *excessiva* (l. 16) is a very infelicitous epithet to apply to the deeds of Can Grande, is simply to overlook the context, since it is evidently intended to echo *excéssum* in the line before, in such a way that no one would be liable to misunderstand it.

(3) As samples of the minute and rather pedantic character of the objections to the Latinity of the Epistle, let us take the following:—'In *Sapientia* de Sapientia legitur' (l. 39) is said to be an affectation. If it be so, one can only say that such verbal affectations are extremely common in Dante, who is almost as fond of them as S. Augustine. A large number will be found collected in Mr. Vernon's *Inferno* on xiii. 25 (i. p. 420).

(*b*) The phrase 'Spiritum Sanctum audiat' is objected to, since it makes Dante quote the Holy Spirit 'as an author[2].' This is assuredly sheer pedantry; since the idea or thought that the language of the writers of Scripture is directly dictated by the Holy Ghost, and, if so, is really His own language, occurs perpetually in Dante, so as amply to justify this expression. Compare especially the words in § 22, 'Dicit Spiritus Sanctus per Hieremiam' with *Mon.* III. xvi. 67 ' haec a Spiritu Sancto [ostensa sunt] qui per Prophetas et Hagiographos ... revelavit.' Add also *Par.* xx. 38 ; xxiv. 138 ; xxix. 41. Note especially *Mon.* III. iv. 84 :—' Non peccatur in Moysen, etc. ... sed in Spiritum Sanctum, qui loquitur in illis,' and two lines below—' Unicus tamen dictator est Deus[3].' Again, add the expression in *Mon.* I. xvi.

good, but that will only be an exception to the general opinion, not a proof against it.'

[1] P. 477.   [2] p. 453.
[3] Compare with this the language of Bacon :—' Moyses the lawgiver and God's first pen,' *Advancement of Learning*, VI. vi. 9.

35 'quum per tubam Sancti Spiritus tibi affletur.' Many other similar passages might be cited.

(*c*) The same kind of answer applies to the objection taken to the phrase 'scriptura paganorum' by which, side by side with two Scriptural quotations, the well-known line of Lucan. is introduced in § 22—'Iuppiter est quodcunque vides, quocunque moveris.' This actual phrase may not be found elsewhere, but the sentiment expressed by it is extremely familiar to all readers of Dante, as I have pointed out in my *Studies,* I. pp. 27, 167 ; and II. pp. 23 *seqq.*[1] Here we need only briefly note *Ep.* VII. iii. 60, where a quotation from Virgil is introduced by the words—'Scriptum etenim nobis est'; and *Mon.* II. iii. 28, where Virgil is quoted side by side with Scripture as 'divinus poeta noster.' Finally, in *Conv.* IV. v. 50, after quoting the authority of the Old Testament for the birth and parentage of David, Dante shows the date of the foundation of Rome by Aeneas to be contemporaneous, 'siccome testimoniano le scritture'; this being in obvious reference to Virgil and Livy. And again in l. 93 we find the expression 'le scritture delle Romane storie,' of which that of Livy is the chief.

In regard to such objections as (*b*) and (*c*) we are surely entitled to ask—Is a writer, when repeating a sentiment perfectly familiar to him, not to be allowed any variation in the expression of it ? Is it not much more likely that such variation should be found, especially if a striking and pregnant phrase such as 'scriptura paganorum' should occur to him? It is obvious that some of the passages above quoted from the *Convito* and *De Monarchia*, would be open to censure if such a principle as this were insisted on.

(*d*) It is further objected that the *Ars Poetica* of Horace is cited in this Epistle as *Poetica*, whereas in the *V. N.*, *Conv.*, and *V. E.* it appears as *Poetria.* As to this it is probably

<hr/>

[1] Gaspary points out that the practice of Dante in this respect was common to many writers of that period. 'It was a time in which the written word was still identical with the infallibly true word, in which authority counted for everything, the authority of the Church and Holy Writ on the one hand, and on the other, that of the classical writers.' *History of Italian Literature*, p. 185 in Oelsner's Translation.

enough to point out that no one pretends that the oldest MS. is the autograph, and such a slight variation might easily have been introduced by a copyist.

(*e*) Scolari and D'Ovidio both object to the phrase 'tenellus gratiae vestrae,' the former chiefly on chronological grounds [1], the latter because the expression in Latin, or even its Italian equivalent, would not be Dantesque (*op. cit.* p. 453). But whether we attach much weight to such objections or not, it is remarkable that in a Munich MS., which however contains only the four introductory or Epistolary sections, but which Dr. Witte (*Dante-Forschungen*, p. 500) holds to be the oldest existing MS., the passage reads quite differently thus: 'Sed zelus gloriae vestrae, quam sitio nostram parvipendens, a primordio metam praefixam urgere ulterius [2].' As this stands, it looks as if the main verb had accidentally dropped out. Witte proposes to insert *facit.* But as he himself in his edition of the Epistles (1827) has a note 'Vulgo, *urgebit*,' why should we not follow that reading [3]? The passage in this form would entirely avoid the above objections as well as one which has been made to the strangely exaggerated expression '*vitam* parvipendens' of the *textus receptus.*

(4) In regard to the language in which similar quotations are referred to, or similar subjects are treated, in this Epistle and in the *Convito*, or elsewhere, the objector oscillates between two different lines of criticism. When the resemblance between such passages is very close, the hand of a forger is said to be betrayed by plagiarism ; when it is less close, or its application is somewhat different, the same inference is drawn from the variations. This seems a little hard. Thus the reference to the popular error as to the dimensions of the Sun is condemned both as 'tolto quasi di peso dal Convivio,' and also as being differently and less appropriately

---

[1] See this further explained *infra*, pp. 359 *seqq.*

[2] There is a MS. in the Ambrosiana at Milan also containing only §§ 1–4, and Dr. Ceriani informs me that it too reads this passage as above, but with *urgebit.* I think the Oxford text should be altered to accord with this MS.

[3] In the absence of further information, it certainly looks as if *urgebit* had been conjecturally altered to *urgebo* to suit the nominative *tenellus.*

ت

employed, so that ' il brav' uomo tradisce il suo giuoco.'
Again, the reference in § 2 to the conditions of friendship
in *Ethics* IX, though it cannot be said to 'contradict'
Conv. III. i, yet it is alleged to be highly suspicious from the
different manner of the application of some of its details.
As however Torraca has acutely pointed out, the difference
in part results from the quotation in the Epistle bearing
a closer resemblance to the Aristotelian original than that
in the *Convito*! Is it likely that any forger would have been
so diligent or so subtle as to have made this change [1]?
Apart from any such answers to these objections severally,
I would observe that objections of this class form a sort
of boomerang argument which is apt to recoil on their author.
For the variations and inconsistencies in detail that have been
alleged are precisely such as a forger would be on his guard
against. The tendency of any but the most consummate
artists in forgery—and it should be observed that both
D'Ovidio and Scartazzini seem to exhaust a singularly rich
vocabulary of abuse and contempt to express their opinion of
the want of intelligence and incapacity of this one [2]—the
tendency, I say, would be rather to obtrude resemblances too
crudely, and to be nervously afraid of falling into differences
or discrepancies. Besides no author is so rigidly bound
to such microscopic uniformity of language or precise accuracy
of detail throughout all his works, as the implied major
premiss of such criticism would assume. Certainly it is
not to be found in the acknowledged works of Dante himself.
See some instances of variation in formulae of quotation given
in *Studies*, II. p. 352 (γ). Thus it is quite absurd to object
to such an isolated phrase as 'tenellus gratiae vestrae' (even
if genuine) as not found elsewhere. This is a palpable abuse of
the argument from ἅπαξ λεγόμενα. If such treatment of ἅπαξ
λεγόμενα were applied to the *V. E.*, almost any page would
afford sufficient evidence to put it out of court. So when the

---

[1] Both these quotations will be found more fully discussed later. See
pp. 337, 338.

[2] As Luzio and Renier have done in reference to the supposed forger of the
Quaestio. See *Studies*, II. pp. 309 *seqq.* Both the writers mentioned in the
text have been entirely distanced in this respect by Dr. Prompt, *v. infra*, p. 323.

expressions *analogo* and *morale negotium* in § 3 are condemned as 'fuori dell' uso Dantesco' the objector seems not
to be aware that the former is simply a direct quotation
from *Nic. Eth.* IX. i. 1 τὸ ἀνάλογον ἰσάζει καὶ σώζει τὴν φιλίαν
(*analogum*[1] being the word found in the *Trans. Ant.*); and
the latter is a scarcely less obvious rendering of πραγματεία
which is several times applied to his Ethical Treatise by
Aristotle (e.g. II. ii. 1; III. ix. 10, &c.), and it is regularly
rendered by *negotium* in the *Translatio*.

Again, D'Ovidio (p. 452) says that the phrase '*pedalis
magnitudinis*' arouses his suspicion, as being (*inter alia*)
'non il solito latino di Dante.' Apart from the fact that
Dante had not often occasion to employ such an expression,
pedalis is in fact the word used by Cicero, *Acad.* II. xxvi. 82,
to express this very thing[2]. Torraca suggests that Dante
(*h. l.* and in the *Convito*) derived the illustration from Cicero
rather than from Aristotle direct. I do not think this supposition either necessary for our purpose, or even probable
in itself. For (1) in *Conv.* IV. viii. 64, Dante expressly
attributes the illustration to Aristotle, and discusses the
meaning he attached to the words, whereas there is no
indication in Cicero of its being a quotation at all; and
(2) Cicero, *l. c.*, says that the *size* of the Sun is more than
eighteen times that of the Earth, whereas Dante in the *Convito*
says that the Sun's *diameter* is five and a half times that of the
Earth. It is true that though thus differently expressed,
the result is much the same, but the statement of Dante
is found (as we might expect) *totidem verbis* in Alfraganus,
Elem. Astr., c. xxii.

Finally, *epigramma* is objected to. But it is remarkable
(as Vandelli (p. 12) has pointed out) that this is just one
of the words that Dante might have learned from his usual
authority, Uguccione. 'Item *gramma* quod est *linea vel
littera*, componitur cum *epy* quod est *supra*, et dicitur hoc
epygramma -tis, id est, *superscriptio*, scilicet titulus vel brevis

---

[1] In the 'Volgare' of the *Convito* the word appears as 'proporzione.' See
Conv. III. i. 59.

[2] To this D'Ovidio replies (p. 478) that whereas Cicero applies *pedalis* directly
to the Sun, the forger inserts *magnitudo*!

annotatio eorum quae diffusius dicuntur in sequenti opere.'
This, it need hardly be pointed out, is precisely the sense
in which it is here used.

Finally (speaking still of the introductory §§ 1–4) it is
objected by D'Ovidio (p. 456) that other self-commentaries of
Dante in *V. N.* and *Convito* were upon works already published (*già divulgate*), whereas in this case the publication
(*pubblicazione*) of the *Paradiso* would be *preceded* by this
'dedicaccia sesquipedale,' and the impression it was to make
'contaminated by premature doctrinal expositions.' This fine
display of question-begging expressions is very imposing,
but it may be fairly reckoned among the κενὰ τοῦ πολέμου [1].
After all, the Dantesque character of the expository process
has to be more or less grudgingly admitted by the objector;
though it is magisterially declared that it is totally out of
place in reference to a work ' not yet published.' But whatever may be exactly meant in those days by 'publication,'
the transmission of a copy of the work, or a portion of the
work, commented on, together with the Commentary (as is
evidently implied), seems entirely to remove any force from
this purely arbitrary *dictum*.

---

[1] It is very much to be regretted that this extravagance of language is
characteristic of the writer throughout. He commonly *introduces* the discussion
of a paragraph or passage by describing it as 'goffaggine,' 'codesta roba,'
'garbuglio,' 'stiracchiatura,' 'quisquilie,' &c. ; or thus : 'l'arfasatto che scrisse
l'Epistola' (463) and so on. The concluding summary of D'Ovidio, p. 473,
consists mainly of a whole series of depreciatory epithets or designations of
this kind. Almost everything throughout is distorted and made to appear
ridiculous in this arbitrary fashion. It would surely be as easy by such treatment to reduce any writing, sacred or profane, to ridicule, as it would be to
silence the most persuasive speaker by simply shouting him down. If we were
to answer such an opponent by his own methods it would only be necessary to
indulge in vague and extravagant laudations of the author, his genius, and his
style, and to insist on the high value of each page or paragraph or statement
of his performance. But such a defence would be just as impotent as such an
attack. Every one would exclaim, 'Non tali auxilio, nec defensoribus istis.'
Yet the process which I have described would be just as easy and just as
effective as it is for D'Ovidio to say (when declaring superfluous any evidence
of the possible relations between the Epistle and the works of other writers or
commentators) :—'It is enough for me that in this Epistle . . . there are many
things absolutely not Dantesque' ('assolutamente non Dantesche,' p. 481).
I regret extremely that a scholar so distinguished as Prof. D'Ovidio should have
allowed his work to be disfigured by such a flaw as this.

* * *

II. i. (*b*) THE DOCTRINAL PORTION (§§ 5-16).

We proceed now to some of the more important objections taken to the sections constituting the second of the above divisions of the Epistle (see p. 286). In the case of the different methods of interpretation in § 7, D'Ovidio drops the charge of plagiarism from the *Convito* II. i, made by some of his allies[1], but insists on two grave discrepancies. (1) In the *Convito* the four senses are treated as coordinate species ; in the Epistle there is a twofold generic division, literal and allegorical (or mystical), and under the latter, allegorical (proper), moral, and anagogical are regarded as species. This, D'Ovidio says, is not a ' plagiarism,' nor a ' correction,' but a ' parody ' ! (2) The second criticism is that the writer forgets two very effective Dantesque examples of these methods in the *Convito* (viz. Orpheus and the three Apostles) and 'strains' the other example, ' In exitu Israel,' to serve as an illustration of all four, ending at last by giving not three senses but only three gradations of a single sense, which is nothing else but ' anagogic ' (p. 462).

Now as regards both of these criticisms we may remark that the passage in the *Convito* occupies so conspicuous a place, and its contents would be so generally known, not only from their occurrence there, but from their being quite a commonplace in numerous other writers, that such variations, which I should say are harmless and natural enough, would be most improbable on the part of a forger, and all the more so in proportion to the serious importance which the objectors suppose to attach to them. But, after all, what does it amount to ?

Why the *Convito* itself recognizes the twofold division as an alternative ! In II. i. 15 Dante indeed *leads off* with the twofold division of *literal* and *allegorical* ; and then adds that

---

[1] He quotes anonymously the criticism of a 'notissimo dantista,' that this illustration from ' In exitu Israel' 'sembra un plagio al Convivio,' and that we cannot possibly admit that Dante plagiarized himself ! This is too much for Prof. D'Ovidio, who justly observes that any author has a right to repeat himself. Scartazzini (*Prol.*, p. 400) also exclaims, ' Era Dante il suo proprio plagiario ? '

there are also as many as four senses possible and appropriate. But, in point of fact, in the exegesis of the *Convito*, to which this is an introduction, we hear no more of any but the two-fold distinction, *literal* and *allegorical*[1], while that forms, as we may say, the framework of the exposition throughout. Moreover, in summing up at the end of this very same chapter of the *Convito*, l. 122, Dante again returns to his first point of view, and says that his Commentary will fall under these *two* heads. So again in I. i. 130-132 ; ii. 123-126 ; also in *Tratt.* II *passim*. See especially c. xiii *init.*, 'Poichè la *litterale* sentenza è sufficientemente dimostrata, è da pro-cedere alla sposizione *allegorica* e *vera*.' Again, in III. x *fin.*, 'Così termina tutta la *litterale* sentenza di questo Trattato ; perchè l'ordine dell' opera domanda all' *allegorica* sposizione omai, seguendo la verità, procedere.'

The cases then are curiously parallel. For in *both* the writer (1) begins with enunciating the two main divisions, *literal* and *allegorical*; (2) proceeds to give the further divisions, amounting to four, with illustrations of each; and (3) ends as he began, by practically retaining only the twofold division.

Besides this, it is surely quite obvious that the *allegorical, moral,* and *anagogical* senses do stand in a natural relation to one another, and in common and equally natural contrast with the *literal*; in short, in the very words of this Epistle (l. 155), 'quanquam isti sensus mystici variis appellentur nominibus, generaliter omnes dici possunt *allegorici*, quum sint a *literali* sive *historiali* diversi.' To this we may add the words of Landino when explaining the plan of his own Commentary : 'Nè solamente apriremo il senso naturale, ma ancora l'Allegorico, Tropologico, e Anagogico ; i quali tre sensi, perchè hanno tra loro molta convenienza, *chiameremo tutti Allegorici*[2].'

So again Buti, after describing almost in the words of the

---

[1] I do not in fact remember that anywhere else in his writings, Dante makes any practical use of the two latter distinctions, *moral* and *anagogic*, unless it be in *Conv.* IV. xvii. 106 where the contrasted conduct of Martha and Mary is interpreted 'moralmente.' Compare 'moralmente' as used in *Purg.* xxxiii. 72.

[2] Landino, *Laudi della Poesia*, &c., ad fin.

Epistle the usual four senses, adds : ' E però esporremo prima
la *lettera*, et appresso secondo l' *allegoria* o vero *moralità*,
secondo ch' io crederò che sia stata l' intenzione dell' autore'
(*Proemio*, ad fin.). Thus again the four senses are practically
resolved into two.

If any further justification be needed, let it be noticed that
both systems of division are found together in the *Summa* I,
Q. 1, Art. 10. After distinguishing ' sensus historicus sive
literalis' (observe these very words at the end of our § 7)
from 'spiritualis,' Aquinas says that this latter *trifariam
dividitur*, viz. allegoricus, moralis, anagogicus. He explains
further that when something in the Old Testament prefigures
something in the New Testament this is *allegorical*; when
what is done in or by Christ figures something that we
ourselves ought to do, this is *moral*; when ' ea quae sunt
in aeterna gloria [significantur],' this is *anagogical*. Further
we may note that ' mystical' as an alternative equivalent for
' allegorical' (in the generic sense) is found again in *Mon.* III.
iv. 47. Notice also how the description of these methods
given by Aquinas is exactly applicable to the examples given
of each in this Epistle, so that if the present writer has 'only
succeeded in tracing three gradations of one sense' (*v. supra*,
p. 306), S. Thomas has failed no less egregiously.

The same method of treatment as here and in Aquinas is
found also in S. Augustine, at least according to the con-
tention of S. Thomas himself, when commenting in this
Article of the *Summa* upon the *locus classicus* of S. Augustine
(*de Util. Credendi*, c. 3), in which he enumerates four senses
as follows : 'secundum historiam, aetiologiam, analogiam,
allegoriam.' When it is objected that these seem different
(' aliena omnino') from the four which S. Thomas himself has
traced (as also Dante in the *Conv. l. c.* and here, § 7), his reply
is that 'illa tria, historia, aetiologia, analogia, ad *unum
literalem sensum* pertinent. . . . Sola autem *allegoria* inter illa
quatuor *pro tribus spiritualibus sensibus* ponitur.' Thus again
the fourfold division is reduced to *literal* and *allegorical*,
though the four several members of the division are both
differently denominated themselves, and the 'gradations of

meaning' are differently classified in relation to the twofold generic division. When the systems of Augustine and Aquinas are compared, the result may be thus exhibited :—

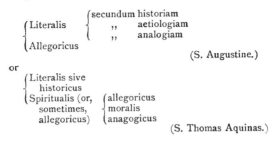

Then again Bede exhibits precisely the same variety of treatment of the subject. He generally sets in contrast the literal and allegorical senses merely. Like Dante also, he sets a far higher value on the latter. It is like wine compared with water, like fruit compared with leaves. But he also recognizes the familiar four senses: (1) Historical, (2) Typical or Allegorical, (3) Moral or Tropological, (4) Anagogical. Sometimes also he gives three senses: (1) Historical, (2) Allegorical, (3) Moral ; or (1) Historical, (2) Allegorical, (3) Anagogic. As Mr. Plummer (to whose notes I owe these details) remarks: 'It is difficult for us to grasp the distinctions between the last three (of the four) senses which we should be inclined to class together as figurative or allegorical.' This shows how perfectly naturally the same writer may recognize and adopt both methods.

If therefore this passage in the Epistle is nothing but a 'parody' of the treatment of the subject in the corresponding passage of the *Convito*, it is one which has been anticipated by some very serious writers.

My apology for treating of this point at such great length is that such very great weight has been attached to this particular objection by the opponents. As to the variation in the examples given—each method having a separate one in the *Convito*, whereas in the Epistle one example differently treated serves to illustrate all the methods—the same answer will avail. The variation of treatment is perfectly legitimate[1], but such variation in a well-known passage is much more likely to have been introduced by the original author than by a forger writing under his name.

It is next objected that in § 9 the use of *rithmi* for 'verses' is inconsistent with *V. E.*, where *rithmus* or *rithimus* is said to be used only in the sense of rhyme[2]. But in any case in *Conv.* I. x. 88 *rima* and *ritmo* are distinguished, and the latter is defined as 'numero regolato[3].' Buti understands the word in the sense of *terzine*, since, paraphrasing this passage in the Epistle, he writes: 'E ciascuno Canto si divide nelli suoi ritimi, o vero ternari, e li ritimi o vero ternari si dividono in versi' (*Proemio*, p. 6, *med.*). Again, Boccaccio, *Com.*, Lez. 1[ma], p. 83 *fin.*: 'essendo tutti i ritmi d'egual numero di sillabe,' &c. This sense therefore of the word seems to have been regarded as quite natural.

The next or tenth section is of considerable importance. It is characteristically introduced by D'Ovidio as 'un altro orrore,' since he thinks that it affords very strong evidence in support of his case. It appears to me rather that it exhibits some of the most convincing characteristics of

---

[1] One might with at least as much reason object to the very different application made in the *Purg.* and in the *Convito* of the incident of the companions of Aeneas being left behind in Sicily. In the former, this is given as an example of *Accidia*, whereby they sacrificed all chance of distinction. In the latter, it is made to illustrate the loving care of Aeneas in releasing from toil those who were no longer capable of bearing it. If so, they could not be described as 'accidiosi.'

[2] See especially *V. E.* II. xiii. 7, with the true reading 'sine rithimis.' The old reading 'sive rithimus' appeared to give an exception to the general use of the word in this treatise.

[3] But even *rima* itself, as well as *ritmo*, is used by Dante in a narrower and a wider sense, as is explained in *Conv.* IV. ii. 101 *seqq.*: 'strettamente' as 'rhyme' and 'largamente' as 'tutto quello parlare che in numeri e tempo regolato in rimate consonanze cade,' in other words 'verses.' Besides, Dante applies *rima* to the Aeneid in the general sense of 'poem,' in *Inf.* xiii. 48—
        'Ciò ch' ha veduto pur con la mia rima.'
So Boccaccio, *Vita di Dante*, § 13, speaks of his composing in 'rima volgare,' i. e. in the poetry of the vulgar tongue: or as we find this in the *Compendio*:—'in fiorentino idioma ed in rima la cominciò.' I am informed by a friend that the same two senses of *rima* are found in Old French and in Provençal. In *Purg.* xxviii. 18 Dante uses *rima* of the song of birds, and in three or four other places in the *Divina Commedia* he uses 'rima' 'largamente' as equivalent to 'verses.'

Dantesque authorship.   First, the derivations of 'tragedy,'
'comedy,' and 'allegory' are cheaply sneered at as 'misplaced Greek erudition' ('sproposita erudizione ellenica,'
p. 463), as if the merest tyros in Dante were not aware that
similar examples, and quite as much 'misplaced,' abound in
the *Convito*.   At least ten such could be quoted.   Further,
as Dr. Toynbee has pointed out, they nearly all come from
the same source—the *Derivationes* of Uguccione—to whom
however Dante only once refers by name (*Conv.* IV. vi).
This is in fact the source of the three etymologies now
under review[1].   As I have argued under a similar circumstance in the *Quaestio*[2], and as Dr. Toynbee has argued in
reference to the case before us, a forger is not likely to have
ascertained this obscure source of Dante's etymologies (which
he only hints at in the case of one of them), and then to
produce from it three fresh examples nowhere else found in
Dante's works.   For D'Ovidio is shortsighted enough to draw
our attention to this fact[3]!   Next, the two quotations from
Horace are stigmatized, the first as inopportune, and the
second as pedantic.   These are purely matters of opinion or
dogmatic assertion, and in the former case a very shallow
opinion.   For the quotation is, on the contrary, quite obviously
'opportune,' since there is very much in the *Paradiso*, though
part of a 'Comoedia,' akin to the *exceptional*, rather than the
normal, style of Comedy, and the 'licence' accorded by
Horace is cited as a justification of this.   As to the 'pedantry'
of the latter[4], it may be paralleled by many similar cases in
the *Convito*, where Dante is led by a single word, or phrase,
or name, to embark on disquisitions which in a modern writer
would be certainly thought both pedantic and irrelevant[5].

[1] This is true besides of the word *polysemus* (also objected to on the same
grounds) which occurs in § 7.

[2] *Studies*, II. p. 352.

[3] p. 464, where it is also dogmatically added that they are *here* introduced
'con una certa ostentazione e senza necessità'!

[4] We may compare §§ 5 and 18 of this Epistle.

[5] The same tendency may be seen in Pietro di Dante, and in Boccaccio.
Thus the latter, commenting on the words 'accenti d'ira' in *Inf.* iii. 26, solemnly
discusses the three different kinds of 'accents' in Greek—'acute,' 'grave,'
and 'circumflex'!

Thus the mention of the sun in Canzone II. l. 19 (in quite an ordinary sense),

'Non vede il sol che tutto il mondo gira,'

is the only peg on which hangs the whole elaborate and intricate astronomical disquisition in *Conv.* III. v[1]; and the simple expression 'in quell' ora,' in the next line of the Canzone, gives rise to the astronomical distinctions of 'ore eguali' and 'ore temporali' in c. vi. So again, in IV. ii, a quite casual occurrence of the word *tempo* leads to a metaphysical definition of 'time,' and also a discourse on the use and proper appropriation of our time[2]. Similarly, the word *mente*, used quite ordinarily, is the basis of an elaborate psychological discussion in *Conv.* III. ii. 79 *seqq.* Any one may call this 'pedantic' if it pleases him, but it is certainly Dantesque. Once more, it is asserted that the account of Tragedy and Comedy is inconsistent with that in *V. E.* II, because in the latter we have nothing either about the derivations here given, or about the unhappy or happy endings respectively. This is simply a grotesque, I had almost said childish, objection. It seems to imply that if Dante knew of these details, he must have inserted all and sundry of them whenever speaking on the subject elsewhere, and that as this writer did not do so, he may be presumed to have been entirely ignorant of them! 'Forse lo avrà ignorato del tutto' is D'Ovidio's own surprising inference (p. 464). But it was no part of the purpose of the *V. E.* to go into these distinctions, but only into those of diction and form. So far as these points are touched on in the Epistle, there is an exact correspondence with the *V. E.*, extending even to some of the words themselves. Thus in *V. E.* II. iv we read that the style of Tragedy is superior, and that of

---

[1] *v. supra*, p. 46.

[2] This no doubt seems very much 'out of place' according to our ideas. If this last example had only occurred in this Epistle and not in the *Convito*, one might perhaps have feared that some opponent would reduce it to ridicule by comparing it—as an example of 'erudizione' no less 'sproposita,' 'superflua,' and 'pedantica'—with Mr. Shandy's well-known disquisition on the metaphysical nature of 'Time,' 'Infinity,' and 'Duration,' which is hung upon a casual remark that a certain short period of time 'seemed an age'!

Comedy is inferior; that the language of the latter is 'quandoque mediocre, quandoque humile'; and that of the former includes 'superbia carminum' and 'constructionis elatio.' Compare the words *humiliter, elate,* and *sublime* in this section of the Epistle.

With equal cogency it is urged that the author of the *Convito* could not possibly have written this section because of the statement that the style employed is 'remissus et humilis, *quia* loquutio vulgaris' in ll. 222–5. For this casts contempt upon that 'Vulgare' which in *Conv.* I. x–xii is so highly extolled. D'Ovidio lays special stress on this 'quia,' and declares that this at any rate is one thing that Dante could not possibly have said, 'dimessa e umile, *perchè* volgare!'

But this absurdly imaginary 'contempt' rests upon a palpable 'Fallacia Equivocationis,' or perhaps one 'a dicto secundum quid,' &c., or both. In the *Convito* Dante is arguing against those who decried and despised the Volgare or the Italian language in contrast with the acknowledged dignity of Latin. In this passage he uses 'vulgare' in the sense of ordinary colloquial language, in no way differing from the means of communication in general use, 'even among women.' If this be 'contempt,' must we not also reject the *V. E.*, where the 'vulgaris loquutio' (the identical expression) is described as that 'qua infantes adsuefiunt ab adsistentibus'; or that 'quam sine omni regula nutricem imitantes accipimus' (I. i. 21 *seqq.*)? Nay, more, the very same supposed 'contemptuous' formula occurs in the first sentence of the *V. E.*, where this 'vulgaris eloquentia' is said to be that on which 'non tantum viri, sed etiam *mulieres et parvuli* nituntur [1].' And yet, a few lines later in the very same chapter, after describing *Grammatica* [2], and saying

---

[1] We may compare with the words under consideration ll. 52–54 of Dante's first Eclogue :—

> 'Comica nonne vides ipsum reprehendere verba,
> Tum quia foemineo resonant ut trita labello,
> Tum quia Castalias pudet acceptare Sorores?'

[2] It should be explained that by *Grammatica* here Dante means a literary language. His words are, 'Est *alia locutio secundaria* nobis, quam Romani

314 STUDIES IN DANTE

how few there are who attain to it, and what long and serious study it demands, Dante adds: 'Harum quoque duarum *nobilior est vulgaris.*'

Now this is at first sight surprisingly inconsistent with *Conv.* I. v. 48 *seqq.* For Dante there states that 'il Latino (exactly = *Grammatica* as used in *V. E.*, *l. c.*) è perpetuo e non corruttibile, e il volgare è non istabile e corruttibile.' How very strongly this has been felt may be seen from Prof. Rajna's note on this passage, and also from the fact that it has even been suggested to read (*e coni.*) *utilior* for *nobilior* in the text of the *V. E.*! Yet I am not aware that any one has proposed to reject as spurious either the *Convito* or the *De Vulg. Eloq.* in consequence of this much more serious difficulty.

Once more, in *V. E.* II. iv. 45, while Comedy adopts the 'vulgare mediocre et humile' the *same* 'vulgare' as employed by Tragedy is declared to be 'illustre.'

Finally (and one is glad to have at last exhausted the prolific list of objections furnished by this tenth section) the supposed forger is censured for having referred to the Dramas of Seneca and Terence as confidently as if he had read them, thus 'unexpectedly going outside the whole classical repertory of Dante.' The confidence of knowledge implied by the word 'patet' (l. 205)[1] is treated as especially shameless (*sfacciato*). But (1) every one knows that this is a formula of quotation very common in the *De Mon.* (to say nothing of the *Quaestio*), and has no such emphatic significance as this. Besides, (2) the only point which is said here 'patere' is the very broad and general one that the Tragedies and Comedies of these authors end in calamity or in prosperity respectively. This might be 'patent' (even in the fullest sense) from common knowledge and without special study. Then (3) what a pre-

---

Grammaticam vocaverunt. Hanc quidem secundariam (*sc.* locutionem) Graeci habent et alii, sed non omnes.' *Grammatica* is explained to mean 'literary language' in c. ix. 94. In the passage just quoted, the two *Grammaticae* referred to are evidently Latin and Greek, and when he says that not all people have *Grammatica*, he clearly means that some dialects never rise to the dignity of a literary language.

[1] Cf. ll. 27, 126; and *Studies*, II. p. 348.

posterous limitation it is upon any writer to say that he
cannot quote any author unless he has quoted him before[1],
or at least elsewhere, even when fresh occasion may have
arisen for doing so. Again, (4) are we on this ground to
reject the *De Mon.* because Galen and Vegetius are quoted
in it alone, they being therefore clearly 'outside the whole
classical repertory of Dante'? Lastly, (5) the case against
the authors just named is really stronger than that against
Seneca and Terence, since other works of Seneca (though not
his Tragedies) are quoted by Dante four or five times in the
Convito[2]; and Terence is mentioned in *Purg.* xxii. 97, and
a passage from his *Eunuchus* is quoted (though, it is true,
almost certainly on second-hand knowledge through Cicero[3])
in *Inf.* xviii. 133–135.

The only other adverse criticism calling for special notice
in this second main division of the Epistle (§§ 5–16), is the
objection raised by D'Ovidio to the statement in § 16 that
the class of philosophy under which the Comoedia falls is
Ethical or Moral, because the work is declared to be undertaken entirely for a practical, and not a speculative, purpose.
He cannot suppose that Dante himself would have admitted
this, in view of the abstruse scientific and philosophical
problems dealt with, nor will he accept the answer given
(l. 275) to this anticipated objection. But surely the purpose
of an essay or a sermon can be said to be 'wholly practical'
even if it contain passages dealing with highly abstract

---

[1] On the difficulty in which an author would be thus involved in every fresh
quotation, compare the quaint dialectical puzzle worked out by Dante in
Conv. IV. xv. 19 *seqq.* about 'Nobiltà.'

[2] It should be admitted, as to these quotations, that in the Middle Ages it was
supposed that there were two Senecas, (1) the author of the Tragedies, and
(2) the author of the philosophical works. (In the latter were included two
works not really by Seneca but by Martinus Dumiensis in the sixth century :
'De Quattuor Virtutibus Cardinalibus' and 'De Remediis Fortuitorum.') It
has been suggested that the expression 'Seneca morale' in *Inf.* iv. 141 may be
intended to point the distinction from 'Seneca tragico.' Still the passage
before us in the Epistle implies no more than the modest amount of knowledge
that there was a 'Seneca tragico.' The distinction between the two Senecas
is found in both Boccaccio and Benvenuto. See Toynbee, *Dante Studies*,
pp. 150 *seqq.*

[3] See *Studies*, I. p. 261.

questions of doctrine. And, in point of fact, Dante has
a very frequent habit of 'improving' (as it is sometimes
called) the most abstruse and even arid discussions of metaphysics or science by drawing attention to their moral or
religious bearing. Thus, to take the very instance advanced
by D'Ovidio as an extreme case, the cause of the Lunar
Spots. The concluding lines (*Par.* ii. 136–148) of the long
digression distinctly draw a general moral lesson from the
particular phenomenon elucidated. We observe the same
habit in the case of other scientific subjects that *prima facie*
'have no flavour of salvation in them'; and that not only in
the *Divina Commedia* but in the *Convito*; e. g. the manner of
the Sun's revolution round the Earth, *Conv.* III. v. 196–
208; the inclination of the Ecliptic, *Par.* x. 13–27; the
process of generation and the development of the embryo,
Conv. IV. xxi, especially ll. 49–58. And I would add besides
the conclusion appended to the very technical discussion in
the *Quaestio* from § 21, l. 62 to the end of § 22. It would
surely under these circumstances be competent to the author
of even such discussions as these to say that they had
a predominantly moral or practical purpose. Much more
is this the case in the *Divina Commedia*, where the digressions
in the way of abstract discussions have mostly to deal with
questions which have a distinct bearing upon Theology.

II. i. (*c*) THE EXPOSITORY PORTION.

We pass on now to the third part of the document (§§ 17–31),
in which the Prologue to the *Paradiso* is explained in detail.
The objections taken to the contents of these sections seem
to be mainly four, or perhaps five.

(1) It is said that from this point the first person is dropped,
and the writer speaks in the third person, and so it is suggested
that this patch or portion was composed by the forger (or
perhaps by some one else) for some different purpose, and
that he was too lazy (*v. pigrizia*, p. 470), when appropriating
it here, to introduce the correction which would have been
needed for uniformity. I think it would be more correct

to say that the first person is practically limited to what D'Ovidio calls the strictly Epistolary portion, viz. §§ 1–4 and 32, 33. There is, I believe, only one exception to this, viz. in § 6, ll. 113 and 123, where it is evident that the use of the first person could scarcely be avoided ; where in fact it might be said 'che per necessità qui si registra.' If so, the principle of the writer would seem to be to use the third person when he is speaking, if one may so say, *ex cathedra*, as an expositor, whether of general principles (§§ 5–16), or of the prologue in detail (§§ 17–31), and to speak in his own name when the style and matter is epistolary in character. But even if no such intelligible principle for interchange of persons were traceable, we might still justify it by the practice of Dante in the *Convito*, where (as Torraca has pointed out) we find almost indifferently, 'io dico, ei dice, il testo dice,' &c. (*op. cit.* p. 33).

(2) A more serious objection is this. Dante (it is said) would surely have been precluded from writing a Latin Commentary on a Poem in the Volgare, by the many strong considerations urged by himself against such a course in *Conv.* I. v–ix. But in reply it is to be remembered—

(*a*) That the Commentary forms in this case part of an Epistle, and that Latin was still (and for much later) the regular medium for Epistolary correspondence.

(*b*) All Dante's Epistles which have any pretence to being genuine are in Latin. That the Epistle purporting to be addressed to Moroello Malaspina (sometimes printed as No. 3) is in Italian, has always been urged (*inter alia*) as a strong argument against its genuineness. Had this present Epistle been in Italian, we cannot doubt that this would have figured as a formidable count in the indictment against it.

(*c*) There is a special reason in this case, since the Epistle itself comprises a formal dedication addressed to a person of high dignity. This at any rate must almost necessarily have been in Latin [1].

---

[1] The occasional use of Latin phrases in the *Divina Commedia* seems generally to be accounted for by the dignity of the speakers : e. g. a Pope, an Emperor, Cacciaguida ; also Angels, Saints, and Doctors. The following is an

(*d*) Moreover, the dedicatory portion is, so to speak, the essential feature of the composition. The partial Commentary is introduced as subordinate and consequential to it. See § 4, l. 87. Had Dante undertaken a formal and independent Commentary on the *Comoedia*, after the fashion of the *Convito*, it is probable that it would have been in the Volgare.

(3) A third difficulty is raised by D' Ovidio in reference to the formulae of citation of other authors, chiefly because the definite *Books* of such works are here specified. D'Ovidio describes this as a ' zelo non frequente in lui (i. e. Dante) di citare il *libro* di ciascuna opera.' I can only say this is a statement of quite astonishing inaccuracy. The real truth is as I have stated it in *Studies*, I. p. 96 : 'In quoting authors like Aristotle, Virgil, Ovid, Cicero, and others, Dante almost always refers to the title of the work quoted, and *generally to the number of the Book*, if the work be so divided [1].' But this is not a matter of opinion on one side or the other. It admits fortunately of being easily tested by the help of my index of quotations. Let us take the works of Aristotle quoted in this Epistle, which are the *Ethics*, *Physics*, *Metaphysics*, and *De Coelo* [2]. Now the *actual facts* are as follows, taking all the cases in the Prose works in which any of these Aristotelian treatises is directly quoted by name. The *Ethics* are so quoted forty-four times. The number of the Book is mentioned in forty cases, and omitted only in four. Moreover, every one of the ten Books is thus definitely cited. The *Physics* are quoted fifteen times. The number of the Book is given in fourteen cases and omitted only in one (viz. *Mon.* III. xv. 13); the *Metaphysics* are also quoted fifteen times. The

---

interesting point that I do not remember to have seen noticed. In *Par.* xxv. 73 Dante, when himself quoting Ps. ix. 11, says 'Sperino in te' ; but the glorified spirits repeating it later (l. 98) say 'Sperent in te.' Witte, probably not observing the reason for this, has printed it in Latin in both cases on the strength of one MS. But out of forty other MSS. which I have examined I did not find a single one that had the Latin words in l. 73.

[1] See further *ib*. p. 37 for the occasional blunders made in the numbers of such Books.

[2] The *Rhetoric* is only named once here and once in all the other works of Dante.

number of the Book occurs in eleven cases ; it is omitted in four only ; the *De Coelo* is quoted eleven times, with the number of the Book eight times, and without it only three times (two of these, as well as one on the other side, being in the *Quaestio*) [1]. *Tant pis pour les faits !*

After this, we can afford to neglect the trifling objection to the alleged peculiarity in the formula ' Plato . . . in suis libris.' The fact is that the writer is not referring to any particular passage or to any particular work, but to a general characteristic of Plato's style [2]. It may be worth while, however, noting that in the only other passage in which Plato is quoted by Dante with a definite reference, his words are—' scrisse in un suo libro, che si chiama Timeo' (*Conv.* III. v. 46).

(4) The objection to which D'Ovidio attaches the greatest weight ('più notevole di tutto') is the interpretation given of l. 4—

> 'Nel ciel che più della sua luce prende
> Fu' io '—

since he declares this to be palpably incorrect, and therefore impossible to have been given by Dante himself. The interpretation in question is that this expression refers to the tenth Heaven or Empyrean, whereas it pleases some modern critics to say that Dante himself meant Paradise generally, in which all the ten Heavens would be included. These are the chief reasons alleged :—

(*a*) The former interpretation is described by D'Ovidio as ' estranea forse ai primi Commentatori,' though now generally prevalent on the strength of this supposed statement of Dante himself.

The cautious insertion of ' forse ' is fully justified by the fact that the interpretation ' Empyrean ' is distinctly given by Buti, Landino, and Vellutello ! That of ' Paradiso ' generally is found in the Ottimo, Benvenuto, and Daniello.

But ' forse ' is dropped afterwards, and the other interpretation is boldly affirmed to be that of the ' primi chiosatori,' and

---

[1] As to the books of the Aeneid, their number is habitually given in the Virgilian quotations.

[2] Compare the general character of the references to Seneca and Terence in § 10.

the writer considers it to be incredible that Dante himself should have preferred this 'worse' alternative (p. 483).

(*b*) The antithesis with *universo* in l. 2 is said to be less complete. I will present the opponents with the quotation

'l' arte
Che mostri in cielo, in terra, e nel mal mondo' (*Inf.* xix. 10, 11)

which would perhaps serve to illustrate their interpretation. But the truth is that either meaning would, from this point of view, suit the passage equally well. For it is perfectly true and clear that the Divine light is most fully present in the Empyrean (as the Epistle goes on to prove) in comparison with any other part of the Universe, even including the other nine Heavens.

(*c*) This interpretation is said to ignore the fact that Dante was also in the other Heavens, that in them also he heard 'unspeakable things' (ll. 5, 6), and that from them also (the 'regno santo' of l. 10) he brought back memories to narrate. The explanation therefore here given is declared to be nothing but a 'wretched oversight' ('misera sfuggita') on the part of the writer.

This is mere trifling. The tenth Heaven does not exclude the others, but it is the climax of the ecstatic vision, where the difficulties of either understanding or remembering or recounting the things revealed are far the greatest. This is specially insisted on in xxxiii. 55–57 :

'Da quinci innanzi il mio veder fu maggio
Che il parlar nostro, ch' a tal vista cede,
E cede la memoria a tant' oltraggio.'

Besides which the Empyrean is the true abode of *all* the Saints in Paradise. Their appearance in any lower Heaven is, so to speak, only 'subjective' to Dante, an accommodation to his intelligence. This is clearly stated in *Par.* iv. 28–39. Compare also *Conv.* II. iv. 30, where the Empyrean *in distinction* from the other nine Heavens is described as 'lo luogo degli spiriti beati.'

I maintain therefore that the interpretation given in the Epistle is far the more probable on considerations quite independent of its own authority. But even those who think otherwise cannot surely be so confident as to say that this explanation is so entirely inadmissible as to condemn the document in which it is found !

(5) Finally, it is urged by D'Ovidio that these petty philosophical glosses ('chioserelle filosofiche') on the opening lines of the Poem are of no help to our exegesis ('non aiutano la nostra ermeneutica'), to say nothing of their actually leading us astray in reference to vv. 4-6. The latter point has just been dealt with. As to the former, it is doubtless true, one might almost say truistic, as a criticism of the exegesis of any age when judged by the requirements or expectations of a much later age. How true is it of all, or nearly all, of the earliest Commentators of the *Divina Commedia* ! How true it is of many of Dante's own comments in his other prose works ! Nay more, how true it is of a large amount of Patristic commentaries on Scripture ! In all these cases we do not find information on just those points which seem to us most urgent and interesting, while we do find pages of disquisition on points 'che non aiutano la nostra ermeneutica.'

Judged in this spirit and by this standard what can be more inept than some of the arguments of the *De Mon.*, or much of the exegesis of the *Convito* ? There is scarcely a feature in the processes of this Epistle which cannot be amply illustrated from these works. It is as futile to condemn them as not ' helpful to our exegesis ' as it is to interpret Dante's relations to Beatrice from a modern standpoint, and then triumphantly insist on the absurdity or impossibility of our believing in their (or her) reality.

The third division, dealing with the exposition of the Prologue in detail, is brought to an abrupt conclusion at the end of § 31, and in the two last sections the Epistolary style with the direct address to Can Grande is resumed. In § 32 (as we have seen in our analysis) the writer breaks off the task, which, if carried out on the same scale to the ' pars executiva ' of the Poem, would have been an enormous one, on the ground that he is hampered by domestic anxieties which he hopes

* * *

that his patron may be able to mitigate, so that his purpose may be carried out. This is stigmatized by D'Ovidio as servile, abject, and humiliating, and altogether unworthy of Dante. But, as Torraca reminds us, it does but exemplify the condition to which Dante confesses in the *Convito*, I. iii, that he was ' peregrino, quasi mendicando,' throughout all Italy[1]. He confesses that in consequence ' sono vile apparito agli occhi a molti.' Compare again the pathetic reference to the painfulness of asking favours in *Conv.* I. viii *fin.*, ' Per che sì caro costa quello che si priega, non intendo qui ragionare.' When it is replied that even if Dante may occasionally have been reduced to such straits in action, he would never have condescended to perpetuate and make public so humiliating a position by committing it to writing, we must remember that this is not a formal treatise but a private letter ; that we have no evidence that it was in any sense ' intended for publication '; and that on the contrary the existence of the Epistle as such was in fact for a very long period unknown. If Dante were ever reduced to ask such favours from a patron in words, there seems no reason why he should not do the same in writing to him.

The further objection as to the alleged want of modesty in the value assigned to the execution of the proposed work, has been sufficiently dealt with already. On the other hand, even these two sections afford in their details evidence favourable to the genuineness of the Epistle, but these, according to our plan, will be considered separately later.

Hitherto I have, for the reasons given above, followed mainly the lines of D'Ovidio's attack. A few words may be added on the far more extravagant outbursts of Dr. Prompt, not that they deserve any serious reply, but as a curious specimen of quite irrational vituperation they may claim a passing notice.

I have already noticed (p. 284) the audacity with which, under the title ' Les Œuvres apocryphes de Dante,' he has

<hr/>

[1] If *Epist.* II. were not one of those now commonly repudiated, we might also appeal to its language in § 3—'nec negligentia neve ingratitudo me tenuit, sed inopina paupertas quam fecit exilium.'

included in one sweeping condemnation the Eclogues, the
Epistle to Can Grande, the *Quaestio*, and even the *De
Monarchia*! He insultingly refers to the author of the
De Monarchia as 'the personage who composed this barbarous and abominable book' (p. 23). The following are
some of the choice flowers of rhetoric which I have gathered
from his attack on this Epistle[1].

'The ignorance of this animal is so great that he is not
acquainted with the *Vita Nuova*, with the *Ars Poetica*, or
with the contents even of the *Paradiso* itself!' This serious
charge in respect of the former two works is based on the
explanation of the invocation to Apollo (§ 31) as being a
prayer for help from a superior being, whereas in *V. N.* § 25
Horace is quoted to show that when a Poet thus invokes
a Muse he is really addressing his own science. This 'contradiction' (!) alone, he claims, would be enough to prove the
forgery.

A still 'more serious' objection is the degradation of the
Divine Poem involved in its designation as a Comedy!
Dr. Prompt endeavours to avert one's obvious appeal to *Inf.*
xvi. 128, and xxi. 2, by declaring that Dante only means to
apply the term to 'certain scenes in the *Inferno.*'

Again, 'the ignorance of this animal is so great that he
does not know the reason of his etymologies,' since that given
in the case of Tragedy is inconsistent with the *Ars Poetica*.
But (as we have seen) the etymology comes direct from
Uguccione, the regular source of Dante's etymologies generally,
so that the argument (?) recoils on its author. The 'animal's'
alleged ignorance even of the *Paradiso* itself rests on a ground
that can only be described as childish, viz. that Dante in
Paradise moves 'di lume in lume,' from planet to planet, from

[1] It is strange that the opponents of the Epistle seem unable to keep their
temper or refrain from vituperation. I have noticed already the frequent
violence of D'Ovidio's language. It will be seen that he is far surpassed in
this respect by Dr. Prompt. Even in the earlier days of the controversy it was
the same. Scolari talks of the 'assurdissima assurdità di quella Lettera
apocrifa, falsa, mendace.' This is quoted by Giuliani, ii. p. 248, and he adds
the well-merited rebuke, 'Tanto improvvide e insolenti grida dimostrano più
che altro il perturbato animo ond' emersero, e non lasciano luogo a risposta.'

star to star, whereas this ignorant writer says 'de coelo in coelum!'

I am sure my readers will agree that it would be waste of time either to quote more of such 'criticism' as this, or to attempt to reply to it seriously. One can imagine how Dante himself would have met it from his language in *Conv.* IV. xiv. 105: 'risponder si vorrebbe non colle parole ma col coltello a . . .' but, though the words are Dante's and not mine, I would rather not proceed with the quotation.

II. ii. THE INTERNAL EVIDENCE AS IT APPEARS TO BE FAVOURABLE.

Thus far we have been occupied almost entirely with objections of opponents based upon 'cose assolutamente non Dantesche' supposed to be detected in the Epistle. I may now venture to adduce some examples of a contrary kind that have occurred to myself, i.e. similarities in thought, expression, and method, as compared with admitted works of Dante. I must premise that I am fully aware of the two-edged nature of such arguments[1], but I also contend that the same character attaches to many of those of a converse kind, as we have already seen[2]. And in any case, *if* Dante were the author such resemblances must certainly be expected[3].

Passing over such general features of similarity as have been indicated already (*supra*, p. 295), I would draw attention, more in detail, to the following points.

II. ii. (*a*) RESEMBLANCES TO OTHER WORKS OF DANTE.

(1) ll. 1–5. Giuliani has pointed out the general similarity of the language here applied to Can Grande with that of *Par.* xvii. 85–90:

> ' Le sue magnificenze conosciute
> Saranno ancora sì, che i suoi nimici
> Non ne potran tener le lingue mute.

---

[1] As I have explained in reference to the *Quaestio*, in *Studies*, II. pp. 327, 328.

[2] *Supra*, pp. 302, 306, 310, and *infra*, pp. 337, 339, 343.

[3] Again see *Studies*, II. pp. 332, 346.

> A lui t' aspetta ed ai suoi benefici ;
> Per lui fia trasmutata molta gente,
> Cambiando condizion ricchi e mendici.'

Compare especially the words of ll. 89, 90 with those of the Epistle: 'distrahit in diversa diversos, ut hos in spem suae prosperitatis attollat, hos exterminii deiciat in terrorem.' This is certainly striking, and a like similarity may again be traced between the next sentence in the Epistle and the following *terzina* in the Canto (ll. 91–3):

> ' " E porteraine scritto nella mente
> Di lui, ma nol dirai :" *e disse cose*
> *Incredibili a quei che fien presente.*'

In the same tone we read that the heralding of Can Grande's prowess was 'facta modernorum exsuperans, tanquam veri existentia latius' (ll. 6, 7).

(2) l. 466, 'Quum omnis vis causandi sit radius quidam profluens a prima causa quae Deus est.' Compare with this the fuller statement in ll. 400–404, and also ll. 378 and 489. That all celestial influences are conveyed by means of the *rays of light* of the several heavenly bodies is an extremely common thought with Dante, e. g. *Purg.* xxv. 89 ; *Par.* vii. 74 ; viii. 3 ; xix. 90 ; xxix. 29 ; *Conv.* II. vii. 90 ; III. xiv. 32 ; IV. xx. 73, &c.

(3) Still more familiar is the combination of the appeals to Reason and Authority occurring two or three times in the Epistle ; e. g. xx. l. 353 ; xxii. l. 412 ; xxvii. l. 510 *seqq.* and xxviii. The process is clearly set out in the words 'ratio et auctoritas manifestat' in § 20 ; and 'Similiter etiam ac *scientia* facit *auctoritas*' in § 22 *init.* We may illustrate this by *Par.* xxiv. 133 ; xxvi. 25, 26, and 46, 47 ; *Mon.* I. v. 11 and 20 ; II. i. 60 ; III. xvi. 64–71 ; *Epist.* IV. iii. 26, &c.

(4) The familiar alternation of sacred and profane examples occurs in the only passage where any such examples are cited, viz. in § 1, the Queen of Sheba and Pallas, but a similar admixture of sacred and profane authors occurs also in the appeals to authority in §§ 22 and 27. This practice of Dante is too common to need illustration[1].

---

[1] *Studies,* I. pp. 26, 118 ; II. pp. 22-25 ; and *supra,* p. 301 n.

(5) We find the same rather depreciatory way of speaking of women (§ 10), which occurs in other works of Dante. Compare *V. E.* I. i. 6 (with the same reference to ordinary language as in this Epistle, § 10, l. 225). Add *V. E.* I. iv. 18–23 ; *Conv.* IV. xix. 88 ; *Purg.* xxix. 24–30 ; *Quaestio* xix. 69.

(6) The habit of refining on the different shades of meaning in similar words is noticeable here as elsewhere in Dante. Thus in § 18 *exordium* and *prologus* ; in § 23 *penetrat* and *resplendet* ; and in § 29 *nescit* and *nequit*. Compare *Conv.* II. xi. 39 *seqq.*, *pietà* and *misericordia* ; III. xiv. 38–48, *lume* (or *luce*), *splendore*, and *raggio* ; IV. xxv, *Vergogna, Verecundia, Stupore* and *Pudore*.

(7) The abstract account of the difference between 'absolute' and 'relative' terms in § 5 may be compared with that in *Mon.* III. xii. 35–44, in which also we find 'pater' and 'dominus' given as examples of ' relative' terms. So again, Dante there says of ' homo ' (which serves as his example of an 'absolute' term), 'homo est id quod est per formam substantialem . . . per quam reponitur sub praedicamento substantiae.' This is in effect much the same as the statement made in the Epistle: ' Eorum vero quae sunt, quaedam sic sunt, ut habeant esse absolutum in se.'

(8) Next let us note the language of § 20, ll. 354–63 as to the dependence of everything that exists on some antecedent cause, except in the case of God Himself, who *alone* exists *per se*. Compare with this *Conv.* IV. xviii. 13–22, and especially the concluding lines as to the impossibility of two things existing *per se*.

(9) The statements about Rhetoric in § 19 correspond exactly in thought (and again without any suspicious repetition of actual phrases) with the sentiments of the *Convito*. The writer says here that the main object of Rhetoric is to please the auditor and secure his good will and his attention, and that the key to this is to arouse in him wonder or admiration. Compare *Conv.* II. vii. 53 *seqq.* : ' In ciascuna maniera di sermone lo dicitore massimamente dee intendere alla persuasione, cioè all' abbellire dell' audienza, siccome quella ch' è principio di tutte l' altre persuasioni, come li rettorici sanno, e potentissima

persuasione sia, a rendere l' uditore *attento*, promettere di dire *nuove e grandiose cose*,' &c. So again, *Conv.* II. xiv. 116: 'la Rettorica è *soavissima* di tutte l' altre scienze, perocchè a ciò principalmente intende.'

(10) Some points in the language used about the Empyrean are to be noticed.

(*a*) In §§ 24, 25, the description of the Empyrean as 'coelum continens corpora universa' (l. 443), and, again, the words 'per suum omnia continere et a nullo contineri' (l. 455), may be compared with *Quaestio* iv. 6 'nobilissimo continenti, qui est coelum primum'; and also *Conv.* II. iv. 35, 'Questo è il sovrano edificio del mondo, nel quale tutto il mondo s' inchiude.'

(*b*) A minor point on which I would not lay too much stress is the explanation of the term Empyrean as in *Conv.* II. iv. 14. But in the Epistle (§ 24) it is added that the 'fire' which the name implies is not to be understood literally but spiritually, as 'amor sanctus sive caritas.' This idea, however, (as Giuliani points out) is found exactly in the gloss upon 'Sua beltà piove fiammelle di fuoco' in *Conv.* III. viii. 147, 'cioè ardore d' amore e di carità.'

(*c*) A more important point is the assertion of its immobility, and the argument based thereupon, which will be discussed under the next head.

(11) The whole of § 26 is thoroughly in Dante's manner both in thought and expression. The first point to notice is the fundamental principle that all motion implies defect[1]; or, as we might put it in a homely way, all that moves does so in order 'to better itself'; i.e. as Dante often expresses it elsewhere, from a desire *ultimately* to become reunited to God (see especially, among many other passages, *Purg.* xvi. 90; *Par.* vii. 143; *Conv.* III. ii. 50–9; IV. xii. 138–176)[2]. Hence the Empyrean Heaven alone is motionless: 'Illud igitur coelum quod a nullo movetur, in se et in qualibet sui parte habet

---

[1] This principle is admitted by Aquinas, *Summa*, I. liii. 1 'Motus est actus imperfecti'; and though this is explained with a qualification in the case of Angels (*Art. cit. ad fin.*), yet the principle is again recognized in the words :— 'Motus existentis in potentia est propter indigentiam suam.'

[2] See further *supra*, p. 24.

quidquid potest modo perfecto, eo quod motu non indiget ad suam perfectionem' (ll. 485–88); and again, 'Si Deus non dedit illi motum, patet quod non dedit illi materiam in aliquo egentem' (ll. 499–501). Precisely the same thought is expressed in rather different language in *Conv.* II. iv. 16, 'pongono esso (*scil.* Empireo) essere immobile per avere in sè, secondo ciascuna parte, ciò che la sua materia vuole.' Add *Par.* xxii. 67, 'non s' impola.' The converse application of the same principle is found in the words following in *Conv. l. c.*, where it is said that the 'velocissimo movimento' of the *Primum Mobile* is due to its intense desire to come to the tranquil rest of the Empyrean which is in close proximity to it. Another aspect of this 'Law of Motion' is found in *Conv.* III. iii. All things, animate and inanimate, elementary or composite, have a natural love to their 'proprio loco,' and consequently an innate tendency to move towards it. They cannot remain at rest anywhere else. On this principle Dante's ascent to Heaven is explained in *Par.* i. 103 *seqq.* See especially ll. 139–41 :

> 'Maraviglia sarebbe in te, se privo
>   D' impedimento giù ti fossi assiso,
>   Come a terra quiete in foco vivo.'

Compare with this Aquinas, *Summa*, I. vi. 3, 'tertia perfectio ignis (he has just stated that "Perfectio alicuius rei triplex est") est secundum quod in loco suo quiescit.' Otherwise it would be in motion striving to reach this. See *Conv.* III. iii. ll. 11 *seqq.*, and ll. 472–80 of this Epistle.

Passing on now to the argument employed in this section, it will be found to be both obscure and highly technical. That will hardly be thought to militate against its claim to be Dantesque. Indeed it bears the strongest resemblance to many such arguments in the *De Mon.* and the *Quaestio.* The reasoning appears to me to proceed thus :—

> All motion implies imperfection. (ll. 472–484.)
> ∴ All that is motionless is perfect. (ll. 485–488.)

in other words,

> All that moves is imperfect.
> ∴ All that does not move is perfect.

Consequently the Empyrean, being motionless, is perfect, and, being perfect, must be in close relation to the Light of God (ll. 488-493).

But here the logical conscience of the writer warns him that though his conclusion is true, he seems to have arrived at it by an unsound argument, in effect, by denying the antecedent of a hypothetical syllogism ('destructione antecedentis'). Thus :—

> If anything moves it is imperfect.
> This Heaven does not move.
> ∴ It is not imperfect.

But, he replies, though the argument is wrong in form it is true materially ('ratione materiae'), (ll. 495-503), because in this case the two terms are *convertible*. We must admit that all that is perfect is motionless, and also that all that is motionless is perfect, because otherwise God would have created something that might be eternally imperfect (l. 498). Thus the terms 'immobility' and 'perfection' are convertible terms, just as much as 'homo' and 'risibilis.' This illustration deserves to be very particularly noted. It is assumed as obvious that 'risibility' is a *differentia* of the species man. Now Dante asserts this *totidem verbis* in *V. E.* II. i, 'quidquid nobis convenit, vel gratia generis, vel *speciei*, vel individui convenit, ut sentire, *ridere*, militare.' And again, *V. N.* xxv. 17 *seqq.*, 'Dico anche di lui che rideva, ed anche che parlava ; le quali cose paiono esser *proprie dell' uomo*, e specialmente esser *risibile.*' We find further that this illustration comes from a book of Aristotle with which Dante was certainly acquainted[1]. It seems then hardly possible to resist the con-

---

[1] Viz. *De Part. Anim.* III. 10. The evidence afforded by Dante's references to this work of Aristotle appears to me significant as to the degree of his acquaintance with it. It will be found from the Index in my First Series of *Studies*, p. 337, that he refers to it more or less distinctly six times, independently of the present passage. If we suppose the illustrations quoted above from *V. E.* and *V. N.* to have come from this source that would add two more possible references. In one case only does he quote it by name, and even then, departing from his usual practice in regard to Aristotle, his reference is vague, and he does not specify the Book quoted. I should infer therefore that he was not so familiar with it as with most of the other works of Aristotle, but that

clusion that this section throughout bears evident traces of the hand of Dante himself. I ought also to have called attention to the curious expression 'destructio antecedentis' in the sense of *denying* the antecedent. Compare *Conv.* IV. xii. 123, 'per la distruzione del conseguente'; *Quaestio,* xii. (*init.*), 'Ad destructionem igitur primi membri consequentis dico'; so again in § 13 *init.* and in *Mon.* II. xii. 60; *Conv.* IV. xiv. 11, 'questa loro ragione anche si distrugge,' &c. The technical phrase is also common in Albertus Magnus.

(12) The words which follow in close connexion with the above, at the beginning of the next section, as a quotation from the *De Coelo* (a work very familiar to Dante) formulate a principle which is recognized also in *Conv.* III. v. 38 *seqq.* and again twice in the *Quaestio,* §§ 4 and 23 [1], these places also bearing distinct evidence of their derivation from the *De Coelo,* though there is no direct quotation acknowledged. (See *Studies,* I. p. 128.) There is a further especial significance about this particular quotation which will be found discussed later (p. 339).

(13) Once more let us note the very remarkable language which the writer applies to himself in the last words of § 28. He is conscious that his own unworthiness of the grace of so

a certain amount of its contents were lodged in his memory. That precisely corresponds with the absence of any acknowledgement of the source of the illustration in the present passage.

[1] I have no hesitation in quoting parallels from the *Quaestio,* since those who hold both that work and this to be forgeries cannot possibly suppose that either forger can have been acquainted with the work of the other. At any rate it is scarcely conceivable that Moncetti can have known this Epistle as such, it never having been published, and the MSS. being extremely rare, even if generally then known at all. Any undoubted coincidences would therefore afford a very strong presumption of the genuineness of both works. And in this relation I am struck with the close resemblance of § 28 of the Epistle and § 22 of the *Quaestio.* Not only is the general aim of these sections and the position they occupy in the two works very similar, but their structure is on the same lines, the repeated quotations being emphatically introduced by the four times repeated *legant* in the former case and the five times repeated *audiant* in the latter. Again, compare ll. 27 and 126 'inspicienti patebit' and 'sicut apparet inspicienti' with *Q.* § x. 10, 'ut subtiliter inspicienti satis manifestum est.' From the frequency of parallels between the two works that are noted in this Essay, it seems to me that they afford mutual support to one another.

great a revelation may impede its acceptation. As Dante himself confesses in *Inf.* ii. 33 :

'Me degno a ciò nè io nè altri 'l crede.'

The bitterness of his self-accusations in the concluding Cantos of the *Purgatorio*, as well as in other isolated passages, lend a pungent force to the admission of the 'peccatum loquentis' here, though he characteristically resents such a censure on the part of *others* as *oblatratio*, and denounces them as *invidi*. But the striking point is the precise language of his apology : He who makes His Sun to rise upon the good and upon the evil, with different intent and in different degrees reveals His glory to those *whose lives may be ever so ill*, '*quantumcumque* male viventibus [1].'

I confidently ask, would any one other than Dante himself have dared to make this characteristically humble [2], and even pathetic confession of unworthiness in his name?

(14) The following are, as it seems to me, some favourable considerations to be derived from the two concluding (Epistolary) sections for which, as we have already seen, the supposed forger has been vehemently censured.

As a minor point of similarity with the words in § 33, 'nec dividendo nec sententiando quidquam dicetur ad praesens,' Giuliani aptly compares *Conv.* II. xiii. 76, 'e non è qui mestiere di procedere dividendo e a lettera sponendo.'

In l. 613 it is declared that supreme Beatitude consists in the intellectual contemplation of Divine Truth. This is very distinctly stated by Dante in *Par.* xxviii. 106–111. The last three lines should be specially noted—

'Quinci si può veder come si fonda
L' esser beato nell' atto che vede,
Non in quel ch' ama, che poscia seconda.'

Compare *Par.* xiv. 40–42 ; and *Summa*, II [1]. iii. 4, r₄.

---

[1] We might compare the language of his apology for addressing the Cardinals in *Ep.* viii. 71 : although he be 'de ovibus pascuis Iesu Christi minima una.' He pleads that 'out of the mouths even of babes and sucklings' God's truth may issue ; and that 'a man born blind' openly professed the truth when the enlightened Pharisees were silent and even hostile.

[2] See *Early Biographers*, p. 147; or *Studies*, II. pp. 75, 328.

Again, in ll. 620, 621 it is stated that enlightenment and information will be sought from time to time by Dante in his progress through Paradise from the glorified spirits, on the ground that they 'see all things in God,' 'ab eis, tanquam videntibus omnem veritatem, multa quaerentur.' How frequently this is the case must be known to every reader of the *Paradiso*. Thus in *Par.* xxiv. 40–42, Beatrice tells S. Peter that he has no need to inquire to what degree Dante possesses the three great Christian Virtues:—

> 'Non t' è occulto, perchè il viso hai quivi
> Dov' ogni cosa dipinta si vede.'

In *Par.* xxvi. 106, Adam explains his knowledge of Dante's thought to be

> 'Perch' io la veggio nel verace speglio,'

and again S. Thomas Aquinas in *Par.* xi. 20, 21 says,

> 'Sì, riguardando nella luce eterna
> Li tuoi pensieri, onde cagioni, apprendo.'

To save space the reference only will be given to several other passages equally apposite. *Par.* iii. 32, 33 ; iv. 116 ; v. 118 ; viii. 87–90 ; ix. 73 ; xvii. 16, 43 ; xix. 28 ; xxiv. 41 ; *Purg.* xxx. 103. Finally we should add *V. E.* I. ii. 13–20, where the knowledge by the Angels of one another's thoughts is accounted for, because 'per illud fulgentissimum speculum, in quo cuncti repraesentantur pulcerrimi atque avidissimi speculantur,' and hence they stand in no need of communication by language.

I gather here a number of minor resemblances of diction.

§ 16. In practical subjects the speculative element is always subordinate to the practical, though ἁπλῶς Dante frequently asserts the pre-eminence of the speculative over the practical. (This is too common to need illustration [1].) But the statement of the present passage will be found again in *Mon.* I. ii. 30–42 : 'in iis (*scil.* practical matters) non operatio propter speculationem, sed propter operationem illa adsumitur,' &c.

---

[1] Perhaps note *Conv.* II. v. 69 *seqq.* ; IV. xvii. 85 *seqq.* ; *Mon.* III. xvi. 43 *seqq.*

§ 25, l. 469. Compare 'magis habet rationem causae' with 'quanto causa est universalior, tanto *magis habet rationem causae*' in *Mon.* I. xi. 130. But we have besides a correspondence of thought as well as of diction between the two works. The principle thus stated in the *De Mon.* is expressly enunciated in the Epistle, l. 379, 'causa prima est magis causa,' and in the present passage (l. 468) that principle is applied to the case of the Empyrean also, since it becomes a more efficacious cause in proportion to its greater proximity to the First Cause.

§ 28, l. 534, 'substantia intellectualis separata,' i. e. Angelic nature. See also § xviii. l. 311, 'a substantiis superioribus.' See *Conv.* II. v. 6, 'Sustanze separate da materia, cioè Intelligenze'; III. vii. 47, 'dalle Sustanze separate, cioè dagli Angeli.' Add 'le Intelligenze separate' in III. xiii. 46 ; and *Purg.* xviii. 49,

> 'Ogni forma sustanzial, che setta
> È da materia.'

This denomination of Angels occurs commonly in Aquinas and also in the Commentary of Pietro. It is further to be noted that the argument in the Epistle, *loc. cit.*, is derived from the fact that human nature has 'connaturalitatem et affinitatem' with this angelic nature, and that is just a point which is insisted on in one of the passages just cited from the *Convito*. See especially ll. 74 *seqq.* of III. vii (perocchè) 'tra l' angelica natura, che è cosa intellettuale, e l' anima umana non sia grado alcuno.' So again, *Mon.* III. xvi. 30, 'Si ergo homo medium quoddam est corruptibilium et incorruptibilium, quum omne medium sapiat naturam extremorum,' &c. But further the employment of 'Intelligenza' itself to designate Angels, which is thoroughly Dantesque, occurs in § 21, l. 401, where the 'intelligentiae superiores' are said to radiate their reflection of Divine Goodness to 'intelligentiae inferiores.' The sentiment is exactly parallel to *Par.* ii. 121–3. Add to the *Convito* passages above quoted, III. vi. 35, 'Le Intelligenze del cielo'; and xiv. 35, 'Nelle Intelligenze raggia la divina luce senza mezzo, nell' altre si ripercuote da queste Intelligenze prima

illuminate'; which is almost verbatim what is stated here.
This is also probably the sense of 'Intelligenza' in *Par.* ii.
136 and certainly in *Par.* xxviii. 78. See also *Summa*, I.
lxxix. 10, r, 'Substantiae separatae, quas nos Angelos dicimus,
Intelligentiae vocantur.'

§ 28, l. 559, 'Si vero in dispositionem . . . *oblatrarent.*'
Compare with this *Conv.* IV. iii. 59 'Conciossiacosachè quasi
tutti così *latrano*[1].'

§ 33, 'Invento principio seu primo, videlicet Deo, nihil
est quod ulterius quaeratur.' Compare *Purg.* xxxi. 23, 24:

> 'Io bene
> Di là dal qual non è a che si aspiri.'

§ 2, l. 48. With the statement that those of superior intelligence 'gregum vestigia sectari non decet,' compare a similar
metaphor in *Inf.* ii. 105. Add *Conv.* I. i. 68, 'fuggito dalla
pastura del volgo'; and II. xvi. 65–7.

§ 21, l. 410. The Trinity is described under the terms
bonitatem, sapientiam, virtutem. Compare *Inf.* iii. 5, 6—

> 'Fecemi la Divina *Potestate*
> La somma *Sapienza* e 'l primo *Amore.*'

It is hardly necessary to explain that *virtus* and *virtute*
are constantly used for *power* by Dante: and further that
bonitas is used here not of moral goodness, but, as generally
in the Vulgate, in the sense of *benignitas*, and therefore
closely akin to *amore*. Among very numerous passages,
see Rom. ii. 4; xi. 22; Gal. v. 22, and often in the Psalms.
Besides, this is the common sense of 'bontà'; e. g. *Purg.* iii.
122 and in the *Convito, passim.* So in *Par.* ii. 136 and 148
the sense of *bontà* is 'beneficence,' or 'beneficent influence.'
Hence *h. l. bonitas* is nearly equivalent to the more usual
Amor. We may add that Aquinas often substitutes *bonitas*
for *amor* as a designation of the Holy Spirit, e. g. *Summa*,
I. xxxix. 8, r_3, and I. xlv. 6, r_2, justifying this by the remark
that *bonitas* is 'ratio et obiectum amoris.'

§ 2, ll. 50–54. Let us now compare 'quam non ipsi [*scil.*

---

[1] Comp. its use by S. Aug., 'Vobis non oblatrantibus securius loquebantur'
(*contr. Iul.* i. 6). The same idea occurs in Soph. *El.* 299, τοιαῦθ' ὑλακτεῖ.

intellectu ac ratione vigentes] legibus sed ipsis leges potius dirigantur,' with *Conv.* IV. xxvi. 128, 'il Vecchio per più sperienza dee esser giusto, e non seguitatore di legge se non in quanto il suo diritto giudicio e la legge è quasi tutt' uno,' &c. We have here a close parallelism of thought without any imitative identity of expression[1].

§ 23, ll. 431–7. This is thoroughly Dantesque, as may be seen from the references given by Giuliani to *Par.* xxxi. 22; *Conv.* III. vii. 15; and *V. E.* I. xvi. 48–52. To these we may add *Conv.* III. xiv. 14–28, and IV. xxi. 47, &c.

§ 8, l. 175. We may compare with the phrase 'iustitiae obnoxius' (repeated l. 245), a passage in *Ep.* V. viii. *fin.*, where Dante, describing how unconsciously men sometimes work out God's designs, says 'voluntates humanae . . . obnoxiae voluntati aeternae, saepe illi ancillantur ignare.'

Before proceeding to the subject of the quotations included in the Epistle, there are two other points to be noticed briefly. I do not know what may be the authority for the division of the Epistle into sections. If the work is genuine this is probably due to Dante himself, like the numbering of the chapters in the *Convito*. It is perhaps significant that this letter introductory to the *Divina Commedia*, and the *Paradiso* in particular, should contain just thirty-three sections, the number of Cantos in each Cantica (Canto i of the *Inferno* being Introductory).

The other point is the use throughout §§ 1–4 of the digni- fied style of address by *vos* and *vester*, instead of *tu* and *tuus*, in accordance with the custom, the origin of which Dante describes, and the disuse of which he laments, in *Par.* xvi. 10. Further, his own discriminating use of this idiom in the *Divina Commedia* should not be overlooked. See the instances of this collected in *Studies*, II. p. 29. I do not think it would have occurred to a forger thus to depart from the more usual Latin idiom of *tu* and *tuus*.

---

[1] Compare this as noticed in the case of the *Quaestio*, in *Studies*, II. pp. 329 *fin.*, 331, and elsewhere.

II. ii. (*b*). The Evidence from Quotations.

The character of the numerous quotations from other authors in the Epistle will I think afford a further strong presumption of its genuineness.

(1) I lay no stress on similarity of the formulae of quotation such as ' ut patet,' &c., since that would be an obvious feature easy of imitation [1].

(2) The great wealth of quotations is characteristic of Dante, there being as many as about forty in these few pages.

(3) These quotations are spread over a great number of authors familiar to Dante, and in much the same proportion as elsewhere, Scripture and Aristotle leading the way with seventeen and sixteen references respectively (counting under the latter the *De Causis*, since Dante would so regard it). Besides these, we have Ovid, Horace, Lucan, Cicero, and Boethius. Would a forger have ventured to omit Virgil altogether, even though in the Epistle, as it stands, there seems to be no natural occasion for any reference to him, since nothing would have been easier than to create one?

(4) The general knowledge of Aristotle which is displayed is equally remarkable and equally characteristic; no less than nine of his works being quoted or obviously referred to, viz. *Ethics, Politics, Rhetoric, Metaphysics, De Anima, Physics, De Caelo, De Part. Anim.*, and *De Causis*. Some of these references are quite unobtrusive, and in no case

---

[1] There is a curious formula used here which I do not think occurs elsewhere in Dante, viz. *insinuatur* (ll. 538, 548), meaning 'it is indicated.' I find this expression similarly used by Richard of St. Victor (*v. inf.* p. 340), e.g. p. 48 E *fin.* (ed. Rothom. 1650) 'manifeste quod sciri oportet insinuare'; and by S. Aug. *de Gen.* I. 27 (describing anthropomorphic language) 'cum Deus insinuatur audientibus parvulis.' So again in his commentary on *De Genesi ad Literam*, II. 24 'nihil aliud his verbis (*scil.* Gen. i. 1) quam materiae corporalis informitatem insinuare [Scriptura voluit].' It is also the word by which παρατιθέμενος in Acts xvii. 3 is represented in the Vulgate. Ducange quotes a large number of instances of its use in Ecclesiastical documents, and gives as its equivalents, ἐμφανίζειν, διδάσκειν, and *docere*. He considers the French *enseigner* (generally connected with *insignare*) to be really derived from *insinuare* in this sense. He quotes a passage from S. Jerome (which I have not been able to verify) 'cum cxviii^m Psalmum tibi insinuare conarer.'

is there any appearance of their being artificially dragged in [1].

(5) It is to be specially noted that among all these quotations and references there are in effect only three that are actually found in any other works of Dante, viz.:

(*a*) The references to *Ethics*, Books viii and ix on the subject of Friendship in §§ 2 and 3, which may be treated together as practically one; i. e. as to the different classes of friendship; the friendship between those of unequal station; and the need of some reciprocity ('analogum' or 'proporzione') to maintain it. These passages are quoted also in *Conv.* III. i. 40 and 56, and III. xi. 80 and 90.

Even in this case it is objected by D'Ovidio that a different turn is given to the application of the passage. He says [2] that in the *Convito* this 'proportion' is supplied by the services of the inferior, and by his devotion to the superior. This no doubt is the case. But then D'Ovidio declares that in the Epistle it is supplied by the 'moral elevation of the inferior,' quoting the words in l. 32, that princes have made friends of men 'fortuna obscuros, honestate praeclaros.' This seems to be an extraordinarily forced and unnatural inference from the words. But yet another twist is given to the screw, when they are said to involve on the part of the writer the bad taste of describing himself as 'honestate praeclarum,' which would 'better have been left to a third person'! But even if 'the moral elevation of the inferior' had been here declared to be a preservative of reciprocity in this kind of friendship, it would only be different from, but by no means inconsistent with, the statement of the *Convito*: and that very difference would be a consideration adverse to the theory of forgery. But if we read only a few lines further on, we shall find exactly the same idea as that in the *Convito*. For in ll. 63 *seqq.*, the writer says that he hopes to requite, so far as his 'inferior' station allows, the benefits he has received from Can Grande, by offering him in return the best at any rate that he has to give: which, best though it be, he modestly

---

[1] The same was noticed in the case of the *Quaestio*, in *Studies*, II. p. 328.

[2] *Op. cit.* p. 452.

* * *

describes as 'munusculum.' This corresponds precisely with *Conv.* III. i. 62–9.

(*b*) The second of these more or less 'duplicate' quotations is the reference (§ 2, l. 44) to the apparent diameter of the Sun being no more than about one foot. This is from Arist. *De An.* III. iii, and is referred to in *Conv.* IV. viii. 51. In both cases, it may be noted, it comes as an illustration merely, and is not explicitly given as a quotation. Dante perhaps did not remember its exact source, though we see from a few lines below in the *Convito* passage that he was aware that it came from Aristotle somewhere. This is a curious coincidence, which may I think fairly be counted as 'an undesigned coincidence,' especially as the opponents have founded an objection again on the different use which is made of the illustration in the two works. Indeed D'Ovidio is quite elated over this, and triumphantly exclaims (p. 454): 'il brav' uomo tradisce per poca avvertenza il suo giuoco.' In the *Convito* (*l.c.*) this is given as an illustration of the distinction between 'errore sensuale' and 'errore razionale.' Here it serves as an example of 'iudicium sine discretione.' But what else is 'errore sensuale' but this? Besides, the very chapter in question in the *Convito* where this reference occurs has for its subject *discrezione*, 'il più bel ramo che dalla radice razionale consurga' (l. 1)[1]; and *discrezione* is described as 'proprio atto di ragione' (ll. 5, 6). When this is absent we have 'errore sensuale' (of which the mistake as to the Sun's diameter is an example); or in the language of the present passage 'sine discretione iudicium'; or as we read again in *Conv.* III. x. 28, 'sensuale giudizio.' But, apart from this single parallel in the *Convito*, we see from other places how thoroughly Dantesque is the thought and expression of the passage before us. Compare *Conv.* I. xi. 18 *seqq.*, where after describing *discrezione* as 'the Eye of Reason,' corresponding in its functions with the eye in the body, he adds:— 'quelli ch' è cieco del lume della *discrezione*, sempre va nel suo *giudicio* secondo il grido,' &c., and again *V. E.* I. iii,

---

[1] Compare Bede's language in *E. H.* III. v *ad fin.* :—'Gratia discretionis, quae virtutum mater est, imbutus.'

'quum . . . ipsa ratio vel circa *discretionem,* vel circa *iudicium,* vel circa electionem diversificetur,' &c. Compare also *Conv.* I. iv. 30, 'lo imperfetto giudicio che non secondo ragione, ma secondo senso giudica solamente.'

(*c*) The third passage is the expression, also in § 2, l. 50, 'intellectu ac ratione vigentes,' which is given as a direct quotation from Aristotle's *Politics* in *Mon.* I. iii. 91. In that case a little more of the Aristotelian context is given, viz. 'aliis naturaliter principari.' Again, in *Mon.* II. vii. 53, we find the same quotation, though in that case the earlier part, 'intellectu et ratione vigentes,' is not cited. Here we have nothing but the phrase, the ring of which was familiar to the writer, not given as a quotation, and the use made of it does not coincide either with the original in Aristotle, or with its application in the *De Mon.* Again, I venture to say that a divergence of this kind is favourable rather than adverse to the genuineness of the work.

(6) There is another quotation which comes near to being a 'duplicate,' but which, from a comparison of its treatment in the two passages, affords a striking evidence of genuineness.

In § 27 a passage is quoted from the *De Coelo* to show that the authority of Aristotle accords with the exalted position assigned in the previous sections to the Empyrean : 'Praemissis quoque rationibus consonanter dicit Philosophus in primo *De Coelo,*' &c. Now compare with this *Conv.* II. iv. 32, where after a long description of the opinion of the Church respecting the tenth Heaven or Empyrean, as being 'above' all the others, Dante adds, 'ed anco Aristotile pare ciò sentire, a chi bene lo intende, nel primo *di Cielo e Mondo.*' There are two or three passages in that Book, including the one quoted in the Epistle, to which this general reference might refer. Would a forger be likely to act on this vague hint, and search the *De Coelo* in order to find some more definite quotation for this place ? Observe that the authority of Aristotle is in both cases adduced for precisely the same point.

(7) The reference in § 21, l. 405 to Dionysius, though

not strictly a quotation, may be considered here. Dante professes his acquaintance with his work (*De Coelesti Hierarchia*) in *Par.* xxviii. 130-2. He refers to an opinion of his in *Conv.* II. xiv. 34. Also the language of the present passage 'ad modum speculorum' (attributed in a general way to Dionysius) may be compared with that upon the same subject in *Par.* xiii. 59[1]. But there is a still more striking point to be noticed in connexion with the mention made in the Epistle of the names of Dionysius (*h.l.*), and those of S. Bernard and Richard of St. Victor in § 28. To their works those who cavil at the contents of the *Paradiso* are referred. I quote the following passages from Mr. Gardner's excellent work on the 'Ten Heavens of Dante,' where they occur without any reference whatever to this Epistle. Speaking of a certain correspondence traceable between each Heaven, and the celestial movers allotted to it from the nine orders of angels, Mr. Gardner observes :—' This is more marked in some spheres than in others, but is seen to some extent in all, and can be traced by comparing Dante's heavens and saints with the *Celestial Hierarchies* of the supposed Dionysius, and with St. Bernard's Angels in his *De Consideratione*. The poet's theory is perhaps mainly a blending of the views of Dionysius [2] and St. Bernard ' (p. 21). Again (p. 219), speaking on another point, Mr. Gardner says :—' Perhaps, however, it should be regarded as derived, *like so many other points in the Paradiso*, from the writings of Richard of St. Victor.'

It is surely very remarkable to find the author of this Epistle indirectly acknowledging, or rather implying, an

---

[1] See also *Par.* ix. 61 ; xxix. 144.

[2] It is well known also that Dante in the *Paradiso* deliberately adopts the Order of the Angelic Hierarchies given by Dionysius in preference to that of S. Gregory the Great, who he says smiled at his own error as soon as he entered Heaven (*Par.* xxviii. 133-5). The Dionysian order is found in Hugh of St. Victor (to whom, as well as to Richard of St. Victor, Lubin has pointed out that Dante was very largely indebted) ; and also in Aquinas, *Summa*, I. cviii. 5, where the two systems are discussed, and preference given on the whole to that of Dionysius, though the difference is recognized as being of slight importance. The principle of the difference is thus explained by S. Thomas :— ' Dionysius exponit ordinum nomina secundum convenientiam ad spirituales perfectiones eorum ; Gregorius vero . . . in expositione horum nominum magis attendere videtur exteriora ministeria.'

indebtedness to three authors, whom a modern writer discovers, by an independent study of the *Paradiso* itself, to
have been important sources of Dante's inspiration in that
poem. It is as if Dante were saying : If any one distrusts
the revelation of heavenly things given by the mouth of one
so unworthy as I am, let him consult the very authorities
from which I have myself derived them. And on looking
into the *Paradiso*, we find that this was in fact the case. Can
we imagine a forger having the diligence to ferret out such
' origines ' of the subject-matter of the poem, on the chance
of some one recognizing their aptitude under these passing
references ?

(8) The significance of the apparent allusion to Aristotle's
De Part. Anim., as bearing on the manner in which Dante
elsewhere treats that particular work in the matter of quotation, has already been discussed (p. 329 n.) and need not
be spoken of further here.

(9) Finally, there are no new authors quoted in the Epistle
beyond those with whom Dante shows himself familiar elsewhere, with just this exception. In one passage we have
seen that cavillers are referred, though without precise quotation of definite passages, to three several works that are named
of Richard of St. Victor, S. Bernard, and S. Augustine [1].
These are works that are not elsewhere mentioned by Dante.
But each of these writers is among those glorified by Dante
in the *Paradiso*, and from that might be inferred some admiration of their works. Such an inference (as we have just
now seen) would be borne out by the contents of the
Paradiso. Of these authors, however, only S. Augustine is
elsewhere quoted at all, and in his case this particular work
is never referred to. But at any rate such a new departure
(though it has been made the ground of an objection) does
not resemble the procedure of a forger. There are two of the
Scriptural quotations on which a word may be added. In
§ 27 *fin.* the prophecy of Ezekiel against ' the prince of Tyre '
is quoted as if spoken of Lucifer. This was a common patris-

---

[1] See *Par.* x. 131 (Richard of St. Victor) ; xxxii. 35 (S. Augustine) ; and
xxxi–xxxiii (S. Bernard).

tic interpretation of the passage. Thus S. Augustine, *Gen. ad Lit.* xi. § 32 :—' In figura principis Tyri per Ezechielem prophetam in diabolum recte intelliguntur ' : and the passage is again quoted in this sense in *De Civ. Dei*, xi. 15. Corn. a Lapide quotes Ambrose, Jerome, Origen, Isidore and Bede as giving the same interpretation. It is also so applied by Hugh of St. Victor, i. p. 437 (ed. Rothom. 1648) ; and by S. Thomas in the *Summa*, I. lxiii. 5 and 6. We need not then be surprised to find it assumed here.

The application made of the passage in Daniel in the next section, l. 560, is more curious. The words in Dan. ii. 3 are :—' Vidi somnium, et mente confusus ignoro quid viderim.' The gloss upon this here is that Nebuchadnezzar had had revealed to him certain things against sinners, and had consigned them to oblivion ('oblivioni mandasse ') ; and the moral is that we should not be extreme to remember one another's faults, and that in particular the unworthiness and sinfulness of the author of the *Paradiso* should not be brought up against him in depreciation of his work. I have searched in vain for any authority for such an application of the words, but such a liberty of exegesis would certainly not be at all unnatural in Dante himself, or in many of the authors familiar to him. It is but an instance of the ' moral' interpretation which is legitimately applicable to all Scripture, as is maintained *supra*, § 7 and *Conv.* II. i. Further, this allusive reference is very like another that occurs concerning this very same chapter of Daniel in the *Paradiso* itself, viz. iv. 13–15 : ' Beatrice did as Daniel did when relieving Nebuchadnezzar of his anger which had made him unjustly cruel ' ; i. e. she interpreted Dante's thoughts. See Dan. ii. 12 :—' For this cause the king was angry and very furious, and commanded to destroy all the wise men of Babylon ' ; and v. 24 Daniel said, ' Destroy not the wise men of Babylon : bring me in before the king,' &c. Dante again refers to the subject of this chapter in *Inf.* xiv. 106 *seqq.*

In conclusion I would ask—Would any forger be likely to have not only general culture and knowledge so extensive as these quotations indicate, but also so nearly co-extensive

with that of Dante himself, especially in reference to Aristotle ? Would any be likely to go behind the quotations
offered by the writings of the author he was imitating, and
study the original works that the latter was acquainted with
in order to find fresh quotations ? Again, would he be so
crafty, or so venturesome, in the rare cases when he did reproduce any reference or quotation from that author's other
works, as to vary the treatment of it in a manner that would
give colour to the charge of inconsistency with those works ?

It seems to me that throughout we find just that amount of
similarity in method and thought combined with independence
in language and treatment as we should expect in the same
author writing at different times and on different subjects.

III

THE EXTERNAL EVIDENCE

WE will now turn to the consideration of the external evidence.

I confess I do not attach much importance to difficulties of external evidence, if they are only of a negative kind. The history of literature presents so many unaccountable anomalies in the fortunes of works admittedly genuine, that this is evidently a field in which the saying of Agathon is amply verified, that ' it is likely that many things should happen that are unlikely.' Of this I have collected many instances in my Essay on the *Quaestio de Aqua et Terra*[1]. But in the case now before us the difficulties go much beyond the mere absence of evidence, and the problem with which we have to deal is exceedingly obscure and complicated. But these difficulties (as is sometimes the case in theological disputes) are not solved by simply assuming a sceptical attitude, and dismissing the Epistle as a forgery. We have still to explain in what way, consistently with the indications of both external and internal evidence, the production of such a document, as a fact, can be plausibly accounted for.

The problem has presented itself in different forms as the facts to be reckoned with have been changed by further investigations. There have been three main stages in the data of the controversy, and corresponding variations in the theories put forward as to the origin of the Epistle.

(1) When Scolari first raised a doubt upon the question, it was believed (*a*) that there was no existing MS. older than the sixteenth century; and (*b*) that there was no evidence of acquaintance with the Epistle in any earlier writers. Hence, the field of external evidence being almost blank, it was argued that the letter was probably a forgery of the early

---

[1] *Studies*, II. pp. 314 *seqq.*

Renaissance period when such literary enterprises were very common.

(2) Next came (*a*) the discovery by Witte at Munich of a much earlier (apparently middle of fifteenth century) MS.[1] containing the first four sections (the dedicatory portion) of the Epistle ; (*b*) the knowledge that F. Villani (appointed Lecturer on Dante 1391, died c. 1400) bears direct testimony to the Epistle by definite citations, as well as by frequent and obvious indebtedness to it ; (*c*) the recognition that passages in the Commentary of Boccaccio bore a resemblance too close to be accidental to passages in the Epistle. But the other early Commentaries being mostly unedited[2] there was not supposed to be any other evidence of this kind. Then it was suggested that the Epistle was forged at an earlier date, and possibly by F. Villani himself, helped by hints from the work of Boccaccio. It was argued that the earlier existence of the Epistle was scarcely credible in view of the silence of so many Commentators on Dante to whom it would have been a document of supreme interest. Beside this, it was argued, how is it credible that so important and unique a document, if it existed, could have remained entirely unknown for seventy or

---

[1] See *Dante-Forschungen*, I. p. 500.

[2] This was before the days when the munificence of Lord Vernon had made accessible to scholars the Commentaries of the *Anonimo* (now known to be Graziuolo de' Bambagioli), those of Jacopo and Pietro di Dante, and the *Chiose sopra Dante* (known as the 'False Boccaccio'). To the liberality and enthusiasm of his son, the Hon. W. W. Vernon, we now owe besides the most valuable of all the early Commentaries, that of Benvenuto da Imola. In regard to the *Comento* of the *Anonimo*, first published in an edition of only 100 copies by Lord Vernon, perhaps I may be pardoned for here recording the fact (though it is a small matter) that I was the first to identify this with the very ancient (c. 1324) and long-lost Commentary of Ser Graziuolo de' Bambagioli. I announced this in a letter to the *Academy* of Oct. 8, 1881. I need not repeat the details there given. I sent a copy of this shortly afterwards to Dr. Witte, and in his reply (dated Dec. 18, 1881) he writes :—'Mi congratulo con Lei che in esso [Articolo] sotto ogni riguardo abbia veduto il vero. . . . Penso di stampare un Articolo . . . che renda conto della scoperta, e ne esponga l' importanza. S' intende che vi si darà dovuto ragguaglio di quanto V. S. contribuì rischiarare i fatti decisivi, e spero di poter spedirgliene una copia.' This I never received, and I do not know whether the Article was ever published. My apology for these personal details must be that a different account of the matter has been more than once published in Italy.

eighty years. Some distinguished modern scholars still think
the idea of a forgery by F. Villani himself not improbable,
e. g. Prof. D'Ovidio and Dr. Kraus.

(3) Finally, it is now discovered that there are very numerous places in other early Commentators[1] besides Boccaccio
offering a close and even *verbatim* resemblance to passages in
the Epistle, amounting to distinct, though unacknowledged,
quotation such as would now be called direct plagiarism
either of one author from another, or of both or all from
one common original. Such a practice was of course quite
common in those days, and Dante himself affords many
instances of it.

Still the facts, though thus changed, continue to be *prima
facie* as adverse as ever to the genuineness of the Epistle.
For so far as they appear to necessitate a much earlier date
for its composition, they seem also to make it even more
impossible to regard it as a work of Dante. Obviously it
could not have so presented itself to the Commentators who
seem to be quoting it, since they would have either eagerly
availed themselves of its authority, or repudiated its claims.
Moreover, there appear to be other reasons why they could
not have known the Epistle at least in anything like its
present form.   For Boccaccio, who apparently quotes it very
frequently, argues in one place[2] that the name 'Commedia,'
though seemingly inappropriate, is not unlikely to have been
applied to the Poem by its author, since the term is used
by him in *Inf.* xxi[3].   But as this title is explicitly given
to it, and the designation defended in § 10 of the Epistle,
Boccaccio must either have been unacquainted with the
Epistle, or he could not have supposed that he had before

[1] In particular, Pietro di Dante, Jacopo della Lana, and Francesco da Buti.
We must now however add, and in a still more remarkable degree, Guido da
Pisa, whose very early Commentary (probably c. 1324) is still unedited.   The
British Museum possesses a beautiful MS. of this very rare work, purchased
a few years ago at the sale of the Sunderland Library.   See further on this
infra, pp. 349, 356.

[2] *Comento*, Lez. 1ma, p. 86.

[3] Buti, *Proemio*, p. 7, uses the same argument, enforcing it by a further
reference to *Inf.* xvi. 128, evidently in entire ignorance of the contents of § 10
of this Epistle.

him the words of Dante himself. Further, in § 15 of the *Vita* he mentions two traditions as to the dedication of the *Paradiso*; one, that it was dedicated to Frederick III, King of Sicily [1] (which Boccaccio mentions first); another, that the whole poem was dedicated to Can Grande della Scala. On this subject (he adds) we have only individual opinions to go by, and further it is one not worth the trouble of investigating [2]. This clearly shows that he could not possibly have been acquainted with the existence of this Epistle, though he is certainly in some way familiar with much of its contents.

From these facts the hypothesis supported by D'Ovidio and others seemed naturally to follow, viz. that the Epistle is a composite document, patched up, whether by Villani or some one else, with the help of those passages in the different Commentaries [3] and elsewhere. Then a head and tail were added associating it with the name of Dante himself.

Putting out of sight for a moment the complications introduced into the question by these fourteenth-century quotations, let us first deal with the simple problem of the possibility of the existence of such a dedicatory letter remaining for so long unknown. That much at least, if it be genuine, seems to be clearly established.

(1) This purports to be a private letter addressed to an individual, not necessarily in any sense 'published' or 'intended for publication.' The recipient may have put it aside among his other papers, and thought no more about it [4].

---

[1] More commonly called King Frederick II.

[2] *Vita*, c. 15 *fin.* In the recension of Boccaccio's *Vita* known as the 'Compendio,' an opinion is expressed in favour of the dedication of the whole to Can Grande on the strength of the statement made a little before (§ 14) that Dante was in the habit of sending six or eight Cantos, more or less, as they were composed, to Can Grande.

[3] These changing hypotheses are curiously like those of the Tübingen School in reference to the Gospel according to S. John. First, the later date of the Gospel was thought to be proved by the absence of quotations in the first half of the second century. Then when quotations were proved to exist in the works of Justin Martyr, it was maintained that the author of the Gospel was really quoting Justin! See p. 351 (2).

[4] This may also explain the silence of Giov. Villani as to this Epistle. It is well known that he mentions three only of the Epistles that have been attributed to Dante, viz. Nos. 6, 7, and 8. All of these are on public affairs, and addressed

(2) He might naturally have done this in any case, but still more so if the dedicatory letter were sent to him before the completion, to say nothing of the ' publication,' of the *Paradiso*. (In relation to this point, the question of the probable or possible date of the Epistle, if genuine, will be found discussed later, pp. 359 *seqq.*)

(3) It is certainly not a thing unknown that documents of even greater importance than this have mysteriously been lost to sight in family archives, and have been brought to light after long periods of oblivion. On the other hand, there undoubtedly did exist a tradition of the dedication of the *Paradiso* to Can Grande, since, as we have seen, it was stated as a matter of common belief by Boccaccio. Further, there is a Sonnet by a Venetian poet, Giovanni Quirini, a contemporary of Dante, which has been lately published for the first time by Prof. Morpurgo. It is addressed to some person of distinction unnamed, but probably and presumably Can Grande. The poet urges him to publish to the world the *Paradiso* of Dante, alleging that he knew it to have been, and still to be, the poet's wish that it should be thus brought out under his auspices[1].

So far then as the merely negative aspect of the evidence goes, if that were all, I should feel no serious difficulty, in the face of what appears to me to be the exceedingly strong internal evidence in favour of the genuineness of the Epistle[2]. But we have now to consider a much more difficult problem than this. It is not merely the *ignorance* of the letter on the part of the early commentators that we have to deal with, but

to persons in authority in connexion with such affairs. These Epistles were naturally in some sense 'published.' The case before us is quite different. The same may be said of the absence of any mention of it by Lionardo Bruni (d. 1444) in his Biography of Dante. (See *Dante and his Early Biographers*, pp. 68, 71.) Bruni professes to have seen several letters written by Dante, whose handwriting he describes. He mentions more or less definitely four of these; one possibly, but none certainly, corresponding to what are now extant.

[1] See a fuller account of this interesting piece of evidence in Mr. Vernon's Preliminary Chapter to his *Readings on the Paradiso*, p. xxx, and also in Messrs. Wicksteed and Gardner, *Dante and del Virgilio*, p. 92.

[2] An opinion, I may add, shared by Ugo Foscolo, Witte, and even Scartazzini. For the last-named see *infra*, p. 359.

it is the combination of *ignorance* and *knowledge* (as implied
by their apparent plagiarism) that complicates the question.
If the Epistle be genuine, how is it possible that so much
of its contents should be known and used by several fourteenth-
century commentators without any suspicion that it was
a work of Dante, as it claims on the very face of it to be ?   If
genuine, how could it possibly (as D'Ovidio puts it) traverse
the whole of the fourteenth century *incognito*?

It here becomes absolutely necessary to have a perfectly
clear perception of the actual *facts*. We must therefore
set out the evidence so as to show precisely (1) *To .what
extent* were the contents of the Epistle actually known ; and
(2) *In what manner* are they used or treated ?

I had intended to introduce here a comparative table of the
quotations from, or resemblances to, the Epistle, found in
several of the old commentators.   But it appeared that while
such a table might have value and interest in view of a study
of the mutual relations of these authors themselves, these
details would have no practical bearing on the particular
question before us, since the existence of these numerous
points of correspondence is fully admitted and beyond dispute.
Now the fourteenth-century Commentators, who show many
and unmistakable points of agreement, such as undoubtedly
imply a connexion either between them and this document,
or between them and it alike with some common original,
are as follows :—

Boccaccio chiefly, c. 1370 ; and next to him perhaps
Guido da Pisa, whose Commentary (still unpublished) seems
from internal evidence to have been written probably within
three or four years of Dante's death ; Jacopo della Lana,
c. 1328 ; Ottimo, c. 1333 ; Pietro di Dante, c. 1340 ; Buti,
in 1393.

The general results of the examination which I and others
have made may, I think, be summarized thus :—

(1) There is no trace of any knowledge of the *Epistolary*
part of the document.

(2) Nor is there any of what has been described as its third
division, viz. the part dealing with the interpretation of the

Prologue to the *Paradiso.* For those Commentators (e. g. *Pet., Lan., Ott.* and *Buti*) who comment on that Cantica, show absolutely no trace of acquaintance with this exposition.

(3) All the resemblances are in fact limited to the second division, i. e. the ' general doctrinal part ' (as some have called it), which treats of the considerations understood to be applicable to any literary work whatever ; these being here displayed in their application to the *Divina Commedia* generally and to the *Paradiso* in particular. The portion in question would include only §§ 6 to 16.

(4) There is yet a further limitation in that we find no allusion to those sections, even within this second division, which relate to the modifications to be applied to these points (or at least to three of them) when the *Paradiso* is exclusively in consideration. These sections are, 6 *fin.*, and 11, 12, and 13, i. e. those in which 'totum' and 'pars' are set in contrast. (See later, p. 354.)

These limitations seem to me to be of the very highest importance, in relation to the problem before us.

(5) It is to be observed that the commentators are generally more diffuse than the Epistle in corresponding sections or passages.

(6) In particular, Torraca has acutely pointed out the contrast between the modest conciseness of the personal reference to the author in Epistle, § 14, and the laudatory effusiveness in which the Commentators indulge [1]. (It is perhaps fair to admit that a moderately skilful forger might have seen the propriety of this.)

Now it appears to me that three different theories might more or less account for these facts.

(1) That the Commentators and the author (i. e. forger)

---

[1] The language of the Epistle is simply—'Agens... est ille qui dictus est' and the description thus referred to is no more than ' Dantes Aligherius, Florentinus natione, non moribus.' The laudatory expansions of Pietro, della Lana, and Boccaccio are quoted by Torraca (*op. cit.* p. 22). But Guido da Pisa enlarges still more on Dante's illustrious descent, his noble character, his scientific and poetic eminence. He adds that he revived Poetry which had been long dead, even as Boethius restored Philosophy.

of the Epistle may have all alike borrowed from some lost
original, in fact from some 'Ur-Kommentar' (as the Germans
would call it) like the Ur-Evangelium which is sometimes
assumed to explain the phenomenon of the Synoptic Gospels.

(2) That the Epistle was subsequent to the Commentaries,
and was compiled out of the passages in them which were at
first regarded as quotations from it.

(3) That the portion of the Epistle, to which all the resemblances are limited (as has just been shown), was itself, so
to speak, the 'Ur-Kommentar' from which they all, directly
or indirectly, borrowed. This portion, it might be supposed,
may have in some way obtained currency, as a detached
fragment, apart from the rest of the document. The last
hypothesis alone leaves room for sustaining the originality of
the Epistle, though some modification of the first may not be
inconsistent with its genuineness. By this I mean that Dante
and all alike may have borrowed to some extent not from
any Ur-Kommentar on the *Divina Commedia* itself, but from
documents of that nature applicable to literary works
generally[1]. Now it is clear that none of these hypotheses
can ever be either proved or disproved. They must remain
matters of pure conjecture. Provided that they appear to
account for the facts, and are not in themselves improbable,
their acceptance will largely depend on the conclusion to
which any one may come respecting the internal evidence.

Holding, as I do, a strong opinion on this point, I will now
endeavour to show that the third suggestion in some form
is at least a reasonably admissible one.

It seems to me that the materials common to the Epistle
and the Commentaries fall under two heads.

(1) A number of familiar literary commonplaces applicable
to any serious work whatsoever, in due relation to which it
was understood that any such work should be capable of being
exhibited.

(2) Certain precise and apparently carefully formulated
definitions of the subject and purpose of the *Comoedia* in
particular.

[1] On this see further the Supplementary note, pp. 363 *seqq.*

Now in regard to the former of these we all know how carefully Dante planned and thought out the scheme of his several works. Witness the elaborate symmetry of construction in the *Purgatorio*, and the frequent references to the subjects of some of the already designed, but unhappily never written, fifteen *trattati* of the *Convito*[1]. Take in connexion with this his habit of analysing his own work, and exhibiting it in connexion or contrast with other related subjects, in fact viewing it all round in every possible aspect (v. *Convito, passim*). Does it not then appear natural or likely that in regard to his *magnum opus*, the *Divina Commedia*, he should have worked out such details as these? He would desire both to satisfy himself and to prove to others that all the rules of art applicable to 'ogni scrittura,' to 'quodque doctrinale opus,' had been strictly complied with; that all was *selon les règles*; that all the commonly recognized features of literary composition were to be duly found in his work; that it could be adjusted in all its details to the conventional framework of such compositions. I think it probable, if we had other contemporary Commentaries and Introductions, that we might find in their method of treatment a great similarity to that of this Epistle and of the early commentators on Dante. Many of these details were common stock before Dante wrote. Such, for example, would be setting out the six points 'quae in *principio cuiusque operis* inquirenda sunt[2]'; or again, indicating the manner in which the familiar four causes are exhibited in a work; or, once more, the famous four methods of interpretation according to which, as Dante says in the *Convito*, 'le scritture si possono intendere e debbono sponere';

[1] There were to be fourteen Canzoni treated of (see I. i. 103), and consequently fifteen Trattati. Hence 'Justice' or 'Righteousness' is announced as the subject of the fourteenth Trattato in I. xii. 87, and as that of the 'penultimo Trattato' in IV. xxvii. 100. Other passages bearing on the subjects projected are—I. viii *fin.*; II. i. 35; III. xv. 144; and IV. xxvi. 66.

[2] I have since met with the following note in Messrs. Wicksteed and Gardner's recently published work (p. 93) in reference to this passage :—'As very notably in the Commentary upon the *Ecerinis* of Mussato . . . which was finished in 1317. The earlier portions . . . are clearly analogous in conception and occasionally almost identical in phraseology with parts of this Epistle.' [See supplementary note on this, *infra*, pp. 363 *seqq.*]

or the scarcely less familiar system by which these four methods may be regarded as falling under two main divisions (*v. supra*, pp. 306 *seqq.*). Equally common also was the practice of heralding any treatise by a commendatory introduction of this character. Torraca gives some interesting illustrations from Aristotle (especially as to the relation of a work to the 'four causes'), from Cicero *de Inventione* (called by Dante *Nova Rhetorica*), from Seneca *Ep. ad Lucilium*, &c., to say nothing of the uniform practice of commentators upon Dante himself. For even if they copied this Epistle when they were composing their Introductions, they had no need thus with one consent to commence with such an Introduction at all, unless it were (as some of them explicitly state) the recognized practice. Other contemporary instances are adduced by Torraca (*op. cit.* p. 20). I see no particular reason in the character of such a fragment as I am supposing, why it might not even have been prefixed by Dante himself to either or both of the already completed *Cantiche*; the modifications by which it was specially adapted to its present purpose being introduced later.

Suppose now that such a sketch or 'memorandum,' more or less in the form now found in this second part of the Epistle, were drawn up by Dante, and were, as we say, 'among his papers,' relating to the scheme of the *Divina Commedia* generally. Some of its contents may very well have become known to persons familiar with him, and in particular to his son Pietro, either in writing or orally. Such a fragment may have easily become divulged, or in some way 'got about'; and, as an anonymous piece of introductory Commentary on the *Divina Commedia* of unknown origin, may have formed a common mine for several later writers. But here I would add two points. First, there is no absolute *necessity* to suppose that it was 'of unknown origin.' Even if the fragment were known by some commentators, or at any rate by the original plagiarist, to be by Dante himself, he would not be at all likely to have acknowledged it, unless he wished to claim Dante's authority, or *ipse dixit*, for some controverted opinion. But this would not be the case in regard to the 'commonplaces'

* * *

which we are at present considering. It could only have occurred in the later sections, viz. § 17 onwards, and of these, as I have shown, no knowledge is ever displayed. Secondly, we need not suppose the fragment or memorandum in question to be precisely in the form in which we have it in this Epistle. It may have been among the 'munuscula' said in § 3 to have been turned over when this dedication was in contemplation [1]. It may have been retouched and modified when embodied in the Epistle. In particular, those sections may have been added which were required to adapt some of the points enumerated to the *Paradiso* specially, as distinguished from the *Divina Commedia* in general. I refer to §§ 6 *fin.*, 11, 12 and 13, and to the expression 'totum et pars' in §§ 14, 15, and 16 [2]. There is no trace of these distinctions, I believe, in the commentators, though in other respects they do distinguish and separate the three parts of the Poem clearly, and sometimes, as one might think, superfluously. May not this be an indication that with the Epistle as such they were not acquainted, though they were with some of the matters embodied in it? The omission of all reference to the part which would be of most practical value to a commentator on the beginning of *Par.* i. (§§ 20–31) is very significant.

Next, (see p. 351 *fin.*) as to the repetition not of general commonplaces, but of precise and apparently carefully formulated statements regarding the subject, literal and allegorical, of the work (§ 8), its purpose (§ 15), and its position in the scheme of philosophical classification (§ 16). All these are reproduced so accurately (e. g. in particular the whole of § 16

---

[1] Observe the words:—'propter hoc munuscula mea saepe multumque conspexi, et ab invicem segregavi, necnon segregata percensui.' &c.

[2] I cannot help thinking there are one or two indications which are, to say the least, consistent with the supposition that the writer is adapting old materials of a more general application. He seems almost nervously anxious to justify the inclusion, in an Introduction to the *Paradiso*, of much that applies to the *Commedia* as a whole rather than to the *Paradiso* itself. See the somewhat elaborate justification for this in §§ 5 and 6. Then, though we have discussed in succession the three out of the six divisions in which a different meaning has to be assigned in the *Paradiso* from that which they bear in the whole work, yet a much larger space is devoted to the general meanings (§§ 8, 9, 10) than to the special (§§ 11, 12, 13).

almost *verbatim* in Guido da Pisa[1]) that there can be no possible doubt of deliberate copying either of the Epistle by the commentators, or of the Commentary by the Epistle, or of some earlier document by both. (By ' copying the Epistle,' I do not of course here mean the Epistle in its present form, but the contents of the special portion of it to which I have referred as possibly having had an independent existence in an approximately similar form.) Now the passages above described are just such set definitions or formal declarations as may well have gained currency (especially those of §§ 8 and 15) even in the lifetime of Dante. They would have almost certainly found a place in such a fragment or memorandum as we have been imagining, if it ever existed. Besides this, Dante may well have given currency to such *dicta*, in conversation, or other communications with his friends or patrons.

I will now compare the suggestion above made with those put forward by Torraca and Vandelli and others. These it partially resembles, though it was in fact made independently of them.

Torraca supposes that Boccaccio had fallen in with an 'acephalous' copy of the Epistle commencing with § 5. He argues that as Witte's Munich MS. contains only the first four sections, so copies may have also existed containing the rest of the Epistle only, commencing, as above supposed, with § 5. As to the references made by Pietro, he thinks that confused recollections of conversations with Dante or possibly a sight of the autograph some years before the date of his Commentary may account for them. Jacopo della Lana[2] (argues Torraca) could not have known the Epistle itself, since he does not refer to it when commenting on the *Paradiso*. But his references might be accounted for by the general currency of some of the formal definitions alluded to above. I confess, with all respect to the learning and industry displayed by Torraca, and with full acknowledgement of very much that

---

[1] I ought to mention that I am indebted for my information as to the Commentary of Guido da Pisa almost entirely to the Monograph of Vandelli, in which the *Proemio* of that Commentary is printed.

[2] This however (as we have seen) would apply equally to other Commentators (*v. supra*, p. 346).

I owe to his monograph, I do not think this solution adequate to explain the facts. (1) Chiefly it takes no account of the Commentary of Guido da Pisa. In that (besides many instances of unmistakable correspondence with della Lana) the coincidences with the matter of the Epistle are far the most striking and extensive of any found in these writers, even more so than in Boccaccio. (2) The resemblances to the Epistle in della Lana are too precise (as it appears to me) to be explained except by access to an actual copy of some portion of the Epistle, or to the work of some writer who had such access. It will be observed that the explanation which I have offered does not suppose the existence of an 'acephalous' Epistle (which it should be observed must have lost its tail as well as its head), but only that a small and detached portion of it (of which alone the commentators show any knowledge) may have had an independent existence, as a fragment composed with a more general purpose.

An hypothesis more nearly resembling my own has been advocated by Vandelli. He thinks (*op. cit.* p. 21) that 'the doctrinal part of the letter' may have been circulated or published (*divulgata*) together with the Poem as a sort of 'introduction' to it. But if we suppose this to have been *extracted from the letter* for the purpose, it seems to me very difficult to explain (*a*) the fact of the existence of the Epistle *as such* having been wholly unknown ; and (*b*) the absence of any association of such an 'introduction' with Dante's own name, whether it were supposed to have been so employed by himself, or by some one else who had seen the Epistle.

Next, we find D'Alfonso (*op. cit.* p. 24) making the following suggestion. He thinks (in view of Epistle, § 10 quoted *supra*, p. 346) that Boccaccio did not know of the Epistle when he wrote the *Vita di Dante*, but that before writing his Commentary he had met with a copy of it, and made free use of it without acknowledgement. Dr. Witte had already made a similar supposition, assigning as approximate dates, 1350 for the *Vita*, and 1373 for the Commentary. That is an opinion held also by Giuliani. But apart from the difficulty of Boccaccio's never claiming the authority

of Dante, or reopening with these new lights anything left
undecided in the *Vita* (e. g. *supra*, p. 347), the explanation fails
to take account of the knowledge of contents of the Epistle
by *earlier* commentators, and especially and in the most
striking degree by Guido da Pisa [1].

I observe that Giuliani boldly argues for the genuineness
of the Epistle from the fact of its being known to so many
of the early commentators, citing for this purpose *Pet., Lan.,
Ott., An. Fior.,* &c. He does not notice the special difficulty that none of them seem to know it as an Epistle of
Dante, or to treat its contents as bearing his authority.

I propose now to add a few words as to the theories
which suppose the Epistle to be a forgery. As regards the
first (see *supra*, p. 350), (*a*) it has the disadvantage of assuming
a document by an entirely unknown author, for the existence
of which there is no external evidence or tradition whatever.
(*b*) The limits of time within which it can have been composed
and got abroad are rather narrow, since the Commentaries of
della Lana and Pietro were not long after Dante's death
(c. 1328 and 1340 respectively), and that of Guido da Pisa
probably about as early as 1324 [2]. (*c*) The supposition appears
to be purely superfluous, since either the Epistle itself, or
some one of the existing Commentaries, might serve equally
well for the original document, and ' causae non sunt multi-
plicandae praeter necessitatem.'

As regards the second theory (viz. that the writer of the
Epistle copied from the Commentaries), it is of course very

---

[1] His Commentary, or at any rate the nature of its contents, was then presumably unknown to Dr. Witte. As far as I know, only two complete MSS. of
this Commentary exist. One is registered by Colomb de Batines as belonging to
the Marchese Archinto, at Milan. This is now in the Library of the late Duc
d'Aumale, who kindly allowed me to consult it in 1888. The other (not known
to Batines) was seen by me in the Sunderland Library at Blenheim, from which
it was purchased by the British Museum. A fragment (in an Italian translation)
containing *Inf.* Cantos i–xxiv is in the Library of Lord Vernon at Sudbury,
the Commentary on the remaining Cantos being supplied by an Italian translation of the Commentary of Graziuolo de' Bambagioli (*v. supra*, p. 345, and my
Article in the *Academy* of Oct. 8, 1881, there referred to).

[2] I state this on the authority of Dr. Witte, who in the letter to myself above
quoted (p. 345), writes : ' La chiosa al v. 112 dell' Inf. xxi ci fa certi che l' opera
sia composta nel 1324.'

difficult indeed to determine the question of precedence in
plagiarism. It is however clear, I think, that as a fact the
tendency of the commentators as compared with the Epistle
is towards expansion [1], and that expansion rather than con-
traction of any material to hand, diffuseness rather than
compression, certainly seem to be generally more characteristic
of writers of that class and period [2]. Hence there is a slight
presumption of priority in favour of the more condensed
of two such related works. Again, to look at this argument
from the other side : why should a writer, who is so apt to go
off at a tangent as this writer often shows himself (this being
true of Dante also), have omitted the diffuse information
about the Greek Drama which he would have found in
Boccaccio ; or about the other classes of poetry, with examples and illustrations, which would have been provided
by Guido da Pisa, especially as in the latter case the subject
is just touched upon at the end of § 10 of the Epistle? It
seems to me far more probable that this brief allusion gave
the hint, or furnished the peg, for the digression, rather than
that a compiler declined to avail himself of all this promising
'copy.' As a point of detail, Vandelli (*op. cit.* p. 20 *n.*) draws
a very ingenious comparison between a passage in the Italian
of Boccaccio and the Latin of the Epistle which Boccaccio has
apparently misunderstood. Vandelli makes it, I think, very
clear, that while the Latin words might easily have been thus
misunderstood, yet if the Italian were the original the Latin
could scarcely have arisen out of it. This is a suggestive line
of argument which might perhaps be worked further. But
these are perhaps points too slender to lay much stress upon.
In fact as regards the second hypothesis, I frankly admit that
there is not much to be said against it, *if* any one regards the
internal evidence as adverse. Undoubtedly many distinguished scholars have done so, such as D'Ovidio and Dr.
Kraus. Not so however Scartazzini, though he felt bound to

---

[1] *v. supra*, p. 96.

[2] Since writing the above, I find that Witte has noted this point in comparing
the Epistle with the Commentary of Boccaccio, and has drawn the same inference as to their relative dates.

yield to the adverse weight (as he considered it) of the external evidence. He frankly admits, 'se non è di Dante, è certamente scritto nel suo spirito[1].' The same conviction as to the favourable character of the internal evidence *per se* was felt by Ugo Foscolo, and by Dr. Witte[2], besides the distinguished living writers whose works I have so often referred to. The case against it cannot be so triumphantly clear as D'Ovidio in particular seems to think, when such names as these are found in the opposite camp.

It behoves us now to show that there is no insuperable difficulty (as has been alleged) in assigning a possible date for the composition of the Epistle by Dante. The chief difficulty is supposed to arise from the expression 'tenellus gratiae vestrae' in § 4, l. 84. It should be observed in the first place that there is an important difference of reading here, which has already been discussed *supra*, p. 302, and that the alleged difficulty attaches solely to the (probably) *lect. fals.* That, however, is declared to give rise to this inextricable dilemma. If Dante were in the early stage of his acquaintance with Can Grande, the *Paradiso* cannot have been ready to offer to him[3]. If, on the other hand, the *Paradiso* were completed or approaching completion, the expression becomes wholly inappropriate, since by that time Dante's intimacy with Can Grande was a thing of the past, and he was comfortably settled at Ravenna under the protection of Guido da Polenta.

This argument involves (1) an entirely unfounded assumption, and also, (2) in the case of some of those who have employed it, a grave error. The error is that the 'Gran Lombardo,' with whom Dante was to find his 'primo rifugio' in his exile (see *Par.* xvii. 71), was Can Grande. This is obviously out of the question, since he was then scarcely

---

[1] *Prolegg.* p. 398.

[2] In *Dante-Forschungen*, I. p. 503, he speaks of 'mirabilem Epistolae cum reliquis Dantis operibus consensum.'

[3] Dr. Witte apparently felt the force of this objection so strongly that he made the rather forced suggestion that 'tenellus gratiae' referred to the intensity of Dante's affection, and not to its recent date. He argues that as some of Dante's contemporaries used 'tener' for 'sollicitus,' so it is possible here 'de studio, quo Canis amicitiam expetit, unice sensisse Dantem.' (From a note in his Edition of the *Epistles.*)

twelve years old. This supposition, however, is not essential
to the argument. The assumption (which *is* essential) is that
this Epistle implies that when it was written the *Paradiso*
was a completed, or nearly completed, work. There is
certainly no internal evidence to necessitate this. Rather,
on the other hand, we find some expressions which, though
not necessitating, certainly might suggest, the inference that
it was sent before the completion of the poem, and indeed
that possibly the letter may have only been accompanied by
Canto i[1]. Thus, in § 4 the writer says 'a primordio *metam
praefixam urgebo* (*al.* urgebit)[2] *ulterius.*' The future tenses
'procedetur,' 'recitabitur,' 'quaerentur,' in the last paragraph
would at any rate come naturally from one who had the
complete plan of his work sketched out, but the details not
yet completely filled in. We are told by Boccaccio that it
was Dante's habit to send a few Cantos at a time to Can
Grande or other friends, and he also mentions a common
tradition that the last thirteen Cantos of the *Paradiso* were
missing at the time of Dante's death, and that consequently
the work was for some time supposed to be even then
incomplete. Now the date of Dante's second visit to Verona
as the guest of Can Grande, though it cannot be determined
with precision, seems most likely to have been about 1315 or
1316. If so, then, or shortly after, the expression 'tenellus
gratiae vestrae' (if we are still to accept that reading) would
be appropriate. We cannot say how far the actual composition of the *Paradiso* had then gone[3], but there can be no

---

I have since learnt that Ponta also has suggested this as possible (*v.* Giuliani,
ii. p. 250). Also I find that Torri (ed. *Epistt.*, p. 144) writes—'Forse la Cantica
che gli intitolava *era appena incominciata.*'

[2] See again *supra*, p. 302, for the *varr. lectt.* found here.

[3] The evidence of the Eclogues shows that in or after 1318 (that date being
fixed by the first Carmen of Joannes del Virgilio, l. 29) the *Paradiso* was still
incomplete, though at any rate ten Cantos seem to have been ready. Note the
often quoted passages in Dante's first Eclogue (ll. 48–50) :—

> 'Quum mundi circumflua corpora cantu
> Astricolaeque meo, velut infera regna, patebunt,
> Devincire caput hedera, lauroque iuvabit:'

and again l. 64 :—

> 'Hac implebo decem missurus vascula Mopso.'

(Mopsus in these poems stands for Giovanni del Virgilio).

doubt both that some progress had been made with it, and also that the whole plan of it was mapped out in Dante's mind, at least quite as much of it as is implied by the concluding section of this Epistle. I fail entirely therefore to see any difficulty as to finding a suitable date for its composition. May we not also fairly add this consideration? If the *whole* of the *Paradiso* were supposed to be referred to in the Epistle, the inconsistency of the phrase 'tenellus gratiae vestrae' would be too glaring to escape the notice of the clumsiest forger. Further, that he would not even venture, by leaving the question of date open, to have run the risk of being so easily detected.

To resume briefly. My suggestion amounts to this. Dante had perhaps composed (as seems to have been then usual) a short statement of the subject, purpose, and general character of the *Divina Commedia*. This may have been retained by himself, being perhaps shown to his son Pietro, or to friends; its outlines, it may be, were repeated in conversation; possibly it may even have been prefixed as a sort of 'Introduction' to the parts of the poem already 'published.' In any case, the plan of his work had been sufficiently formed before its execution to make such a sketch possible. Shortly after his settlement at the court of Can Grande, c. 1316 [1], ('tenellus gratiae vestrae') [2] he desired to offer some token of gratitude and esteem to his patron. The other two Cantiche had probably already been dedicated to others who had befriended him. He had no doubt several compositions, such as *Canzoni*, Trattati of the *Convito*, or other works, which might have been among possible 'munuscula' (see § 3). He resolved, however, now to offer to Can Grande the crown of his great work, the Cantica of the *Paradiso*. It was still in hand and unfinished, though its outline and main features could be indicated. Possibly only the first Canto may have been ready. (Even that would be enough to

---

[1] I have seen since writing this that Messrs. Wicksteed and Gardner (who firmly believe in the genuineness of this Epistle) place the date of composition as probably not earlier than 1317 or 1318 (*op. cit.* p. 93). Torri (ed. *Epistt.*, p. 144) suggests 1318; and Witte (*Dante-Forsch.* i. p. 503) 1318 or 1319.

[2] I do not however admit this reading to be genuine. *V. supra*, p. 302.

satisfy the conditions of the Epistle.)   Dante, we may imagine, first wrote a formal Dedication.   Then he took the (supposed) general Introduction already written, working in such modifications as would adapt it specially to the *Paradiso*. Finally, he added a minute Commentary on the Prologue to the *Paradiso*, as a sample of an exposition that he hoped, should leisure and more favourable circumstances permit, to carry out for the rest of the work.   Of its contents he sketched a very brief outline in the concluding paragraph.

I cannot see that such a hypothesis involves any improbable assumption, while it does seem to afford a possible means of escape from the difficulties surrounding the subject, for those who on *other* and *internal* grounds are led to believe in the genuineness of the Epistle.   It would at any rate account for the Epistle, *as such*, long remaining unknown, while certain portions of its contents were familiar to many.   For after all it is to be remembered that, *as far as external evidence is concerned,* the defenders of the Epistle are only bound to show that there is nothing in respect of date or other conditions to make it *impossible* that it should have been written by Dante. They are not required to make everything appear quite natural and straightforward, as to how or when the letter was composed, or what its subsequent vicissitudes may have been.   That would often be a hopeless task in regard even to many admittedly genuine works.   One need only turn in illustration of this to the interminable controversies respecting the date of the *De Monarchia* and those of the several Trattati of the *Convito*.   It seems as if none of the various dates that have been suggested are consistent with all the conditions of the problems offered by the contents of those works, or that any are ever likely to be.   Yet we continue notwithstanding to receive them without hesitation as genuine works of Dante.

SUPPLEMENTARY NOTE

*On some early Commentaries on the ' Ecerinis' of Mussato, and on the
' Eclogues' of Petrarch.*

I HAVE suggested in the text (*supra*, p. 352) that if we had examples of
contemporary commentaries on other works we should probably find
evidence that many of the supposed coincidences or plagiarisms between
this Epistle and the earliest Commentaries on the *Divina Commedia* were
independent embodiments of the generally recognized plan and methods
of such comments. This seems pointed at by the words (l. 119) 'quae in
principio cuiusque doctrinalis operis inquirenda sunt.' I certainly did not
expect to find such a remarkable confirmation of this anticipation as is
afforded by the independent contemporary commentary on the *Ecerinis*
of Mussato. I have to thank Mr. Wicksteed for kindly directing my
attention to this[1].

The *Ecerinis* is a 'tragedy,' in the mediaeval sense (for which *v. infra*,
p. 365), i. e. a poetic narrative of the deeds and crimes and horrible
deaths of the two tyrants Ezzelino (or Azzolino) da Romano and his
brother Alberico. The former is mentioned in *Inf.* xii. 109, and alluded
to by his sister Cunizza in *Par.* ix. 28 *seqq.* The name 'Ecerinis'
is a Latinized form of Ezzelineis (cf. Achilleis, Thebais, &c.). The
'tragedy' was finished and publicly *recited* at Padua in December, 1314
or 1315[2]. Its author was highly honoured and received the coveted
'poetic crown' with great pomp in his native city. The poem was in
Latin, and formed on the model of Seneca's Tragedies, many passages of
which are directly imitated.

Let us now compare its early history with that of the *Divina Commedia*.

(1) In the first place, it was *immediately* made the subject of an
elaborate Commentary. This was at once commenced by a Bolognese,
Guizzardo, and was amplified and completed *in the year 1317* by
Castellano of Bassano. So in the case of the *Divina Commedia*, it seems
probable that the *Chiose Anonime* on the *Inferno*, published by Selmi,
were written in 1320, while Dante was still living[3].

Very shortly afterwards, probably within three or four years, followed
the Commentaries of Bambagioli and also that of Guido da Pisa[4], the
probable date of the latter being (as we have seen) c. 1324. Within twelve

---

[1] The Commentary is published in Padrin's excellent edition of the 'Eceri-
nide.' This includes also a valuable monograph by Carducci.

[2] Mr. Wicksteed inclines to the former date, Prof. Carducci to the latter.

[3] *Auct.* Karl Hegel, *Über den historischen Werth*, &c., p. 2.

[4] For these Commentaries *v. supra*, pp. 345, 349.

years at any rate of Dante's death were written also the Commentaries of Jacopo di Dante, Jacopo della Lana, and the *Ottimo* ; and these were quickly followed by that of Pietro di Dante.

(2) But, more than this, the practice of an author himself supplying a commentary to his own compositions (as in this Epistle, in the *V. N.*, and in the *Convito*) receives an illustration from the case before us and others. Guizzardo's Commentary was written 'sublimis autoris venia[1].' Also the very early *scholia* in the principal MS. of the poems of Del Virgilio afford evidence of having been at least in many places inspired by Del Virgilio himself. On this Mr. Wicksteed observes : 'It appears not to have been unusual for the author of a poem containing difficulties of any kind to put some friend in possession of the information necessary for writing elucidating notes.'

(3) This Commentary, which, be it remembered, is precisely contemporary with the Epistle (1317), and relates to an entirely independent work, offers the most extraordinary number of points of similarity in general character, and also in numerous details, with the Dedicatory and Expository Epistle ascribed to Dante.

(i) First, we have six points which, as the Epistle says, 'in principio cuiusque doctrinalis operis inquirenda sunt' (l. 119). In the *Ecerinis* Commentary we read :—' In libri huius principio, . . . *ut moris est commentantibus*, sex solita sunt dicenda : quippe causa *efficiens, finalis, formalis, materialis* : cui *parti philosophyae* supponatur, et quis sit libri *titulus*.' These, it will be observed, do not correspond throughout with those of the Epistle, but they are found thus almost *totidem verbis* in the Commentary of Pietro (p. 3). Della Lana says there are four such points, viz. the four causes, but he brings in the 'Title' under the 'formal cause' and the 'part of philosophy' under the 'final cause,' so that again the six are recognized. Boccaccio[2] resembles della Lana, giving the four causes first (p. 82), and introducing the title (p. 83) and part of philosophy (p. 91) as two other 'cose principali' which have to be explained.

In Guido da Pisa we again meet with the six divisions, as in this Epistle, but in a different order, and the first four are arranged under the four causes[3]. For Benvenuto see what is said later, pp. 367 *seqq.*

Thus while the same six introductory heads seem to be practically recognized throughout, the early commentators on Dante follow more closely the arrangement of the Mussato Commentary than that of Epistle x.

It is clear that it was generally assumed that these 'six points' were a necessary part of the introduction 'cuiusque doctrinalis operis.'

(ii) But the detailed treatment of some of these six heads affords evidence that the general agreement as to the 'set form' of any such introductory commentary went further still. I do not propose to follow up

---

[1] Wicksteed, *op. cit.* p. 270.

[2] *Comento*, ed. Milanese.

[3] See extract from this Commentary printed by Vandelli in the *Bullettino della Società Dantesca*, N. S. VIII. pp. 137 *seqq.*

these points in the early Commentaries on the *Divina Commedia* itself, since the coincidences between them and the Epistle are admitted, and also can be variously explained. My present point is to show that they are to be found in an entirely independent Commentary on a totally different work.

(*a*) Thus we have the 'forma' divided, just as in Epistle x. 9 (*init.*). For in the Mussato Commentary [1] we read in almost identical language, 'Formalis duplex: forma tractatus et forma tractandi.' The former (as in Dante) is 'compositio partium libri,' and the latter (not quite the same) is the 'modus agendi,' and this is explained to be 'tragicus,' with the usual derivation and Horatian and other citations.

(*β*) Tragedy is defined as 'tractatus altae materiae de miseriis et ruinis insignium et excellentum.' Here it should be noticed how widely the medieval conception of Tragedy and Comedy had departed from Greek and even Roman originals. The dramatic element had disappeared [2]. They were written merely for recitation, not for acting [3]. Thus we read that the *Ecerinis* was introduced to the Paduan audience by a public 'recitation,' not 'performance.' The type of $\tau\rho\alpha\gamma\omega\delta\iota\alpha\iota$ $\dot{\alpha}\nu\alpha\gamma\nu\omega\sigma\tau\iota\kappa\alpha\iota$ which prevailed at Alexandria has entirely superseded the original idea of a Drama. The distinction between Tragedy and Comedy depended on the dignity of the subject narrated, and the character of the issue. Hence Dante's appellation of 'Commedia' as applied to his own great work (as well as that of 'Tragedia' to the Aeneid of Virgil) ceases to be surprising, and the censure of nineteenth-century critics (like much else of their criticism of this Epistle) is seen to be purely anachronistic. Carducci accurately characterizes the *Ecerinis* as 'epos tragico-scolastico [4].' The definition of Tragedy given by Isidore (to which Carducci refers) is this:— 'Tragoedi sunt qui antiqua gesta atque facinora sceleratorum regum luctuoso carmine, spectante populo, concinebant' (*Etym.* xviii. 45).

(*γ*) Again (p. 83); 'parti philosophyae supponitur *ethice*, nam bonis exemplis virtus accenditur ... Nec minus et *theologe* supponitur, quia poetica est profecto ars divina, sicut Philosophus dicit in principio Metaphysicae.' Compare with this Epist. § 16—'*Genus* vero *philosophiae*, sub quo hic in toto et parte proceditur, est morale negotium, sive *Ethica*.'

(*δ*) Then we read:—Libri titulus: 'Albertini Musati poetae Paduani tragoedia Ecerinis incipit.' Compare Epist. § 13, 'Patet etiam *libri titulus*.... Incipit Cantica tertia Comoediae Dantis, quae dicitur Paradisus.'

(*ε*) After the preliminary explanations of these general points we have 'Descensus ad literam' (p. 92). See Epist. § 17, 'His itaque praemissis ad expositionem *literae* ... accedendum est.'

---

[1] p. 80. On p. 98 we find the figure 'transumptio' explained. See 'transumptivus' in Ep. *l. c.*

[2] See Carducci's monograph, *op. cit.* p. 251.

[3] So in this Commentary, we are not told what is said or done by the actors, but 'Autor in persona Adeleytae describit,' &c., and so on *passim*.

[4] *op. cit.* p. 277.

(iii) Another similarity is found in the repeated divisions and sub-divisions of the subject, which we have seen to be so prominent a feature of the Epistle. For this see the scheme drawn out upon p. 291. Let us compare with this the skeleton outline of the treatment of the subject-matter of the *Ecerinis*. It is first divided into three main heads, which the commentator says might almost be called Books :—I. the birth ; II. the reign ; and III. the downfall, of the two brothers. I need only, as I say, give a skeleton of the divisions and subdivisions which are worked out in the course of the Commentary. I have traced these out with some labour, and I am not prepared to say that I may not have overlooked some other subdivisions. These however at any rate occur, and they are quite enough to indicate the similarity of method between this Commentary and that of Epistle x in this respect also. Moreover, they are introduced in a similar manner throughout by quoting the initial words corresponding to each division.

```
                i. . . .  { α
                          { β
                          { γ
I. . . . {
                          α . . .  { a
                                   { b
                                   { c
         ii. . . . { β
                   { γ
                   {
                   { δ . . .  a . . .  { a
                                       { b
                              b . . .  { a
                                       { b

                          α . . .  { a
                                   { b
                                   { c
         i. . . . { β . . .  a . . .  { a
                  {                   { b
                  {                   { c
                  {          b
                  { γ
II. . . . {
          ii. . . . { α . . .  { a
                    {          { b
                    { β . . .  { a
                               { b
                               { c

          iii. . . .  { a
                      { β

                          α . . .  { a
                                   { b
                                   { c
          i. . . . { β
                   { γ . . .  { a
                   {          { b
                   { δ
III. . . {
          ii. . . .  { a
                     { β
```

(iv) We have a fine display of what D'Ovidio calls ' spropositata eru- dizione ellenica ' when, in Ep. x, the derivations of certain words from the Greek are introduced. I have counted nearly twenty such in this Com- mentary, and I believe[1] they are all (as was natural at that time) taken from the *Magnae Derivationes* of Uguccione da Pisa, though I do not think his name is mentioned more than once. It will be remembered that Dante owes all his etymologies to this source, though he also only mentions him once. It is needless to point out how frequently these often grotesque derivations occur in the early commentators on Dante, e.g. Pietro, Boccaccio, Benvenuto, Buti, &c. We find also in this Commentary some instances of the minute distinctions between nearly synonymous words, of which examples occur both in Epistle x[2] and in the recognized works of Dante—e.g. ' patens ' and ' patulus ' (p. 108),' continuus ' and ' contiguus ' (p. 90).

(v) Once more the Commentary bristles with classical and scriptural quotations. Seneca is naturally most prominent, as his Tragedies are the model on which the *Ecerinis* is framed. We also find many references to Aristotle (*Philosophus*), Virgil, Horace, Ovid, Statius, Lucan, Cicero, and Boethius. This, with the exception of Seneca, implies much the same range of reading as we find in Dante and in the early commentators on the *Divina Commedia*, in whom also, especially Pietro and Ben- venuto[3], such quotations are extremely numerous.

We have here then a specimen of the work of a contemporary scholar— indeed the Epistle and Commentary may quite well have been written in the very same year, 1316–7—a scholar of very similar culture and engaged upon a similar work. If the Epistle be genuine, there can be no suspicion of any communication or connexion between them[4]. It is instructive and significant to observe on what very similar lines the two writers worked.

I have next to thank Dr. Paget Toynbee for a reference to another four- teenth-century Commentary by Benvenuto da Imola on the Eclogues of Petrarch, in which we again find the same familiar features repeated. The work is described as ' Francisci Petrarchae poetae *nuper laureati.*' Now as this coronation of Petrarch took place in 1341 and his death was not till 1374, the Commentary must almost certainly have been written in his lifetime, as indeed the context in the Introduction seems to imply, and probably very soon after the publication of the work com- mented on. This we have already seen to have been a common practice. Indeed there is an extant letter[5] purporting to be addressed by Benvenuto to Petrarch, which, if genuine (as there seems no sufficient reason to doubt),

---

[1] *v.* notes in Padrin's ed.   [2] *v.* Epistle, §§ 18, 23, 29.

[3] See an exhaustive Index to the authors quoted by Benvenuto compiled by Dr. Toynbee in the Report of the American Dante Society for 1899–1900.

[4] Nor, it may be added, between this Commentary and those of the early Commentaries on Dante, which also have so many points of resemblance with it.

[5] Dr. Toynbee informs me that only a part of the letter is extant, which was printed by Claricio in his edition of Boccaccio's *Amorosa Visione*, Milan, 1521.

would settle the question definitely. He there writes:—' Nonnulla hortatu Ioannis Boccatii ... pro tuarum Eclogarum interpretatione reposuisse scias velim. Quae ei placuerint, ea ad te mitto, rescribas quid animi habeas etiam atque etiam te oro.' The Commentary begins :—' In principio huius libri, *quemadmodum in principio aliorum librorum*, sex per ordinem sunt videnda. Primo, quis fuerit auctor : Secundo, quae materia : Tertio, quae intentio : Quarto, quae utilitas : Quinto, cui parti philosophiae supponatur : Sexto, quis sit libri titulus.' Though there is no mention of the 'four causes,' yet it is easy to see the relation of the first four heads to that classification (*v. supra*, p. 364). In any case the passage quoted corresponds almost *verbatim* with the six heads as they occur in Benvenuto's Commentary on the *Divina Commedia* (i. p. 11).

Next we meet with the usual trifling speculations as to the fitness of the author's name, Franciscus Petrarcha, just as we find in most of the early commentators on the *Divina Commedia* (and in Benvenuto among others) respecting the name of Dante. This is a point of resemblance which we could hardly expect to find in the Epistle, if it were the work of Dante, as he would naturally be precluded from indulging in it.

' Dicitur Franciscus quasi *francus* et liber ab omni vitiorum servitute, uti illustris poeta Dantes Beatum Franciscum solem appellat. Dicitur Petrarcha, quasi *petra* et *archa*. *Petra*, i. e. basis et firmamentum : *Archa* dicitur quasi continens sapientiam. Dicitur *poeta* a professione eius.'

Under the second head, the words ' bucolic ' and ' eclogue ' are explained much as Tragedy, Comedy, Allegory, &c., are in the works we have already noticed. Thus ' *Ecloga* dicitur ab *egle*, quod est "capra," quod quoddam animal est utilissimum.' Under the fourth head we are told that ' utilitas est triplex,' and the third kind of ' utility ' is, ' ut delectet animos auditorum,' which may be an echo of the passage in the *Nova Rhetorica* of Cicero quoted in the Epistle, § 19. Under the fifth head we read, as in the Epistle and the Commentaries on the *Divina Commedia* generally, and in that on the *Ecerinis* :—' iste liber supponitur philosophiae morali, nam totus de moribus est.' Then we have the divisions of the Book, which are simple enough in this case, being twelve, corresponding to the number of Eclogues. Finally, we have some more of the typical etymological speculations as to the names of the interlocutors in Ecl. I, viz. Sylvius and Monicus. ' Monicus ' is explained to be the name of an ancient giant who had one eye, and who was so called from ' *monos* quod est "unum," et *oculus*.' In this case, however, the name is equivalent to Monachus ; and a monk is also appropriately so called because he has a *single eye* to divine things !—' ideo appellavit Monicum, quum respiciebat solum divina.'

Thus, as I said, we have again the familiar features repeated, which in the case of the Epistle and the Commentaries have been thought to imply direct copying. It really seems as if any one in those days proposing to write a commentary was somewhat in the position of a lawyer having to draw up a lease or other legal document. The general form would be provided for him, and he would only have to fill in the blanks according to the special subject in hand.

Two concluding remarks may be made :—

(1) The striking points of similarity both in the Mussato Commentary and in that of Benvenuto on Petrarch would account for at least many of the like features appearing in the early Commentaries on Dante. I do not hereby imply that there is no evidence of acquaintance on their part with some of the contents of the Epistle, or of some document related to it. Still the force of the argument which was based upon a 'cumulus' of points of resemblance is very much weakened, when so many of these are found to be common to entirely independent documents also.

(2) Not only are all the main features of Epistle x repeated in these Commentaries, but most of those 'peculiarities' or 'weaknesses' which have offered an easy mark to the jibes of nineteenth-century criticism are seen to be natural at the date of such compositions, not to say inevitable. It is perfectly easy for a modern critic to say that the 'erudition' is pedantic, the etymologies childish, the digressions disproportionate, the arguments inconclusive, the exegesis unenlightening. But these we have seen to be defects not so much of the author as of his age ; and almost as much of a necessity as his adoption of the Ptolemaic Astronomy. No doubt our best modern Commentaries would have seemed equally perverse and uninteresting to a mediaeval schoolman. It is to be hoped that twentieth-century critics will take a sounder view, and will judge this and other fourteenth-century writings by the standard of their own age and environment, and not by that which would be suitably applied to 'recent literature.' This is, no doubt, a very trite and obvious suggestion, but one feels tempted to apply to it the words of Dante in the *De Mon.*—'multi habent in ore, in intellectu vero pauci.' For assuredly to the neglect of it may be distinctly traced a great deal of the destructive criticism by which for some years past the minor works of Dante have been assailed.

PS.—Most of this was written before reading the notes of Giuliani ; but I have since been able to work in several more references which I owe to the unrivalled knowledge of Dante's works in detail possessed by that scholar. I gladly also acknowledge the help I have derived from the monographs of Torraca, Vandelli, D'Alfonso, and from that of the venerable Professor D'Ovidio. I have unfortunately been compelled on this subject to treat him as an antagonist.

The monograph of D'Alfonso contains an excellent Bibliography, and also a list of the existing MSS., of which there seem to be four. Besides these there are two which contain only the first four paragraphs of the Epistle (*v. supra*, p. 302).

* * *

ADDITIONAL NOTES

P. 62, l. 4. It is not an unnatural objection to the explanation of the 'three crosses' which I have advocated, that the term 'crosses' is not strictly applicable to the intersection of lines forming such very acute angles as some of those indicated. It is generally assumed that 'croce' implies an intersection of lines at right angles. This is maintained both by Rizzacasa and by Angelitti, though they are entirely at variance as to the circles by which such crosses are supposed to be formed. Rizzacasa thinks that the circles are the Equator and the two tropics, which form three crosses by their intersections with the Equinoctial Colure. It is an obvious objection that in this case there is no one point or passage (*foce*) of intersection. Note *quella* in l. 38. Angelitti gives two alternative explanations[1], in each of which two pairs of great circles intersecting at right angles furnish *two* true crosses, but he cannot find a *third*. Hence he is driven to the rather desperate expedient of proposing to read *due* for *tre* in l. 39.

In the explanation offered in the text the 'crosses' may be of imperfect form, but there are clearly three of them, and they also fulfil the condition of intersecting in one point or *foce*.

Pp. 102, 103. There is an allusion to the shortness of the summer nights in Cicero *pro Roscio*, § 19. He says that the news of the murder of Sextus Roscius was conveyed to his enemy Capito at Ameria within 'decem nocturnis horis.' As the murder was in the summer, the indecent haste with which the intelligence was conveyed is thus emphasized. Chaucer distinguishes the 'equale' and 'inequale' hours in his *Treatise on the Astrolabe*, Part II. §§ 7–10, and the day made up of a varying number of 'equale' hours is termed the 'artificial' day. See also passage quoted in the following note.

P. 137, l. 2. Pietro di Dante (p. 286) states that 'secundum Isidorum est [Purgatorium] in alio emisphaerio sive orbe, in cuius summitate est Paradisus terrestris.' I have failed however to find this passage in Isidore.

P. 144 *fin.* We might compare the way in which Chaucer feigns the 'Vision of the House of Fame' (which contains many imitations of the *Divina Commedia*) to have occurred on the night of December 10, but he leaves the year to be inferred by his readers from allusions in the poem. It is in this way found to be 1383. In the *Canterbury Tales* also, Chaucer has frequently been at the pains to indicate the month and day and hour of parts of the action. It is curious to find that these indications (generally astronomical) have been almost as fruitful of doubt and dispute as in the case

---

[1] From the *Bullettino*, &c., N. S., vol. x. pp. 232 *seqq.*

of Dante. When Chaucer gives precise astronomical *data* for a particular day of the month, we must not overlook the ten or eleven days difference in the still uncorrected calendar. Also when references to the sun's position in the zodiac occur, there is the possible confusion between signs and constellations ; and we must also note that Chaucer was aware that the 'signs' were entered on the twelfth or thirteenth day of the month and not on the twenty-first. This is stated in the *Treatise on the Astrolabe*, Part II. §§ 1-3.

The following may be taken as a specimen, from the Introduction to the 'Man of Law's Prologue,' ll. 1-14 :—

> Owr Hoste sey wel that the brighte sonne
> Th' ark of his artificial day had ronne
> The fourthe part, and half an houre, and more ;
> And though he were not depe expert in lore,
> He wiste it was the eightene[1] day
> Of April, that is messager to May;
> And sey wel that the shadwe of every tree
> Was as in lengthe the same quantitee
> That was the body erect that caused it.
> And therfor by the shadwe he took his wit
> That Phebus, which that shoon so clere and brighte,
> Degrees was fyve and fourty clombe on highte;
> And for that day, as in that latitude,
> It was ten of the clokke, he gan conclude.

P. 161 *fin.* Prof. Gambèra in his *Note Dantesche* (Salerno, 1903), an early copy of which I owe to his courtesy, has founded an argument for the date 1300 from the prophecies both of Ciacco (*Inf.* vi) and Cavalcante (*Inf.* x.).

In the former, ll. 64-69, 'Verranno al sangue' is referred (as is usually the case) to the first bloodshed between the factions on May 1, 1300, as is recorded by G. Villani (viii. 38) ; the expulsion of the Neri by the Bianchi (*la parte selvaggia*) taking place on June 24 of that year. The next words, 'Poi appresso convien che questa caggia Infra tre soli,' relate to the expulsion of the Bianchi in January, 1302, and among them Dante himself, who was exiled by the decree of January 27. The objection generally taken to this explanation is that the limit of time was less than two years, but Gambèra suggests that the word *sole* is not here equivalent to 'anno,' but is to be taken astronomically, i.e. that the three *soli* are those marking the years 1300, 1301, and 1302, each year, so to speak, having a 'New Sun.' If the events are in fact those above given, and they seem to correspond perfectly with Dante's language, it is evident that the assumption of the date 1301 would be quite unsuitable, and even more so if 'sole' be taken as 'a year.' I may add that if this explanation of 'sole' be correct we gain collaterally some support for the view advocated *supra*, p. 150, that Dante's year began according to the Roman and not the

---

[1] *Var. lect.* eighte & twenty.

Florentine use, otherwise we should not obtain the Suns of *three* years but only of *two*.

Then, again, as to the prophecy of Cavalcanti in Canto x. 79-81 :

> ' Ma non cinquanta volte fia raccesa
> La faccia della donna che qui regge,
> Che tu saprai quanto quell' arte pesa.'

This prophecy Prof. Gambèra supposes (as I do also) to have been uttered on the assumed date of April 9, 1300. It declares that before fifty New Moons Dante should have experience of the difficulty of being able to return from exile. The first of these New Moons would occur on April 20 or 21, 1300, the fiftieth ($29\frac{1}{2}$ days × 50) about April 4, 1304, and the forty-ninth about March 5, 1304. Now precisely between these two dates, viz. on March 10, began the abortive mission of Cardinal Niccolò da Prato, sent to Florence by Benedict XI as peacemaker (Paciarius) to reconcile the rival factions and to secure the restoration of the exiles. He completely failed, though Epistle i of those commonly attributed to Dante, to be assigned probably, if genuine, to this very month of March, shows how keen were the hopes entertained from his efforts. Here again we seem to have an exact and suitable fulfilment of a 'prophecy' on the assumption of the date 1300. I am not aware of any event so strikingly *calzante al caso* for the date 1301.

Pp. 172-174. While these sheets are being finally revised for the Press, I observe in the current number (August, 1903) of the *Bullettino della Società Dantesca Italiana* a notice of the *Quarterly Review* article which forms the basis of Essay III in this volume. The writer is Prof. Boffito, who is already well known from his two very learned and exhaustive *Memorie* on the *Quaestio de Aqua et Terra* (1902 and 1903). In this review he appears to accept unhesitatingly the arguments, both historical and astronomical, in my Essay, with a single exception, viz. that which relates to the position assigned by Dante to Venus as a Morning Star in 1300. This he regards as unconvincing, and as savouring rather of 'special pleading.' But he himself overcomes the astronomical anomaly by means of a discovery which he has just made of a Calendar for the year 1300, which is found in two MSS. in the Laurentian Library, one of which is stated to be itself contemporary with Dante. In this Calendar Venus is actually entered, whether by oversight or error of calculation, as a *Morning Star*, and in the constellation Pisces, in March–April of that year. Prof. Boffito thinks that such a Calendar may have fallen into Dante's hands and misled him. For, as I have pointed out on p. 173, Dante is not describing an actual scene or historical event of which he was a spectator. I think it is extremely probable, indeed almost certain, that he would have taken his astronomical information generally for that year (already ten or twelve years past) from a Calendar for the year, as I have maintained respecting the Lunar *data* throughout the *Divina Commedia*, in my explanation of the 'Time References.' At the same time, I do not, in regard to an ideal picture such as that in *Purg.* i. 13-21, consider it *necessary* for him to have claimed any such authority for all its details. But it is very interesting to find that this curious discovery clearly opens the way even to this line of defence, and removes the strongest objection (one might almost venture to say, the last remaining objection), on astronomical grounds, to the acceptance of the year 1300 as the assumed date of the Vision. I thank Prof. Boffito for this important help in support of my argument, as well as for the kindly tone of his review of an article, which though anonymous, he has rightly assigned to me.

P. 188 *sub fin.* I find that I have omitted to notice an incident of some little difficulty in the beginning of Canto xxxii. 'Troppo fiso,' 'too fixed a gaze,' the attendant angels exclaim, when Dante's gaze continues to be intently centred on Beatrice. Perhaps in an ordinary writer we might be content to suppose that this meant no more than that his attention was required for the other sights and scenes about to be displayed by the mystic procession. In Dante, however, we naturally suspect something more than this, some hidden and deeper meaning underlying the outward act or words. I think it may perhaps be this. Here in this life there are other duties to attend to besides contemplation, however exalted and blessed a thing in itself. If so, this is a call back to active work and duty, like, 'What doest thou here, Elijah?'

Or perhaps thus:—For one who is still in the flesh, through the prolonged contemplation of Divine Truths, or continued poring over the mysteries of Revelation, the mental eye may become dazzled and blinded; even as Dante represents himself to have been, by too steadily gazing at the glory of S. John in Paradise (*Par.* xxv and xxvi). For us mortals, excess of light may bring darkness, even as Milton says:—

'Dark with excessive bright thy skirts appear.'   (*P. L.* iii. 380.)

In *Par.* x. 59, 60, Dante states that his mind became so intently fixed on God Himself,

'Che Beatrice eclissò nell' obblio,'

and he adds that this did not displease Beatrice, but that she smiled in approval of it. Similar passages occur in *Par.* xviii. 20, 21; and xxiii. 70-72.

P. 191. Ruskin (*M. P.* iii. p. 112), speaking of 'true' and 'false' griffins, says of the former: 'Thus signed the winged shape becomes at once one of the acknowledged symbols of the Divine power; and, in its unity of lion and eagle, the workmen of the middle ages always meant to set forth the unity of the human and divine natures.' He then refers to *Purg.* xxix, &c.

P. 274. Roger Bacon in his Greek Grammar (lately published by Messrs. Nolan and Hirsch, Cambridge University Press, 1902) writes:— 'Sciendum est quod greci et hebrei computat (*sic*) per litteras.' He then explains that by this method the following four Greek names have been suggested, as corresponding to the number of the Beast, viz. 'Arnoyme; Antemos, quod est *tyrannus*; Teitan, quod est *sol*; Gensirikos, quod est *seductor'* (p. 194). Similarly on p. 83 *fin.*, where Bede is quoted as an authority for the first three of these names.

Pp. 324 *seqq.* In the list of ' Resemblances to other works of Dante,' in Epistle x, I might well have noticed the insistence in § 29 on the twofold difficulty of communicating 'heavenly things,' viz. the failure of the *mind* to grasp them, and the failure of *language* to express them (*v. supra*, p. 294, on the words 'nescit et nequit'). The following references will show how familiar was this thought to Dante.

Beside *Par.* i. 6 (the passage commented on) we have *Par.* xxxiii. 55–57 :

> Da quinci innanzi il mio veder fu maggio
> Che il *parlar* nostro, ch' a tal vista cede,
> E cede la *memoria* a tant' oltraggio.

Inf. xxviii. 4–6 :

> Ogni lingua per certo verria meno
> Per lo nostro *sermone* e per la *mente*,
> Ch' hanno a tanto comprender poco seno.

Conv. III, Canzone ii. 9–13 :

> E certo e' mi convien lasciare in pria,
> S' io vo trattar di quel ch' odo di lei,
> Ciò che lo mio *intelletto* non comprende,
> E di quel che s' intende
> Gran parte, perchè *dirlo* non saprei.

See also the commentary on these lines in *Conv.* III. iii, 103–127, in which these two causes of failure are expounded at length as *due ineffabilità.*

PS.—I have just received from a Dutch Dante scholar the following suggestion in modification of my explanation of the number 515.

He supposes Dante to have recognized the fact that there were no vowels in Hebrew ; and to have assigned to the Latin or Italian vowels in order the values 1, 2, 3, 4, 5.

In that case (see *supra*, p. 271) the word Arrico would give the number 508, and then Arrico VII would give the exact number required, 515.

This is certainly ingenious, but that Dante never elsewhere (I believe) employs a numerical title of this kind, seems to me to be a strong *prima facie* objection. (It is clear that 'il secondo Federico' in *Inf.* x. 119 cannot be cited as a case in point.)

FURTHER *ADDENDA* TO THE FIRST SERIES OF STUDIES

[See Studies, II. p. 376.]

b.	*Purg.* xxii. 154	. . . .	Matt. xi. 11.
c.	xxxii. 46	. . . .	Dan. iv. 17 (*Vulg.*)
b.	*Par.* i. 78 .	. . . . .	Cic. Somn. Scip. xviii.
b.	iv. 129.	. . . .	Ar. Nic. Eth. I. ii. 1 (1094 *a* 21).
b.	v. 10–12	. . . .	Boeth. Cons. IV. Pros. vi. *med.*
c.	72	. . . . .	Lucr. i. 84, 102.
b.	83	. . . . .	Prov. vii. 22 (*Vulg.*).
b.	vi. 38	. . . . .	Virg. Aen. i. 272.
c.	xi. 1–12	. . . .	Lucr. ii. 1–13.
c.	xvi. 37-42	. . . .	Boeth. Cons. V. Pros. vi. *med.*
c.	*Conv.* II. v. 114	. . . .	Ar. Nic. Eth. I. vii. 20 (1098 *a* 22).
c.	xvi. 40-47 .	. .	Ecclus. iv. 17, 18.
b.	III. i. 20	. . . .	Boeth. Cons. III. Pros. xi. *med.*
b.	xv. 78 .	. . .	Ar. Nic. Eth. I. ii. 1 (1094 *a* 21).
c.	*Mon.* I. iv. 9 .	. . . . .	Ecclus. xxxviii. 25 (E.V. 24).
b.	*Epist.* X. vii. 154 .	. . .	Rom. viii. 21.

CORRIGENDA TO THE SECOND SERIES OF STUDIES

Page 29, note, l. 2 from bottom, *for* ' illusion ' *read* ' allusion '

,, 133, ll. 26, 27, correct the quotation thus :—
' Presenting Thebes or Pelops' line
Or the tale of Troy divine '

,, 162, in the list of sins in the *Inferno*, ' Avarice' *should come between* ' Gluttony' *and* ' Anger '

,, 173, l. 14, the same change should be made.

,, 174, ll. 23–25, read the sentence thus :—For *there* Accidia is *above* Anger, and therefore *better* than it ; *here* it would be below it, and therefore *worse.* *Dele* the rest of the sentence from 'also' to 'above it.'

,, 181, l. 8, *insert* ' either ' *after* ' arise '

,, 195, l. 2, *for* ' below' *read* ' above '

,, 225, l. 15, *for* ' another ' *read* ' and he '

,, 226, l. 4 from bottom of text, *for* ' Centaurs ' *read* ' Antaeus (xxxi. 126) '

,, 227, l. 22, *for* ' frequently ' *read* ' presently '

,, 241, l. 6 from bottom of text, ' eats and drinks ' should be in *italics.*

,, 248, ll. 6, 7, *for* ' growing narrower ' *read* ' becoming of less diameter '

,, 327, l. 21, *for* ' xxiv ' *read* ' xxi '

,, 329, l. 20, *for* ' snsuale ' *read* ' sensuale '

,, ,, ll. 24–26, as this quotation does not correspond with the sense in its context, it should be omitted.

,, 368, note 2, l. 1, *for* ' Arezzo ' *read* ' Ristoro '

,, 386, col. 1, l. 14, *for* ' 359 ' *read* ' 259 '

LIST OF THE PRINCIPAL PASSAGES DISCUSSED OR EXPLAINED IN THE PRESENT VOLUME

INDEX

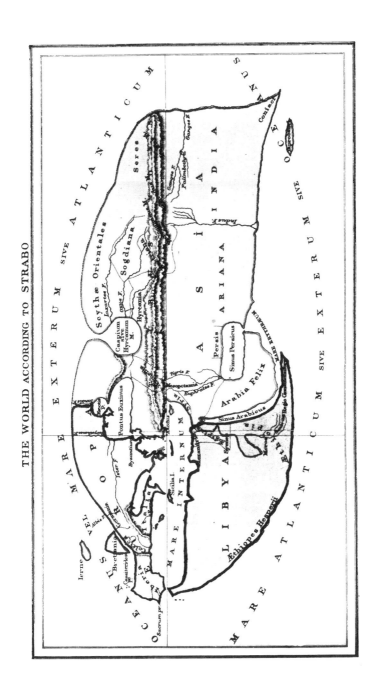